AN INTRODUCTION TO SWAMINARAYAN HINDU THEOLOGY

Since its inception over 200 years ago, Swaminarayan Hinduism has flourished into a transnational movement described as one of the fastest-growing Hindu groups in the world. Despite being one of the largest and most visible Hindu traditions both in India and the West, surprisingly little is known about what the Swaminarayan fellowship believes.

An Introduction to Swaminarayan Hindu Theology provides a comprehensive doctrinal account of the Swaminarayan tradition's belief system, drawing on its rich corpus of theological literature, including the teachings of Swaminarayan himself and classical commentaries on canonical Vedāntic texts. Part I delineates the sources and tools of Swaminarayan Hindu theology, while Part II systematically expounds upon its distinctive five eternal entities – Parabrahman, Akṣarabrahman, māyā, īśvara and jīva – and mukti (spiritual liberation). In presenting these key themes theologically and lucidly, Swami Paramtattvadas makes the Swaminarayan Hindu belief system intelligible to scholars, students and serious readers.

SWAMI PARAMTATTVADAS was ordained as a Hindu monk in 1992 by His Holiness Pramukh Swami Maharaj. After studying in India for fourteen years, including for a Master's in Sanskrit, Paramtattvadas returned to England in 2006 to read for a Master's in Religion at Oxford. After a further year of pre-doctoral studies focussing on Christianity, he completed his PhD in Hindu theology under Gavin Flood at the Oxford Centre for Hindu Studies and Maharaja Sayajirao University of Baroda, India. Swami Paramtattvadas has written and spoken extensively on Swaminarayan history, doctrine and teachings around the world, and is currently a scholar at the Oxford Centre for Hindu Studies.

AN INTRODUCTION TO SWAMINARAYAN HINDU THEOLOGY

SWAMI PARAMTATTVADAS

CAMBRIDGE
UNIVERSITY PRESS

CAMBRIDGE
UNIVERSITY PRESS

University Printing House, Cambridge CB2 8BS, United Kingdom

One Liberty Plaza, 20th Floor, New York, NY 10006, USA

477 Williamstown Road, Port Melbourne, VIC 3207, Australia

4843/24, 2nd Floor, Ansari Road, Daryaganj, Delhi – 110002, India

79 Anson Road, #06–04/06, Singapore 079906

Cambridge University Press is part of the University of Cambridge.

It furthers the University's mission by disseminating knowledge in the pursuit of education, learning, and research at the highest international levels of excellence.

www.cambridge.org
Information on this title: www.cambridge.org/9781107158672
DOI: 10.1017/9781316666005

First published 2017

Printed in the United Kingdom by TJ International Ltd. Padstow Cornwall

A catalogue record for this publication is available from the British Library.

Library of Congress Cataloging-in-Publication Data
NAMES: Paramtattvadas, Sadhu, author.
TITLE: An introduction to Swaminarayan Hindu theology / Sadhu Paramtattvadas.
DESCRIPTION: New York : Cambridge University Press, 2017.
IDENTIFIERS: LCCN 2016056416 | ISBN 9781107158672 (hardback) | ISBN 9781316611272 (paperback)
SUBJECTS: LCSH: Swami-Narayanis – Doctrines. | BISAC: RELIGION / Hinduism / General (see also PHILOSOPHY / Hindu).
CLASSIFICATION: LCC BL1289.245 .P37 2017 | DDC 294.5/56–dc23
LC record available at https://lccn.loc.gov/2016056416

ISBN 978-1-107-15867-2 Hardback
ISBN 978-1-316-61127-2 Paperback

The enlightened [Guru] comprehensively reveals that brahmavidyā . . . by which Akṣara and Puruṣ[ottama] are truly known.

Muṇḍaka Upaniṣad 1.2.13

Parabrahman, that is Puruṣottama Nārāyaṇa, is distinct from Brahman and also the cause, support and inspirer of Brahman. Having understood this, and having developed oneness of one's soul with that Brahman, one should subserviently offer upāsanā [devotion informed by correct theological knowledge] to Parabrahman. Understood as such, brahmajñāna is also an unhindered path to realising the highest spiritual goal.

Swaminarayan, Vacanāmrut Gaḍhaḍā 2.3

My manifestation is to make souls brahmarūpa [like Brahman] and grant them ultimate liberation. That is why I, Puruṣottama, who transcends even Akṣara, have become like a human.

Swaminarayan, Ātyantik Kalyāṇ p. 76

Contents

Figures

Tables

Foreword

Many years ago Religious Studies distinguished itself from Theology as an objective discourse about religion in contrast to Theology's insider perspective. On the one hand, on this view, we have the science of religion, while on the other, we have confessional attestation. We now know that things are more complex than this distinction implies and Theology can function as a critical discourse that engages with a secular Religious Studies just as much as Religious Studies has critiqued the biases or presuppositions of Theology. Until recent times, Theology was largely understood to be Christian, although Jewish and Islamic voices have now emerged and, along with Christianity, form the 'Abrahamic religions'. While this term is itself contested, the point is that discourses that reflect on the sources of their tradition within 'circles of faith' or express confidence in the values of those traditions, developed in a post-critical moment in the history of Western religious discourse. Now, new voices are emerging distinct from Abrahamic traditions to join this academic discussion. Swaminarayan Hinduism is one such newly emerging voice. Indeed the category of Hindu Theology is itself relatively new. In this welcome introduction to Swaminarayan Hindu Theology, Swami Paramtattvadas has succeeded in presenting in a lucid, meticulous and methodical exposition, the fundamental beliefs of his tradition. In some ways this book is similar to any 'Religious Studies' enterprise in expounding the views of a particular perspective, but yet intends to go beyond such an essentially descriptive endeavour in taking the claims of tradition with intellectual seriousness. Rather than bracketing the truth claims of the Swaminarayan religion, the author trusts those claims and functions within their horizon.

This book is a welcome contribution to Hindu Theology and to the emerging discussion of Comparative Theology. It assumes much of the critical discussion that has developed within post-colonialism and might be seen as a kind of thinking that could only come after that critique. While this book is a display of Swaminarayan Theology, it is also a claim to the legitimacy of a non-Christian systematic theology. Indeed, while many Christian theologians would wish to distance themselves from the very idea of a systematic theology in the twenty-first century, this book sees the systematic exposition of Hindu theological ideas as crucial to the intellectual development of the tradition in Western academic circles and to showing other readers, other theologians, how this particular Hindu system of thought functions. It is not polemical in the sense of attempting to convince the reader to inhabit a certain kind of Swaminarayan interiority, but it is sympathetic to tradition and pays attention to its claims as a coherent and valuable way of living in the world. It presents confidence in the Swaminarayan world view and argues for the centrality of a higher dimension informing human life. The outsider will read this book with a sense of gaining an insight and understanding into the Swaminarayan thought world, while the reader from within the circle of faith will gain clarity and depth of understanding of her own tradition. The values of the Swaminarayan religion come to life in its pages.

But now the tradition must ask itself, where to go from here? Swami Paramtattvadas has laid out the foundations of a particular Hindu Theology and other traditions may do likewise, but the challenge lies in the way in which an intellectual discourse is generated that engages with contemporary conditions of late modernity, with environmental concerns, with social justice, with issues raised by contemporary technology – especially medical technologies – and with ideas about the nature of the human as some proclaim the emergence of the post-human world. Swami Paramtattvadas's theology lays the foundations for Hindu ways to approach these issues and others important to Swaminarayan and Hindu Theology.

MacIntyre once described three rival versions of moral inquiry: the enlightenment model of detached, rational inquiry that claims objectivity; the genealogical critique of those assumptions stemming from Nietzsche; and a kind of discourse that stands within the values and horizon of tradition, such as Catholic thought. This book, while standing within Swaminarayan Hinduism, seeks to engage with a broader, rational discourse and to stimulate discussion beyond the bounds of Hindu communities. The writing of this book has been a large scholarly task, aiming to systematise key themes from an extensive network of the tradition's authoritative texts in Gujarati and Sanskrit. As such it is an important contribution to Theology and Religion and, to my knowledge, is the first Hindu systematic theology written in English. I am sure it will find a wide readership among both the academic and Hindu communities. I look forward to further developments in this promising new discussion.

PROFESSOR GAVIN FLOOD FBA
University of Oxford

Acknowledgements

Ancient authors began their works with benedictory verses invoking God, gurus and sages. Less eloquently, but no less sincerely, I wish to follow in this auspicious tradition by beginning with a heartfelt expression of my gratitude to those who have helped me in this work.

Firstly, my thanks to Gavin Flood, formerly Professor of Hindu Studies and Comparative Religion at the University of Oxford, who provided invaluable guidance, support and encouragement at every stage of this project, especially in its initial form as my doctoral thesis. Alongside him stands Shaunaka Rishi Dasa, Director of the Oxford Centre for Hindu Studies, whose encouragement, counsel and friendship have helped make my time at Oxford a great pleasure.

I have also benefitted from the astute guidance of several other scholars from around the world. To name a few of those who were kind enough to spare the time in reading my outline and sharing their input through correspondence and personal discussions, they are Francis X. Clooney, S.J. (Harvard University), Raymond Brady Williams (Wabash College), Parimal Patil (Harvard University), Chakravarthi Ram-Prasad (Lancaster University), Mark Edwards (University of Oxford), Graham M. Schweig (Christopher Newport University), Patrick Olivelle (University of Texas at Austin) and Ravi M. Gupta (Utah State University).

I wish also to acknowledge here my indebtedness to my tutors at Oxford University, including Mark Edwards, Johannes Zachhuber, Phillip Kennedy, John Muddiman, George Pattison, Yannis Papadogiannakis, Benno van den Toren, Christopher Tuckett, Christopher Rowland, Paul Joyce, Peter Harrison, Brian Leftow and Mark Chapman, under whom I studied for my Master of Studies in the Study of Religion and for a subsequent year of pre-doctoral studies, all of which proved vital training for this endeavour. Prior to this, my tutors and mentors at BAPS Swaminarayan Sanskrit Mahavidyalaya in Sarangpur, India, provided the essential grounding in Nyāya, Vyākaraṇa, Vedānta and Sanskrit literature, without which this further study would simply not have been possible. I therefore wish to offer my special thanks to Swami Gnaneshwardas, Swami Narayanmunidas, Swami Aksharcharandas, Swami Brahmadarshandas, Swami Bhadreshdas and Swami Bhaktisagardas, as well as to my former classmates with whom I spent over twelve happy years of learning there. Among them, I am especially indebted to Swami Atmatruptdas for his patient listening and insightful comments during our many discussions on the topic of Swaminarayan Hindu thought and practice.

Special thanks are also due to Swami Yogvivekdas, Head Swami at BAPS Shri Swaminarayan Mandir, London, where I lived and worked for the duration of my recent studies and research, for his untiring support and encouragement. My fellow swamis at the Mandir in London and elsewhere also deserve my grateful respect; their brotherhood was and continues to be a constant joy and blessing.

My extended stays in Gandhinagar, India, at AARSH (the Akshardham centre for Applied Research in Social Harmony) call for me to also appreciate, among several others, Swami Anandswarupdas, Swami Shrutiprakashdas and Swami Vishwaviharidas, along with Dinesh Patel, the ever-smiling librarian.

In bringing this book to its material form, I have been fortunate to have worked with an outstanding team of production, design and publishing experts. Of these, Laura Morris, Beatrice Rehl, Mary Catherine Bongiovi and Sri Hari Kumar Sugumaran, through the assistance of Yogesh Patel, provided timely instruction and continuous support. To them and everyone at Cambridge University Press, I am extremely grateful.

This book, of course, is not the first scholarly work on Swaminarayan Hinduism. It follows and is indebted to the decades of rigorous scholarship in Sanskrit, Gujarati and Hindi from several eminent scholars within the tradition. I wish to thank all of them, in particular Swami Ishwarcharandas and Swami Viveksagardas, who have enriched the field of Swaminarayan Studies for over fifty years with their insightful writings and discourses.

Finally, to whom I owe my greatest debt of gratitude, not only for their constant care, support and encouragement, but also for their profundity and clarity of scriptural exegesis, are my gurus, Pramukh Swami Maharaj and Mahant Swami Maharaj, and their guru, Shastriji Maharaj, whose incisive scholarship defined by relentless fidelity to and careful elucidation of Swaminarayan's teachings has informed my understanding of

Swaminarayan Hindu theology throughout this exposition. It is thus to them and all my teachers that I dedicate this book.

> Yad atra sauṣṭavaṁ kiñcit tad guror-eva me na hi |
> Yad atrā'sauṣṭavaṁ kiñcit tan mamaiva guror-na hi ||

> Whatever is good here [in this work] is attributable
> only to my teachers, not to me.
> Whatever is bad here [in this work] is attributable
> only to me, not to my teachers.

Notes on Text and Translation

Italics

I have chosen not to italicise Sanskrit and Gujarati words or titles of key sources, such as those abbreviated below. The sheer number of their occurrence would have made for cumbersome reading.

Quotations from Primary Sources

Quotations from primary sources, of whatever length, have been indented to highlight their primacy.

Translations

All translations from Sanskrit and Gujarati works are my own. For the Vacanāmrut, I used the latest Gujarati edition, published in 2015 with extensive footnotes and appendices (696 pages), but also consulted the revised English version, for which I was a part of the team of translators and a member of the editorial committee.

Sanskrit and Gujarati words of special interest or importance are provided, in transliteration, within curly brackets alongside their English translation. This heuristic device will help Sanskrit and Gujarati readers see how the translation was rendered and to appreciate key terms that may not be immediately apparent in translation.

Transliteration

For the Romanisation of Sanskrit text from the Devanagari script, I have used the standard scheme established by the International Alphabet of Sanskrit Transliteration.

On the whole, I have followed the same rules when transliterating Gujarati. However, it should be noted that there is a loss in phonemic length of vowels, especially the 'a' when conjoined with the final consonant of a morpheme. Thus, in practice, although one might write 'પ્રગટ', for example, it is usually pronounced in Gujarati as 'pragaṭ' (as opposed to 'pragaṭa' in Sanskrit). Also, the 'ઋ' is more commonly pronounced as 'ru', so 'Vacanāmṛta', 'Prakṛti' and 'kṛpā', for example, are pronounced in Gujarati as 'Vacanāmrut', 'Prakruti' and 'krupā'. This may cause some confusion for words that are written identically in Sanskrit and Gujarati, but are pronounced differently. As a rule, I have kept the Sanskrit as the default pronunciation, except when citing words explicitly from Gujarati sources. For accuracy, I have transliterated these words as they are commonly pronounced in Gujarati. With the absence of the retroflexive 'ળ' in Sanskrit, but which is common in Gujarati, I have denoted it with 'ḷ', which should not be confused with the rare Sanskrit vocalic 'ḷ'.

As is becoming common innovation, I have sometimes applied English suffixes to Sanskrit and Gujarati words to form such modifiers as māyic, śāstric, sampradāyic, brahmic, etc. Their spellings thus follow English conventions rather than the Sanskrit or Gujarati, as in 'Vedic', 'yogic' and 'Upaniṣadic', etc., rather than 'Vaidika', 'yaugika' and 'Aupaniṣadika', as it would be otherwise. Only occasionally have I extended this rule to beyond adjectives, e.g., for such useful adverbs as 'sampradāyically'.

Finally, for non-English names of people and places, I have generally used the common Anglicised spelling, providing the Sanskrit or Gujarati pronunciation in parentheses at the first occurrence of each. However, for non-recurring names of people, I have used only the diacritically marked spelling.

Abbreviations

Titles of key texts and, in the case of the Vacanāmrut, its major sections have been abbreviated as below when used in citations and sometimes within the text.

AU	Aitareya Upaniṣad
BG	Bhagavad-Gītā
BP	Bhāgavata-Purāṇa
BS	Brahmasūtras
BU	Bṛhadāraṇyaka Upaniṣad
CU	Chāndogya Upaniṣad
IU	Īśā Upaniṣad
KaU	Kaṭha Upaniṣad
KeU	Kena Upaniṣad
MāU	Māṇḍūkya Upaniṣad
MuU	Muṇḍaka Upaniṣad
PU	Praśna Upaniṣad
SB	Svāminārāyaṇa-Bhāṣya
SU	Śvetāśvatara Upaniṣad
SV	Svāmīnī Vāto
TU	Taittirīya Upaniṣad
Vac. Amd.	Vacanāmrut Amdāvād
Vac. Gaḍh. 1	Vacanāmrut Gaḍhaḍā I
Vac. Gaḍh. 2	Vacanāmrut Gaḍhaḍā II
Vac. Gaḍh. 3	Vacanāmrut Gaḍhaḍā III
Vac. Jet.	Vacanāmrut Jetalpur
Vac. Kār.	Vacanāmrut Kāriyāṇī
Vac. Loyā	Vacanāmrut Loyā
Vac. Pan.	Vacanāmrut Pancāḷā
Vac. Sār.	Vacanāmrut Sāraṅgpur
Vac. Var.	Vacanāmrut Vartāl
VR	Vedaras

CHAPTER 1

Prolegomenon

Background and Rationale

This book seeks to provide a theological exposition of the Swaminarayan (Svāminārāyaṇa) Hindu tradition's belief system.

The Swaminarayan tradition, or Swaminarayan Hinduism, takes its name from its founder and deity, Swaminarayan, earlier known as Sahajanand Swami (Sahajānanda Svāmī).

Swaminarayan was born on 3 April 1781 in northern India. After a childhood of prodigious learning and the passing of his parents, he renounced his home at the age of eleven to travel alone as a child-yogi, wearing only a loincloth and carrying little besides a staff and gourd. His journey took him to the Himalayas, into Nepal and Tibet, through present-day Myanmar (formerly Burma) and Bangladesh, and around India. After seven years and almost 8,000 miles (12,000 kilometres), he settled in western India, in what is currently the state of Gujarat. There, at the age of twenty-one, he founded what came to be known as the Swaminarayan Sampradāya. Over his twenty-eight-year ministry, he introduced many social and religious reforms and initiated 3,000 sadhus {ordained monks}, 500 of whom were of the highest order, called paramhansas. He built six large temples and inspired scores of religious works in Sanskrit and vernacular languages. His works of public edification and social reform also attracted the attention of British officials and Christian clergy, including the Governor of Bombay Sir John Malcolm and the Bishop of Calcutta Reginald Heber. By his followers he was worshipped as Parabrahman, the supreme existential reality. He passed away on 1 June 1830.[1]

[1] For a comprehensive biographical account of the life and work of Swaminarayan, see Harshad T. Dave's *Bhagvān Śrī Svāminārāyaṇ*, 5 vols (Ahmedabad: Swaminarayan Aksharpith, 2013). For a concise introduction in Gujarati, see Swami Adarshjivandas's *Sarvāvatārī Bhagvān Svāminārāyaṇ: Jīvan ane Kārya* (Ahmedabad: Swaminarayan Aksharpith, 2005), 240 pages, and in English, Yogi Trivedi's *Bhagwan Swaminarayan: The Story of His Life* (Ahmedabad: Swaminarayan Aksharpith, 2014), 497 pages, and Swami Mukundcharandas's *Bhagwan Swaminarayan: An Introduction* (Ahmedabad: Swaminarayan Aksharpith, 2007), 106 pages. For a short summary,

More than 200 years since its founding, Swaminarayan Hinduism has flourished into a transnational movement described as one of the 'fastest-growing'[2] Hindu groups in many parts of the world and certainly one of the 'most visible forms of contemporary Hinduism'[3] in India and the West. For example, the 'largest comprehensive Hindu temple in the world'[4] has been built in the Indian capital of New Delhi by BAPS Swaminarayan Sanstha, one of the tradition's largest denominations, also described as 'the single largest identifiable Hindu community in the West'[5]. The hundred-acre temple complex's opening ceremony in 2005 was attended by both the Prime Minister and the President of India. The first traditional Hindu stone temple built in modern times outside of India is in Neasden, London. Built by the same Swaminarayan group, it opened in 1995 and annually receives around 400,000 worshippers, pilgrims and visitors, including over 30,000 students from schools, colleges and universities coming to learn about Hinduism. The 'Neasden Temple', as it is popularly known, has also been visited by royalty, celebrities and religious and political leaders. In recent years, the same group has built similarly large and intricately carved stone temples in North America, in Chicago and Houston (2004), Atlanta and Toronto (2007), Los Angeles (2012) and Robbinsville, near Princeton, New Jersey (2014). Together with several other denominations of the tradition, Swaminarayan Hinduism has thousands of temples and centres in Britain, parts of mainland Europe, North America, Africa and the Middle East, the Asia-Pacific and of course all over India, with an estimated global fellowship of over five million followers.

But for all its global presence, public engagement and continuing growth,[6] surprisingly little has been written in English about what the Swaminarayan fellowship believes. What are the tradition's core beliefs underpinning all

see Raymond Brady Williams, *An Introduction to Swaminarayan Hinduism* (Cambridge University Press, 2001), pp. 12–32.

[2] Williams, *Swaminarayan Hinduism*, pp. 54, 64, 201, 217 and 218.

[3] Raymond Brady Williams, 'Introduction' in Raymond Brady Williams and Yogi Trivedi (eds.), *Swaminarayan Hinduism: Tradition, Adaptation, and Identity* (New Delhi: Oxford University Press, 2016), p. xix.

[4] *Guinness World Records 2009* (London: Guinness World Records, 2008), pp. 270–1.

[5] J. Gordon Melton and Constance A. Jones, 'Reflections on Hindu Demographics in America', p. 7; accessible at www.thearda.com/asrec/archive/papers/Melton_Hindu_Demographics.pdf.

[6] See, for example, Arun Brahmbhatt, 'The BAPS Swaminarayan Community' in Helen R. Ebaugh and Stephen Cherry (eds.), *Global Religious Movements Across Borders: Sacred Service* (Farhnam, UK and Burlington, VT: Ashgate, 2014), pp. 99–122; Hanna Kim, 'Transnational Movements: Portable Religion and the Case Study of the BAPS Swaminarayan Sanstha' in Brian A. Hatcher (ed.), *Hinduism in the Modern World* (New York: Taylor & Francis/Routledge, 2015), pp. 48–64; and Hanna Kim, 'The BAPS Swaminarayan Temple Organisation and Its Publics' in John Zavos, Pralay Kanungo, Deepa S. Reddy, Maya Warrier and Raymond Brady Williams (eds.), *Public Hinduisms* (New Delhi, India: Sage, 2012), pp. 417–39.

their temples and charitable works of community outreach and, presumably, driving its growth? Are these beliefs rooted in canonical Hindu texts? Indeed, how do these beliefs make this relatively young Hindu tradition a distinct school of thought within the larger expanse of classical Vedānta?

This book addresses these questions by providing a systematic and thorough doctrinal account of the Swaminarayan Hindu tradition's core beliefs. Presenting them within a theological framework helps make the belief system intelligible to scholars, students and serious readers.

Hindu Theology

As a discipline committed to the study of God (and God-related topics) relying primarily on scriptural authority and, for practitioners if not scholars, a faith-based inquiry amenable to reason in the quest for greater understanding, theology is a natural and highly fruitful way to expound the belief system of Swaminarayan Hinduism. Indeed, the idea of presenting Hindu beliefs theologically has recently been gaining traction in Western academia. In his chapter in *The Blackwell Companion to Hinduism*, Francis X. Clooney, S.J. calls for 'Restoring "Hindu Theology" as a Category in Indian Intellectual Discourse'.[7] With its emphasis on Scripture and other religious authorities, it is theology rather than philosophy, Clooney argues, which 'most accurately describes some of the major trajectories of Hindu thought'.[8] He also adds: 'It must be the theologians of the Hindu tradition who must take the lead in maintaining and fostering Hindu theology.'[9]

Clooney reiterates his argument and hope for Hindu theology in his seminal work on comparative theology, *Comparative Theology: Deep Learning Across Religious Borders*.[10] He writes: 'Since we are speaking of *Hindu* theology and not a *theology of Hinduism*, the final test must occur in the Hindu context, if and when there are thinkers willing to identify themselves as both "Hindus" and "theologians." They must decide whether to agree that there is Hindu theology; I hope they do.'[11]

Clooney, though, is not the first to advocate the category of Hindu theology. Julius Lipner wrote in 1986: 'The time has come, I believe, to rehabilitate "theology" as an apt description for a substantial part of the

[7] Gavin Flood (ed.), *The Blackwell Companion to Hinduism* (Oxford and Malden, MA: Blackwell, 2003), pp. 447–77.

[8] Clooney, 'Restoring "Hindu Theology"', p. 449. [9] Ibid., p. 463.

[10] Francis X. Clooney, S.J., *Comparative Theology: Deep Learning Across Religious Borders* (Oxford and Malden, MA: Wiley-Blackwell, 2010).

[11] Ibid. p. 79 (emphasis original).

intellectual tradition of the Hindus.'[12] More than a decade before him, John Carman had already written *The Theology of Rāmānuja*,[13] while perhaps the first exploration of theology in an explicitly Hindu sense was conducted much earlier, in 1930, by the German Lutheran theologian Rudolf Otto in his *India's Religion of Grace and Christianity Compared and Contrasted*.[14] Academic interest in Hindu theology has noticeably grown in recent years, evidenced by dedicated panels at international conferences[15] and more recent works such as *Hindu Theology and Biology*,[16] *Hindu Theology in Early Modern South Asia*[17] and *A Hindu Theology of Liberation*.[18]

In advancing this exciting, developing new discipline, this book is an attempt by a practitioner-theologian to articulate the Swaminarayan tradition in theological terms according to recognised scholarly standards and conventions, aiming not just at describing or justifying Hindu theology, but also at constructively and systematically *doing* theology. In other words, it is a serious attempt to engage with Western theology from a Hindu standpoint using a Hindu example and working from within that tradition. Thus theologising within Swaminarayan Hinduism not only establishes itself as a theological system and a good example of Hindu theology, it also *a posteriori* affirms the viability, validity and value of Hindu theology more generally.

In self-consciously dealing with theology in a Hindu context *as* 'Hindu theology', this effort will inevitably take Hindu theology beyond its usual national and linguistic borders; the fact that this is in English and uses terms previously reserved solely for Christian theology makes it immediately comparative and relevant. Yet it also presents an opportunity to compare classical Hindu Vedānta with contemporary Western understandings of theology. This not only opens up more fruitful ways of

[12] *The Face of Truth: A Study of Meaning and Metaphysics in the Vedāntic Theology of Rāmānuja* (State University of New York Press, 1986), p. ix.

[13] John Braisted Carman, *The Theology of Rāmānuja: An Essay in Interreligious Understanding* (New Haven, CT and London: Yale University Press, 1974).

[14] (New York: Macmillan, 1930). Graham Schweig provides some historical background to the use of 'theology' in a non-Christian, Vaiṣṇava context in his conclusion to *A Living Theology of Krishna Bhakti: Essential Teachings of A. C. Bhaktivedanta Swami Prabhupada* by Tamal Krishna Goswami (New York: Oxford University Press, 2012), pp. 205–8.

[15] For example, at the American Academy of Religion's Annual Meeting in 2008, in Chicago.

[16] Jonathan Edelmann, *Hindu Theology and Biology: The Bhāgavata Purāṇa and Contemporary Theory* (Oxford University Press, 2012).

[17] Kiyokazu Okita, *Hindu Theology in Early Modern South Asia: The Rise of Devotionalism and the Politics of Genealogy* (Oxford University Press, 2014).

[18] Anantanand Rambachan, *A Hindu Theology of Liberation: Not-Two Is Not One* (State University of New York, 2015).

understanding traditional Hindu thought, but also broadens and enriches the category of theology as a whole. The promise lies in the opportunity of developing a shared intellectual space and respect for Hindu theology among scholars, students and serious readers, both in the academy and in Hindu and other religious communities.

Methodology

Alister McGrath writes in his popular introduction to Christian theology that 'questions of method have dominated modern theology, not least on account of the challenge of the Enlightenment to establish reliable foundations of knowledge'.[19] However, he quotes Jeffery Stout of Princeton University as he observes: 'Preoccupation with methodology is like clearing your throat; it can go on for only so long before you lose your audience.'[20] David Kelsey, in prefacing his two-volume *Eccentric Existence: A Theological Anthropology*, too bemoans 'today's methodologically hyper-self-conscious world of technical academic theology'.[21] He therefore confesses that identifying any methodological commitments to a complex theological project can be 'largely retrospective', warning that we should be sceptical of any efforts to reduce the work of theology to producing an 'instructions booklet' about how to assemble one's very own conceptual structure. Theology, he believes, 'is too much of an art form to be regulated in that way'. Besides, so diverse are the intellectual and imaginative challenges peculiar to different theological topics that any set of methodological rules claiming to cover them all would have to be so general as to be ineffective.[22] Daniel Migliore similarly warns of the 'growing danger' that 'the work of theology is being replaced by the work of *preparing* to do theology'.[23]

This book is squarely committed to the *work* of theology. However, without indulging too far in any methodological technicalities, some basic notes on how I have intended to go about this theological project are nonetheless necessary.

[19] Alister E. McGrath, *Christian Theology: An Introduction*, 4th edn (Oxford and Malden, MA: Blackwell, 2007), p. 112.

[20] Ibid.

[21] David H. Kelsey, *Eccentric Existence: A Theological Anthropology*, 2 vols (Louisville, KY: Westminster John Knox Press, 2009), I, p. 12.

[22] Ibid.

[23] Daniel L. Migliore, *Faith Seeking Understanding: An Introduction to Christian Theology*, 2nd edn (Grand Rapids, MI and Cambridge, UK: William B. Eerdmans, 2004), p. xiii (emphasis added).

In attempting to identify and locate theology within a Hindu context, the task, as Clooney observes, 'involves a reflection on Hindu intellectual discourses and an intelligent re-use of ideas rooted in Christian and Western intellectual sensitivities'.[24] Specifically, I am adopting the style of 'Systematic Theology' to formulate a clear, orderly and coherent overview of the Swaminarayan tradition's key doctrinal themes.

I am aware that systematic theology has come under some suspicion in the postmodern era, specifically for its attempts to offer neat, doctrinal packages, often dismissed as 'mere dogmatics'.[25] The shift of authority from the theologian to the individual has especially raised questions about whether any useful, meaningful understanding of God can be systematised, which, according to the critiques, attempts to box him into categories with an arrogant sense of finality. After all, the Bible is not itself systematically structured. It is a diverse collection of writings and, even while believed by many Christians to be God's inerrant word, is not a mere handbook of doctrine and morals. As eminent theologian Charles Hodge wrote, 'the Bible is no more a system of theology than nature is a system of chemistry or of mechanics'.[26] Like the Bible, neither the Vacanāmrut (the principal theological text of Swaminarayan Hinduism) nor the Upaniṣads or Bhagavad-Gītā are organised according to doctrinal loci.

Nevertheless, as Migliore defends, 'the effort of theology to be "systematic" should be affirmed insofar as it expresses trust in the unity and faithfulness of God in all God's works'. Patterns and continuities can emerge from his revelation giving shape and coherence to our theological reflection.[27] He goes on to engage David Tracy's argument that 'fragments' rather than 'totalities' best describe the form of our knowledge of God. Even so, a provisional 'gathering of fragments' is still possible and fruitful.[28] The corralling, organising and contextualising of key passages and discussions into as coherent an account as possible is the task of the

[24] Clooney, 'Restoring "Hindu Theology"', p. 449.

[25] See, for example, Mark Taylor's *Erring: A Postmodern A/theology* (Chicago University Press, 1984). For more on this topic, see Kevin J. Vanhoozer (ed.), *The Cambridge Companion to Postmodern Theology* (Cambridge University Press, 2003).

[26] Charles Hodge, *Systematic Theology*, 3 vols (Grand Rapids, MI: William B. Eerdmans, 1940), I, p. 1.

[27] Migliore, *Faith Seeking Understanding*, p. 12.

[28] David Tracy, 'Form and Fragment: The Recovery of the Hidden and Incomprehensible God', *Reflections: Centre of Theological Inquiry*, 3 (Autumn 2000), 62–88, cited in Migliore, *Faith Seeking Understanding*, p. 12.

systematic theologian.[29] Hodge explains: 'This is not an easy task, or one of slight importance.'[30]

Many of my decisions in undertaking this important task have been guided by the appreciation that this is the first such systematic theological account of Swaminarayan Hinduism in English and perhaps one of very few of a living Hindu tradition. By design, I have therefore kept the scope of the project broad so as to provide a thorough – though by no means exhaustive – overview of the Swaminarayan system as a useful example of Hindu theology at work. This has necessitated an exposition of all its main themes, as is the nature and demand of systematic theology, which has sometimes precluded an in-depth exploration of each of them in a limited single-volume work.[31] Nevertheless, I have attempted to demonstrate the possibility of deep theological reflection and analysis at various junctures, for example, in the technical, hermeneutical study of certain statements from the Upaniṣads and Bhagavad-Gītā in relation to the ontological distinction of Akṣarabrahman from Parabrahman (see Section 'Akṣarabrahman as Ontologically Distinct from Parabrahman' in Chapter 7). To employ a photographic analogy, I have used both a wide-angle lens to set the scene of the landscape and then also, at useful and interesting points in the expanse, shifted to a telephoto lens to zoom in on the finer details. This should provide an adequate 'lay of the land' while also demonstrating the scope of depth possible.

The expansive nature of this project has also led it to be largely descriptive in style. The deliberate intention has been to lay the groundwork, ready for subsequent rounds of theologising and critical analysis. I believe it was vital at this nascent stage of Swaminarayan studies in the Western academic setting to concentrate on carefully expounding the Swaminarayan system rather than critiquing it, though, of course, not at the expense of any academic rigour or clarity.[32] (See also the Afterword, for opportunities of new scholarship to which this introductory exposition now leads.)

[29] It shall become apparent that I do not see theology as an exclusive enterprise performed by a cadre of professional theologians in the academy or ministers in 'Church' (or pundits and priests in a temple) – although as both a scholar and ordained monk I see the great worth of both these roles – but an *active* exercise for every member of a religious community in which they participate by reflecting upon and practising their faith in search of greater understanding. See also Nicholas M. Healy, 'What is Systematic Theology?' *International Journal of Systematic Theology*, 11 (2009), 24–39 on his three types of 'systematic theology': (1) 'official', produced by the institutional church; (2) 'ordinary' theological reflection, engaged in by virtually all believers; and (3) 'professional', performed by academics.

[30] Hodge, *Systematic Theology*, 1, p. 2.

[31] This would be in contrast to the expansive, multivolume works of systematic theology produced by, for example, Karl Barth, Charles Hodge, Paul Tillich and Wolfhart Pannenberg.

[32] See Lipner's similar observation in *The Face of Truth*, p. xi.

is conceived as being inherently pure but in need of liberation from a false self-understanding?

This also raises the politically charged question of who *owns* theological words, such as 'God' and 'salvation', even 'theology'? Does salvation *have* to presuppose original sin? If not, what will the Christian be saved from? How distinct is the concept of being 'saved' from being 'freed'? Or can soteriology also mean being *liberated* from the bondage of sin? Conversely, can jīvas {the spiritual self} be *saved* from māyā {binding ignorance}? But can that which is not damned be saved? If not, how proper is it to speak of the 'salvation' of the jīva? Can indeed doctrines be argued on words? For example, can that which is not hidden be revealed? If not, how accurate is 'revelation' in referring to scriptural descriptions about God in Hindu theology?

Those who brazenly dismiss such debates as 'mere semantics' would do well to remember that theologians for centuries have argued zealously over meaning and interpretation, from the early ecumenical councils debating the union of the two natures in Christ and his consubstantiality with God the Father to disputes among the Vedāntic schools arguing for which type of non-dualism is accurate – pure, qualified, singular or none at all.

In an effort to increase accuracy and intelligibility, one alternative to using Sanskrit terms, such as 'mukti mīmāṃsā', could be to employ their Latin or Greek equivalents, such as *līberātiō*. Extending this to parallel various derivatives, we can have 'liberation' (for 'salvation'), 'liberatology' (for 'soteriology'), 'liberatological' (for 'soteriological'), 'liberative' or 'liberatific' (for 'salvific') and 'liberator' (for 'saviour'). But this still does little to clarify the different and nuanced doctrinal meanings underlying such terms.

Another option could be to apply Greek suffixes to Sanskrit terms. Like Christology, could we have 'Brahmology', for example? When suggesting 'Buddhology' or 'Dharmology' for Buddhist theology, José Ignacio Cabezón observed that 'new nomenclature … besides being infelicitous, will become meaningful only through consensual use, which in any discipline is difficult to achieve'.[35] A more prevalent practice has been to form adjectives and even adverbs from popular Sanskrit nouns, such as 'yogic' and 'yogically' from 'yoga'.[36]

[35] José Ignacio Cabezón, 'Buddhist Theology in the Academy' in Roger Jackson and John Makransky (eds.), *Buddhist Theology: Critical Reflections by Contemporary Buddhist Scholars* (Richmond, UK: Curzon, 2000), p. 25.

[36] See Notes on Text and Translation for further examples of such usage in this book.

What should be apparent is that there does not (yet) appear to be a consensus among scholars on the best or accepted way to proceed on this matter. Until there is, and possibly even thereafter, there will need to be a patient learning process for both readers and authors. Readers will have to avoid, as far as possible, (dis)colouring their understanding of new concepts with already known ideas from their own faith. If I use 'salvation', to recall our earlier example, can I be sure that the Christian will not assume that the Hindu soul is also born of original sin which needs to be 'saved' rather than liberated? Equally, authors will be called to adopt new terms and ways to express their theological ideas, often learning from other systems, all the while being true to the ideas themselves, without compromising, as far as possible, their complexity, richness, profundity and subtle nuances.

In an effort to make Hindu theology intelligible and appreciable, I struggled, as perhaps was inevitable, towards a 'happy middle' between the two extremes of stubborn adherence to native terminology and wilful ascension to over-translation. While thus happily and humbly appreciating the power and limitation of words, I also had to concede to Parimal Patil's pragmatic observation that 'Hindu intellectuals will be forced, at least for the present, to conform to the vocabulary and genre conventions of contemporary philosophical theology'.[37] I have therefore used words from a theologically familiar vocabulary as a starting point, qualifying them sufficiently to lead the reader into understanding something which is analogous to what she might already know yet would require some reasonable modification. This careful explaining and reading (and rereading) is itself a deeply inter-religious, comparative and dialogical task of learning.

Structure

The contents of this book are sectioned into two broad parts, each divided more finely into discrete chapters and sub-chapters.

As aforementioned, this book is committed to *doing* Hindu theology rather than simply discussing or defining it. But before embarking upon any theologising within the Swaminarayan tradition, the sources and tools of Swaminarayan theology will need to be delineated. This is covered in Part I.

[37] Parimal Patil, 'A Hindu Theologian's Response: A Prolegomenon to "Christian God, Hindu God"' in Francis X. Clooney, S.J., *Hindu God, Christian God: How Reason Helps Break Down the Boundaries between Religions* (Oxford University Press, 2001), p. 188.

With theology so rooted in revelation – indeed, it is what distinguishes it from philosophy and perhaps all other intellectual disciplines – the crux of this section will deal with the revelatory sources of theology within Swaminarayan Hinduism. It will begin with an understanding of revelation in Swaminarayan Hindu theology and how this relates to Parabrahman, the Guru, the soul and 'Scripture', by which I refer mainly to Swaminarayan's own teachings documented in the Vacanāmrut, the principal theological text of the tradition. I shall examine its determinant features as a revelatory source, including, importantly, how it is to be read and interpreted. Additionally, I will touch upon the position and role of three tools of theology – reason, tradition and praxis – especially in relation to the primacy of Scripture.

With tools in hand, the discussion will then be able to proceed to the heart of the book in the form of Part II. I begin by introducing the Swaminarayan theological system as comprising *five* eternal metaphysical entities – Parabrahman, (Akṣara)Brahman, māyā, īśvara and jīva – which immediately sets it apart from other schools of Vedānta. Each entity is then systematically expounded within its own chapter, covering its nature, its relationship with other entities, and important clarifications and discussions also relevant to the wider field of Hindu theology and possibly also theology. It will end, fittingly, with a section on the goal and climax of theological understanding and practice, the liberation of the soul. This format also allows the book to cover the three key topics associated with classical Vedāntic inquiry: pramāṇa-mīmāṃsā (epistemology; Chapters 2–4), tattva-mīmāṃsā (metaphysics; Chapters 5–10) and mukti-mīmāṃsā (soteriology; Chapter 11).

At relevant junctures, I also raise challenges to some of the abovementioned themes and explore how they are addressed theologically – though, to be clear, this book is neither intended to be polemical in style nor apologetics in genre. Rather, such a study will provide useful insights into the exegetical discussions that can ensue in Swaminarayan Hindu theology, and Hindu theology more broadly, when difficult questions are raised and answered from within the tradition.

Since this book is envisioned as opening up new avenues of theological reflection, analysis and description, both within the Swaminarayan tradition and beyond, the Afterword will consider possible ways forward from this introduction. The epilogical chapter touches upon some of the exciting and challenging opportunities for new scholarship on the Swaminarayan Hindu tradition, in Hindu theology and Hinduism, and especially in comparative theology. It explores a variety of possibilities within theology and also where it meets, intersects and collides with secular concerns and concerns of modernity. The intention and hope is to broaden and enrich not only Swaminarayan Hindu theology and Hindu studies, but the discipline of theology and religion as a whole.

Finally, the book is appended with a glossary of useful Sanskrit, Gujarati and English terms commonly encountered in Swaminarayan Hindu theology and a summary of the key theological principles of the Swaminarayan Hindu tradition as distilled by Pramukh Swami Maharaj (further explained below). Though brief, both shall prove helpful for readers wishing to better understand the belief system presented in this book.

Sources

With theology so deeply attentive to scriptural analysis, it is both natural and necessary that this book on Swaminarayan Hindu theology be similarly grounded in and guided by Hindu revelatory texts. In particular, I rely upon two sets of textual sources. The primary sources from the Swaminarayan corpus include the Vacanāmrut, Vedaras, Svāmīnī Vāto and other Guru teachings, all of which are in Gujarati. These will be closely substantiated with the three Sanskrit texts commonly referred to collectively as the 'Prasthānatrayī' – the Brahmasūtras, Upaniṣads and Bhagavad-Gītā – and their respective commentaries.[38] I also draw upon the extensive existing scholarship from within and on the Swaminarayan tradition (found mainly in Gujarati, with some works in Sanskrit, Hindi and English), along with other secondary sources, including writings in English from the academic discipline of theology in general.

Some further description is warranted to introduce the main primary texts.

Vacanāmrut: This is a collection of 273 discourses[39] delivered by Swaminarayan towards the end of his life, between 1819 and 1829 CE (see cover image). These discourses were meticulously documented and

[38] The polysemantic nature of the Prasthānatrayī texts makes commentaries a necessary and integral part of Vedāntic literature. Traditionally, each of the Vedānta schools formulated their own interpretations in their commentaries to validate their doctrines as being in consonance with the original revelatory sources.

[39] The version I am using is the original Gujarati text published by Swaminarayan Aksharpith, which itself is a letter-to-letter, printed version of the original manuscript, containing 262 discourses, published in 1928 under the auspices of Acharya Shripatiprasad of the Vartal diocese. A further eleven discourses accepted as canonical by the Ahmedabad diocese are appended as 'Additional Vacanāmruts', making 273 in total. The useful doctrinal letter titled 'Bhūgoḷ-Khagoḷ' is included in another appendix.

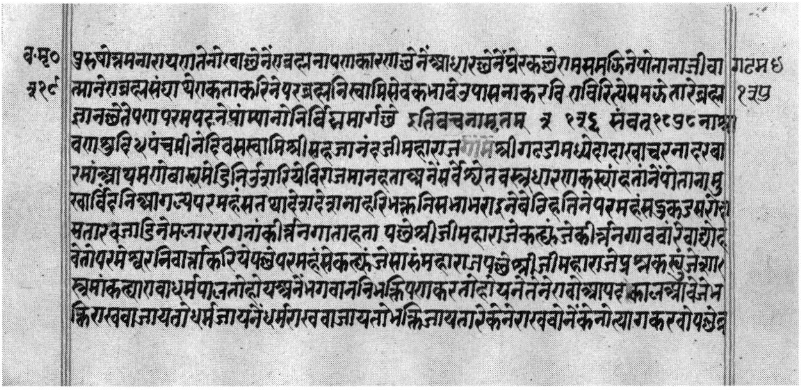

Figure 1 One of the oldest extant manuscripts of the Vacanāmrut, dated 1833. The folio shown is of Gaḍhaḍā 2.3, in which Swaminarayan explains the ontological distinction and relationship between Akṣarabrahman and Parabrahman. (Photo courtesy of Akshardham centre for Applied Research in Social Harmony, Gandhinagar)

compiled by four of his most learned and senior disciples – Gopalanand Swami (Gopālānanda Svāmī), Muktanand Swami (Muktānanda Svāmī), Nityanand Swami (Nityānanda Svāmī) and Shukanand Swami (Śukānanda Svāmī) – and later presented to him for review and personal verification (see, for example, the mention in Vac. Loyā.7 and Prasādānand Svāmīnī Vāto 42). This compilation came to be known as the 'Vacanāmrut', literally 'immortalising ambrosia in the form of words' (Figure 1).

The text is divided into ten sections, based on the various villages and towns in which the discourses were delivered. The sections are chronological in order and named as follows: Gaḍhaḍā 1, Sāraṅgpur, Kāriyāṇī, Loyā, Pancāḷā, Gaḍhaḍā 2, Vartāl, Amdāvād and Gaḍhaḍā 3. Two additional sections include eleven discourses from Amdāvād, Aślālī and Jetalpur, and a letter, traditionally titled 'Bhūgoḷ-Khagoḷ', dictated from Gaḍhaḍā containing a cosmological description of the world. Each individual discourse is also called a 'Vacanāmrut', and these are arranged chronologically and numbered sequentially within each section. Hence, 'Vacanāmrut Vartāl 11' (abbreviated to 'Vac. Var.11'), for example, is the eleventh recorded discourse delivered by Swaminarayan in the town of Vartāl.

Ingeniously, each Vacanāmrut opens with an introductory paragraph meticulously describing the setting of the assembly in which the discourse was delivered. Swaminarayan instructed Muktanand Swami to include the precise date of each discourse and the names of those who asked questions in the assembly.[40] Even at the risk of sounding repetitive, the compilers also recorded the place and a mention of the audience seated in each assembly. In many instances, they also noted the time of day and described the clothes and adornments Swaminarayan was wearing. In some instances, they even described the seat upon which he was seated and the direction in which he was facing. This lends the text considerable historical authenticity.

In literary style, the Vacanāmrut is highly dialogical and didactic, with most discourses taking the form of a question-and-answer session, where either Swaminarayan asks the questions or members of his audience do, sometimes at his bidding. Even if he begins a sermon unprompted, he would sometimes question his own explanation to confirm if his audience had understood him correctly or to proleptically counter opposing views. More often, though, his aspiring seeker-followers, ranging from senior monks to lay farmers, would be braced with questions from their current readings of Hindu texts or their own personal application of those teachings. As Swaminarayan would answer, sometimes a series of follow-up questions or counter-questions would ensue as they probed for further clarity or refinement in their understanding of his teachings. This orality and reciprocal aurality between Swaminarayan and his disciples situates the Vacanāmrut in the ancient Upaniṣadic tradition of a guru-disciple dialogue.[41]

Swaminarayan spoke in the local language of Gujarati, presenting complex concepts in simple, lucid terms, drawing extensively on popular stories from the Purāṇas and epics and employing analogies and day-to-day examples, perhaps in an attempt to make his teachings as accessible as possible to his wide-ranging audience. He also cited profusely from the Upaniṣads, Bhagavad-Gītā, Bhāgavata-Purāṇa and various other authoritative Hindu texts.[42]

Most importantly, the Vacanāmrut is accepted within the Swaminarayan tradition as the primary revelatory text by which its doctrines are established and articulated. As we shall see in Part I, this abiding status of the Vacanāmrut is predicated on the distinctive belief of the faith community that Swaminarayan, as the self-manifestation of God, is both the source and the subject of revelatory knowledge comprised within it.

[40] Swami Prasadanand, *Sadguru Prasādānand Svāmīnī Vāto* (Ahmedabad: Shri Swaminarayan Mandir Kalupur, 1995), p. 208.

[41] For a detailed and insightful introduction to the Vacanāmrut, see Swami Brahmadarshandas's *Vacanāmrut Rahasya*, vol. I (Ahmedabad: Swaminarayan Aksharpith, 1999), 242 pages.

[42] See Section 'Primacy of Scripture' in Chapter 3 for more on this topic.

Vedaras: Swaminarayan also sent an extensive, preceptive letter addressed to his paramhansas. Apart from high moral instruction for a monastic way of life, the letter included considerable doctrinal elucidation. The opening reads:

> I write thoughts related to brahmavidyā for you in this letter. These thoughts are my innermost essence and the essence of all the Upaniṣads. (VR 2)

This letter has been published under the title 'Vedaras' {Essence of the Vedas}.

Swaminarayan is also believed to have authored the *Śikṣāpatrī*, a 212-verse work in Sanskrit. I should be clear about why I have not included it as a primary source. As the title reveals, the *Śikṣāpatrī* is an 'epistle of precepts', giving primarily *moral* injunctions. It is not a *theological* treatise of doctrinal elucidation. It thus proved unhelpful to me for this particular exposition. Nevertheless, any relevant portions of it have been elaborated and clarified with the help of other sampradāyic texts, as the *Śikṣāpatrī* itself instructs in verse 203.

Svāmīnī Vāto: Gunatitanand Swami (Guṇātītānanda Svāmī; 1785–1867 CE) was one of Swaminarayan's most eminent ordained monks and, according to some denominations within Swaminarayan Hinduism, was revealed by Swaminarayan as the personified human form of Akṣarabrahman on earth.[43] He is thus regarded as the first spiritual successor of Swaminarayan and the first in the lineage of Brahmasvarūpa Gurus continuing to this day. He preached extensively over his forty-year ministry, with many of his most important teachings being recorded by followers who lived and travelled with him. In his lifetime, these notes were compiled and even discoursed upon after being reviewed by Gunatitanand Swami, thereby giving the compilation the status of an authentic text. It came to be known simply as 'Svāmīnī Vāto', the 'talks of [Gunatitanand] Swami'. Eventually this was published, first in five chapters and later in seven chapters.[44]

[43] For detailed accounts with historical evidence, see Swami Brahmadarshandas, *Vacanāmrut Rahasya*, vol. III (Ahmedabad: Swaminarayan Aksharpith, 2001), pp. 106–73, 415–38 and Swami Shrutiprakashdas, *Akṣarbrahma Nirupaṇ: Vaidik tathā Sāmpradāyik Śāstronā Ādhāre* (Ahmedabad: Swaminarayan Aksharpith, 2009), pp. 217–52. Both draw extensively from the original research of Shastriji Maharaj, especially eye-witness accounts of Swaminarayan's contemporaries, noted, for example, in his letter of 7 December 1938 – see *Lī. Śāstrī Yajñapuruṣdāsjī* (Ahmedabad: Swaminarayan Aksharpith, 2007), II, pp. 374–82 – and a recording of his discourse from 1950, transcribed as 'Brahmasvarūp Svāmīśrī Śāstrījī Mahārājnī Divyavāṇī', *Svāminārāyaṇ Prakāś*, 469–70 (November–December 1977), 462–9.

[44] I am using the most recent version of the Gujarati text published by Swaminarayan Aksharpith (21st edition, 2015; 388 pages), which takes advantage of the latest research and a critical study of the original manuscripts.

The 'talks' themselves range from short, pithy sayings, some just one or a few lines long, to extensive explanations running over several pages. A key feature of the style of instruction is that it makes good use of parables and vivid imagery, drawing freely from quotidian occurrences and scriptural examples. The lucid, colloquial Gujarati language belies the sophisticated concepts it addresses and the practical guidance it provides in living out those concepts, an important emphasis of the teachings. It draws extensively from the Vacanāmrut and also cites several other Hindu texts. In elucidating, elaborating and providing further insight upon many of the important teachings of the Vacanāmrut, the Svāmīnī Vāto serves within the tradition as a 'natural commentary' upon it.[45]

Guru Teachings: Following Gunatitanand Swami in the lineage of Brahmasvarūpa Gurus of the BAPS Swaminarayan tradition are a further five generations of exponents of Swaminarayan Hindu theology: Bhagatji Maharaj (Bhagatjī Mahārāj; 1829–1897), Shastriji Maharaj (Śāstrījī Mahārāj; 1865–1951), Yogiji Maharaj (Yogījī Mahārāj; 1892–1971), Pramukh Swami Maharaj (Pramukh Svāmī Mahārāj; 1921–2016) and presently Mahant Swami Maharaj (Mahant Svāmī Mahārāj; b. 1933). Their teachings provide further layers of vital interpretation, clarification and elucidation of Swaminarayan's sermons, becoming, as with the Svāmīnī Vāto, 'natural commentaries upon the Vacanāmrut.

Swaminarayan himself repeatedly stressed, as we shall cover in some detail in Section 'Receiving Scripture through the Guru' in Chapter 3, that it is only when Scripture is received from the Brahmasvarūpa Guru that its revelations are fully accessible. This applies to his own words too. It was therefore essential to call upon these Guru teachings to ensure a clear and accurate reading of the Vacanāmrut. Thus, even though not cited explicitly, these teachings have necessarily informed all theological reflection in this book. It is only appropriate, then, that I acknowledge their vital role by briefly introducing here six key sources of these teachings, noteworthy for their exceptional historicity and theological content.

1. *Brahmasvarūp Śrī Prāgjī Bhakta*. This is a 590-page biography of Bhagatji Maharaj authored by Harshad T. Dave, one of the most prolific and eminent scholars of the Swaminarayan tradition, based on the copious notes and diaries of Shastriji Maharaj and contemporaries. Within the historical narrative, the biography includes Bhagatji

[45] For a useful introduction to the Svāmīnī Vāto, see Swami Brahmadarshandas, *Brahmavidyānā Amūlya Grantho: Vacanāmrut ane Svāmīnī Vāto* (Ahmedabad: Swaminarayan Aksharpith, 2008), pp. 72–150.

Maharaj's extensive oral exegesis upon the Vacanāmrut, portions of his other discourses and even a dialogue he had with scholars of other schools of thought, thereby providing useful elucidation on Swaminarayan doctrine.

2. *Lī. Śāstrī Yajñapuruṣdāsjī* is a two-volume collection of letters written by Shastriji Maharaj and his contemporaries between the years of 1888 and 1951. The internal correspondence among votaries of Swaminarayan Hindu theology, as well as those who were challenging its interpretations, provides an invaluable window into the history of BAPS Swaminarayan Sanstha and, more importantly for us, vital source material about Swaminarayan doctrine and practice. Among this compilation, of special significance are Shastriji Maharaj's own words and the letters of Swami Nirgundas, a leading scholar of the Swaminarayan tradition at the time. His indefatigably handwritten letters, sometimes spanning several scores of pages, contain renderings of Shastriji Maharaj's teachings scrupulously based on the Vacanāmrut.
3. *Brahmasvarūp Svāmīśrī Śāstrījī Mahārājnī Divyavāṇī*. This is the only extant audio track of Shastriji Maharaj, recorded in 1950 in Ahmedabad, Gujarat. In it, we hear him narrating eye-witness accounts of Swaminarayan's contemporaries recalling Swaminarayan's revelations on the nature of Akṣarabrahman and on Gunatitanand Swami as its personified form. A full transcript of this recording was published in the *Svāminārāyaṇ Prakāś* periodical in 1977.[46]
4. *Yogī Vāṇī*. This is a compilation of Yogiji Maharaj's teachings on Swaminarayan doctrine and praxis, distilled from the six-volume biography *Brahmasvarūp Yogījī Mahārāj* written by Swami Ishwarcharandas, a personal attendant of Yogiji Maharaj for over twenty years. The 364-page book of Yogiji Maharaj's sayings, captured in his original conversational style and characteristically colloquial words, contains extraordinarily profound theological clarifications.
5. *Yogī Gītā*. Some of Yogiji Maharaj's key teachings, including a letter dated 28 March 1941 and a transcript of a prayer said at Shastriji Maharaj's birthplace on 9 December 1966, have been compiled into this small, handy booklet. This, too, contains some invaluable interpretations of Swaminarayan's teachings from the Vacanāmrut.
6. *Svāminārāyaṇ Darśannā Siddhāntono Ālekh*. This is a creedal statement by Pramukh Swami Maharaj summarising the key theological

[46] 'Brahmasvarūp Svāmīśrī Śāstrījī Mahārājnī Divyavāṇī', *Svāminārāyaṇ Prakāś*, 469–70 (November-December 1977), 462–9.

principles of the BAPS Swaminarayan denomination. It prefaces recent editions of the Vacanāmrut published by Swaminarayan Aksharpith, along with the original handwritten words of Pramukh Swami Maharaj, indicating the statement's position as an exceptionally valuable and venerable source of theological revelation for those of the BAPS Swaminarayan fellowship. As a useful summary of Swaminarayan Hindu theology, the statement has been included whole, in English, as an appendix.

Svāminārāyaṇa-Bhāṣya: This voluminous set of commentaries on the canonical texts of Vedānta forms an important *magnum opus* of the Swaminarayan Hindu tradition. It provides a detailed, word-by-word explication and elaboration of the root text as well as a thorough elucidation and defence of the theological and philosophical concepts interpreted to be embedded therein. Though published relatively recently, between 2009 and 2012, the Svāminārāyaṇa-Bhāṣya is very much composed in the genre of other, much older, classical Vedāntic commentaries: It is written in Sanskrit and is rich in ratiocination; while religiously protecting the revelatory status of its sources, it foresees and forestalls contestations by offering *prima facie* views before consummately dismantling them and advancing the one, exegetically sound and conclusive interpretation according to the Swaminarayan school of thought.

Comprising five volumes and spanning more than two thousand pages, the Svāminārāyaṇa-Bhāṣya commentates on the foundational Vedāntic texts as follows:

1. Brahmasūtra-Svāminārāyaṇa-Bhāṣyam (462 pages)
2. Īśādyaṣṭopaniṣat-Svāminārāyaṇa-Bhāṣyam (476 pages)
   This contains a commentary on the following eight Upanishads:
   - Īśā Upaniṣad
   - Kena Upaniṣad
   - Kaṭha Upaniṣad
   - Praśna Upaniṣad
   - Muṇḍaka Upaniṣad
   - Māṇḍūkya Upaniṣad
   - Taittirīya Upaniṣad
   - Aitareya Upaniṣad
3. Bṛhadāraṇyakopaniṣat-Svāminārāyaṇa-Bhāṣya (389 pages)
4. Chāndogyopaniṣat-Svāminārāyaṇa-Bhāṣyam (419 pages)
5. Śrīmad-Bhagavad-Gītā-Svāminārāyaṇa-Bhāṣyam (404 pages)

All five volumes have been authored by Swami Bhadreshdas.[47] As the authoritative interpretation of Vedāntic texts in the BAPS Swaminarayan tradition, the Svāminārāyaṇa-Bhāṣya forms the basis of all readings of the Brahmasūtras, Upaniṣads and Bhagavad-Gītā used in this book.

Theological Scholarship in Swaminarayan Hinduism

Having introduced the primary texts in some detail, I move on now to provide an overview of, and pay tribute to, some of the other theological material that is available on the Swaminarayan Hindu tradition and which has provided a sturdy foundation upon which to construct this exposition.

Apart from a vast corpus of devotional literature, comprising thousands of hymns and scores of sacred biographies, both in prose and verse, a great deal of attention was also given to technical treatises and commentaries during Swaminarayan's own time. As Arun Brahmbhatt writes:

> Though Sahajanand Swami never authored a commentary on Vedanta canonical texts, his sacred biographies, writings, and teachings indicate his deep engagement with the Vedanta system and the earlier commentators and theologians. He left the task of writing commentaries to his disciples, who commenced a robust commentarial tradition comprising the authoring, translating, editing, and publishing of these texts for the edification of members of the Sampradaya, as well as entering into a conversation with a wider Vedanta and Indian intellectual audience.[48]

These commentaries (and sub-commentaries), mainly in Sanskrit and Gujarati but also Braj Bhasha, include those on the Brahmasūtras – *Brahmasūtrabhāṣyaratnam* by Muktanand Swami, *Vyāsasūtrārthadīpa* by Gopalanand Swami, *Brahmamīmāṃsā* attributed to Muktanand Swami, with *Pradīpa* thereon attributed to Gopalanand Swami; the Upaniṣads – *Īśāvāsyopaniṣadbhāṣyam* by Gopalanand Swami; the Bhagavad-Gītā – *Śṛī Bhagavad Gītā Bhāṣya* by Muktanand Swami, *Śrī Bhagavad Gītā Saṭīk* by

[47] Swami Bhadreshdas is an eminent scholar of the Swaminarayan Hindu tradition, with a string of academic qualifications and accolades to his name, including: Ṣaḍdarśanācārya (the equivalent of a Master's degree in each of the six orthodox schools of theistic Indian thought), Navyanyāyācārya (a Master's in neo-classical Indian logic), Vyākaraṇācārya (a Master's in classical Sanskrit grammar), a PhD in Philosophy based on the Bhagavad-Gītā, and a D.Litt. in Vedānta. More recently, he was conferred the titles of 'Mahāmahopādhyāya' by Kavikulaguru Kalidas Sanskrit University, Nagpur; 'Darśanakesarī' by the Akhil Bhartiya Vidvat Parishad, Varanasi; and 'Vedānta-Mārtaṇḍa' by Silpakorn University, Bangkok at the 16th World Sanskrit Conference – all in recognition for his contributions to Indian philosophy and Sanskrit literature by way of these commentaries.

[48] 'The Swaminarayan Commentarial Tradition' in Williams and Trivedi (eds.), *Swaminarayan Hinduism*, p. 151.

Nityanand Swami, *Bhagavadbhāvadīpikā* by Gopalanand Swami and *Gītāgūḍhārthadīpikā* by Shukanand Swami; and the Sāṇḍilyasūtras – *Śrīśāṇḍilyasūtrabhāṣyam* by Nityanand Swami. It is especially noteworthy that all these scholars also documented and compiled Swaminarayan's teachings as the Vacanāmrut.

Considerable work was also produced on the Bhāgavata-Purāṇa, in various languages and genres. Some of the Sanskrit commentaries and glosses on various portions of it include the following by Gopalanand Swami: *Śukābhiprāyabodhinī* (second canto), *Nigūḍhārthaprakāśikā* (tenth canto), *Śrutyarthadīpikā* and *Anvayārthadīpikā* (Vedastuti, i.e. 10.87.14–41) and *Śrīkṛṣṇābhiprāyabodhinī* (eleventh canto).

With the establishment of traditional pāṭhaśālās in Vadtal and later Ahmedabad and Gadhada, the commentarial enterprise continued even after Swaminarayan's passing. Scholars such as Kṛṣṇamācārya and Aṇṇaṅgarācārya oversaw new works, like the *Bhaktarañjanī Vyākhyā* gloss on the Bhāgavata-Purāṇa by Bhagavatprasādjī Mahārāj, as well as the translation and printing of unpublished manuscripts, such as the commentaries listed above.[49]

Besides commentaries, standalone philosophical treatises in Sanskrit were also produced, such as *Śrījñānavilāsa* by Caitanyānanada Svāmī and *Śrīpraṣnottarasāgara*, a catechism, by Yogānanda Svāmī. Sometimes such discussions were embedded within sacred biographies, such as with Nityanand Swami's *Śrīharidigvijaya*, which received its own commentary in the form of *Vijayadundubhi* by Acintyānanda Brahmacārī and Bholānātha Śarmā. Śatānanda Svāmī's *Śrīharivākyasudhāsindhu*, a Sanskrit versification of the Vacanāmrut, is another work of value. This was glossed by Raghuvīrjī Mahārāj with the especially useful *Setumālāṭīkā*, and later by Keśavprasādjī Mahārāj with the *Anvayadīpikā*.

As the Swaminarayan tradition branched into different dioceses and denominations, scholars within each offshoot produced scholarship of their own. One renowned and especially prolific author, active from Varanasi and Junagadh, was Kṛṣṇavallabhācārya. He has over fifty titles to his name, including celebrated treatises on Nyāya (Indian logic), Mīmāṃsā (ritual) and poetics, apart from on the Swaminarayan tradition.[50]

[49] For a complete catalogue and study of Sanskrit literature in Swaminarayan Hinduism, see Swami Adarshjivandas, 'Svāminārāyaṇ Sampradāymā Saṃskrut Sāhitya: Ek Adhyayan', unpublished PhD thesis, Sardar Vallabhbhai Patel University, Vallabh Vidyanagar (2009).

[50] For a complete list of Kṛṣṇavallabhācārya's works, see *Akhila-Bhūmanḍalīya-Sāmpradāyika-Mukti-Vyvasthā*, 4th edn (Jamvanthali, India: Shri Harisharanagati Mandal, 2005), pp. 200–2.

Towards the end of the nineteenth century and the turn of the twentieth, Shastriji Maharaj, founder of the BAPS denomination, rose as a key proponent of Swaminarayan's teachings. An acclaimed scholar himself, Shastriji Maharaj was especially attentive to history and Swaminarayan's oral revelations about Akṣarabrahman and Gunatitanand Swami as its human manifestation. His investigative research, historical interrogation and punctilious reading of the Vacanāmrut – discernible in his numerous letters, for example – singled out Shastriji Maharaj as the chief exponent of Swaminarayan's system as Akṣara-Puruṣottama siddhānta or Akṣarabrahma-Parabrahma-Dar śana (Figure 2).

After Shastriji Maharaj's passing in 1951, new scholarship proliferated under Yogiji Maharaj, who encouraged training in Vedānta, Sanskrit and English for young ordinands. He established the 'Akṣara-Puruṣottama Saṃskṛta Pāṭhaśālā' in Mumbai in 1961, which delivered a steady stream of doctoral research in the 1960s and 1970s, including Swami Viveksagardas's seminal work on *Śrīgopālānandasvāmikṛtiṣu Śrīsvāminārāyaṇīyam Akṣarabrahma-Parabrahma-Darśanam*, Swami Bhaktipriyadas's *Bhagavat-Svāminārāyaṇīya-Dharma-Darśanam*, Swami Shriharidas's *Śrīsvāminārāyaṇa-Jñāna-Mīmāṃsā* and Swami Bhagwatpriyadas's *Śrīsvāminārāyaṇa-Bhakti-Vicāra.*

Lay scholars also contributed with their works. An exceptional example of this was Harshad T. Dave, one of the most prolific writers in the tradition. His voluminous publications and dozens of articles, in Gujarati and English, included several works of history and sacred biography as well as philosophy and theology, such as *Life and Philosophy of Shree Swaminarayan*, first published in 1974 by George Allen and Unwin. He also helped edit a two-volume anthology, *New Dimensions in Vedanta Philosophy*, published in 1981, marking the bicentenary of Swaminarayan.

Serious scholarship within the Swaminarayan tradition received further impetus with the beginning of Pramukh Swami Maharaj's guruship in 1971. He established formal teaching centres – such as the BAPS Svāminārāyaṇa Saṃskṛta Mahavidyālaya (formerly called Śrī Yajñapuruṣa Saṃskṛta Vidyālaya) in Sarangpur in 1973 and the Akshar Purushottam School of Philosophy in Ahmedabad in 1975; and two research institutes – AARSH (Akshardham centre for Applied Research in Social Harmony) in Gandhinagar in 1992 and the BAPS Swaminarayan Research Institute in New Delhi in 2010. These have served as hubs for teaching, scholarly engagement (such as seminars and conferences), research and new textual production. A prime example of the last has been the five-volume *Svāminārāyaṇa-Bhāṣyam* commentary on the Brahmasūtras, Upaniṣads and Bhagavad-Gītā by Swami Bhadreshdas introduced earlier. He has followed

Figure 2 Swami Yagnapurushdas (1865–1951), known within the fellowship as Brahmaswarup Shastriji Maharaj, is regarded among the BAPS Swaminarayan tradition as the chief exponent of Swaminarayan's theology as Akṣarabrahma-Parabrahma-Darśana. (First known photo of Shastriji Maharaj, taken in Vadodara, 1916. Photo courtesy of Swaminarayan Aksharpith)

this with the compendious *Svāminārāyaṇa-Siddhānta-Sudhā*. A similar recent addition is Swami Shrutiprakashdas's *Svāminārāyaṇa-Siddhānta-Candrikā*, a compilation of the theological portions from his five-volume, 19,000-verse Sanskrit epic, *Akṣara-Puruṣottama-Māhātmyam*, styled in the genre of purāṇic texts. One of his latest works, *Svāminārāyaṇa-Pramāṇa-Ratnākara*, is a classical epistemological treatise.

In Gujarati, no less extensive or robust, is the five-part *Vacanāmrut Rahasya* by Swami Brahmadarshandas. It provides in-depth analyses and cross-referencing from the Vacanāmrut to explain its primacy as a scriptural source (Part I), exposit the five eternal entities (Part II and Part III), and outline key aspects of praxis (Part IV and Part V). This work stands as an excellent example of 'systematic theology' conducted within Gujarati, and to which this book is indebted throughout. Other Gujarati works of exceptional theological and historical insight include, for example, Shrutiprakashdas's *Śrī Svāminārāyaṇ Sampradāymā Avtār-Avtārī Nirupaṇ* and *Akṣarbrahma Nirupaṇ: Vaidik tathā Sāmpradāyik Śāstronā Ādhāre*. I am greatly indebted to the outstanding scholarship of all these eminent theologians, as we can justly call them so, for their commitment to so rigorously elucidating Swaminarayan's original teachings.

I hope this makes clear that this book is not the first such work of theological merit on the Swaminarayan belief system. As a theistic, devotional tradition steeped in and committed to the pursuit of seeking to understand and articulate its faith, Swaminarayan Hinduism has been producing theological scholarship for almost two hundred years. By the end of this book, I hope it is equally clear that this effort continues to be grounded in scriptural authority while employing tools of reasoning, draws upon canonical Hindu texts such as the Bhagavad-Gītā and Upaniṣads, and is resolutely based on the teachings of Swaminarayan himself, thus affirming this introduction as a work of theology, *Hindu* theology and, above all, *Swaminarayan* Hindu theology.

PART I

Sources and Tools of Swaminarayan Hindu Theology

CHAPTER 2

Introduction

The Imperceptibility and Ineffability of God

A good starting point for the study of a theological system is the basis upon which its ideas are established and articulated. Thus, before venturing into an exposition of Swaminarayan Hindu theology, we should ask: What are its sources and the tools by which we can understand its theological foundations and, indeed, can theologise within the tradition? This early part of the book is dedicated to answering this fundamental epistemological question.

But before we can proceed to answering 'How can we know about God?', a still more fundamental and provocative question awaits us: Can God be known at all?

The Upaniṣads famously extol the imperceptibility and ineffability of the highest reality. For example:

> From where speech returns with the mind having not grasped it. (TU 2.4.1)
>
> It cannot be grasped by the eyes, nor even by speech, nor by other senses or by austerities or work. (MuU 3.1.8)
>
> Not by speech, not by mind, nor by the eyes is it possible to reach him. (KaU 6.12)
>
> There the eyes go not. Speech goes not. Nor the mind. (KeU 1.3)

In picking up on each of the three key tools of perception mentioned in this last verse – eyes, speech and mind – Bhadreshdas offers a basic epistemological analysis of why perception, worldly testimony and inference cannot serve as independent means to valid knowledge of God. In summary, he explains:

- 'Eyes' are representative here of all cognitive senses, which are instrumental in directly cognising tangible objects. For example, the sense of sight allows eyes to perceive physical form; the sense of hearing allows ears to perceive sounds; and so forth with the senses of touch, taste and smell and their respective sense organs, the skin, tongue and nose. However, their scope is firmly confined within the realm of the physical world, composed as it is of māyā, like the senses and sense organs themselves. They cannot possibly perceive anything that is beyond māyā, such as the form and virtues of the divine, transcendental and limitless Parabrahman. Parabrahman is thus beyond the senses {atītindriya} – intangible.

- 'Speech' represents the faculty of speech and the capacity of words. While everyday patterns of speech or vivid descriptions may be able to elucidate the qualities of worldly objects and events, they cannot fully describe God, his form and his qualities, because he is absolutely not of this world. Besides, Bhadreshdas adds, worldly testimony still relies on the senses of perception and physical organs, whose limitations have already been identified above.
- The 'mind' is the 'inner sense', and here it indicates the means of inference. With inference also predicated upon direct perception, it, too, suffers from the same limitations highlighted above.[1, 2]

While spelling out the scope and limitations of these means of cognition and articulation, Bhadreshdas is careful to make two important points. Firstly, in his refutation of sensory and mental means, he is sure to qualify them with the term 'laukika' {relating to this world}, i.e. anything composed of māyā. This has important implications for the authority of divinely inspired and divinely spoken words that constitute Scripture, or revelation, and also for the state of liberation when the liberated soul is endowed with brahmic mind and senses by which it enjoys the direct realisation of Parabrahman. A more general denial of sensory perception of Parabrahman would preclude this climactic experience as well as the possibility of Scripture as an authentic source of theological knowledge.[3]

Secondly, Bhadreshdas invariably adds that the senses and mind return from Parabrahman not entirely empty-handed, so to speak, but having not grasped him fully.[4] With each of the three means mentioned at KeU 1.3, for example, Bhadreshdas adds 'sampūrṇatayā', 'sākalyena' and 'kārtsnyena' – each meaning 'completely' – to emphasise that the eyes, speech and mind cannot have a *complete* perception of Parabrahman. But this does not deny

[1] KeU-SB 1.3, p. 36.
[2] The role of 'reason' as a tool for theological knowledge is discussed in more detail in Chapter 4.
[3] Both of these topics are covered in some detail in Chapter 11, on Mukti, and the following chapter, respectively.
[4] TU-SB 2.4.1, p. 370.

them *any* perception of Parabrahman whatsoever. After all, Bhadreshdas adds, if that were not the case, the following scriptural statements instructing individuals to know, see, realise or contemplate upon Parabrahman would be rendered futile:

> Verily, that Self [Paramātman] is to be realised, heard, reflected and contemplated upon. (BU 2.4.5, 4.5.6)
>
> Seek to know that. That is Brahman. (TU 3.1.1)
>
> Seek indeed to know that Truth [Parabrahman]. (CU 7.16.1)
>
> Know that Puruṣa who should be known. (PU 6.6)

Equally, descriptions of knowing, seeing and realising Parabrahman would also have to be non-veridical. For example:

> Your most auspicious form, that I see. (IU 16, BU 5.15.1)
>
> When he knows him thus. (CU 1.9.2)
>
> It [the Self] is seen by the pointed, subtle intellect of those discerning seers. (KaU 3.12)
>
> The wise who perceive him residing within the soul, theirs alone is eternal peace, not others'. (KaU 5.13)
>
> They continuously extol me. (BG 9.14)[5]

But then how can these two sets of statements be reconciled? On the one hand, they attempt to describe God and urge that he should be known, and yet, on the other, he is described as ineffable and not completely knowable. But that is precisely the thrust of the Vedāntic argument, Bhadreshdas observes. Even after knowing all that one can know about God, what one really needs to know – indeed, what one *can* know – is that he is unlimited, unfathomable. In fact, when concluding this comment, Bhadreshdas questions whether the limited human mind and senses can ever fully grasp even meagre, tangible objects such as a pot or rag. What, then, can be said of their inadequacy in comprehending someone as subtle and transcendental as Parabrahman?[6] What this ensures is that any authentic

[5] Bhadreshdas also cites many of these passages in response to the objector's claim at BS 1.1.1 that it is futile to desire to know 'Brahman', simply because 'Brahman' is unknowable. See BS-SB 1.1.1, pp. 11–12.

[6] KeU-SB 1.3, pp. 35–7. See also BS-SB 1.1.1, pp. 11–12.

knowledge or description of Parabrahman, even while being useful and meaningful, is never exhaustive; he remains that much beyond the limited capacity of māyic faculties and this-worldly means of cognition and articulation. In other words, any knowledge of God does not subvert his unlimited nature (or 'mystery').[7] Even the fullest realisation will always be of the form *neti neti* – 'Not this much; not this much'.[8] The experience is so staggeringly overwhelming that any sincere attempt to articulate it in words seems woefully inadequate. Whatever eloquence one can muster and however many superlatives one can summon, human language and devices of expression seem certain to fall short of fully describing the greatness, power, knowledge, splendour, benevolence and auspiciousness of God.

This seems to be the inevitably humble realisation candidly shared by the seers of the Kena Upaniṣad:

> We know not, we cannot understand how one can expound him. (1.3)

Bhadreshdas explains here that the sheer transcendence or other-worldliness of Parabrahman means that there is no known tangible reference point with which to begin describing him. He is simply incomparable to anything that can be found in this māyic world or can be perceived by māyic senses. Swaminarayan emphasises these two points at considerable length in Vac. Pan.4 when he begins:

> The Vedas, the Purāṇas, the Mahābhārata, the Smṛtis and the other scriptures proclaim that the original form of God . . . is not like any form that can be seen by the eyes. His sound is not like any sound that can be heard by the ears. His touch is not like any touch that can be felt by the skin. His smell is not like any smell that can be smelt by the nose. The tongue cannot describe that God. He cannot be conceived by the mind {manas}. He cannot be contemplated upon by the citta {inner faculty that allows contemplation}. He cannot be comprehended by the intellect {buddhi}. Nor can the ahaṃkāra {literally 'I-maker'; inner faculty that allows sense of identity} fully claim, 'I am God's, and God is mine'. In this manner, God remains beyond the reach of the senses and inner faculties.
>
> Moreover, the form of that God is such that it cannot be compared to any other object in this brahmāṇḍa {'world' or planetary system} – including

[7] The unlimited nature of Parabrahman is expounded in detail in the Section 'Limitless Greatness of Parabrahman's Own Being' in Chapter 6.

[8] While still apophatic, this interpretation is markedly different from the entirely negating 'Not this; not this'. The difference is between totally (and lazily) denying any descriptive power or worth to theological language, and realistically and humbly acknowledging its inadequacy even while continuing to endeavour in theology (or 'God-talk').

> everything from Brahmā to the smallest blade of grass. His sound is such that it cannot be compared to any other sound in this brahmāṇḍa. The smell of God is such that it cannot be compared to any other smell in this brahmāṇḍa. The touch of God is such that it cannot be compared to any other touch in this brahmāṇḍa. The tastes related to God are such that they cannot be compared to any other taste in this brahmāṇḍa.

Swaminarayan then goes on to explain the basis of this incomparability. It is because all forms in this brahmāṇḍa that have evolved from Prakṛti-Puruṣa {a configuration of māyā instrumental in the protological process} are māyic, whereas God is divine. So, since the two are totally different, how can they possibly be compared? Swaminarayan thus concludes: All scriptures claim, God is beyond the reach of the senses and the inner faculties.

But if God is not knowable as an object of sensorial perception, empirical investigation or intellectual speculation, how indeed – even in the limited sense possible – can he be known? Swaminarayan provides the answer himself in Vac. Pan.4 and other sermons, but before we go on to discuss this in detail, let us firstly see a more general answer from Vac. Gaḍh. 1.24 that will help frame this discussion. Swaminarayan explains that the conviction of a devotee with intense faith is always of the form:

> The manifest form of Puruṣottama has compassionately revealed his form to me. (Vac. Gaḍh. 1.24)

This is similar to a statement found identically in the Muṇḍaka Upaniṣad and Kaṭha Upaniṣad:

> This Self [Paramātman] cannot be attained by instruction, nor by intellectual power, nor even through much hearing [i.e. learning]. He is attained only by the one whom the Self [Paramātman] chooses. To such a one, the Self [Paramātman] reveals his own form. (MuU 3.2.3, KaU 2.23)

Quite simply, both statements explain, God can be known only when *he* chooses to be known, or, to paraphrase them even more closely, when God graciously 'reveals' himself. We find here the clearest possible reference to what is commonly termed in theology as 'revelation'.

With this groundwork in place, the following chapter can now present the complex doctrine of revelation as it is found in its various forms within the Swaminarayan tradition and explain its role as the exclusive source of Swaminarayan Hindu theology.

CHAPTER 3

Revelation
The Exclusive Source of Swaminarayan Hindu Theology

Acknowledging the limited scope of human cognition impaired by māyic senses and mind is the first step in accepting revelation as the exclusive source of authentic theological knowledge. The divine, transcendental and unlimited nature of God means that he is hardly accessible by human intelligence, imagination and ingenuity. So we need to be *told* what God is like. Indeed, *God* needs to tell us what he is like. Better still, God needs to *show* us who he is. And so he reveals himself.

For Swaminarayan Hinduism, this points to the three modes of revelation discernible within the tradition. They are as follows:

1. Revelation as the self-manifestation of Parabrahman in the person of Swaminarayan
2. Revelation as Parabrahman being substantively present in and made known by the Brahmasvarūpa Guru
3. Revelation through Scripture, i.e. Swaminarayan's sermons documented in the Vacanāmrut and the Brahmasvarūpa Gurus' teachings, such as the Svāmīnī Vāto

As each mode is expanded in turn, the following sections shall also look to address some important questions and useful discussions that will be further developed in Part II concerning the major themes of Swaminarayan Hindu theology.

Revelation as Self-manifestation

The actual appearance or 'self-manifestation' of Parabrahman on earth in an accessible, endearing human form is the most decisive, explicit and direct form of revelation possible. It allows God to not only tell us and show us what that ultimate reality is, but to present it in himself. This self-presenting to humanity of the God who cannot be seen or reached by human effort alone is thus a supreme act of God's loving and liberative grace. Swaminarayan iterates this repeatedly throughout his sermons (for example, in Vac. Pan.7, Gaḍh. 3.31, Gaḍh. 3.37 and Gaḍh. 3.38), most often while explaining the purpose of this human manifestation in terms of granting ultimate liberation to countless souls. To quote just one of those statements:

> That God himself . . . becomes like a human for the purpose of granting liberation to the jīvas. (Vac. Gaḍh. 3.37)

Added to this is the distinctive, fundamental belief of Swaminarayan Hinduism that this earthly manifestation of Parabrahman occurred in the person of Swaminarayan between 1781 and 1830 CE. The specificity of Parabrahman *as* Swaminarayan is what lends the concept of revelation its power and authority to the faithful of the tradition. For them, Parabrahman *is* Swaminarayan; or, even more personally, Swaminarayan *is* Parabrahman. He appeared *himself* so that humans may identify who God is and begin to know and relate to him, even within their limited human capacity.

As we shall see in some detail towards the end of Chapter 6 on Parabrahman, followers find instances of Swaminarayan referring to himself as this highest reality in several of his sermons (Vac. Gaḍh. 2.9, Gaḍh. 2.13, Gaḍh. 3.38, Amd.6, Amd.7). At this point, it will suffice to quote just one statement cited from old manuscripts of the tradition, personalising the more general statements excerpted above. It reads:

> While other avatāras had manifested to fulfil a particular task, my manifestation is to make souls brahmarūpa ['like Brahman'] and grant them ultimate liberation. That is why I, Puruṣottama who transcends even Akṣara, have become like a human.[1]

The striking but apparent contradiction of Parabrahman being beyond eyes {parokṣa}, speech and mind, as described in the Upaniṣads and by Swaminarayan himself, suddenly becoming manifest before the eyes {pratyakṣa}, as Swaminarayan also claimed, was not lost on his followers. Were both forms real? How indeed could that same imperceptible, transcendental Parabrahman be visible on earth? This appears to be the pointed question posed by Daharānanda Svāmī in Vac. Gaḍh. 1.78. He asks:

> God transcends Akṣara; he is beyond mind and speech; and he is imperceptible to all. Why, then, can everyone see him as manifest before the eyes?

[1] Nandkishor Swami, *Ātyantika Kalyāṇa* (Bhuj, India: the author, 1958), p. 76.

Swaminarayan replies:

> God – who transcends Akṣara, who is beyond mind and speech, and who is imperceptible – himself, out of compassion, resolves: 'May all the enlightened and unenlightened people on earth {Mṛtyuloka} behold me.' Having resolved in this manner, God – whose will always prevails – becomes perceivable to all people on earth out of compassion. (Vac. Gaḍh. I.78)

Swaminarayan thus confirms that the human manifestation of Parabrahman is indeed wholly real and transcendental, made possible only by his loving and gracious will.

A similar question initiates the discussion in Vac. Gaḍh. I.51. After establishing the māyic composition of human senses and the inner faculties (by which we think, reason, contemplate and identify), Pūrṇānanda Svāmī asks:

> God, however, transcends māyā. How, then, can one cultivate the conviction of God through the māyic inner faculties? How also can one perceive God with one's māyic eyes and other senses?

Swaminarayan first sought to clarify the question by asking:

> Māyic objects can be realised by māyic means, and if one has realised God through the same māyic inner faculties and senses, then it implies that God must also be māyic. That is your question, is it not?

After Pūrṇānanda Svāmī and the other paramhansas in the audience confirmed that 'that is precisely our question', Swaminarayan began a lengthy exposition of the impassable supremacy of Puruṣottama, the highest being among all other realities and cosmic elements. He then concluded:

> It is this very God who, out of compassion, for the liberation of the jīvas, gives darshan [i.e. becomes visible] in a manifested form to all of the people on earth.

Then moving to explain how it can be possible for humans to not only perceive that God but hold a firm conviction of him, he states:

> At that time, if a person realises this greatness of Puruṣottama Bhagavān by profound association with the Sant [i.e. Guru], then all of his senses and inner faculties become divine like Puruṣottama Bhagavān's senses and inner faculties. Then, through those senses and inner faculties, he can develop the conviction of that God.

To help his audience understand, Swaminarayan employs a useful analogy.

> For example, a diamond can be cut only by a diamond; it can never be cut by anything else. Similarly, the conviction of God can only be cultivated through God. In the same way, the darshan of God is possible only through God, but it is not possible through the māyic senses and inner faculties.

Swaminarayan's explanation here is relevant to our understanding of his conceptualisation of revelation because it confirms that, firstly, revelation leads to a resolute conviction or realisation of God, and, secondly, that such a realisation is made possible only by God himself or through the help of the Guru, whom Swaminarayan refers to here and elsewhere as 'the Sant'. This has important implications for the ontological position of the Guru within the five-reality system of the Swaminarayan School, which shall be considered at length in Chapter 7 on Akṣarabrahman. The role of this Guru in leading devotees to a realisation of Parabrahman is something that will be discussed shortly in this chapter.

The striking revelation also worth noting from both these last sermons is the declaration of the utterly transcendental becoming wholly personal – he is *different* yet *among us* – which is something that makes this self-manifestation especially gracious and powerful for the followers of the tradition and, unsurprisingly, what permeates and guides the whole of Swaminarayan Hindu theology. It is the self-expression of the supremely divine on māyic earth, the eternal in time, the universally pervasive in a particular human form.

This leads us to an associated discussion about the receptivity of revelation from the perspective of the individual soul.

Revelation as Unveiling of the Soul

Members of the Swaminarayan faith community will see the self-manifestation of Parabrahman on earth as a supremely significant, gracious and unprecedented[2] event. Apart from being an objective occurrence, though, it is also a subjective experience for all those who encounter that revelation (in its various modes), even today. Seen from the perspective of

[2] According to the Swaminarayan theological system, as we shall learn in Part II, the avatāras are metaphysically īśvara, whereas Swaminarayan is believed to be Parabrahman, the Avatārin (or source of the avatāras). The ontological distinction and supremacy of the latter make Parabrahman's manifestation on earth all the more unique, significant and powerfully liberative. Swaminarayan is recorded as revealing that this self-manifestation of Parabrahman has never occurred before in this brahmāṇḍa (planetary system), nor shall it ever occur again (SV 4.10, SV 4.13). Gunatitanand Swami and other ordained and lay disciples have also noted this revelation several times in their own works. See Sadhu Shrutiprakashdas, *Svāminārāyaṇ Sampradāymā Avatār-Avatārī Nirūpaṇ*, 2nd edn (Swaminarayan Aksharpith: Ahmedabad, 2010), pp. 194–215.

the individual soul, we are offered an opportunity to understand 'revelation' anew from within a Hindu theistic context, especially if we are to take the basic meaning of *apokalypsis*, the Greek word usually translated as 'revelation', as the 'removing of a veil so that something can be seen'.

The basic idea is this: If God is indeed hidden, as the term 'unveiling' would presuppose, it is not God who is doing the hiding under some intractable disguise or sheath of darkness. Rather, it is the *soul's* veil of ignorance – māyā – which is obstructing or obscuring a full vision of Parabrahman. In other words, the veil that is removed in *apokalypsis* is shrouding not Parabrahman but the individual ātman. In unveiling (or 'de-veiling') the soul of its ignorance, God is there to be seen, as he always was. The realisation thus does not take the form of God saying, 'Look, here I am!', but rather of the soul discovering God: 'Oh, there you are!' That is why 'sākṣātkāra' or 'darśana' – the highest state of enlightenment, possible upon liberation from māyā – is, literally, the direct realisation or vision of God, as if 'before the eyes'. Swaminarayan describes this state as follows:

> One who has attained God-realisation ... experiences the following: Wherever he casts his eyes – among all the mobile and immobile forms – he sees the form of God as if it is before his eyes, the same form that constantly remains in Akṣaradhāma even after the dissolution of the body, the brahmāṇḍa and Prakṛti-Puruṣa. Other than that form, he does not perceive even an atom.[3] (Vac. Kār.7)

We have already seen above that it is by the gracious resolve of Parabrahman that he manifests on earth and makes himself perceptible to humans, notwithstanding their still-māyic senses. Since this is also a subjective experience, how well one appropriates this grace of revelation determines the final outcome of realising Parabrahman in all his transcendental glory. In between these two points on the spiritual journey – from revelation to realisation – lies the process of religious praxis, or sādhanā {literally, 'means'}.[4]

A good example of the soul's need to properly appropriate the grace of God's revelation can be found in the eleventh canto of the Bhagavad-Gītā, often cited by Swaminarayan in the Vacanāmrut (Vac. Kār.8, Pan.6, Var.18; especially Gaḍh. I.25 and Pan.4,). When Arjuna prays Kṛṣṇa show him his divine, lordly form (BG 11.4–5), Kṛṣṇa reveals his cosmic manifestation. But even then, Arjuna is unable to see it with his own eyes. Kṛṣṇa states:

[3] The translation of 'aṇu' as atom throughout this book is used in its pre-modern or philosophical sense, meaning an infinitesimally minute particle.

[4] The interesting discussion of divine grace and the role of human effort in being able to properly receive that grace has rightly been reserved for Chapter 11, when expounding upon mukti.

> It is not possible to see me with these [māyic] eyes of yours. I therefore grant you divine eyes. [Now] see my yogic powers. (11.8)

We see here two rounds of grace at play: firstly, the gracious revealing of the transcendental form and, secondly, the gracious granting of divine eyes by which to see that form that is otherwise 'very hard to see {sudurdarśa}' (11.52) and 'difficult to discern {durnirīkṣya}' (11.17). Arjuna, however, was unable to properly receive that grace and hence could not appreciate the divine form. He found the vision astounding and terrifying (11.20, 11.23, 11.24, 11.25, 11.35, 11.45). Unnerved and bewildered, he beseeches Kṛṣṇa once more, this time to retract the revelation and appear to him as he was (11.45–46). Kṛṣṇa does so, explaining that this vision is not attainable by mere scriptural study, nor by severe austerities, generous gifts, sacrificial rites or any other means (11.48, 11.53). He explains:

> O Arjuna the Oppressor! Only by singular devotion is it possible to thus perfectly see me, know me and enter into me. (11.54)

Here we must summon an important verse from the final canto of the Bhagavad-Gītā to make better sense of the method suggested by Kṛṣṇa. He explains how such singular devotion, of the very highest form, can be attained:

> He who becomes like Brahman [i.e. brahmarūpa] ... attains the highest devotion to me. (18.54)

Arjuna was thus unable to enjoy the divine form of Kṛṣṇa so graciously revealed to him because he was not ready to fully receive that type of grace. He was not yet brahmarūpa – spiritually pure and mature like Brahman – which, according to BG 18.54, is the prerequisite to offering the highest devotion to Parabrahman. And only with such devotion, according to BG 11.54, is the perfect 'vision' or realisation of Parabrahman possible. In many ways, this is, as we shall learn, the core doctrine of Swaminarayan Hindu theology: One must become like Brahman to perfectly realise and offer devotion to Parabrahman. Conversely, as Arjuna's example shows, even if God is fully in sight, he cannot be appreciated if the māyic veil has not been removed.

Swaminarayan explains in Vac. Pan.7:

> When an ignorant person looks at that manifest form of God before the eyes with a māyic vision, he perceives a human like himself. Just as he himself is born, becomes a child, becomes a youth, becomes old and dies, in the same way, he believes God to undergo the same process. But when one sincerely

> worships God having faith in the words of the Ekāntika Sant of God, one's māyic vision is resolved. Thereafter, one realises that same form of God as being the supreme conscious being, characterised by eternal existence, consciousness and bliss.

Swaminarayan clearly distinguishes between those who are ignorant, whose perception of God's fully divine reality is clouded by their māyic vision, and the devotees who have learned from the Brahmasvarūpa Guru how to correctly see and serve that God. With the use of an extended analogy here and also in Vac. Amd.4, which we shall discuss in detail later,[5] Swaminarayan goes on to elaborate at great length the absolute divinity of the revealed, self-manifested God while reiterating the erroneous perception of him as born of the seer's own ignorance. This is in contrast to the correct and complete theological knowledge of a true devotee made possible by the Ekāntika Sant, or Brahmasvarūpa Guru.

This neatly leads us to the next mode of revelation: God revealed in and by the Guru.

Revelation in and by the Guru

A thorough study of the Vacanāmrut leads to a patent observation that Swaminarayan did not intend the words 'manifest form of God before your eyes' to be restricted to his own relatively short time on earth. Nor did he wish to limit the promise of final liberation to only those who had encountered revelation through his own self-manifestation of Parabrahman. For Swaminarayan Hindu theology, revelation is not a one-off event, but a continuing occurrence. This is because Swaminarayan reveals the continuing substantive presence of Parabrahman through Akṣarabrahman, which presents itself on earth in human form as the Brahmasvarūpa Guru (referred to variously in the Vacanāmrut and Svāmīnī Vāto as 'Sant', 'Sādhu', 'Bhakta' and 'Satpuruṣa', and often qualified with such terms as 'Ekāntika' {ultimate; perfect}, 'great', 'God's' or alongside the soteriological imperative). The reality of Akṣarabrahman in its various forms is a central aspect of Swaminarayan Hindu theology, but one that may seem novel to even those familiar with other schools of Vedānta. We shall have ample opportunity to discuss this topic and question its assertions in the following chapters. Here, we can proceed to briefly introduce it in light of the doctrine of revelation, reserving the more detailed elucidation for its proper context.[6]

[5] See Section 'Absolute Divinity of the Embodied Form' in Chapter 6.

[6] See, for example, Section 'Akṣarabrahman as Brahmasvarūpa Guru' in Chapter 7.

If the self-manifestation on earth of Parabrahman himself is a supremely gracious and benevolent act of revelation, this revelatory grace is vividly demonstrated and made available through the Brahmasvarūpa Guru. This is seen to be active within the faith community in two highly related ways that are sometimes difficult to tell apart. Nevertheless, they can be explained in simple terms thus: firstly, the Guru is the 'vessel' that perfectly holds the complete presence of Parabrahman and therefore through whom Parabrahman liberatively works and relates to humans. Because of this, the Guru is, secondly, by whom others can know God, i.e. relate to and serve him, as correctly and completely as possible. God is thus made known both *in* the Guru and *by* the Guru.

To briefly elaborate upon the first of the Guru's revelatory roles, we see numerous references in the Vacanāmrut, where Swaminarayan reveals Parabrahman living on and working through the Guru, and therefore making it possible to personally encounter God via 'the Sant'. For example, Swaminarayan states:

> Since it is God who sees through his [the Sant's] eyes . . . Since it is God who walks through his legs . . . Since it is God who resides in all of the senses and limbs of such a Sant, (Vac. Gaḍh. 1.27)

it therefore follows that

> When one has the darshan of such a Sant, one should realise, 'I have had the darshan of God himself'. (Vac. Sār.10)

This striking proclamation by Swaminarayan confirms that even while the Guru neither is nor ever becomes God, God is substantively revealed in the Guru. Quite simply, according to Swaminarayan, to see the Guru is to see God; to relate to the Guru is to relate to God.

This revelatory presence is the reason why Swaminarayan and Gunatitanand Swami repeatedly and emphatically reiterate in the Vacanāmrut and Svāmīnī Vāto the need to know, serve, love, obey, trust and surrender to the Guru as one would to God (when he is not personally present on earth), the fruit of which is still realising God, overcoming māyā and securing liberation. For example, in Vac. Var.10 Swaminarayan states:

> One who aspires for liberation should recognise God through these characteristics and seek the refuge of that God . . . However, when God is not manifest on this earth before the eyes, one should seek the refuge of the Sant who is absorbed with that God, because the jīva can also secure liberation through him.

This clearly evidences Swaminarayan's intention that the liberative work of God is to extend beyond his own self-manifestation on earth and continue by way of the Guru.

As another example, in Vac. Jet.1 Swaminarayan firstly describes the insurmountability of the binding forces of māyā. But then adds:

> When the jīva meets the manifest form of Śrī Puruṣottama Bhagavān – who is beyond māyā and who is the destroyer of māyā and all karmas – or the Sant who is absorbed with that God, then, by accepting their refuge, the jīva can transcend māyā.

What is important to note is that both God and Guru are invariably mentioned in tandem in these important soteriological statements. This liberative function of the Guru confirms his person as Akṣarabrahman[7] and his direct, complete and substantive relationship with Parabrahman. Indeed, Swaminarayan explains in Vac. Gaḍh. 3.27 that such a Sant has a direct relationship {sākṣāt saṃbandh} with God.

Gunatitanand Swami reinforces this relationship in his sermon at SV 5.392 when he states:

> The association of the Sādhu is a direct relationship with God and leads to the bliss of God. Why? Because God fully resides in the Sādhu.

That it is possible to experience the bliss of God when associating with the Guru implies it is God who is granting the bliss through the Guru. This is an idea that can also be found in the Bhagavad-Gītā. Bhadreshdas notes that while God is described in the final verse of the fourteenth canto as the 'foundation of the highest, eternal bliss' (14.27), it is stated at 5.21:

> He who has joined his soul with Brahman [i.e. the Brahmasvarūpa Guru[8]] enjoys undiminishing bliss.

The two statements find their internal coherency, according to Bhadreshdas, in the proof that it is God who is granting the blissful experience to the soul through his presence in the Guru.[9]

The same blissful, liberative experience is also reiterated in the Praśna Upaniṣad. When asked by Satyakāma about the afterlife upon meditating on 'Aum', Pippalāda replies:

[7] This will be further corroborated in Chapter 7.

[8] This is a unique reading of the term 'Brahman' in Swaminarayan Hindu theology, which shall be clarified in Chapter 7, on Akṣarabrahman.

[9] BG-SB 5.21, pp. 126–7. Note the important observation from the BG-SB that 'Brahman' *never* refers to God anywhere in the Bhagavad-Gītā.

> That which is the sound of 'Aum', O Satyakāma, is verily the higher and lower Brahman. Therefore, with this support alone does the knower attain either. (PU 5.2)

After showing that the dual classification of 'higher' and 'lower' Brahman confirms the ontological distinction between Parabrahman and Akṣarabrahman, and the superiority of the former over the latter, Bhadreshdas emphasises that this verse also enjoins the meditation of Akṣarabrahman on par with that of Parabrahman, since 'Aum' is *equally* denotative of both Parabrahman *and* Akṣarabrahman. Furthermore, because the fruit of such meditation is described as the attainment of 'either' {ekatara} of them, this is further evidence of Parabrahman's liberative presence in Akṣarabrahman. The meditation of Akṣarabrahman leads to no lesser an experience or result than that of meditating on Parabrahman himself.[10]

We therefore see similar calls to serving the Guru in order to attain God in final liberation. For example, Swaminarayan instructs in Vac. Gaḍh. 3.26:

> Those who are eager to secure their liberation should thus serve such a Sant.

Why? Because

> such a Sant should not be thought to be like a human nor should he be thought to be like even a deva . . . Such a Sant, even though he is human [in form], is worthy of being served like God.

Swaminarayan elaborates with examples in Vac. Var.5 on how to serve the Guru 'like God' by instructing perfectly 'equal service' of both, further establishing the revelation of God in the living Guru. Serving the Guru is thus serving God.

Such an instruction of 'equal service' resonates with the famous declaration at the end of the Śvetāśvatara Upaniṣad:

> All objectives declared [in the sacred texts] shine forth [i.e. become attainable] for the great soul who offers the highest devotion to God and, as he does to God, also to the Guru. (SU 6.23)

Swaminarayan further explains:

> Intense love for the Satpuruṣa is itself the means to realising one's ātman, is itself also the means to realising the greatness of the Satpuruṣa, and is itself also the means to having the direct realisation of God. (Vac. Var.11)

[10] PU-SB 5.2, pp. 214–16.

Again, the remarkable and instructive revelation here is that devoutly relating to the Guru leads to the realisation of God.

Because Parabrahman is revealed *in* the living Guru, it seems natural that he should also be an authentic and vital source of theological knowledge. This is the second revelatory role of the Guru, *by* whom God is revealed or made known. The Guru leads the faithful to the realisation of God, without whom such a realisation would remain elusive. Swaminarayan thus instructs that one should develop faith in Parabrahman – or 'the conviction of God' {niścaya or niṣṭhā}, as he often terms it – through the Brahmasvarūpa Guru. Indeed, he bases his very definition of resolute faith on the Guru. After asking the question,

> What is the conviction of God?

Swaminarayan goes on to say in Vac. Gaḍh. 3.27:

> The Sant . . . has a direct relationship with God. Therefore, one should develop the conviction of God based on his words. In fact, to have firm faith in the words of the Sant is itself the conviction of God.

One is properly convinced about the existence and nature of God only after having faith in the Guru, because, again, it is in the Guru that God himself chooses to be fully present and so by whom God can be revealed. In fact, Swaminarayan goes as far as to omit the causal connection and equates the two: Faith in the Guru *is* the conviction of God.

Of course, God is not restricted to the Guru and is still free to reveal himself independently, though, as shall be explained, the Brahmasvarūpa Guru remains his most accessible and endearing medium through which to personally interrelate with humans.

Nor, of course, does Swaminarayan mean to discount the role of Scripture in revealing God, as we shall shortly learn. There, too, though, the role of the Guru in relation to scriptural revelation will become evident when Swaminarayan stresses the 'reading' of Scripture only through the Guru if one is to arrive at the most accurate understanding of God. If Swaminarayan is not elevating the Guru above Scripture, he is surely positioning him as a living Scripture of the most authoritative kind.

It comes as no surprise that the Upaniṣads and Bhagavad-Gītā – themselves treatises richly steeped in the ancient Vedic tradition of guru–disciple learning – also emphasise the need of the Guru in order to avail of true theological knowledge, or, in other words, to realise God and be liberated. For example:

> Only knowledge learned from the Guru leads one to the goal. (CU 4.9.3)

> Arise, awake, and understand [this liberative knowledge] having approached the best [teachers, i.e. the Gurus]. (KaU 3.14)

Some of these calls to imperatively seek the Guru also include vital hints about the essential credentials of such a bona fide spiritual teacher, as opposed to others of an 'inferior' sort.

> It [liberative knowledge] is difficult to grasp when taught by an inferior man, even though one may be highly contemplative. Yet there is no way to it without it being taught by the non-inferior [i.e. superior teacher, the Brahmasvarūpa Guru], [for] it is subtler than an atom [and] beyond the realm of reason. Nor can this knowledge be grasped by argumentation. Yet, Dearest [Naciketas], it is well known when taught by the other [the Brahmasvarūpa Guru]. (KaU 2.8–9)

> To realise that [higher knowledge], imperatively surrender, with sacrificial wood in hand, to only that guru who has the realisation of revealed texts, who is Brahman and who is ever steadfast [in God]. (MuU 1.2.12)

> Learn that [knowledge] by obeisance, inquiry and service. Those enlightened [Gurus] who 'see' the truth will teach you that knowledge. (BG 4.34)

While we shall be discussing these later in much more detail, it is important to note here that in all these verses Bhadreshdas stresses that they refer only to the Brahmasvarūpa Guru, for only he is capable of making God known perfectly because of his own perfect, eternal and sublimely inherent God-realisation.

This returns us to the Upaniṣadic statement with which we began this discussion of revelation.

> This Self [Paramātman] . . . is attained only by the one whom the Self chooses. To such a one, the Self reveals his own form. (MuU 3.2.3, KaU 2.23)

Bhadreshdas explains that God is attainable by grace alone {kṛpaikasādhya}, and only when and how he chooses to reveal himself. Apart from his self-manifestation on earth, one way that Parabrahman chooses to graciously reveal himself is by providing earnest seekers of the truth the association of the Brahmasvarūpa Guru, within whom he substantively resides, who can then lead them to him. Therefore, when elaborating upon the form that God's grace takes, Bhadreshdas states:

> God, the ocean of grace that he is, grants that devotee access to the profound association of the Akṣarabrahman Guru . . . so that his devotee can easily realise him [Paramātman].[11]

[11] KaU-SB 2.23, p. 119.

In conclusion to this section, we can end with a simple analogy to help summarise and further elucidate the unique revelatory dual-function of the Guru and his relationship with God. Consider a cup of water. The cup itself is not made of water, but as its container, it is normal to refer to it, especially when full, as 'a cup of water'. Without dismissing the value of the cup itself, it is its contents to which attention is drawn. Similarly the Guru, though 'composed of' Akṣarabrahman, holds – is brimming with – the divine presence of Parabrahman. Only such a Brahmasvarūpa vessel can perfectly hold Parabrahman, and that, too, only by Parabrahman's will, and so it is the God within who ultimately becomes the focus of devotional attention. Nevertheless, the cup and contents never become one. In the same way, the Guru *never* becomes God; he forever remains ontologically distinct and infinitely subordinate to God.

This also means that earnest seekers can be liberated and can enjoy the limitless bliss of God by associating with the Guru, just as those who drink from the cup experience the contents, not the cup. The Guru becomes the indispensable means, or medium, by which to encounter God. Without the cup though, such an experience or encounter would hardly be possible, for how else would one partake of the water considering its fluidity? While water in its various forms may be available elsewhere – in freshwater lakes or even in the air as vapour – it is found in its fullest, most 'handy' form when contained in the cup. Here, too, God, otherwise resident in his transcendental abode and pervasive throughout creation, becomes available and readily accessible by his substantive presence in the Guru.

Consider further now a perfectly transparent cup. It not only holds the water but also reveals what it is holding. In a similar way, the eternally māyā-free, all-divine Guru makes God known through his own perfectly pure Akṣarabrahmic being.[12]

Revelation through Scripture

The third mode in Swaminarayan Hindu theology by which God reveals himself is through teachings, which, for ease and consistency, we can refer to as 'Scripture'. In this section, we can address the scope of Scripture within Swaminarayan Hinduism as pertaining to the Vacanāmrut and the wider Vedic canon, and its role as the cornerstone upon which all doctrines

[12] Like all analogies, the similarity breaks down when considering the wider, active role of the Guru. The Guru is not a passive vessel; as we shall see, he plays an important dynamic function in leading seekers to liberation and bestowing his brahmic qualities in making them brahmarūpa.

of the faith are articulated. The section will also address the determinant features authenticating these texts as revelatory sources and, importantly, how Swaminarayan instructs them to be read and interpreted. First, then, what do the faithful of the Swaminarayan tradition primarily mean when they speak of 'Scripture', and why is it so important to them?

Swaminarayan's manifestation on earth in human form allowed for him to teach his ideas about God, liberation and the meaning of life. It is not difficult to appreciate the extraordinary religious significance of this event for members of the Swaminarayan faith. The sacred perennial wisdom of the Vedas, Upaniṣads, Bhagavad-Gītā and other canonical texts, which ancient seers had received by way of divine inspiration, was now available *in person*. Parabrahman was not inspiring those wise words remotely through some distant medium, but speaking them himself, here on earth, in human form. These spoken words were meticulously documented by some of Swaminarayan's most learned and closest disciples, themselves also advanced seekers of liberation, and the compilation later presented to him for personal authentication (see, for example, the mention in Vac. Loyā.7). This set of 273 sermons is the Vacanāmrut, 'the immortalising words'. Its abiding status in the Swaminarayan tradition as the most authentic source of scriptural revelation lies in the distinctive belief that Swaminarayan, as the self-manifestation of Parabrahman, is both the source and the subject of revelatory knowledge comprised within the Vacanāmrut. For the Swaminarayan community, this means, quite literally, it is *God talking about God* – theology, if essentially 'God-talk', in its fullest sense.

Equally, the Vacanāmrut attests to the self-manifestation of Parabrahman as Swaminarayan, but its faithful readers would see it as more than a witness to that revelation. As a receptacle of the spoken words of Swaminarayan, the Vacanāmrut is not a mere book. A footing for this belief can be found in an important sermon where Swaminarayan implicitly identifies himself as 'the avatārin', not a form of the past avatāras, but 'the cause of all of the avatāras'. In conclusion, he adds:

> Although these talks are extremely subtle, even a person of average intelligence can understand them. It is as if these talks are personified {mūrtimān}. (Vac. Gaḍh. 2.9)

Swaminarayan's emphasis here seems to indicate that the sermons are not to be considered a dead letter, because they speak of a living God 'manifest before the eyes' in person, in human form {mūrtimān}, rendering even the most abstract of ideas tangible and easier to grasp. Elsewhere he adds that

'My words are my form',[13] implying that a proper engagement with these teachings can be evocative of relating to God in person, and should, in fact, lead to a personal encounter with his living form.

Of course, 'revelation' as the manifestation of Swaminarayan cannot itself be equated to the text of the Vacanāmrut. It is Parabrahman self-revealed as Swaminarayan who lends the Vacanāmrut its authority and sanctity, not vice versa. And it is God who grants liberation, not a text. In this sense, it might be more accurate to say that the theological truths of the Swaminarayan faith are revealed not *in* the text but *through* the text, by Swaminarayan himself. If the Vacanāmrut as a 'book' is holy, it is because of its divine author, or rather, orator.[14]

The above can also be applied to the sermons of Gunatitanand Swami compiled in the Svāmīnī Vāto and other teachings of the subsequent Brahmasvarūpa Gurus. The community of faithful recognises the authority that these texts already inherently hold on account of them being spoken by Parabrahman and Akṣarabrahman. This authority is not imposed upon them by any external source; their veridicality is intrinsically certified, i.e. they are svataḥ-pramāṇa. This divine oratory is why other religious works – such as the biographical accounts of Swaminarayan and the Gurus, or the thousands of devotional songs of praise and moral teaching composed by Swaminarayan's disciples – while still rich in theological content, cannot, strictly speaking, be considered a direct source of theological knowledge on par with 'revelation'. They can certainly be useful tools that help one reflect upon and illumine revelation (as we shall see in the next chapter). But alone, they are not the foundation upon which the faith of the Swaminarayan tradition stands and grows. To reiterate, the revelatory value of the Vacanāmrut, Svāmīnī Vāto and Guru teachings as authentic and authoritative sources of theological knowledge is undergirded by the self-manifestation of Parabrahman as Swaminarayan (the first mode of revelation we saw in this chapter) and his continued revelation in and by the Akṣarabrahman Guru (the second mode of revelation we saw). Thus, it is always Parabrahman who is

[13] Monier Williams (ed.), 'Sanskṛit Text of the Śikshā-Patrī of the Svāmi-Nārāyaṇa Sect', *Journal of the Royal Asiatic Society of Great Britain and Ireland,* New Series 14.4 (1882), 749, verse 209.

[14] Although the Vacanāmrut comes to us in textual form, it is regarded and revered within the tradition for the *spoken* words of Swaminarayan it holds. Correspondingly, it receives its authority from *Swaminarayan* speaking and authenticating the words that are documented in it, not the transcribers or compilers of those words (even if they were assumed to be divinely inspired to complete their task as accurately as possible). The Vacanāmrut thus follows in the wider aural tradition of Hindu sacred literature, where revealed texts are śruti – heard, not read. 'Scripture' in Hinduism is thus not necessarily limited to something written.

revealing knowledge of himself, *through* the text of Scripture. It is in this sense that Scripture (the third mode) serves as 'revelation'.

For Swaminarayan Hinduism, this extends the boundaries of scriptural revelation beyond the ancient canon of the Vedas, Upaniṣads, Bhagavad-Gītā, Brahmasūtras, Purāṇas, etc. In fact, for his devotees, Swaminarayan's teachings in the Vacanāmrut represent the most direct and authentic source possible of knowledge about God. What may have been germinal, scattered and abstract in other texts has been brought together more clearly and concretely than ever in the Vacanāmrut. To be even more explicit, for the Swaminarayan tradition, the Vacanāmrut – personally delivered by the self-revealed Parabrahman and 'heard' (i.e. received) via the Brahmasvarūpa Gurus (as we shall shortly learn) – is *the* climactic revelatory text by which its theological doctrines are established and articulated.

This, however, in no way relegates the Vedic corpus to a secondary canonical tier; the revelatory status of the Vedas, Upaniṣads, Bhagavad-Gītā and Brahmasūtras remains intact. The Vacanāmrut simply provides the proper perspective with which to correctly read them now. What may have been dim and blurry before is now bright and clear. With the Vacanāmrut, Swaminarayan has shone a new light onto the ancient teachings and brought them into sharper focus. The freshly illumined texts suddenly reveal meanings that appear as if anew. Of course, they have always been there, but this act of rereading is the seeing of what was in sight but had been hitherto overlooked. So if we are to return to the Upaniṣads and Bhagavad-Gītā to read them in light of what is learned from the Vacanāmrut – for example, that Akṣarabrahman (or 'Akṣara' and 'Brahman') is an ontologically distinct entity apart from Parabrahman – it can lead to an 'Aha!' moment of insightful theological discovery.

In this sense, the Vacanāmrut serves as a natural commentary on the Upaniṣads, Bhagavad-Gītā and Brahmasūtras, as it interprets, illuminates and sometimes expands upon many of the key themes and ideas latent within the ancient texts. As we shall see throughout the exposition in Part II, the major themes of Swaminarayan Hindu theology find resonance and grounding in these classical, canonical sources.

This is also attested to in the Vacanāmrut when Swaminarayan presents his teachings as a distillation of the many Hindu texts. For example, he proclaims in Vac. Gaḍh. 3.10:

> From all the Vedas, Purāṇas, Itihāsa and Smṛti scriptures, I have gleaned the principle that jīva, māyā, īśvara, Brahman and Parameśvara are all eternal.

In another sermon, when addressing another point, he states even more emphatically:

> In the four Vedas, the Purāṇas and the Itihāsa scriptures, there is but one central principle, and that is that only God and his Sant can grant liberation. (Vac. Gaḍh. 2.59)

When in Vac. Gaḍh. 2.21 Swaminarayan similarly stressed 'the manifest form of God before the eyes and the manifest form of the Sant before the eyes as being the only grantors of liberation', he concluded:

> This very fact is the essence of all of the scriptures.

On the same topic again, Swaminarayan completed his address in Vac. Gaḍh. 2.28 with the following emphatic addendum:

> What is this sermon like that I have delivered before you? Well, I have delivered it having heard and having extracted the essence from the Vedas, the Śāstras, the Purāṇas and all other words on this earth pertaining to liberation. This is the most profound and fundamental principle; it is the essence of all essences. For all those who have previously attained liberation, for all those who will attain it in the future, and for all those who are presently treading the path of liberation, this discourse is like a lifeline.

Properly understood, then, it is not a question of whether the Vacanāmrut supplants or supersedes other Hindu texts. For the Swaminarayan tradition's faithful, it provides the vital light and perspective needed to understand them correctly and completely in consonance with the revelation of Swaminarayan himself.

Having thus understood Scripture, particularly the Vacanāmrut, as a mode of revelation within the Swaminarayan tradition, we can now move on to understanding its primary position as a source of theological knowledge.

Primacy of Scripture

The priority and authority placed on the Vacanāmrut within the Swaminarayan tradition as a source of theological knowledge can also be traced to Swaminarayan's own emphasis on appealing to authentic texts whenever possible. He often corroborated important points within his sermons by citing widely accepted scriptures. In the sermons compiled within the Vacanāmrut, 98 scriptural references are directly quoted a total of 110 times, including 45 verses or verse-portions from the Bhāgavata-Purāṇa and 33 from the Bhagavad-Gītā. Other scriptures directly referenced include the

Aitareya Upaniṣad, Bṛhadāraṇyaka Upaniṣad, Chāndogya Upaniṣad, Muṇḍaka Upaniṣad, Subāla Upaniṣad, Śvetāśvatara Upaniṣad, Taittirīya Upaniṣad, Taittirīya Āraṇyaka (Yajur Veda), Mahābhārata, Skanda Purāṇa, Hiraṇyakeśīyaśākhāśruti, Carpaṭapañjarī and Maṇiratnamālā. Indirectly, Swaminarayan refers to more than fifty works of religious and other significance, including some extremely remote texts, such as Sūryasiddhānta and Siddhāntaśiromaṇi.

When engaging his audience with theological questions, he would similarly insist that they, too, offer answers supported by scriptural testimony. For example, when asking in Vac. Gaḍh. 1.69,

> What exactly is dharma?

he follows up immediately by requesting the respondents to

> Please base your reply on the scriptures.

Similarly, in Vac. Gaḍh. 1.71 he requests:

> Therefore, please base your answer on the principles of the scriptures.

When in reply to one of his questions the sādhus did not substantiate their answer, Swaminarayan quickly responded:

> From what principle in the scriptures do you claim that . . . ? Please quote any reference from the scriptures. (Vac. Gaḍh. 1.78)

At the heart of this insistence to root all reflection in Scripture lies the principle of scriptural revelation as the only authentic knowledge-source of all things Godly. Swaminarayan makes this explicit in Vac. Sār.13 when describing how to develop faith in God.

> Whosoever develops faith in God does so only through the scriptures. Why? Because the scriptures describe the characteristics of God as well as the characteristics of the Sant. So, only faith developed through the scriptures remains steadfast. On the other hand, faith developed by one's own mind, without the help of the scriptures, eventually dissolves.
>
> Only one who has faith in the scriptures is able to develop unshakeable faith in God, and only such a person attains liberation.

In Vac. Gaḍh. 3.27, Swaminarayan further asserts Scripture as the ultimate source of all theological knowledge. In other words, all theological knowledge, wherever it exists, has its root in Scripture.

For Swaminarayan, then, scriptural testimony is the only knowledge-source {pramāṇa} among all the epistemological means whereby one can properly know the nature of the transcendental, otherwise imperceptible Parabrahman (and Akṣarabrahman).[15] To this, there is a useful (though untraceable) Sanskrit verse that reads:

> Anekasanśayocchedi parokṣārthasya darśanam |
> Sarvasya locanam śāstram yasya nāstyandha eva saḥ ||
>
> Scriptures dispel several doubts and reveal intangible truths [literally, make visible that which is beyond the eyes]. Scriptures are the eyes of all. Without them, a person is indeed blind.

Here, though, we must pause to face a contention raised by Bhadreshdas in his extensive commentary of BS 1.1.3. The sūtra itself – Śāstrayonitvāt | – affirms that Scripture is that by which one can know 'Brahman', which has already been identified as the subject of the Sūtrakāra's inquiry (BS 1.1.1) and minimally referred to as the cause of the world's origination, sustenance and dissolution (BS 1.1.2).

The objection takes this form: Upaniṣadic statements such as

> From where speech returns . . . having not attained it (TU 1.4.1, 2.9.1);
>
> This Self, the immortal indweller, is the unseen seer, the unheard listener . . . (BU 3.7.23);

and

> That which is unseeable, ungraspable . . . (MuU 1.1.6)[16]

confirm that God is beyond the subject of speech and sound; he cannot be described nor can he be heard. He is therefore unknowable by scriptures, which, after all, are nothing but 'a pile of words'.

To this Bhadreshdas retorts that these are the ramblings of those who have not grasped the true import of the scriptures and rely solely on the imagined proficiency of their flawed reasoning. Statements such as the above serve simply to affirm the unlimited nature of God and the limited scope of human means. Indeed, it is by these very scriptures that this is established! How can those same scriptures, which you, too, cite, then become invalid? If you argue, on the basis of these statements, that God is not the subject of verbal testimony, then what will you make of other statements, in those same

[15] We shall be considering in the following chapter the means of reason, praxis and tradition as, not *sources* of theology but, *tools* to illuminate and better receive revelation.

[16] According to Bhadreshdas, these last two statements refer in particular to Akṣarabrahman, but can also apply to Parabrahman.

set of scriptures, which describe him as knowable through scriptures? Such statements include the following:

> That Self extolled in the Upaniṣads . . . (BU 3.9.26)

> I alone am to be known by all of the Vedas. (BG 15.15)

They assure that, even with all their usual limitations and imperfections, words, when divinely spoken or inspired, can invaluably serve as a reliable source of knowledge about God.[17] As always, though, we must also accept that this revelation, even though adequate, is never exhaustive.[18]

Receiving Scripture through the Guru

As direct as the Vacanāmrut and the Svāmīnī Vāto are the words of Swaminarayan and Gunatitanand Swami, the inescapable fact remains that they still come to us as words, fraught with the potentiality of being misread by frail, imperfect human minds. Unlike ordinary texts, however, they are, according to the tradition, words spoken by Parabrahman and Akṣarabrahman – divine speakers – and so any interpretation of them must also be faithfully undertaken. Indeed, reading and interpreting the Vacanāmrut as the authentic, normative source of theological knowledge for the Swaminarayan Hindu community is an endeavour that must adhere to certain guidelines. The correct methodology of reading theological texts is a complex topic, though, deserving a lot more detail and discussion than is available here. Nevertheless, it is necessary to cover the most important guideline Swaminarayan repeatedly emphasised in the Vacanāmrut itself, that is, the 'reading' or 'listening' of Scripture from the Brahmasvarūpa Guru.

Firstly, it is important to clarify that we are allowed here a broader meaning of the terms 'reading' and 'listening'. It is, of course, highly desirable to hear first-hand the Guru reading and exegetically elaborating upon Scripture. But if that is not possible, when reading personally or even when listening to a text-based discourse from another expert, the exegetical import is always derived from the Guru. The final, decisive responsibility of valid interpretation is invariably deferred to the Brahmasvarūpa Guru, because it is only he, as Brahman and being fully established in Parabrahman ('brahma niṣṭham'), who has the most direct and perfect realisation of scriptural truths ('śrotriyam') and is thus the most qualified and able to convey them.[19]

[17] Condensed from BS-SB 1.1.3, pp. 17–18.

[18] See Chapter 2 on the imperceptibility and ineffability of God.

[19] See MuU-SB 1.2.12, pp. 253–6 for an elaboration of the words and this point. See also BS-SB 1.1.3, pp. 22–4.

The Guru, to be precise, is not only a knower of the revealed truth ('jñānin') but a direct *seer* ('tattvadarśin')[20] and embodiment of it.

These attributes become all the more vital when one appreciates the multivalency of scriptural words, and thus the potentiality of their misreading, alongside the primacy of Scripture above all other sources of theological knowledge. Others, even erudite scholars, who are without a direct experience of God, would be prone to misinterpret or incompletely understand scriptural teachings, and would therefore be unable to fully and properly explain them as God intended them to be understood. This would mean that experts theologising upon first-order and second-order texts can still be innovative and imaginative in their exegesis, insofar as it conforms to the overarching reading provided by the Guru. Anything contradictory to or divergent from the original revelation, however, would be deemed inauthentic.

What is further clear from Swaminarayan's sermons is that, in his mind, the reading of Scripture is not a barren, academic activity. When Gopalanand Swami asks in Vac. Var.11,

> Why is it that despite reading the Śāstras, the Purāṇas and other scriptures, the pundits of the world still do not understand the greatness of God and the Sant as it really is?

Swaminarayan explains that the fault lies in their lack of refuge in God. As a result, the pundits, as learned as they may be, are 'overpowered' by their own 'inner enemies' of 'lust, anger, avarice, jealousy', etc., leading them to arrogantly misunderstand God and the Guru.

> So, even though they read the Śāstras and Purāṇas, they fail to realise the greatness of God and his Sant as it really is.

To capitalise on its inherent liberative benefits, scriptural reading thus needs to be conducted with a firm grounding in faith. In the very next sermon, Swaminarayan warns against hearing the holy scriptures from faithless exponents. He likens someone who 'does not have such firm faith coupled with the knowledge of God's greatness' to an 'impotent' person, from whom no woman can ever beget a child. 'Similarly', Swaminarayan explains,

> no one attains liberation by hearing even holy scriptures such as the Gītā and the Śrīmad-Bhāgavata from one who does not have faith in God coupled with the knowledge of his greatness. (Vac. Var.12)

[20] See BG-SB 4.34, p. 110.

It is thus the fertile intercourse of *faith* with Scripture that bears the liberative and joyous understanding of God.

Going even further in Vac. Var.12, Swaminarayan warns that receiving the holy texts from faithless readers can not only be fruitless but gravely dangerous to one's faith.

> Just as death is assured to whoever drinks sweetened milk into which a snake's venom has fallen, similarly, no one can ever attain liberation by listening to the Gītā or the Śrīmad-Bhāgavata from a person who does not have faith in God coupled with the knowledge of his greatness. On the contrary, it can be detrimental.

The natural culmination of this instruction can be found in Vac. Loyā.11, where Swaminarayan states simply and concisely:

> One should only hear the sacred scriptures from the Satpuruṣa, but never from an unholy person.

Swaminarayan emphasises even more clearly in Vac. Gaḍh. 2.13 the essentiality of the Guru in helping access revelatory truths from the scriptures. After delivering an exceptionally important sermon on the nature of God, in particular alluding to himself as Parabrahman, Swaminarayan appends his address with the following reminder:

> However, such discourses regarding the nature of God cannot be understood by oneself even from the scriptures. Even though these facts may be in the scriptures, it is only when the Satpuruṣa manifests on this earth, and one hears them being narrated by him, that one understands them. They cannot, however, be understood by one's intellect alone, even from the scriptures.

In another sermon, Swaminarayan adds categorically:

> The words of the scriptures cannot be [fully] understood by anyone except an Ekāntika Bhakta. (Vac. Gaḍh. 1.66)

Thus, in Swaminarayan's mind, the Vacanāmrut or any other scriptural text is only correctly interpreted when it is read under the faithful tutelage of the Guru. Reading from the Guru ensures that each detail is understood 'sampradāyically' (as in ecclesiastically), so to speak, in conformation with the norms, faith and history of the tradition. The living Guru, and faith in his words, thus becomes the essential hermeneutical tool in Swaminarayan Hindu theology by which to make sense of Swaminarayan's revelation and live by it (Figure 3).

Figure 3 Swami Narayanswarupdas (1921–2016), known within the BAPS Swaminarayan fellowship as Brahmaswarup Pramukh Swami Maharaj, discoursing on Swaminarayan's teachings from the Vacanāmrut, in Bangalore, 1989. Receiving Scripture from the living Brahmasvarūpa Guru is considered one of the surest, most direct forms of theological revelation. (Photo courtesy of Swaminarayan Aksharpith)

In conclusion to this chapter, this is what can be succinctly said of 'revelation' in Swaminarayan Hindu theology: God, out of his loving grace, has chosen to be revealed in person as Swaminarayan, in and by the Brahmasvarūpa Guru and through Scripture, which most specifically means the Vacanāmrut when faithfully received via the Guru. It is by these means only that God can be directly, most easily, and authentically known. Understood as such, revelation thus serves as the exclusive source of veritable theological knowledge in the Swaminarayan Hindu system.

CHAPTER 4

Reason, Praxis and Tradition
The Tools of Swaminarayan Hindu Theology

If it is by revelation alone – the gracious, loving act of God revealing himself in person or through Scripture and the Guru – that God can be known, the question then remains, what place do human reason and endeavour, both past and current, have in the quest to better understand that revealed God? This shall be the subject of inquiry in this chapter. In particular, it shall address the role of reason, praxis and tradition in the Swaminarayan system in understanding God and progressing towards the goal of liberation.

First, though, it is important to note the function of these factors as *tools* in relation to revelation; that is, unlike revelation, they are not independent *sources* of theological knowledge. Nor are they complementary or supplementary to it, for revelation is not necessarily deficient in any way that they could add anything missing or new to whatever is already inherent within revelation.

What the tools do provide, however, is a new vigour of light with which to better appreciate revelation and its latent beauty and power. They help illuminate revelatory truths, so that seeing the same in a new perspective sometimes leads to a discovery of what had previously been missed. In this sense, these tools can function like spectacles, bringing into sharper focus what – due to defects or deficiencies in the observer, not the object (i.e. revelation) – may have seemed obscure or indistinct. Rather than enhancing revelation, they enhance the capability of the reader to access and receive revelation more intensely. They serve to clarify and fortify its meanings, helping unlock deeper chambers of truth that may not be immediately apparent. These highly complex topics warrant far more detail and discussion than is possible here, but we may be able to fleetingly point to their basic function in the sections below as we briefly introduce each in turn.

Reason

In his extensive commentary on BS 1.1.3, Bhadreshdas strongly defends the primacy of verbal testimony {śabda pramāṇa} and its irreducibility to an inductive expression. In particular, he argues in some detail about the limits and defects of rational induction when employed independently of Scripture to prove the creatorship of Brahman. He firstly draws upon the basic reasoning used by the Nyāya school of Indian logic to deduce such creatorship. Their syllogism takes the form: All effects have an agent; the world (comprising of sprouts, etc.) is an effect; therefore it must have an agent, as with a pot. Bhadreshdas then systematically dismantles each technical constituent of the argument and rejoins a series of counterarguments before issuing a warning: an overzealous application of reasoning or confidence in one's intellect can blind one from seeing one's own limitations and fallacious argumentation, leaving one empty of higher, more subtle truths.[1]

Elsewhere,[2] Bhadreshdas adds that adeptness in argumentation alone is inadequate, simply because the divine, not-this-worldly and sensorially imperceptible God can never become the subject of reason alone – just as the ears can never grasp the visual beauty of a rose and the eyes fail to apprehend the sweet song of a nightingale. Besides, all instances of inference are predicated on perception, and therefore the senses, whose limitations have already been well established.

The Kaṭha Upaniṣad, for example, clearly states that the highest theological knowledge is 'beyond suppositional reasoning {atarkyam}' (2.8) and thus not fully comprehendible by the intellect alone. The very next verse begins:

> Nor can this knowledge be grasped by argumentation. (KaU 2.9)

As Bhadreshdas affords some extra elaboration on this topic, he again warns that reasoning left to its own devices can be dangerous, because, after all, argumentation is a skill. A strong argument can always be thwarted by a stronger argument. So there is no telling which incisive piece of logic might be superseded by a yet more rational objector or by the same thinker at a different time or place. Such contestations and disputes are endless and ultimately meaningless, he asserts, for this is not the way to decide or judge established principles {siddhānta}. Besides, reasoning is designated as a quality of the intellect {buddhi}, which the Kaṭha Upaniṣad later concedes is increasingly inferior to the soul, Akṣarabrahman and Parabrahman (KaU 3.10–11). It is thus a futile if not perilous and

[1] BS-SB 1.1.3, pp. 19–22, esp. p. 20.

[2] The following is based on BS-SB 1.1.3, pp. 17–24; BS-SB 1.1.5, pp. 29–31; BS-SB 2.11, pp. 164–6; KaU-SB 2.9, pp. 92–4; and KaU-SB 6.12, pp. 164–5, with added personal reflection.

ridiculously arrogant venture to attempt to grasp knowledge of the supremely divine by that which is still shackled by māyā.

In conclusion, Bhadreshdas asks: how can there be any other reliable means of knowing that which is not fully perceptible to human senses and graspable by human intellect? Therefore, rather than perception or inference, it is the intrinsically certified, divinely spoken or divinely inspired words constituting Scripture which we must solely rely upon to form a valid understanding of God. Among all the sources of knowledge, Scripture is thus 'the principal knowledge-source {paramapramāṇa}',[3] and God is, simply, 'understandable by Scripture alone {śāstraikagamya}'.[4]

Even so, while the above places reasoned argumentation in its proper epistemological position, it need not be totally abandoned in order to defer to scriptural authority. In the same comment on KaU 2.9, Bhadreshdas makes the crucial distinction between correct reasoning {sattarka} and incorrect reasoning {dustarka}.[5] The former is that which is informed by and undergirded by śraddhā, which he describes in BS-SB 2.1.11 as 'utmost faith in the Brahmasvarūpa Guru and the śāstra and siddhānta he propounds'.[6] Conversely, incorrect reasoning is that which is uncommitted to and independent of Scripture and Guru. Reason alone may be blind, but holding the hand of faith, it is able to reliably explore the wider contours of theological reflection. Faith gives it direction, leading it safely to fruitful ends.

Reason, therefore, becomes a valuable tool in understanding revelation when properly grounded in and guided by Scripture and the Guru. It helps not necessarily in discovering theological ideas anew, for their roots can always be traced to revelation, but exploring those ideas further and excavating from them deeper truths that had been within sight but not really seen. This is what is meant by reason providing 'insight', as it opens one to fresh, deeper, richer understandings of revelation.

Reason can also help in confirming and consolidating what has already been learnt from Scripture and refuting claims contradictory to it. Early on, in the Brahmasūtra-Svāminārāyaṇa-Bhāṣya, an objection is raised about the inquiry into 'Brahman'. The question is this: if śāstra (Scripture) is the supreme authority of brahmic knowledge (theology), it is futile, then, to debate upon it because now there is no room for doubt and therefore there are no doubts to dispel. Bhadreshdas rejects that idea, asserting realistically that doubts can still occur even within Scripture. Moreover, he adds, once doubts are dispelled, it is useful and even

[3] KaU-SB 6.12, p. 165. [4] BS-SB 1.1.3, p. 22. [5] KaU-SB 2.9, p. 93. [6] BS-SB 2.1.11, p. 166.

necessary to test and consolidate what one knows, just as one shakes a peg that has been freshly hammered into the ground.[7]

The very project of the Brahmasūtras testifies to the faithful employment of reasoned argumentation to harmonise meanings, clarify ambiguous content, refute contradictory interpretations and rebut objections. Reason thus serves to consolidate and clarify that which has already been established by Scripture, to protect and embolden faith. Bhadreshdas too defends his interpretations in the Svāminārāyaṇa-Bhāṣya as being 'śrutiyuktisammata', that is, in agreement with both revelation and reasoning.[8] Ratiocination is still permissible and profitable, when deployed on the basis of Scripture.[9] Applying reasoned reflection, therefore, is not in contradistinction to the concept of *sola scriptura*, insofar as it is in consonance with and submission to revelation. Indeed, reason often works in the service of revelation, bolstering its authority and justifying its priority.

Praxis

Validation for reasoned argumentation or faithful inquiry can also be found in BG 4.34. The first half of the verse reads:

> Tad-viddhi praṇipātena paripraśnena sevayā |
>
> Learn that [knowledge] by obeisance, inquiry and service.

Importantly, though, inquiry is bookended by humble obeisance and sincere application. That is, Bhadreshdas explains,

> only such an inquiry is herein advocated that is doubly bound and refined by being preceded by surrender and succeeded by service. Otherwise, any questioning divorced of a faithful obeisance to begin with and not followed by a subsequent commitment to practice is not conducive to theological understanding; it is verily averse to it.[10]

True inquiry must thus not only be grounded in revelation; it must also follow through into 'sādhanā' {literally 'means' or liberative endeavours}, also referred to as praxis.[11] Indeed, a sincere application of theological ideas is an integral and necessary part of the process of understanding theological teachings. It becomes clear from Swaminarayan's sermons that he did not intend theological beliefs to be simply articles of faith for subscription.

[7] BS-SB 1.1.1, pp. 10–11. [8] BS-SB 1.1.1, p. 8. [9] BS-SB 1.1.3, p. 22. [10] BG-SB 4.34, p. 110.
[11] This should not be confused with the 'praxis' of Liberation Theology, which binds together action, suffering and reflection.

Rather, they are to be lived out and deeply integrated into every aspect of one's actions, thoughts, intentions and being. They are to be experienced, because, as Swaminarayan stressed, only when one experiences what one has learned from Scripture by faith is one's knowledge truly complete (Vac. Loyā.7).

In fact, Swaminarayan taught that theological concepts *grow* in their meaning as they are translated into personal theological praxis (which can take a physical and mental form). For example, in Vac. Sār.17 Swaminarayan states:

> As the vision of a person who worships God becomes increasingly subtle, he realises the unlimited nature of God and he increasingly realises the greatness of God.

He goes on to elaborate:

> When that devotee identifies himself with the body, he sees God as the witness of his waking, dream and deep sleep states. Later, when he realises himself as transcending the waking, dream and deep sleep states, he realises God as transcending them too. Then, as his vision becomes increasingly subtle, he realises God as being far beyond himself and understands the greatness of God even more. Then, as he becomes more and more lovingly attached to God, his upāsanā [i.e. loving worship informed by theological understanding] of God becomes even more firmly established.

Swaminarayan's import here is that one's understanding of God is predicated on how well one understands one's self. Importantly, as one progresses in a correct spiritual self-understanding, one grows not only in understanding God but, naturally and inevitably, in a deeper loving relationship with him. In effect, Swaminarayan is saying: along the path of theological understanding, one can only see from where one stands; as the seeker walks further and rises higher, she advances in her theological vision and insights upon what had been accepted on trust from Scripture. This is the role of praxis in the task of theology.

Another example can be drawn from a particularly important sermon wherein Swaminarayan expounds the crux of his theological system with notable brevity and simplicity. He begins by explaining the nature and function of Brahman and then its ontological distinction from and subordination to Parabrahman. Swaminarayan then states:

> Having understood this [i.e. having accepted these beliefs], one should develop a oneness between one's jivātman and that Brahman, and worship Parabrahman while maintaining a master-servant relationship with him.

What is noteworthy here is that Swaminarayan immediately calls for the highly theological concept (the Brahman–Parabrahman distinction and connection) to be implemented by way of a living relationship with Brahman (i.e. the Brahmasvarūpa Guru) and God. Furthermore, he brings even such an application into the domain of 'understanding' as he goes on to conclude the sermon thus:

> With such *understanding*, 'brahmajñāna' also becomes an unobstructed path to attaining the highest state of enlightenment. (Vac. Gaḍh. 2.3; emphasis added)

This interplay between understanding and praxis is a key feature of Swaminarayan's teachings, revealing that he never intended faith to be passive. True faith is not an exercise in intellectual excogitation, but calls one to act, sincerely and devoutly. That is why Swaminarayan advocated and indeed engaged his followers in such endeavours as temple-building (Vac. Gaḍh. 2.27) and works of religious service and public welfare (Vac. Gaḍh. 1.31, Vac. Var.17). He admonished those who 'sat idly', and urged those who wished 'to attain the highest state of enlightenment' to 'make an effort, but . . . not relax or lose courage' (Vac. Gaḍh. 2.12). In one sermon he categorically stated:

> All deficiencies that do remain in a devotee are due to his own lethargy. (Vac. Gaḍh. 1.20)

Moreover, Swaminarayan added, the location of this praxis is the crucible of the faith community itself. Reading of Scripture may be a deeply personal endeavour, but imbibing its teachings in daily life becomes inescapably a communal enterprise. To be clear, this remains an individual effort, but one made within a living community of practitioners. In fact, Swaminarayan emphasised patient praxis within the community as a mark of faith, whereas those who sought to escape the community and practise in isolation were lacking in an essential understanding of God and what it meant to be a person of faith (Vac. Var.5).

Swaminarayan thus often integrated the theoretical and practical aspects of theology to bring seemingly abstract concepts to fruition through ways of practical application. For example, to gain in spiritual strength, Swaminarayan prescribes sincerely serving devotees of God through word, thought and deed (Vac. Gaḍh. 2.63). To control or win over the mind, one should engage in acts of reverent devotion (Vac. Gaḍh. 3.11). Dispassion towards material pleasures can be achieved by observing the basic code of conduct prescribed in religious texts, including physically serving other devotees, listening to scriptural discourses and performing other acts of devotion (Vac. Gaḍh. 3.34). And after describing the essentiality of a correct, spiritual understanding of the self, Swaminarayan emphatically asserts that observing the commands of the Guru is indeed tantamount to realising oneself as the ātman (Vac. Gaḍh. 2.51).

This emphasis on the pragmatic is also discernible in the questions posed by his disciples, who sought not only answers to their theological queries but clear guidance for their sādhanā in progressing towards liberation. For example, when Muktanand Swami asks Swaminarayan in Vac. Kār.8,

> Mahārāj,[12] the Vedas, the Śāstras, the Purāṇas and the Itihāsa scriptures have described the saguṇa form of God and have also described his nirguṇa form. So how should one understand the nirguṇa form and how should one understand the saguṇa form of Śrī Puruṣottama?

his question is not complete until he concludes with the following:

> How much does a devotee of God benefit by understanding the nirguṇa form of that God, and how much does he benefit by understanding the saguṇa form of that God?

What is apparent is that the question being asked is not for mere data collection. It is not enough to simply know a concept. Rather, the seeker is keen to incorporate the concept into his daily practice, and hence is striving to understand its practical significance as well. As mentioned above, in between the starting point of faith (based on revelation) and the finishing line of realisation (i.e. experience) lies this journey of praxis, of physically and mentally applying theological concepts until they come to full consummation.

This emphasis stems from the conviction that these theological ideas or beliefs are true, and the truth is to be lived. As shall be apparent throughout the exposition of the main themes of Swaminarayan Hindu theology, Swaminarayan insists upon not just 'knowing *about* God', as in accumulating cerebral information concerning him, but actually '*knowing* God' personally, that is, developing an intimate, personal relationship with him and his living medium – the Guru. Theology, for Swaminarayan, is not simply about ideas but the transformation of the individual – progressing from material to spiritual, from bondage to liberation, from māyic to brahmic.

This is why sheer textual information or theoretical knowledge was never enough for Swaminarayan (Vac. Gaḍh. 1.35, Gaḍh. 1.50, Gaḍh.

[12] This is an honorific name often used to address Swaminarayan.

1.56, Var.11, Gaḍh. 3.2, Gaḍh. 3.36, Gaḍh. 3.27). He insisted that only those who were making the sincere effort to reflect upon his teachings and imbibing them would be able to understand them (Vac. Gaḍh. 1.18). Faith, then, which is operative, is attended by sincere and patient praxis, by which faith itself is fostered and fortified and revelation is sharpened.

Tradition

If praxis is the application of scriptural teachings, how these theological ideas have been implemented and practised over time provides further insight into their finer meaning. Tradition, as the continuous receiving and transmitting of revelation, thus becomes another useful tool in better understanding revelation itself. A verse from the Mahābhārata (Ādi Parvan 1.267) often cited to substantiate this concept reads:

> Itihāsapurāṇabhyām vedam samupabṛhayet |
>
> The Vedas should be consolidated by the Itihāsa and Purāṇa texts.

It calls us to draw upon historical and epical literature to clarify and consolidate the meaning of revelatory sources.

Vedic literature itself also attests to the tradition of drawing upon previous authorities of verified knowledge, whose lineage is often narrated as a way of substantiating its authenticity. We see this in practice in the beginning of the Bhagavad-Gītā's fourth canto when Kṛṣṇa recounts preaching the yogic knowledge to Vivasvān, who in turn passed it on to Manu, who subsequently conveyed it to Ikṣvāku. He confirms:

> Thus this [knowledge] received by succession is known by the royal sages. (BG 4.2)

Similarly, in the Muṇḍaka Upaniṣad (1.1.1–2), the author traces the transmission of brahmavidyā from Brahmā (not to be confused with Brahman) to his eldest son Atharvan, then successively on to Aṅgir, Bhāradvāja Satyavāha, Aṅgiras and, finally, Śaunaka.

In other Upaniṣads we find the more general acknowledgement:

> Thus we have heard from past [teachers], who explained it to us. (KeU 1.4; similarly also IU 10 and IU 13)

Indeed, the very term 'Śruti' {literally 'hearing'}, used synonymously with the Vedas and to describe revelatory literature in general, pays further testimony to this emphasis on 'tradition'. The fact that the transmission of knowledge from guru to śiṣya is framed as an *aural* tradition, rather than an *oral* tradition, is telling. One would assume that the guru as speaker, being of much higher authority and learning than his audience of disciples, would be the protagonist in the guru–śiṣya dialogue, and thus the revealed texts should be more aptly termed 'Vakti' {speaking}. The fact that they are not, and instead called 'Śruti', affirms, as above, that even the teacher has *heard* whatever knowledge he is imparting from his own previous teachers, extending the lineage indefinitely to, presumably, the initial divine revelation by God himself.

Within Swaminarayan Hinduism, this idea of drawing upon 'tradition' and the transmission of divine knowledge takes on a more specific meaning revolving around the human personhood of Swaminarayan and, in particular, the Guru Paramparā, the unbroken succession of Brahmasvarūpa Gurus in and by whom Parabrahman chooses to be revealed and to remain liberatively active. As perfect devotees, their lives serve as the ideal example of how theological principles should and must be practised, of living out faith in all aspects of everyday life.

Swaminarayan thus urges his devotees to 'reminisce' the 'divine incidents and actions {līlā}' of God who lived among them, sometimes alluding to himself (Vac. Gaḍh. 2.35; see also Vac. Gaḍh. 1.3 and Vac. Gaḍh. 1.38) and also the Brahmasvarūpa Gurus (Vac. Gaḍh. 2.66). In Vac. Gaḍh. 2.58, he explicitly instructs Muktanand Swami, one of his most senior monastic disciples, to 'continuously preach and write' about 'your īṣṭadeva {chosen deity} for the rest of your life', because it is in the texts that narrate the life of one's own īṣṭadeva that 'dharma {righteous or "right" living} as well as the glory of that īṣṭadeva are naturally revealed'. In other words, if the Vacanāmrut is the 'textbook', the biographies of Swaminarayan and the Gurus are the 'workbooks' wherein we find real-life examples of theological ideas being put into practice, calling also the faithful to emulate them. This is important because, as seen above, practices can be a useful tool when understanding or interpreting beliefs, since how one prays and worships reflects what one believes (and, correspondingly, what one believes affects how one prays and worships).

The Guru-centric nature of tradition, and its continuous flow over time, ensures that tradition itself is not a fossilised view of 'how things were done', but becomes an active process of reflection and interpretation, by which theological and spiritual insights are valued, tested and transmitted. The very definition of 'sampradāya', even if translated as 'tradition', points both ways – not just to the past but, ironically, also to the future. The Halāyudhakośa, a famous Sanskrit lexicon, offers the following entry under the term 'sampradāya':

a lineage of successive gurus. (2.402)

When elaborating upon the second half of the Bhagavad-Gītā verse cited above,

> Upadekṣyanti te jñānam jñāninas tattvadarśinaḥ ||
>
> Enlightened seers shall preach that knowledge to you (BG 4.34),

Bhadreshdas is also keen to point out the use of the future tense in the verb 'upadekṣyanti' {will preach} and the plurality in the nouns 'jñāninaḥ' {knowers} and 'tattvadarśinaḥ' {seers}. He interprets this as a clear affirmation of the succession of Brahmasvarūpa Gurus, who will continue to transmit this revelatory knowledge to generations of seekers indefinitely. This perpetual transmission of revelation serves to bolster revelation itself by continuously opening up new opportunities for theological reflection, inquiry and application.

Properly understood, then, tradition along with reason and praxis do not relegate revelation to an equal or lesser authority but secure its position as the primary theological source even while establishing themselves as useful tools in the task of theology.

PART II

Themes of Swaminarayan Hindu Theology

CHAPTER 5

Introduction
The Five Eternal Entities of Swaminarayan Hinduism

A discussion of any classical Hindu school of thought invariably begins with an inquiry (mīmāṃsā} into, or discussion of, its basic entities or realities {tattvas}: How many metaphysical entities does it accept as real and which ones? The answer to this fundamental question more often than not reveals much about the school's basic premises and beliefs. For example, within Śaṅkara's absolute monism, the singular attribute-less {nirguṇa} entity of Brahman necessarily requires the visible world to be unreal and illusory. In contrast, Rāmānuja's acceptance of cit {sentient} and acit {non-sentient} entities in addition to Īśvara {God} allows for both the world to be real and for individual souls to be distinct from God.

Subsequent questions for each entity include inquiries into its essential nature, characteristics, role, relationships, etc. These questions and their answers will occupy the discussion of the following chapters for each of the metaphysical entities of the Swaminarayan school of Vedānta. But first it will be necessary to identify these basic entities. They are the following five:

1. Parabrahman (or Puruṣottama)
2. Akṣarabrahman (also Akṣara or Brahman)
3. māyā
4. īśvara
5. jīva

Swaminarayan explicitly lists these in two sermons of the Vacanāmrut:

> Puruṣottama Bhagavān, Akṣarabrahman, māyā, īśvara and jīva – these five entities are eternal. (Vac. Gaḍh. 1.7)

> From all the Vedas, Purāṇas, Itihāsa and Smṛti scriptures, I have gleaned the principle that jīva, māyā, īśvara, Brahman and Parameśvara are all eternal. (Vac. Gaḍh. 3.10)

To further emphasise that all five of these entities are indeed real {satya}, that is, that they truly exist and are not illusory, Swaminarayan writes in the Vedaras:

> Some claim that jīvas and māyā are imaginary {kalpita}. But O Paramahansas! The jīva is real, māyā is real, īśvara is real, Brahman is real, Parabrahman is real. (VR 177)

He reiterates this point in Vac. Gaḍh. 1.39 and Gaḍh. 1.42 in response, more explicitly than above, to claims from the Advaitins that 'Brahman alone exists and all else besides – jīva, īśvara, māyā, etc. – is unreal {mithyā}'. Rather, Swaminarayan explains, along with the highest two entities, even jīva, īśvara and māyā are real but not illusory.[1]

For anyone familiar with other Vedānta schools, what is immediately striking is that there are *five* tattvas in the Swaminarayan system, in contrast to, say, Śaṅkara's one (Brahman), Madhva's two (svatantra-tattva and asvatantra-tattva) and Rāmānuja's three (Īśvara, cit and acit) – and this is indeed a distinguishing feature of Swaminarayan Hinduism. It also raises a number of important and sometimes difficult questions of the system. For example:

1. Is the 'Brahman' of the Swaminarayan School the same 'highest reality' as that of the other schools?
2. If so, then what/who is 'Parabrahman'?
3. If not – and 'Parabrahman' is the name simply applied to what others call Brahman – then what/who is this other 'Brahman'?
4. Are there *two* 'highest realities' in the Swaminarayan School? Clearly not, for this, by definition of the superlative, is implausible. But then how are 'Brahman' and 'Parabrahman' related? Indeed, how are the two distinct?
5. Furthermore, what is the difference between 'īśvara' and 'Parabrahman'? Is not 'īśvara' God and divine? If not, how do(es) it/he/she/they relate to both God and individual souls (jīvas)?
6. What role do the two seemingly superfluous entities of 'Brahman' and 'īśvara' play, within creation and for God and individual souls?

All of these and many other questions will be addressed in the proceeding chapters as and when each of the entities is discussed. However, to assist in a primary understanding of the five entities as we begin and progress

[1] These five entities are described as eternal and real by Bhadreshdas as well. See, for example, KeU-SB 2.4, p. 47; TU-SB 1.1.1, p. 330; and TU-SB 1.9.1, p. 350.

through this detailed exposition, the succinct overview below (provided in reverse order) shall hopefully prove useful.

- Jīvas are distinct, individual souls, minute in size and innumerable in quantity. Each one is bound by māyā, which shrouds the jīva's radiant self essentially characterised by existence {sat}, consciousness {cit} and bliss {ānanda}.
- Īśvaras are higher beings endowed with special powers for fulfilling various functions within a particular brahmāṇḍa {'universe'}, of which there are countless millions. But like the jīvas, īśvaras, too, are shrouded by māyā.
- Māyā is an instrument of Parabrahman that constitutes the base substance from which this material world is formed. It also forms the ignorance that shrouds jīvas and īśvaras.
- Akṣarabrahman, also called Akṣara and Brahman, is forever untouched by māyā and so jīvas and īśvaras must associate with Akṣarabrahman to transcend their ignorance. Akṣarabrahman takes the form of the abode of Parabrahman, known as Akṣaradhāma, and also appears in human form as his ideal devotee, the Brahmasvarūpa Guru. In this form, Akṣarabrahman leads jīvas and īśvaras to the highest elevated state (akṣararūpa or brahmarūpa) wherein they experience the infinite, undisturbed bliss of Parabrahman. Akṣarabrahman also has an all-pervading form, as ethereal space, known as Cidākāśa, and another form as the ideal servant of Parabrahman within Akṣaradhāma
- Parabrahman, or Puruṣottama, is God Supreme; the one and unparalleled cause, controller and support of the entire world; omnipotent, omniscient, omnipresent and omnibenevolent. Eternally human in form yet fully divine, he manifests on earth with Akṣarabrahman to release seekers of spiritual liberation from their ignorance and elevate them to an enlightened state, finally granting them an eternal place in Akṣaradhāma, his transcendental abode.

The enumeration of these entities as explicitly five – and five only – confirms that all matter, whether material or spiritual, will be subsumed within one of these five categories. In other words, there is nothing that is not one of the five, but the five categories themselves are irreducible. Moreover, everything can be only one of the five but never a hybrid of any two or more of them, since all five of the entities are ontologically and eternally distinct from one another. That one entity can never become any other entity, and that none is ever destroyed (because it is endless), means that there will always be five categories; hence, again, they are explained as 'the five eternal entities'.

Being eternal, of course, must mean that each entity is not only without end {ananta} but also without beginning {anādi}, i.e. that it has always existed and will forever continue to exist; there never has been and never will be a time when it did not. A term closely related to this concept and confirming that the entities are truly real {satya} is trikālābādhita, meaning literally that they are unaffected by 'the three times', the past, the present and the future.[2] It is in this sense that all five entities are said to be eternal {nitya}.

However, the permanence of all five is not the same, and it will be useful in this discussion of 'eternal' entities to briefly touch upon the three types of permanence in Hindu metaphysics.

The first type is 'kūṭastha nityatā', or immutable permanence. Parabrahman, Akṣarabrahman, īśvaras and jīvas are all permanent in their being and immutably so; they never undergo any modifications in their essential nature or form.[3] Māyā, however, does metamorphose into the myriad forms of the material world, yet all the while still being essentially māyā itself. This is called 'pariṇāmī nityatā', or mutating permanence. Finally, not immediately relevant to the five entities but useful for later, is 'pravāha nityatā', or flowing permanence. This relates, for example, to the incessant cycle of creation, from origination through to sustenance and dissolution and back again to origination, meaning that the world will permanently be in some state of this process of creation although any one state is not permanent.[4] In this way, the immutability of Parabrahman, Akṣarabrahman, īśvaras and jīvas groups them against the mutability of māyā.

The same entities are also contrasted by nature of their sentiency. Of the five, Parabrahman, Akṣarabrahman, īśvaras and jīvas are caitanya {sentient or spiritual}, whereas māyā is essentially jaḍa {non-sentient or material}.[5]

A further straightforward categorisation of the entities also useful to emphasise at the outset is their ontological position to māyā. As is apparent from the sequence in which they are usually listed, Parabrahman and Akṣarabrahman are 'above' or transcendent to māyā, whereas īśvaras and jīvas are 'below' or within it (see Figure 4).

[2] The chapter on Parabrahman, in particular, contains a brief discussion about his relationship with time. See Section 'Time' in Chapter 6.

[3] Even so, the immutability of Parabrahman and Akṣarabrahman differs to that of the īśvaras and jīvas, as we shall see in their respective chapters.

[4] Another example of pravāha nityatā, using a contemporary analogy, is that of a prime minister or president. The position is permanent, but its occupancy 'flows' from one person to another.

[5] Māyā can also be described as 'jaḍacidātmikā', but its sentiency is only by way of association with jīvas and īśvaras. See Section 'Characterised by Insentience and Sentiency' in Chapter 10.

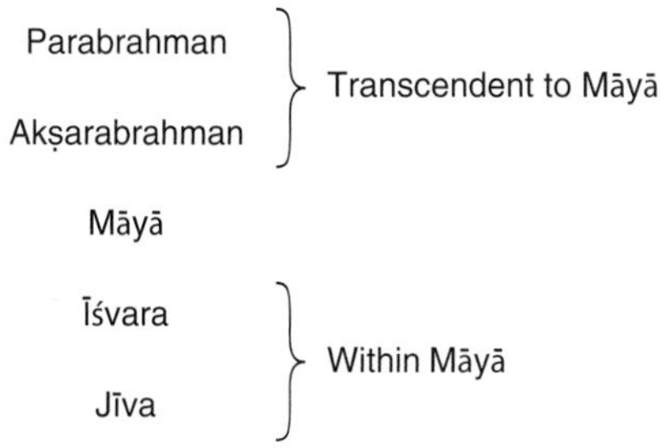

Figure 4 Ontological position of the eternal entities in relation to māyā

The meaning and significance of these characteristics will become more apparent as each entity is discussed in the subsequent chapters of this part.

What needs to be clarified first, however, is how expounding upon all five entities is relevant in this exposition of Hindu theology.

The answer is twofold.

Firstly, the other four entities are revealed and explicated alongside God in the theological texts of the Swaminarayan tradition, hence making their study both unavoidable in and immediately relevant to a discussion of Swaminarayan Hindu theology.

Secondly, and the reason why all five entities are discussed in Swaminarayan theological texts, is because they are related to – in fact, a necessary part of – the study of God. Most obviously, a study of Parabrahman is the study of the nature of God, but alongside that the other four entities are inextricably tied to God and the ultimate goal of human life. A study of the five entities thus involves the following:

Parabrahman	–	the study of the form, nature, function, significance, etc. of God
Akṣarabrahman	–	the study of God's abode and how to become eligible to experience God therein after death and also now
māyā	–	the study of God's creation and its function as ignorance, which needs to be transcended to fully realise God
īśvara	–	the study of empowered beings and their role in God's creation
jīva	–	the study of individual souls and their relationship with God

This composite approach to the study of God is made all the more necessary by Swaminarayan's own definition of 'jñāna', or theological knowledge. In concluding an important epistemological discussion in Vac. Loyā.7, he offers a summary of what constitutes 'knowing God' or the 'knowledge of God' and the characteristics of one who has such knowledge. He explains:

> A jñānin is one who precisely knows God through the senses, mind and experience . . . Such a jñānin is one who singularly serves God manifest before the eyes – who eternally has a form – realising him as transcending Prakṛti-Puruṣa and Akṣara, and as being the cause and support of all. Such understanding constitutes jñāna, and such jñāna leads to ultimate liberation.

Here we find associated with the definition of jñāna (true knowledge of God) all four of the other entities: knowing God as transcending Prakṛti-Puruṣa (a configuration of māyā) and Akṣara necessitates the knowledge of these two entities; and those who must singularly serve God with this knowledge to secure liberation, and whose cause and support is God, points to the jīvas and īśvaras. In all, if theology is, in its most basic and literal sense, the study of God, then for a complete and correct understanding of God, the study of all five metaphysical entities is an essential part of the theological project within the Swaminarayan Hindu tradition.

In turn now, the following chapters will expound upon each of the five metaphysical entities of Swaminarayan Hinduism – Parabrahman, Akṣarabrahman, jīva, īśvara and māyā – ending with an inquiry into the nature and way of liberation {mukti}. Like all intricate theological systems, the deeply interwoven themes of Swaminarayan Hindu theology mean that each theme will require an understanding of the others, and so each will almost always remain a little incomplete until the final theme is fully unravelled, calling for a patient, assiduous and often reflexive reading of the text. As Keith Ward recognises at the very beginning of his series on the key theological issues within the world's major religions: 'There is no one proper starting-point in theology, since every question leads on to every other . . . Only when the study is complete will one be able to check back to see if such a preliminary analysis was correct.'[6]

[6] Keith Ward, *Religion and Revelation* (Oxford: Clarendon, 1994), p. 1.

CHAPTER 6

Parabrahman

We begin our exposition of the Swaminarayan system's five entities at Parabrahman, the ontologically highest reality.

Returning to Swaminarayan's formulation of 'jñāna' from Vac. Loyā.7, we find not only how the other entities contribute to the understanding of God but also an indication of the aspects of God that constitute that theological knowledge. As a reminder, that summary is as follows:

> A jñānin is one who singularly serves God manifest before the eyes – who eternally has a form – realising him as transcending Prakṛti-Puruṣa[1] and Akṣara, and as being the cause and support of all. Such understanding constitutes jñāna, and such jñāna leads to ultimate liberation.

Thus, in effect, true knowledge of God constitutes the knowledge of the following:

1. God as manifest before one's eyes
2. God as eternally having a form
3. God as transcending Prakṛti-Puruṣa (i.e. māyā and liberated souls) and Akṣara (also known as Akṣarabrahman or Brahman)
4. God as the cause and support of all

This corresponds neatly to the four aspects of knowing God traditionally used within Swaminarayan Hinduism, referred to by the following four terms:

1. Pragaṭa {manifest}
2. Sākāra {with form}
3. Sarvopari {supreme}
4. Kartā {doer}

[1] 'Prakṛti-Puruṣa' is a shorthand term referring to the combined form of primordial māyā [Mūla-Prakṛti] and a liberated soul in Akṣaradhāma [Mūla-Puruṣa], who together initiate the creative process, as willed and commanded by Parabrahman. See Section 'Creative Process' in Chapter 10 for further elaboration on the protological process.

These four broad terms, though in a slightly different order,[2] will provide the framework for the four main themes under which aspects and characteristics of Parabrahman can be grouped to aid in a coherent, systematic exposition of the nature of God as found within the Swaminarayan Hindu tradition. It is not a strict framework, and there will inevitably be some overlap and double-berthing between the aspects of God's nature, but all of the most important aspects shall be covered. As perhaps with any intellectual endeavour, the framework itself is not as important as the ideas it supports and contains.

Absolute Essentiality of Knowing God

Before we delve into a detailed exposition of the nature of Parabrahman, it would be useful to begin with a brief understanding of the absolute essentiality of knowing God's nature as held within Swaminarayan Hinduism. While the need for God within a theological system may seem obvious, this emphasis on *knowing* him is significant and will prove helpful when later discussing Akṣarabrahman and liberation.

In the above reference from Vac. Loyā.7, after providing a formulation of jñāna, Swaminarayan is quick to conclude that 'such jñāna leads to ultimate liberation'. This follows from other śāstric statements cited in that same discourse:

> There is no liberation without jñāna (Hiranyakeśīyaśākhā Śruti[3]),

and

> Only by knowing him [Parabrahman] does one pass beyond death; there is no other path for attaining [liberation]. (SU 3.8)

Swaminarayan thus makes it clear that knowledge of God is essential for securing liberation.

Such 'jñāna' is often used synonymously in sampradāyic literature with terms such as 'niścaya' {resolute faith} or 'svarūpaniṣṭhā' {literally, 'conviction of [God's] nature'}, and upāsanā, i.e. worship and faith informed by correct theological knowledge. For example, in Vac. Gaḍh. I.56, Muktanand Swami asks a question about how one can form an abiding conviction that the ātman is distinct from the non-ātman, i.e. the physical

[2] On this occasion, the order is insignificant. Besides, English syntax has not allowed the order from the original Gujarati to be retained in the translation.

[3] This is a non-extant Vaiṣṇava text, but the phrase is attributed to it in the *Setumālā* commentary on the *Harivākyasudhāsindhu* at 115.7.

body, senses, mind, etc. He queries that such a spiritual understanding remains elusive even after learning about it from sermons and scriptural reading. Swaminarayan prefaces his reply with the following emphasis on upāsanā:

> Some become accomplished yogis, some become omniscient, some become devatās, and thus attain countless types of greatness, including the highest state of enlightenment. All this is achieved on the strength of the upāsanā of God, but without upāsanā, nothing can be accomplished.

He then goes on to reply to the original question by explaining that the distinction between ātman and non-ātman cannot be realised by mere study of scriptures or personal resolve, but only by faith in God informed by correct theological knowledge. 'In fact', Swaminarayan reinforces, 'no spiritual endeavours can be fulfilled' without such faith and knowledge (Vac. Gaḍh. 1.56). It is upāsanā, then, above all else, which leads to and fulfils all other spiritual endeavours.

This is explained further in sermon 6.294 of the Svāmīnī Vāto, where Gunatitanand Swami is asked the following question by an unnamed devotee:

> Please tell me one thing within which all spiritual endeavours are subsumed and by which one can attain the highest liberation.

Gunatitanand Swami replies:

> If one has upāsanā and the highest faith in God, then all else will follow from that. (6.294)

In three other key sermons – Vac. Gaḍh. 2.13, Gaḍh. 2.14 and Pan.7 – Swaminarayan reiterates the same point at some length. To cite the first only:

> When you firmly understand the nature of God as such, you will encounter no obstacles on the path to liberation. However, without such firm understanding of the nature of God, one will never be able to overcome one's weaknesses, regardless of however much one renounces [worldly objects] or the number of fasts one observes. . .
>
> A person [with such a firm understanding of God] has nothing left to accomplish; he is fulfilled and has reached the culmination of all spiritual endeavours. If one has such a firm belief in the nature of God, then even if a slight flaw remains in the observance of the vows of non-egotism, non-avarice, non-lust, non-taste or non-attachment, there is still nothing to worry about. Conversely, if any deficiency remains in understanding the nature of God, then in no way will one ever be redeemable. Therefore, one should attempt to understand this profound principle by any means within this lifetime. (Vac. Gaḍh. 2.13)

In all three sermons, Swaminarayan is unequivocal in emphasising not only the absolute need to know God for liberation but also the relative futility of everything else if one does not know God perfectly.

Gunatitanand Swami similarly emphasises both the need for complete theological knowledge, i.e.

> If there is any deficiency in upāsanā, one might attain other pleasures but will not be redeemed of the miseries of entering the womb [i.e. the cycle of births and deaths], (SV 5.73)

and the pre-eminence of this knowledge above all other religious endeavours:

> However much one may have endeavoured otherwise, if one does not have proper upāsanā, then one will not be liberated. (SV 5.126)

In another typically laconic sermon, Gunatitanand Swami reiterates this thus:

> God is the 'one' and religious endeavours are all 'zeros'. (SV 5.192)

Gunatitanand Swami means that while religious endeavours are important and necessary, if they are not preceded by a correct theological understanding of God, they will be as worthless as a long string of zeros lacking the digit '1' in front of them. Just as the '1' gives value and meaning to all the zeros, it is God who gives value and meaning to all other religious endeavours and brings them to fruition. The knowledge of God, then, must be prioritised so that it is first and foremost among all endeavours.

Going even further, Gunatitanand Swami adds:

> He who has a firm conviction of the nature of God has accomplished all spiritual endeavours; he has nothing left to achieve. (SV 1.123)

Swaminarayan similarly explains that after knowing God, not only is there nothing else to know, but there is also nothing else to achieve.

> A person who has realised the form of God perfectly has nothing left to realise . . . Time, karma and māyā are incapable of binding a person who has developed in his heart such firm faith coupled with an understanding of God's greatness. Therefore, he who realises God perfectly in this way has nothing left to achieve. (Vac. Gaḍh. 1.63)

These statements echo some of the famous Upaniṣadic proclamations about 'knowing the one by which all can be known' (e.g. CU 6.1.3 and MuU 1.1.3).

Together these statements from the Vacanāmrut and Svāmīnī Vāto emphasise the primary importance and absolute indispensability of knowing God within Swaminarayan Hindu theology, especially in relation to other theological understanding and religious practice. As a summary, then, knowledge of God is

- Foundational – all religious practice and theological understanding must be grounded in the knowledge of God
- Central – all religious practice and theological understanding revolves around the knowledge of God
- Apical – the aim and culmination of all practice is to know God as fully as possible

Sarvopari: God as Supreme

Ontologically, Parabrahman is the highest, most transcendental entity. As the term 'sarvopari' {literally, 'above all'} suggests, no other being or thing can ever surpass him in any way whatsoever. The Upaniṣads proclaim:

> There is nothing greater than Puruṣa [i.e. Puruṣottama or Parabrahman]. (KaU 3.11)
>
> There is nothing at all greater than [Puruṣa, i.e. Parabrahman]. (SU 3.9)
>
> There is nothing greater than [Parabrahman]. (PU 6.7)

All three of these statements use 'param' {supreme or best}. Apart from this, other terms found in the Upaniṣads and Bhagavad-Gītā that describe Parabrahman's pre-eminent position include 'uttama' {highest or best}, 'utkṛṣṭa' {best}, 'śreṣṭa' {best} and 'kāṣṭā' {ultimate}.

Superlatives such as 'supreme' or 'best' invite two questions: firstly, 'Best among whom?' and, secondly, 'Best at what?' As we look to expound upon the supremacy of Parabrahman in this section, specific aspects of his supreme nature have thus been grouped into two sets broadly corresponding to these two questions. The first set deals with topics showing Parabrahman's transcendence over other entities: how exactly is he greater than all other beings and things? We answer this through the following topics:

- Parabrahman, the one without second
- Parabrahman, the lord of all beings and realms
- Parabrahman, the soul of all beings and things

- Parabrahman the avatārin, the cause of all avatāras
- Parabrahman as Akṣarātīta (greater even than Akṣarabrahman)

The second set of topics deals with the transcendence of God in his own mode of being. In this, we shall be exploring some of Parabrahman's most important inherent qualities and seeing how they are the best they could possibly be. While Parabrahman has infinite qualities and each one of them is infinitely excellent, for the purposes of our exposition, we shall limit our focus to seven aspects of his limitless nature: Parabrahman with respect to time, space, knowledge, power, splendour, bliss and virtues.

Superiority of Parabrahman over All Others

We begin to expound upon Parabrahman's supremacy by examining his position in relation to the other entities.

One without Second

In all senses of the term, Parabrahman is unique. He is one and one of a kind, quite literally in a class of his own, *sui generis*. But that in and of itself does not make him supreme, for this description also applies to Akṣarabrahman. Rather, it is by virtue of his infinite greatness that no other entity can even approximate him. Upaniṣadic statements, such as in CU 6.2.1, thus proclaim God as being 'eka' {one} and 'advitīya' {without second}. A similar emphasis can be found in the Vacanāmrut on both the uniqueness and peerlessness of God. Citing this same phrase, Swaminarayan explains:

> Only God is like God; no one can become like him. The Vedic verse 'ekam evādvitīyam Brahma' also explains that God alone is like God. This is the principle of all of the scriptures. (Vac. Loyā.13)[4]

In the last documented sermon of the Vacanāmrut, where Swaminarayan again reiterates the singularity of God, we also find his argument for a monotheistic system.

> Only God is like God. Many have attained qualities similar to his by worshipping him, yet they certainly do not become like God. If they did become like God, this would suggest the existence of several Gods. As a result, the governance of the world would not remain orderly. One God would say, 'I will create the world', while another God

[4] See also Vac. Loyā.4 and Gaḍh. 3.37, which are similar in tenor to SU 6.8: 'There is nothing equal to or superior than him [i.e. Parabrahman].'

> would say, 'I will destroy the world'. One God would say, 'I will make it rain', while another would say, 'I will not'. One would say, 'I will instil human instincts in animals', while another would say, 'I will instil animal instincts in humans'. A stable state would not be possible in this situation. But see how orderly everything functions in the world! There is not even the slightest irregularity. Thus, the governor of all activities and the lord of all is one God. Not only that, it seems that no one can ever challenge him. Therefore, God is definitely one, and no one can become like him. (Vac. Gaḍh. 3.39)

Swaminarayan alludes at the beginning of this statement to those liberated souls who have attained qualities similar to those of God. How this is possible and what these qualities are will be discussed in detail in Chapter 11 on liberation, but it is important here to reiterate that this in no way challenges or undermines God's greatness. For example, even when Swaminarayan goes as far as in Vac. Gaḍh. 3.37 to say,

> A devotee in the abode of God who has attained qualities similar to God also possesses a form similar to that of God,

he immediately clarifies:

> nevertheless, that devotee is still puruṣa [i.e. a finite being], and God is, after all, Puruṣottama {literally, the 'highest being'}. Indeed, God is supreme among everyone. (Vac. Gaḍh. 3.37)

Similarly, in another sermon, Swaminarayan explains that by the grace of God devotees may rise to the ranks of Śukadeva and Nārada, or become like Brahmā and Śiva, or may even become like Akṣara (i.e. akṣararūpa, fully enlightened).

> However, no one is capable of becoming like Śrī Puruṣottama Nārāyaṇa. (Vac. Kār.10)

Thus, the outright supremacy and uniqueness of Parabrahman is never challenged or undermined. Ontologically, Parabrahman is one, matchless and unsurpassable. He is supreme.

Lord of All Beings and Realms

A recurring motif found in the Vacanāmrut conveying Parabrahman's infinite supremacy is a description of him as the 'king of all kings' or 'lord of all lords' reigning over the entire universe. For example, in an extended explanation in Vac. Pan.4, Swaminarayan begins:

> That God is the great king of all kings {mahārājādhirāj}, he is surrounded by countless divine luxuries and countless divine attendants, and he is the lord {pati} of countless millions of brahmāṇḍas.

Then, perhaps to help his varied audience grasp this rather esoteric concept, he literally brings it 'down to earth' with an analogy to which they can relate.

> For example, suppose there is a great world-emperor whose kingdom stretches from where the sun rises to where it sets . . . So powerful is this world-emperor that it is not possible to count the villages in his empire, as they are innumerable. Nor can the chiefs of these villages be counted, as they too are innumerable. Furthermore, the countless chiefs of those villages come to his court to make requests. The emperor's money, property, pleasures, palaces and wealth are also countless. Similarly, God is the king of the kings of countless villages in the form of brahmāṇḍas.
>
> Moreover, the chiefs of those villages in the form of brahmāṇḍas are Brahmā, Viṣṇu and Śiva. Just as in one village one chief is senior and the whole population of that village bows before him and follows his command, and just as the chief in turn bows before the king, similarly, in each brahmāṇḍa, Brahmā, Viṣṇu and Śiva are superior, and the others in that brahmāṇḍa, that is the devas, demons, humans, seers and prajāpatis of that brahmāṇḍa, worship them and follow their command. But Brahmā, Viṣṇu and Śiva in turn worship Puruṣottama Bhagavān and follow his command.
>
> Furthermore, all of the Brahmās, Viṣṇus and Maheśas of all of the brahmāṇḍas pray to God, 'Mahārāj! Please have compassion on us and visit our brahmāṇḍa' – just as the chief of a village requests the world-emperor, 'Mahārāj! I am poor. Please visit my house. I shall serve you to the best of my ability.' In the same way, Brahmā, Viṣṇu and Śiva pray to that God: 'Mahārāj! Please have mercy upon us and grace us with your darshan; do visit our brahmāṇḍa.' Only then does God assume a body in that brahmāṇḍa. (Vac. Pan.4)[5]

A number of points emerge from this description. Firstly, Swaminarayan adds an important element to the understanding of God as 'world-emperor' – as not just lording over a vast dominion of land and wealth but having subjects over whom he reigns. He is not merely a landlord but indeed the sovereign emperor.

Secondly, these subjects include īśvaras such as Brahmā, Viṣṇu and Maheśa – used in the plural by Swaminarayan to emphasise that he is speaking about multiple brahmāṇḍas over which Parabrahman reigns – who themselves are 'chiefs of the brahmāṇḍs' yet 'poor' in comparison to

[5] See also Vac. Gaḍh. 3.39 for a similar analogy.

'the great king of all kings'. The supplication presented in their prayer to Parabrahman, beseeching him to grace them with his audience, further reveals their utter subordination before him.

That these authoritative īśvaras – themselves worshipped and obeyed – worship and obey Parabrahman adds a third and important message to be drawn from the analogy. While elsewhere Swaminarayan explains that

> God is very powerful; even the devas such as Brahmā and others live under his command (Vac. Gaḍh. 2.66),

here, as if to impress that such obedience is not mere fearful compliance, Swaminarayan adds that the īśvaras *worship* Parabrahman, for he is eminently worthy of their highest reverence and adoration.

> Indeed, God is supreme among everyone and is fit to be worshipped by everyone. (Vac. Gaḍh. 3.37)

These subjects who accord Parabrahman their highest reverence, adoration and humility include some of the most exalted, powerful and holy of all the worlds.

> Even the great such as Brahmā, Śiva, Lakṣmījī, Rādhājī, Nārada, Śuka, the Sanakādika and the nine Yogeśvaras apply the dust of God's holy feet upon their heads. They put aside all of their self-importance and constantly offer devotion to him. (Vac. Gaḍh. 3.39)

Together, this confirms Parabrahman's paramount lordship over all other beings and realms.

Soul of All Beings and Things

A key doctrine of the Viśiṣṭādvaita school of Vedānta is Śarīra-Śarīri-Bhāva – the analogous body–soul relationship between the universe and God. The belief is: just as the physical body is to its soul, so is the world to God; and, vice versa, just as the soul is to its body, so is God to the world. An almost identical doctrine can be found within Swaminarayan Hindu theology.

In narrating the nature of Parabrahman, Swaminarayan often drew upon this relationship to explain that God was the 'omnisoul' {Sarvātman} or 'supersoul' {Paramātman} of the entire world:

> God is the soul {ātman} of all. (Vac. Loyā.7)

> That very God is the soul of countless brahmāṇḍas. (Vac. Gaḍh. 2.17)

In another sermon, when recounting all the material elements of the infinite worlds and then adding īśvaras, māyā, the liberated souls of Akṣaradhāma and even Akṣarabrahman, he adds:

> All of these constitute the body of God. (Vac. Kār.8)

Then in Vac. Sār.10, Swaminarayan brings this to an individual level, citing an expression of what a correct understanding of this doctrine would be:

> Just as the soul resides in the body, God resides within my soul. My soul is the 'śarīra' {body}, and God is the 'śarīrin' {embodied soul} of my soul.

But how exactly is God the soul of all these beings and things and how are they his body?

Swaminarayan asks this question to his audience in Vac. Gaḍh. 1.64. He begins with an objection to including ātman (referring here to finite sentient beings, i.e. jīvas and īśvaras) and Akṣara as the body of God. His point is that a body {śarīra} – even by its etymological meaning {from 'śīr', to decay}, i.e. that which decays – is normally expected to be that which undergoes modifications and which ultimately perishes, whereas the soul is immutable and imperishable. So while identifying Parabrahman as the soul is agreeable because he is immutable and imperishable, it is not so when considering jīvas, īśvaras and Akṣara as his body, for they do not decay and perish, because they, too, are immutable and eternal. He thus asks:

> How, then, can that ātman [i.e. jīvas and īśvaras] and Akṣara be described as the śarīra of God?

When no satisfactory answer is offered, Swaminarayan himself explains:

> All finite sentient beings {ātman, i.e. jīvas and īśvaras} and Akṣara constitute the body of Puruṣottama Bhagavān in that they are pervaded, dependent and powerless. In what way? Well, by means of his antaryāmin powers, God pervades all finite beings and Akṣara, whereas they are the pervaded. He is independent, whereas all finite beings and Akṣara are supported by God and dependent upon him. Furthermore, he is extremely powerful, whereas all finite beings and Akṣara are utterly powerless before him. In this way, God is the embodied soul {śarīrin} of both all finite beings and Akṣara, and they both are the body {śarīra} of God.

In his explanation, Swaminarayan picks on three pairs of terms to define the body–soul relationship, where a body is not just a physical vessel which is born and which grows, decays and eventually dies, but, more broadly, is that which is empowered by, pervaded by and dependent on a sentient being within. This makes even jīvas, īśvaras and Akṣara – and everything in between, i.e. māyā in all its myriad forms – the 'body' of Parabrahman for they are totally empowered by, pervaded by and dependent on him.

Continuing his elucidation of the relationship between God and the other entities, Swaminarayan adds:

> Furthermore, [Puruṣottama Bhagavān] is the inspirer of both the finite souls and Akṣara, is independent from them, and is their controller. He also possesses all spiritual powers. He is greater than even Akṣara, which is greater than everything. (Vac. Gaḍh. 1.64)

Swaminarayan substantiates these points in Vac. Loyā.7 by citing from various classical sources. He begins by quoting the Taittirīya Āraṇyaka of the Yajur Veda,

> The omnisoul, entering within, is the controller of all beings, (3.11)

and ends with passages from BU 3.7 (of the Mādhyandina recension), famously known as the Antaryāmī Brāhmaṇa:

> He, whose body is the earth and who controls it from within, is your soul, the immortal indwelling controller. (3.7.7)

> He, whose body are the souls and who governs all souls from within, is your soul, the immortal indwelling controller. (3.7.30)

As the soul, then, Parabrahman becomes the very life-source of the entire universe, the cause for its existence and the ontic ground {ādhāra} upon which it can function. Just as a physical body perishes once separated from its soul, so, too, the world of material and spiritual realities cannot survive even momentarily without Parabrahman. Even if alive, the body is wholly incapable of doing anything without the will, knowledge and strength of the inner self. As the Kena Upaniṣad and Aitareya Upaniṣad both confirm: Parabrahman is the Self {ātman} of the self {jīva} – the ear of the ear, the eye of the eyes, the mind of the mind (KeU 1.2) – by which it can see, hear, smell, speak and taste (AU 3.1). Thus, all beings are totally dependent on Parabrahman to enliven them and bring them to action. Swaminarayan states, for example, in Vac. Gaḍh. 3.37:

> Indeed, God is the very life of all jīvas. Without him, those jīvas are not capable of doing anything or indulging in anything.

Swaminarayan emphasises this utter dependence of the other entities on Parabrahman in a way that describes him as their 'ādhāra' {support}, the

Table 1 *Relationship between Parabrahman and the other entities*

Parabrahman	Other entities in relation to Parabrahman
Extremely powerful/empowering	Utterly powerless/empowered
Independent	Dependent
Pervading	Pervaded
Controller	Controlled
Inspirer	Inspired
Support	Supported

fundamental Being underlying all beings, the ultimate reality undergirding all things. He says, for example:

> It is God who supports the entire earth along with its mobile and immobile forms of life. (Vac. Gaḍh. 1.78)

> That manifest form of God before the eyes is such that he is the support of both the eight material elements [i.e. earth, water, etc.], which are pervaded, as well as of the spiritual element that pervades therein [i.e. the souls]. (Vac. Loyā.7)

> He [God] is the support of countless millions of brahmāṇḍas. (Vac. Gaḍh. 2.53)

In Vac. Gaḍh. 1.72, Swaminarayan draws together 'Parabrahman as the soul' with 'Parabrahman as the support' as integral to one another.

> Just as God is the soul of 'kṣara' [i.e. māyā and all finite beings],[6] he is also the soul of Akṣarabrahman . . . With his own powers, God supports both kṣara and Akṣara.

Together, these excerpts provide a clearer picture of the relationship between Parabrahman and the other entities, as summarised in Table 1.

Briefly returning to the last excerpt above from Vac. Gaḍh. 1.72, it reads more fully:

> With his own powers, God supports both kṣara and Akṣara, *yet he himself is distinct from them both.* (emphasis added)

[6] While 'kṣara' literally means perishable, it is translated here to include all finite beings, i.e. jīvas and īśvaras, whose bodies perish in every lifetime during transmigration though they themselves are eternal. This interpretation helps maintain semantic consistency with verses such as BG 15.16, which distinguishes all perishable beings {kṣaraḥ sarvāṇi bhūtāni} from the immutable {kūṭastha} Akṣara.

This additional statement leads us to an important clarification necessary in this discussion, one that Swaminarayan provides elsewhere as well. A natural corollary of the body–soul relationship is that in being so closely associated with imperfect and mutable objects, Parabrahman will be assumed to be contaminated by their mutations and imperfections. However, Swaminarayan was sure to include in his description above that while Parabrahman is the soul of all that is perishable and imperishable, 'he himself is distinct from them both'. So, just as the distinct self is not affected by the imperfections of the body it ensouls, neither, too, do the imperfections of māyā, etc. affect God, who ensouls those entities. He makes this absolutely clear in Vac. Gaḍh. 2.17. Using the body–soul analogy, Swaminarayan firstly states that Puruṣottama Bhagavān is the 'soul of all souls' before immediately clarifying,

> but he is still immutable; the mutations of māyā and other mutable objects, etc. do not at all affect [literally 'touch'] Puruṣottama Bhagavān.

He then goes on to add:

> In fact, if the mutations of the gross, subtle and causal bodies do not affect a person who has realised himself as the inner soul, what can be said about them [māyic mutations] not affecting [literally 'touching'] Puruṣottama Bhagavān? Therefore, God is indeed immutable {nirvikārin} and untainted {nirlepa}.[7]

In Vac. Gaḍh. 1.64, when distancing God from any of the undesirable corollaries associated with him being the omnisoul, Swaminarayan also described God as 'independent'. He seems to have in mind that while the physical body is necessary for the soul to experience and enjoy (and also suffer), the same is not true for Parabrahman. He does not need the jīvas, īśvaras, māyā or even Akṣara for anything. He can survive absolutely alone, independently. In taking this important difference to the highest possible degree, Swaminarayan explains in Vac. Loyā.13:

> If [Puruṣottama Nārāyaṇa] wishes, he can eclipse all of the liberated souls of Akṣaradhāma by his own divine light and prevail alone. Also, if he wishes, he can accept the devotion of the liberated souls and reside with them. He can eclipse even Akṣara, in the form of the Akṣaradhāma in which he dwells, and preside alone independently. If he chooses, he is capable of supporting the countless liberated souls by his own lordship, without even needing Akṣaradhāma ... [T]hrough his own lordship, God reigns as supreme. (Vac. Loyā.13)

7 For more on this discussion in the Svāminārāyaṇa-Bhāṣya, see BG-SB 13.31–32, p. 290; KaU-SB 5.11, p. 154; and the Ubhayaliṅgādhikaraṇa in BS-SB 3.2.11–25, pp. 291–302.

The body–soul doctrine thus elaborated is especially useful in Swaminarayan Hindu theology for a consistent understanding of God's nature because it can help reconcile texts which may identify other things as 'the highest' or as 'God'. Technically, everything can be denoted as being 'God' because the soul within everything is Parabrahman, and it is usual, as with people, to identify the distinct body by the name of the person (the living entity within). In Vac. Loyā.7, for example, Swaminarayan explains why even anna {food}, manas {the mind}, vijñāna {knowledge} and ānanda {bliss} have been described as 'Brahman' in various Vedāntic texts.[8]

> Even those things have been called Brahman because God is the cause of all and the support of all. However, they are all the body {śarīra}, and their soul {śarīrin} is the manifest form of Śrī Kṛṣṇa Puruṣottama.

This doctrine is also brought into sharp use by Bhadreshdas on several occasions in his commentaries of the Vedānta canon. For example, in commenting on the famous Upaniṣadic text

> All this is verily Brahman (CU 3.14.1),

he writes:

> It is because Paramātman is the controller and soul of everything that statements placing him in identical predication {sāmānādhikaraṇya} with other things can be reconciled.[9]

Similarly, when explaining another *locus classicus* from the Upaniṣads,

> Tat tvam asi (CU 6.8.7),

Bhadreshdas writes:

> Both the terms 'tat' {that} and 'tvam' {you} . . . are placed in identical predication because 'tat' pervades, controls and is the very soul of the entire sentient-insentient world, including 'tvam'.[10]

Parabrahman thus undergirds, pervades, empowers and controls – indeed, he enlivens – the entire universe, all the while remaining totally distinct from and unaffected by any of the imperfections of the entities he ensouls. This body–soul relationship again affirms the outright supremacy of Parabrahman in relation to all these other entities.

8 See, for example, Chapter 2 (the Anandavallī) of the Taittirīya Upaniṣad.

9 CU-SB 3.14.1, p. 132.

10 CU-SB 6.8.7, p. 278. Note that according to Bhadreshdas, 'tat' here is denotive of both Parabrahman *and* Akṣarabrahman. For another example of Bhadreshdas calling upon this doctrine, see his commentary on the Ananyatvādhikaraṇa in BS 2.1.14–21, pp. 168–73.

Source of All Avatāras

A sterner test of Parabrahman's supremacy, beyond being superior among all māyic objects and minor beings, would be in seeing how he stands in relation to other 'Gods', or avatāras.

Avatāravāda, the doctrine of God manifesting (or, literally, 'descending') on earth in human or other form, is a familiar feature of most theistic Hindu traditions. However, a closer study of the Vacanāmrut, Svāmīnī Vāto and other theological and historical texts of the Swaminarayan tradition reveals that this doctrine takes on a more nuanced form within Swaminarayan Hindu theology. Perhaps one of the most striking features is that the avatāras are considered to be not of Parabrahman directly, but of īśvaras. That is, Parabrahman and the avatāras are ontologically distinct.

How, then, is Parabrahman related to the avatāras? Swaminarayan explains this in Vac. Gaḍh. 2.9, an important sermon for understanding the supremacy of God. After emphasising the need for an accurate understanding of God's nature, Swaminarayan states precisely the belief that a devotee should have.

> One should also intensely maintain the strength of conviction in God's form, i.e. 'I have attained the very form of God who reigns supreme, who forever possesses a divine form, and who is the avatārin, the cause of all the avatāras.'

He reiterates this point with greater force a little later in the sermon, this time adding a stern note of warning as well.

> One should realise the manifest God that one has attained to forever possess a divine form and to be the avatārin, the cause of all the avatāras. If, however, one does not realise this, and instead realises God to be formless or like the other avatāras, then that is regarded as committing blasphemy against God.

What is clear from these words is that Parabrahman is *not* the same as the other avatāras. Rather, he is their cause. The term Swaminarayan uses for Parabrahman in this context is 'avatārin', meaning 'lord or master of the avatāras'.[11]

That the avatāras are ontologically distinct from Parabrahman will become clearer when expounding upon īśvara and the process of creation in the subsequent chapters on īśvara and māyā, respectively.[12] Immediately, though, it will be useful to cite a dialogue from the Svāmīnī Vāto that

[11] The 'in' suffix (see *Aṣṭādhyāyī* 5.2.115) applied to 'avatāra' is in the sense of 'belonging to' (see *Aṣṭādhyāyī* 5.2.94).

[12] See especially Sections 'Distinction from and Relation to Parabrahman' in Chapter 9 and 'Creative Process' in Chapter 10.

explains this ontological distinction more explicitly with the help of various analogies. Gunatitanand Swami once asked in an assembly:

> How should one understand the distinction between the avatāras and the avatārin?

Someone answered:

> Like that of an actor and his character.

Gunatitanand Swami corrected:

> No, that is not how the avatārin is distinct from his avatāras. Rather, one should understand the distinction as like that between a king and his minister, an archer and his arrow, the moon and the stars. (SV 6.33)

The thrust of Gunatitanand Swami's examples seems to be twofold: firstly that the two sets of analogues are different from each other, i.e. the king, archer and moon are different from the minister, arrow and the stars; and secondly that the former are more powerful than the latter. Importantly, he rejects the analogy of the actor and his character, which would imply that it is Parabrahman himself who personally transforms into the avatāras or takes on their role.

But this then leads to the question that if Parabrahman is indeed ontologically different from the avatāras, how can the avatāras be said to be 'avatāras of God'? Moreover, if the avatāras are ontologically īśvara, how, then, can they be considered divine, since we learned at the beginning that even īśvara as a category was 'below' or within māyā?

Both questions can be answered conjointly by understanding more closely the relationship between the avatārin and the avatāras.

In an extensive discussion in Vac. Gaḍh. 2.31 about Virāṭa Puruṣa (sometimes called Vairāja Puruṣa), the very soul and executive administrator of each created brahmāṇḍa, Swaminarayan reveals:

> It is said in the scriptures[13] that the avatāras emanate by way of that Virāṭa Puruṣa.

Swaminarayan then clarifies that only when Parabrahman (referred to in that sermon as Vāsudevanārāyaṇa and Vāsudeva Bhagavān) 'enters' into Virāṭa Puruṣa can avatāras be possible.

> It is when Vāsudevanārāyaṇa resides in Virāṭa Puruṣa . . . that there are said to be avatāras.

[13] E.g. BP 1.3.5.

Conversely,

> When that Vāsudeva Bhagavān withdraws himself and separates from Virāṭa Puruṣa, then it is not possible for an avatāra to emanate through Virāṭa Puruṣa alone . . . In fact, when Vāsudeva the over-soul had not yet entered him, that Virāṭa Puruṣa was not even capable of performing any of his own activities.

And yet, Swaminarayan adds, because of this special 'entering' by Parabrahman:

> Thus all those avatāras are Vāsudeva Bhagavān's only.

What Swaminarayan seems to be emphasising from this sermon is three things:

1. Firstly, all avatāras actually emanate by way of Virāṭa Puruṣa
2. Secondly, this emanation is only possible when Parabrahman enters into Virāṭa Puruṣa; in fact, without Parabrahman, Virāṭa Puruṣa is incapable of doing anything
3. Thirdly, because of Parabrahman's special presence in Virāṭa Puruṣa, the avatāras can be said to be emanating from Parabrahman

The technical term used to describe Parabrahman's presence in Virāṭa Puruṣa for the emanation of avatāras is 'anu-praveśa' {literally, 're-entering'}, signifying a specific empowering presence of Parabrahman above and beyond the blanket antaryāmin presence in all things and beings. Swaminarayan explains this in more detail in Vac. Pan.7 with the help of two more analogies.

> In whomever that Puruṣottama Bhagavān 'enters' for the purpose of fulfilling many types of tasks, he eclipses that entity by his own divine light and he himself reigns preeminently through that entity. Moreover, in whomever he resides, he suppresses their own light and manifests his own divine light – just as when fire enters iron, it suppresses the quality of coldness and the black colour of the iron and exhibits its own quality; or like when the sun rises, the light from all of the stars, the moon, etc. merges into its own light, and only the sun's light remains. In the same way, in whomever God 'enters', he overpowers their light and exhibits his own divine light to a greater degree. Then, after completing the task for which he had 'entered' that entity, he separates from it. Thereafter, the other entity remains as it was before. Thus, the additional powers that that entity appeared to have should be known to actually be Puruṣottama Bhagavān's powers. In this way, the manifest form of Puruṣottama Nārāyaṇa is the cause of all.

It is this empowering presence of Parabrahman that makes him the cause of the avatāras; that allows the avatāras themselves to be called 'avatāras of

God', and therefore be fully divine for their tasks on earth and be venerable by all others; and that also helps reconcile statements that speak of avatāras 'emanating from Puruṣottama' or God 'assuming' the form of various avatāras.[14]

As he who empowers, inspires and divinises the various avatāras across the countless brahmāṇḍas, Parabrahman is further established as the supreme reality among all.[15]

Transcendent to Akṣara

A thorough study of the Vacanāmrut makes apparent that Swaminarayan repeatedly describes Parabrahman's supremacy in relation to Akṣarabrahman. For example:

> There is only one form of God. This God is extremely powerful and no one, *including Akṣara*, is capable of becoming like him. (Vac. Loyā.4; emphasis added)

> Puruṣottama is the soul of all, yet no one *up to and including Akṣara* is capable of becoming as powerful as him. (Vac. Kār.8; emphasis added)

Similarly, in Vac. Kār.10, Swaminarayan begins a list of beings that a devotee of God may become like by the grace of God. He begins with Brahmā and Śiva before moving onto sages such as Śukadeva and Nārada. Then, after including other realised souls, he ends:

> Or he may *even* become like Akṣara [i.e. akṣararūpa, fully enlightened]. However, no one is capable of becoming like Śrī Puruṣottama Nārāyaṇa. (emphasis added)

It is as if Akṣarabrahman is the highest benchmark by which to measure Parabrahman, but one which he still surpasses.

In other sermons, Swaminarayan states the greatness of Parabrahman in relation to Akṣarabrahman more directly. In Vac. Gaḍh. 1.64, for example, he clearly states:

> Puruṣottama is greater even than Akṣara, who is greater than all else.

[14] For a full scholarly discussion of this and other related topics, drawn extensively from a wide range of theological and historical sources, see Shrutiprakashdas's *Svāminārāyaṇ Sampradāymā Avatār-Avatārī Nirūpaṇ*, 2nd edn (Ahmedabad: Swaminarayan Aksharpith, 2010), 521 pages with charts and appendices.

[15] The 'descent' or manifestation of avatāras is well narrated in Hindu texts such as the various Pūrāṇas, and well explained in technical texts such as the Bhagavad-Gītā (see especially 4.7–8). For the extraordinary event of Parabrahman the avatārin himself manifesting on earth in human form, see Section 'Pragaṭa: God as Manifest' further in this chapter.

This seems to be a direct translation of the phrase in MuU 2.1.2:

> Akṣarāt parataḥ paraḥ |

While a fuller discussion of this Upaniṣadic passage will be covered in the following chapter on Akṣarabrahman,[16] it is sufficient to simply note here Bhadreshdas's comment in relation to Parabrahman.

> In this way, Akṣara is greater than all the jīvas, īśvaras, māyā and akṣara-muktas {liberated souls in Akṣaradhāma} ... And with Paramātman being greater {para} even than such a great Brahman by virtue of being his controller, master, inspirer, support, soul, etc. ... it is fitting that Paramātman is also called 'Parabrahman' {literally, 'greater-Brahman'}.[17]

In another comment, Bhadreshdas explains why the adjective 'great' {mahāntam} found in verse 2.22 of the Kaṭha Upaniṣad is appropriate in qualifying Parabrahman. He writes:

> Parabrahman is great, indeed the best {utkṛṣṭa}, because he is greater even than Akṣarabrahman, who is greater than Prakṛti [i.e. māyā] and its effects, all jīvas and īśvaras, countless emanations such as Matysa, Kaccha, etc., and countless akṣara-muktas who are brahmarūpa.[18]

Drawing upon a familiar analogy, Swaminarayan explains in Vac. Gaḍh. 1.63 how to understand God's greatness.

> Consider the analogy of a great king. If even his servants and maids stay in seven-storey mansions, and their gardens, horses, carriages, ornaments, and other such luxuries make their houses appear as majestic as Devaloka, then imagine how majestic the palace and its luxuries of that king must be. Similarly, consider the realms of the lords of this brahmāṇḍa – Brahmā and the other devatās – who follow the commands of Śrī Puruṣottama Bhagavān. If there is no limit to those realms and their opulence, then how can one possibly comprehend the extent of the opulence of Virāṭa Puruṣa from whose navel Brahmā was produced? Furthermore, the master of countless millions of such Virāṭa Puruṣas is Puruṣottama Bhagavān, whose abode is Akṣara. Within that abode, countless millions of such brahmāṇḍas float like mere atoms in each and every hair of Akṣara. Such is the abode of God.

He then goes on to conclude:

> So, how, then, can one possibly comprehend the extent of God's greatness? One with faith understands God's greatness in this manner. (Vac. Gaḍh. 1.63)

[16] See Section 'Akṣarabrahman as Ontologically Distinct from Parabrahman' in Chapter 7.
[17] MuU-SB 2.1.2, p. 260. [18] KU-SB 2.22, p. 118.

Swaminarayan seems to imply that, ultimately, the most accurate understanding of Parabrahman's unfathomable greatness can be formed only in comparison to his abode – that he is greater even than Akṣara. In fact, in several sermons (i.e. Vac. Gaḍh. 1.31, Gaḍh. 1.42, Gaḍh. 1.51, Gaḍh. 1.66, Gaḍh. 1.78, Sār.5, Gaḍh. 2.13, Gaḍh. 2.18 and Gaḍh. 2.31), even when other topics are under discussion, Swaminarayan uses the term 'Akṣarātīta' {transcendent to Akṣara} to qualify Parabrahman. In other sermons, Swaminarayan underscores the supremacy of Parabrahman over Akṣarabrahman when describing various aspects of God's nature. For example:

> The God present within this Satsaṅga fellowship is ... the cause even of Akṣarabrahman. (Vac. Amd.6)

> Parabrahman Puruṣottama Nārāyaṇa is ... the cause, support and inspirer of even Brahman. (Vac. Gaḍh. 2.3)

> This manifest form of Puruṣottama Bhagavān before your eyes is the controller of all, including Akṣara. (Vac. Gaḍh. 3.38)

> The nirguṇa [i.e. all-pervasive] form of God is ... the soul of even Akṣara. (Vac. Kār.8)

> [Puruṣottama Nārāyaṇa] can eclipse even Akṣara ... and preside alone independently. (Vac. Loyā.13)

The use of 'even' {'paṇ' in Gujarati} and 'including' in these excerpts is especially instructive. It reveals Akṣarabrahman as an otherwise unsurpassable extreme – the highest of the high, the greatest of the great – but such is the extraordinary greatness of Parabrahman that he transcends even that. He is, quite simply, Akṣarātīta. In other words, Akṣarabrahman provides the fulcrum with which to fully understand Parabrahman, and it is to Akṣarabrahman that we shall turn after completing this exposition on Parabrahman.

*

So far, in attempting to understand the nature of Parabrahman, we have been looking at the first of four aspects, his supremacy, i.e. Parabrahman as sarvopari. Within that, the discussions of Parabrahman as one and without second, the supreme lord, the soul of the entire world, the cause of the avatāras and, now, as greater even than Akṣarabrahman have been primarily concerned with his supremacy in relation to others, i.e. who is he greater than and how.

We now move on to understanding his greatness on its own terms.

Limitless Greatness of Parabrahman's Own Being

Swaminarayan repeatedly emphasises in the Vacanāmrut that God's greatness is unfathomable (e.g. Vac. Gaḍh. 3.37 and Kār.8) and indeed limitless (Vac. Gaḍh. 2.67), and thus beyond the reach of even the most intellectual and talented beings in all the worlds.

> Not even Śeṣa, Śāradā, Brahmā or the other devatās – in fact, not even the four Vedas – can fathom the vastness of God's greatness, his virtues, his actions, his birth, his power, his splendour, his blissful nature, or his countless other redemptive characteristics. (Vac. Gaḍh. 2.67)

In so saying, Swaminarayan provides a clue here as to how we can begin to understand Parabrahman as limitless, even if only to an infinitesimally limited degree. Drawing upon the list in the above passage, with some expansion and simplification, we can arrive at a framework of seven aspects of God's limitless nature upon which to further expound. These seven aspects are:

1. Time
2. Space
3. Knowledge
4. Power
5. Splendour
6. Bliss
7. Virtues

In the following sections, we shall briefly elaborate upon each to see how Swaminarayan theological texts describe God as being unbound by time and space and as having infinite knowledge, power, splendour, bliss and virtues.

Time

When initially delineating the five metaphysical entities of the Swaminarayan Vedānta school, we noted that Parabrahman is one of the five entities which is eternal {nitya}, i.e. without beginning {anādi} as well as without end {ananta}. Swaminarayan says specifically of God, for example:

> Puruṣottama is eternal. (Vac. Loyā.14)

We also noted that another term used to explain eternal existence is satya, meaning 'truth' or 'being', implying that God truly exists and is characterised by existence.

> God's form is supremely true {param satyasvarūp}. (Vac. Pan.7)

In Vac. Loyā.4, Swaminarayan brings God's existence together with time to explain:

> The form of God is true at all times.

That is, God exists at all times and, by the Vedāntic definition of 'satya', he is trikālābādhita, i.e. totally unaffected by the three forms of time – the past, the present and the future. Swaminarayan thus declares:

> Time devours everything except God; that is to say, time's powers are incapable of affecting God. (Vac. Gaḍh. 3.37)

So not only does God exist at all times, but he exists *as he is* at all times, because he is immune to the ravaging effects of time. In other words, God is forever immutable.

> God remains as one form at all times during the creation, sustenance and dissolution of the universe, but does not undergo any changes as māyic objects do. (Vac. Kār.7)

Apart from time, there are other ways as well in which God's immutability might be challenged, especially when he assumes a human form, so this important discussion will be covered more fully in the section on Parabrahman as pragaṭa {manifest}.[19] However, since Swaminarayan mentioned 'birth' among the list of God's limitless aspects in Vac. Gaḍh. 2.67, it will be relevant and useful to cite here from Vac. Pan.7.

> The phases of childhood, youth and old age apparent in God, as well as his birth and death, are all perceived due to his yogic powers {yoga-māyā}. In reality, God remains exactly as he is . . .
>
> One who is said to have perfectly realised the nature of God understands God to be eternal and imperishable – absolutely unchanging.

Swaminarayan thus explains that God, despite taking birth even, remains totally outside the otherwise inescapable influence of time; he is unborn, unchanging and undying.

In another sense, God is not only unaffected by time when he enters the world or is immanent within it, but he is also *beyond* time in his eminently distinct, transcendental self. More about this transcendental self is introduced below in the immediately following section on space.

[19] See especially Section 'Absolute Divinity of the Embodied Form' in this chapter.

Space

To say that God is unbound by space is to mean that God is omnipresent. Swaminarayan often describes Parabrahman as being sarvavyāpaka, i.e. pervading all places and entities, as we saw, for example, in the discussion on God being the soul and inner-controller of the entire universe.[20] However, Swaminarayan is keen to stress that this indwelling within all is by Parabrahman's extraordinary 'yogic powers' {variously called yoga-śakti, yoga-māyā and yoga-kaḷā}, because, in fact, he still has a distinct and definite form forever residing in his abode.

> God possesses a definite form in his Akṣaradhāma, but through his antaryāmin powers, he pervades the jīvas. (Vac. Kār.4)

> God reveals himself in the countless millions of brahmāṇḍas wherever and however he needs to be revealed, yet he himself is forever in his Akṣaradhāma ... To thus remain in one place and at the same time to appear in infinite places is itself God's pervasive form by way of his yogic powers {yoga-kaḷā}. (Vac. Gaḍh. 2.64)

Swaminarayan similarly explains in Vac. Var.13 that Parabrahman is, by his powers, sarvadeśin {in all places} while eternally being ekadeśastha {situated in one place}. This is how, he argues, scriptural statements describing God as 'sarvagata'[21] {omnipresent}, 'vibhū'[22] {pervasive} or 'vyāpaka'[23] {pervasive}, etc. should be interpreted. 'But he is not pervasive in the sense of being formless like space' (Vac. Var.13 and Gaḍh. 2.64). Swaminarayan reiterates this to avert what he believes is the grave blasphemy of misunderstanding God as existing only formlessly, that is, without having a distinct, definite and transcendental form in his abode.

That Parabrahman can be within all and yet distinct and, conversely, distinct yet within all, is another idea relevant here and important in Swaminarayan's theology that needs to be noted. He uses the terms anvaya {immanent, existing concomitantly within all} and vyatireka {transcendent, existing distinctly alone}, respectively. For example, in Vac. Gaḍh. 1.78, Swaminarayan states:

> [Puruṣottama Bhagavān] is distinct {vyatireka}, yet is immanently present within everything {sarvamā anvaya}, and while being immanent, is still distinct from everything.

[20] See Section 'Soul of All Beings and Things' in this chapter and, for example, Vac. Gaḍh. 1.64.
[21] E.g. SU 3.21. [22] E.g. BU 6.3.4. [23] E.g. KaU 6.8.

Again, in Vac. Var.7 he explains:

> God's form is such that he is immanent within māyā and yet, at the same time, he still exists as distinct.

This also accounts for, as we saw above in the section about God as the omnisoul, how Parabrahman can remain, despite being immanent within all, unaffected by the imperfections of all that he is immanent within (e.g. Vac. Gaḍh. 2.10).

Parabrahman is thus immanent in all only while having an eternally transcendent form entirely distinct from everything else. But by being present in everything everywhere, even while having such a distinct form, ensures that he is unbound by the confinements of physical space. Furthermore, when we expound upon Parabrahman's distinct form in more detail in the section on sākāra, we shall see that since he transcends all human physicality, it is not possible to 'measure' him by any physical measurements. Hence, physical boundaries do not apply to Parabrahman even in his distinct form in Akṣaradhāma. Thus, in both his forms, immanent and distinct, he is spatially limitless.

Knowledge

Closely related to God being unbound by time and space is the idea that God has unlimited knowledge, for if God can be in all places at all times, and if he is a perfectly conscious (knowing) being, it follows that it is possible for God to always know everything from everywhere. Swaminarayan affirms this in Vac. Jet.5, for example, by revealing that God is omniscient, knowing 'all happenings from the three times – the past, the future and the present'. In Vac. Gaḍh. 2.53, he describes this more vividly.

> God sees [i.e. knows] all of the jīvas and īśvaras who dwell in the countless millions of brahmāṇḍas as clearly as he sees a drop of water in his palm.

Swaminarayan indicates from this statement that God's knowledge is complete and effortless. Additionally, because 'all of the jīvas and īśvaras . . . in the countless millions of brahmāṇḍas' are infinite in number, knowing them all perfectly means God's knowledge is also infinite in measure.

Gunatitanand Swami elaborates on what such infinite knowledge means by citing in SV 3.15 the following phrase from a Pañcarātric text:

> He who simultaneously knows everything as if before his eyes, always and independently. (Pārāśarya Saṃhitā 3.20)

This all follows because Parabrahman is indeed a conscious, knowing being. Swaminarayan describes God as 'paramacaitanya', the supreme conscious being (Vac. Pan.7), and confirms in Vac. Gaḍh. 2.17:

> He who realises God's nature to be replete with pure consciousness, free of māyic elements, is correct in his understanding.

The extra emphasis applied with 'supreme' on God's consciousness is perhaps to distinguish him from the other sentient beings (Akṣarabrahman, īśvaras and jīvas), for they, too, are caitanya, i.e. composed of and characterised by consciousness. And since each of the jīvas and īśvaras is also a knower {jñātā} within its own field of scope, Swaminarayan often calls the soul of the finite being the 'kṣetrajña' {literally, 'knower of the field'}. For Parabrahman, however, Swaminarayan emphasises that his knowledge is far superior to that of any other conscious being. He declares:

> Puruṣottama Bhagavān is the kṣetrajña of all kṣetrajñas. (Vac. Gaḍh. 2.17)

This relates back to Parabrahman being the inner soul of everything, of even the knowing beings, including Akṣarabrahman. But by using a term explicitly denotative of a knowing agent – literally, 'the knower of all knowers' – rather than simply 'the ātman of all ātmans', Swaminarayan emphasises that, just as God is 'the lord of all lords', he is the sole supreme knower. In fact, the body–soul relationship in this context also helps to confirm God as the supreme all-knower. Just as the jīvātman (soul of a being) pervades its entire body and is the source of consciousness throughout that body, allowing it to know (feel, see, hear, etc.) – that is to say, the soul is the knower of its entire body – in the same way, God, as the soul of the entire universe, pervades it and is the source of all consciousness throughout the universe; he is the knower of everything because he ensouls everything.

Furthermore, when commenting on KeU 1.6–9, Bhadreshdas adds that Parabrahman does not need inner faculties or cognitive organs to know, as bound souls need the mind, eyes, ears, etc. This is because his knowledge is 'sadā svataḥsiddha' – always self-accomplished or independent.[24]

By drawing together these as well as some previous and other corollary ideas, we are able to arrive at a basic overview of God's omniscience within Swaminarayan Hindu theology. God having infinite knowledge means:

[24] KeU-SB 1.6, p.40.

- God knows everything there is to know
- God knows everything perfectly
- God knows everything immediately
- God knows everything simultaneously
- God knows everything continuously
- God knows everything directly, 'as before his eyes', not by inference, analogy, testimony or any other means
- God knows everything independently; he does not require any senses, organs or mental faculty for cognition
- God knows everything effortlessly; he does not need to exert himself in any way to know anything
- God's knowing is always fruitful and meaningful; it is never useless.

Power

In many ways, several of the aspects of Parabrahman's nature discussed so far are also aspects of his powers. We have already seen, for example, Swaminarayan talking about God's 'antaryāmin śakti', the power to dwell within everyone and everything as their inner-controller, and his other yogic powers, for example, to exist distinctly within his transcendental abode and yet be immanent throughout the universe.

When discussing Parabrahman as the avatārin, the cause of the various avatāras, we also saw how he, by his 'anu-praveśa' (special 're-entering') of Virāṭa Puruṣa, empowers selected īśvaras to become divinised avatāras.

Before that, we learned that Parabrahman is the soul of the entire universe. He not only pervades all that he ensouls but also supports, empowers and inspires it.

Going back even further, we looked at Parabrahman as the supreme lord, reigning over the entire universe. The term used by Swaminarayan to denote Parabrahman's lordship was 'aiśvarya', which is also used synonymously with powers associated with his lordly rule, i.e. supreme and divine powers.

Ahead, as we expound upon Parabrahman as the all-doer {sarvakartā} and all-cause {sarvakāraṇa}, especially in his relation to the material creation, it will become apparent that these, too, are powers of Parabrahman. And when expounding upon the jīva, we will cite from Vac. Gaḍh. 1.65, where Swaminarayan describes God's 'jñānaśakti', 'iccha-śakti' and 'kriyā-śakti', which allow finite beings to know, will and act.

So in this sense, all of these are a part of Parabrahman's extraordinary, godly powers.

Swaminarayan also speaks more generally about these powers. For example, in Vac. Gaḍh. 1.64, Puruṣottama Bhagavān is described as being 'replete with all lordly powers', which are 'innumerable' (Vac. Loyā.1), 'infinite' (Vac. Gaḍh. 3.37) and 'extremely limitless' (Vac. Gaḍh. 2.67).

In Vac. Sār.14, Swaminarayan adds:

> After all, God is extremely powerful; whatever he wishes, occurs.

Swaminarayan indicates here – as we saw with God's power to know all things – the absolute effortlessness with which Parabrahman applies his power of conation. By his mere will do all things happen. There is no exertion on his behalf whatsoever.

A text that deserves particular mention in this discussion of Parabrahman's powers is Vac. Loyā.13. We have seen parts of it earlier in describing God's independence over and above all other entities. An earlier portion of that same excerpt reads:

> Puruṣottama Nārāyaṇa is the all-doer, the cause of all, the controller of all; he is extremely attractive, extremely radiant, and extremely powerful. He possesses the powers of kartum, akartum and anyathā-kartum. (Vac. Loyā.13)

What are these three powers? Literally, they mean that Parabrahman is '[able] to do', '[able] to not do' and '[able] to do otherwise'. While the first already establishes him as powerful enough to do everything, the second answers questions of his undiminished overall authority over his own laws and even over powers he may have devolved to the īśvaras. For example, if something is destined to happen by way of the law of karma, or if an īśvara has determined something to happen in the brahmāṇḍa over which he is presiding,[25] Parabrahman, by his akartum śakti, can prevent it from happening, i.e. to not do it.[26] This is his inviolable superiority and independence at work, for it is only by his command in the first place that the īśvaras are administrating their assigned realms, though one must hasten to add that Parabrahman seldom overrules the īśvaras or the law of karma in this way. The final power, anyathā-kartum śakti, is even more rarely wielded. It implies a superlative power by which Parabrahman can do absolutely anything, including even the outright impossible. Swaminarayan gives a hint of this in Vac. Sār.14:

> By his will, that which is inert can become conscious, and that which is conscious can become inert.

[25] Section 'Roles and Functions of Īśvaras' in Chapter 9 will discuss the role and function of īśvaras in more detail.

[26] See also Vac. Gaḍh. 2.21, discussed in more detail in the following section on Parabrahman as the all-doer.

It must be stressed again that this is a *potentiality* of Parabrahman – he is *able* to do this – but one that he never actually exerts in a way that would disturb the normal flow of reality. It is, rather, to stress the absolute omnipotence and complete authority of Parabrahman; he has unlimited powers, each to an unlimited degree, allowing him to do everything and anything he so wills, by his mere will.

Splendour

In the upcoming section on Parabrahman as sākāra, we shall be looking in detail at how Swaminarayan describes God's divine, human-like form and the stress he lays on understanding it as such. Here, though, as we continue to follow the list of aspects of God's limitless nature mentioned by Swaminarayan in Vac. Gaḍh. 2.67, we come now to briefly understand the nature of God's splendour {saundarya} or charm and beauty {rūpa}.

Swaminarayan describes Parabrahman as 'exceedingly beautiful' (Vac. Loyā.13) and 'extremely arresting' (Vac. Gaḍh. 2.13), going further in Vac. Loyā.18 to say:

> God is so handsome that he puts even millions of Kāmadevas to shame. (Vac. Loyā.18)

Swaminarayan draws upon the attractiveness of the Hindu deity of love, a conventional exemplar of allure and charm in Indic literature, and multiplies it millions of times over to impress upon his audience the overwhelming excellence of God's attractiveness, before which even those innumerable Kāmadevas feel utterly insignificant and humbled.

But in fact, Swaminarayan acknowledges, even such hefty comparisons are inadequate, because

> the beauty of God cannot be found anywhere else (Vac. Pan.3),

and

> the beauty [or form] of that God is such that it cannot be compared to any other object in this brahmāṇḍa – up to and including everything from Brahmā, etc. to the smallest blade of grass. (Vac. Pan.4)

This is, of course, as Swaminarayan explains in Vac. Gaḍh. 2.67, cited above, because Parabrahman's splendour is 'extremely limitless'.

Bliss

For Swaminarayan, an important aspect of Parabrahman's nature is his blissfulness. He elucidates and emphasises it in various ways in several of his sermons, making it deserving of a closer look as we seek to understand Parabrahman's unlimited nature and supremacy within Swaminarayan Hindu theology.

In Vac. Pan.1, Swaminarayan qualifies Parabrahman as 'formed of bliss' {sukharūpa; literally, 'whose form is bliss'}, and in Vac. Pan.7 as 'formed of extreme bliss' {atiśay sukhasvarūpa; whose form is extreme bliss}. In Vac. Gaḍh. 3.27, Gaḍh. 3.28 and Gaḍh. 3.39, he also describes God as being 'replete with bliss' {sukhamayā}.

Swaminarayan explains the nature of this bliss more extensively in sermons such as Vac. Sār.1. He states there:

> If one were to gather all of the sensorial pleasures[27] of countless millions of brahmāṇḍas, even then it would not equal even one millionth of a fraction of the bliss that is present in just one pore of God.[28]

In reiterating that Parabrahman's bliss is far superior to anything else that a person could ever attain, Swaminarayan often draws upon a common analogy. For example, he states in Vac. Gaḍh. 3.39:

> An extremely wealthy man enjoys a great variety of food at home. Then, after finishing the meal, he throws a leftover piece of rotlo {unleavened millet bread} to a dog. In this case, the leftover piece of rotlo can be considered utterly inferior, and the various delicacies that the wealthy man enjoys can be considered to be full of pleasure. In the same way, God has given the countless jīvas of the brahmāṇḍas the sensorial pleasures. But they are inferior like the piece of rotlo thrown to the dog, whereas the bliss of God himself is far superior.

In Vac. Pan.1, Swaminarayan extends this analogy to beyond the pleasures available to ordinary people.

> Compared to the bliss of God, the pleasures of Brahmā and others are like that of a poor man who begs with an earthen vessel at the door of a rich householder. (Vac. Pan.1)

Swaminarayan's point from this is not to degrade the devas to the level of paupers and beggary, but rather to stress the utter superiority of God's bliss and, in turn, inspire devotees away from this high-though-ultimately-finite happiness to instead the highest, infinite bliss of Parabrahman. Elaborating upon the above from Vac. Pan.1, Swaminarayan goes on in that sermon to

[27] Throughout, 'pañcaviśaynu sukh', literally, pleasures derived from the subjects of the five senses, i.e. sights, sounds, smells, tastes and touches, has been translated as 'sensorial pleasures' for brevity and simplicity. Where only 'pañcaviśay' or 'viśay' is used, this is translated more generally as 'sense-objects'.

[28] See also Vac. Var.16 and Loyā.18.

way, we shall encounter a number of challenges to this claim and to the perfect nature of God as a result of his doership or divine agency. These we shall understand with their refutations as addressed in the commentarial tradition.

Emphasis on Knowing Parabrahman as the All-Doer

Some of Swaminarayan's most emphatic instructions to know the true nature of God concern descriptions of Parabrahman as sarvakartā, the all-doer. These include, for example, Vac. Kār.10, where he frames this understanding as a key soteriological tool. He says:

> The jīva's liberation is attained only by the following understanding: 'All that happens is by the doing of the manifest form of [Parabrahman], but nothing at all is done by any of time {kāḷa}, karma, māyā, etc.' In this manner, understanding God alone to be the all-doer is indeed the supreme cause of liberation. (Vac. Kār.10)

The last sentence of this excerpt is especially emphatic in its original Gujarati with its use of multiple accentuations; 'ek' {one; alone} and 'param' {supreme} as well as two instances of 'ja' {only; denoting exclusivity or certainty}, all indicate the imperative need in Swaminarayan's mind for such an understanding. We see the same intensity and a similar array of certainty-stressing modifiers in another sermon, which he prefaces this time with śāstric corroboration.

> I have listened attentively to all of the scriptures written by Vyāsajī regarding the attainment of liberation. The conclusive principle {siddhānta} prevalent in all those scriptures, and the only principle for the liberation of the jīva, is simply this: The sole doer {kartā} of this entire universe is God. (Vac. Gaḍh. 2.21)

This calls for an important clarification: jīvas, īśvaras and Akṣarabrahman, by way of being sentient beings themselves, are also able to do, see, hear, enjoy, experience, etc.; that is, they too have individual agency. However, this agency is predicated on Parabrahman – who pervades them, supports them, empowers them – without whom they would not be able to do anything at all. It is in this sense that Parabrahman alone is the *independent* doer of everything; the others are all doers, though not independently. Furthermore, even while Parabrahman is the all-doer, he does not necessarily intervene upon the actions of the jīvas and īśvaras; he allows the natural course of events and effects to unfold. As we shall see in their respective chapters, Parabrahman delegates power and authority to īśvaras and allows jīvas the freedom of choice over their actions.[38]

Equally emphatic as Swaminarayan's advocacy that God is the all-doer is his reproof of the belief that anyone or anything besides God could be this independent agent. When asked by a leading devotee about how God is pleased, he simply replied:

> If one does not malign God, then God is pleased.

Continuing, he said:

> Then you may ask, 'What does it mean to malign God?' Well, God is the all-doer of this world. However, if one does not understand him to be the all-doer and instead believes that it is time that is the all-doer of this world, or that it is māyā, or that it is karma, or that it is nature {svabhāva} that is the all-doer, then one is maligning God. This is because actually God is the all-doer. To ignore this and to claim that only time, karma, māyā and nature are the all-doers of this world is severe slander against God. (Vac. Var.2)

Swaminarayan adds a string of further admonishments in Vac. Kār.10, where he censures such a person as the worst of sinners, and warns others to 'not even stand in such a person's shadow' nor 'even mistakenly listen to any words from such a person's mouth'.

If we look closely at these statements above, what emerges from them is not so much Swaminarayan's insistence that God is the all-doer, but rather, more specifically, that it is *only* God who is the all-doer. Swaminarayan emphasises this by firstly reinforcing his statements in favour of God with such terms as 'only', 'alone' and 'sole' (often with 'ek' and 'ja' in Gujarati) and secondly by explicitly naming that which should *not* be considered to be the independent all-doers, i.e. time {kāḷa}, karma, māyā, nature {svabhāva}, etc. With this, Swaminarayan is implicitly countering the various non-theistic schools of thought which propound that all that happens is not by the will and strength of God, but independently of him,

- by time in the inevitable unfolding of events in temporal succession;
- or as determined by the karmas of the individual beings, which are capable of administering their own rewards and punishments;

[38] See Sections 'Roles and Functions of Īśvaras' in Chapter 9 and 'Relationship with Parabrahman: Dependent and Free' in Chapter 8, respectively.

- or by simple illusion {māyā} because nothing besides the One or Nothingness is real;
- or by inherent nature {svabhāva}, since all phenomena are naturally bound to happen anyway.[39]

This very much resonates with the debates played out in the Brahmasūtras in adhikaraṇas such as Janmādyadhikaraṇa (BS 1.1.2) and Īkṣatyadhikaraṇa (BS 1.1.5–12). It would be useful to see how Bhadreshdas, based on Swaminarayan's teachings, offers his exegetical argumentation on this topic. However, to appreciate that argumentation more fully, we shall first have to unpack what Swaminarayan means by the term 'all-doer' and its other related terms.

Parabrahman as the All-Doer and All-Cause

When Swaminarayan insists that Parabrahman is the all-doer, what does he mean? What does Parabrahman actually 'do'?

A study of the Vacanāmrut reveals that Swaminarayan includes a number of aspects in the agency of God. As 'kartā', Parabrahman:

- Creates, Sustains and Dissolves
- Supports
- Controls
- Inspires
- Empowers
- Permits
- Dispenses karmic fruits

We shall look at the first set of aspects in some detail, and then most of the others will follow collectively more briefly.

Parabrahman as Creator, Sustainer and Dissolver and Both Efficient and Material Cause

In several sermons, Swaminarayan explains Parabrahman is responsible for the creation, sustenance and dissolution of the world. For example:

> Beyond that Akṣara is Akṣarātīta Puruṣottama Bhagavān, who is the all-doer – responsible for the creation, sustenance and dissolution of everything. (Vac. Gaḍh. 1.51)

[39] To this list is often added the Sāṃkhya school of thought which asserts that all things happen by the inert Pradhāna, which is activated by the conscious Puruṣa. See also SU 1.1–3 for an allusion to these ancient schools of thought and their refutation to affirm God as the sole cause of the world and all beings, not time, inherent nature, necessity {niyati}, chance {ṛccha}, māyic elements, or Puruṣa.

> That greatness [of God] should be understood as follows: [Puruṣottama Bhagavān] is responsible for creating, sustaining and dissolving countless millions of brahmāṇḍas. (Vac. Gaḍh. 1.78)[40]

Strictly speaking, though, Parabrahman does not himself directly engage in the process of creation, sustenance and dissolution. As we shall see in more detail in the chapter on māyā and the 'evolving' of the physical world {jagat}, it is by Parabrahman's mere will {sankalpa} that the entire creative process {utpatti-sarga} is initiated. Nevertheless, it is also completely true to say that without Parabrahman's will, there would be no creation, sustenance or dissolution, and hence, it is correct to describe Parabrahman as, *ultimately*, the creator, sustainer and dissolver.

Moreover, māyā is the actual material from which the physical world is composed, and it is also one of the five eternal entities of the Swaminarayan metaphysical system. This means, if māyā has always existed, it is questionable how God can have actually *created* anything new and be justifiably called the 'creator'. Again, we shall be addressing this very valid query at its proper juncture in the chapter on māyā. There we shall be drawing upon various analogies – such as the sculptor's statue created from a boulder of stone – that help Parabrahman to be properly understood as 'the creator'.[41]

Here, though, it is important to observe that when discussing Parabrahman's doership, Swaminarayan also emphasises God as being the 'kāraṇa' – i.e. the *cause* of all things, including creation – often alongside him being the 'kartā'. For example:

> What is that God like? Well, . . . he is indeed the cause of all causes {sarva kāraṇnā paṇ kāraṇ}. (Vac. Gaḍh. 3.31)

> One who is wise realises, 'God appears like a human, but, in fact, he is the cause of all and the doer of all.' (Vac. Loyā.2)

> Puruṣottama Nārāyaṇa is the all-doer, the all-cause, the all-controller. (Vac. Loyā.13)

In fact, in the first excerpt cited in this section, the complete sentence reads:

> Beyond that Akṣara is the Akṣarātīta Puruṣottama Bhagavān, who is the all-doer – responsible for the creation, sustenance and dissolution of everything – and the cause of all. (Vac. Gaḍh. 1.51)

[40] In several other statements, we often find the word 'kartā' being used conjointly with 'hartā' – as 'kartā-hartā', literally, the 'doer-and-taker' – connoting, at a cosmological level, both the creative and terminative aspects of God's work, and by extension everything in-between. At a personal level, individuals can understand God as both their 'giver and taker'.

[41] See Section 'Parabrahman as Creator and Cause' in Chapter 10.

Technically, though, there are two types of causes for every creative event: the *efficient* cause {nimittakāraṇa}, which refers to the agent who effects the creation, and the *material* cause {upādānakāraṇa}, which refers to the very material from which the object is created. So, for example, in the making of an earthen pot, the potter is the efficient cause while the clay is its material cause. Of these two types of causes, maker and material, which one does Swaminarayan mean? The answer is both; Parabrahman is the abhinnanimittopādānakāraṇa, the 'combined {literally, "non-distinct"} efficient and material cause'. While some of the above statements indicate Parabrahman as the efficient cause of the universe, others point to him being the material cause. For example, the excerpt above from Vac. Gaḍh. 1.51 immediately goes on to mention:

> A cause always pervades its effect, and simultaneously, also remains distinct from it. Thus, if one looks from the perspective of Puruṣottama Bhagavān – the cause of all – then nothing else appears to exist except Puruṣottama Bhagavān.

The causality referred to here by Swaminarayan is of the material type, thus bringing together descriptions of Parabrahman as both the efficient and material cause in one sermon. This does, however, raise a number of questions about how this is possible for Parabrahman and, even if it is, how it may affect his perfect nature.

Some Challenges to Parabrahman's Omnidoership and Perfect Nature

Parabrahman as intelligent world-maker, the efficient cause, seems plausible enough. But how can Parabrahman be the *material* cause of the universe? As briefly explained above, māyā is the primordial matter from which the world is made. So does Parabrahman 'take the form of māyā' and literally *become* the physical world with its myriad objects of myriad names and forms? Surely not completely, for we have already learned that Parabrahman has a definite, distinct and transcendental form in his abode which he never forsakes. So then does that Parabrahman only partially become the visible world, still remaining in part in his transcendental form? But that would make him fragmentary, divisible and effectively mutable, whereas the śāstras, including the Vacanāmrut, proclaim Parabrahman to be whole, without parts {niraṃśa}, indivisible {akhaṇḍa} and immutable {avikārin} (e.g. SU 6.11; Vac. Pan.2). These are, in fact, the objections presented in the commentary of BS 2.1.27. The objectors' challenge can be summarised thus: If you insist on Parabrahman being the material cause of the world, then you will either have to accept him as having parts or being without a distinct transcendental form.

This apparent theological dilemma is resolved by Bhadreshdas by firstly taking recourse in śāstric revelation. As we saw at the very beginning when discussing sources and tools of Swaminarayan Hindu theology, revelation is the only authoritative way by which to accurately determine the nature of God. Bhadreshdas thus insists that that which is beyond the limited grasp of our senses and mind cannot have any other means of confirmation except Scripture. The basic reasoning is: If the Śrutis reveal Parabrahman as being the material cause as well as being whole, indivisible, immutable, etc., then who are we to argue?[42]

To corroborate this position, and to help explain how Parabrahman can indeed be the combined cause of the world, two key doctrines shall need to be summoned. Firstly, since Parabrahman is the inner soul of the world, he pervades, controls and empowers his entire 'body'. However, this pervading is by his antaryāmi-śakti, or special yogic powers, allowing him to therefore be immanently present within all while still being distinctly transcendental. For the task of creation, specifically, Parabrahman specially 're-enters' māyā and the various elements, overpowering their own identity and reigning supreme within them. It is in this sense that Parabrahman is said to 'take the form of māyā'.[43] Swaminarayan explains this in Vac. Gaḍh. I.41. After establishing that 'Puruṣottama Bhagavān creates and enters the various types of life-forms as their cause and as their indwelling controller {antaryāmin}', he adds, as if countering the above objection:

> There is only one Puruṣottama Bhagavān, and it is he who enters all and resides in them as the indwelling controller. But, he does not himself become the jīvas and īśvaras by assuming many forms.

The second doctrine concerns the view of causality adopted by Swaminarayan, which has as its starting point the satkāryavāda of the Sāṃkhya School. In brief, it is the belief that an effect is pre-existent in its cause as a different state {avasthāntara}. In other words: states change, but new substances are not created. So what one sees as 'new' is not a new or different substance, but merely the causal substance (i.e. the material cause) in a different state. For example, a gold necklace is nothing but the gold it is made of in a different form; it is not a new substance apart from gold. At a cosmological level, then, creation is the changing of māyā from its causal state {kāraṇāvasthā} to its effected state {kāryāvasthā}. Conversely, dissolution is the opposite; the returning of māyā from its effected state {kāryāvasthā} to its original causal state {kāraṇāvasthā}.

[42] BS-SB. 2.1.27–8, pp. 177–9. [43] See especially Vac. Pan.7.

Combining this with the crux of the argument that Parabrahman is the very soul of māyā – entering it, controlling it, empowering it – Parabrahman is said to be non-different {ananya}[44] from māyā (even while being ontologically distinct). Therefore, he does not have to change in *substance* to become the effect which is the world, but only change *states* – from 'Parabrahman as māyā in its causal state' to 'Parabrahman as māyā in its effected state'. This is how Parabrahman can be the material cause of the world. Swaminarayan brings some of these points together in Vac. Loyā.2 when he explains:

> God, who is the cause of all, appears like a human being, yet by his yogic powers, he is able to create countless millions of brahmāṇḍas from his body [i.e. māyā] and is able to absorb them back into himself.

The famous Sadvidyā instruction to Śvetaketu by his father in the sixth chapter of the Chāndogya Upaniṣad also refers to this idea. As Bhadreshdas explains, the opening –

> Dear son, in the beginning there was verily only this Being, one, without second (6.2.2) –

refers to Parabrahman as being the material cause, the primordial Being from which all springs forth. The immediately following verse,

> That [Being] thought {literally, 'saw'}, 'Let me be many', 'Let me propagate' (6.2.3),

points to an intelligent being, establishing that primordial Being as also the efficient cause who wills, inspires and thereby initiates each new cycle of creation.[45]

The same twofold representation of Parabrahman is made in TU 2.6.3–2.7.1 and AU 1.1.1.[46] Both passages contain similar words to the Sadvidyā instruction above, with the latter being especially useful because it uses the term 'ātmā' instead of 'sat', i.e.

> In the beginning there was only this one Self {ātmā} . . . He thought {literally, 'saw'}, 'Let me create the worlds'. He thus created the worlds (AU 1.1.1),

thus explicitly tying in Parabrahman's omnisoulship with his dual causality.

[44] This alludes to the Ananyatvādhikaraṇa in BS 2.1.14, which argues for the non-difference between Parabrahman and māyā on account of the former being the latter's cause, indweller, controller and support. See BS-SB 2.1.14–21, pp. 168–73.

[45] CU-SB 6.2.1–3, pp. 252–8. [46] And in BU 1.4.10 for Akṣarabrahman.

The causality of the world is also rigorously debated at the beginning of the Brahmasūtras. After the opening aphorism instructs that an inquiry into Brahman should be conducted, the Sūtrakāra goes on to define in this next aphorism,

> Janmādyasya yataḥ (BS. 1.1.2),

that Brahman is 'that from which [occurs] the origination, etc. of this [world]'. Here, too, when the objectors argue that 'Brahman' could plausibly refer to such beings as a Brahmin, or Brahmā the īśvara, or a jīva or liberated soul, or even the Vedas, Bhadreshdas is quick to emphasise that it is impossible for any of them to be both the efficient *and* material cause of the world, because only God[47] can enter, control and empower the whole world as its soul. Thus, only God can be the complete cause of everything, not anyone or anything else.[48]

However, believing Parabrahman to be both the efficient cause and material cause of the world raises a serious and potentially irredeemable challenge against the perfect nature of God. It stems from the idea that a causal substance (the material cause) is not dissimilar from its effect, just as a pot is similar to the clay from which it was produced and a piece of cloth from its threads. This leads to the following challenge: Since the world is composed of things that are inert, in flux, mutable, ordinary, sorrow-filled, sullied by the impurities of māyā and always constituted of the three māyic qualities (sattvaguṇa, rajoguṇa and tamoguṇa), how can it be that God is its material cause? The objectors are effectively saying: If you insist on Parabrahman being the material cause of the world, you will have to accept that he is no longer conscious, unchanging, immutable, divine, replete with bliss, pure and forever transcending māyā.[49]

In response, the Brahmasūtras state:

> But it can be seen. (2.1.6)

That is, Bhadreshdas explains, there are examples – both around us and mentioned in texts – that disconfirm the thesis that the effect is necessarily of the same nature as its cause. For example, hairs grow from a person, and as stated in the Taittirīya Upaniṣad, 'From space came air; from air, fire', etc. (2.1.1). Space is without any of the tactile qualities found in air, nor

[47] We shall learn in the chapter on Akṣarabrahman that 'Brahman' in this aphorism also denotes 'Akṣarabrahman'.

[48] BS-SB 1.1.2, pp. 12–14. The same arguments are also employed in the Īkṣatyadhikaraṇa, which takes its cue from the Chāndogya Upaniṣad verses cited above. See BS-SB 1.1.5–12, pp. 29–36.

[49] BS-SB 2.1.4–5, pp. 159–61.

does air have the form or appearance of fire. Thus, there is nothing inordinate in Parabrahman being the material cause and still being different in nature from the world and unsullied by all its imperfections. This is possible by virtue of him being the indweller, controller, support and soul of everything, including of māyā from which the world is composed.[50] Swaminarayan explains this in Vac. Var.7 by further elucidating upon the concept of God as anvaya and vyatireka – that Parabrahman can be immanent within and non-different from māyā as its soul and yet be wholly distinct from it in his abode. He says:

> The principle of anvaya-vyatirek is not that God has become half immanent within māyā and remains half distinct in his abode. Rather, God's form is such that he is immanent within māyā and yet, at the same time, he is distinct. God is not afraid, 'What if I enter māyā and thereby become impure?' Instead, when God associates with māyā, even māyā becomes like Akṣaradhāma [his abode]; and if he associates with the 24 [māyic] elements [of creation], then they also become brahmarūpa [i.e. like Brahman].

Thus, there is no question of Parabrahman becoming imperfect. He can safely be the material cause of the world as well as its efficient cause without endangering his purity.

Still one more challenge can be levelled at Parabrahman's pure nature. It stems more generally from his omnidoership, that is: If he is the all-doer, by whose wish and inspiration all things happen, do the consequences of those actions (i.e. karmas) return to affect him? Swaminarayan anticipates this question and answers it in a number of sermons. For example, in describing one of the six types of higher understandings regarding God, he includes in Vac. Loyā.12 that Parabrahman 'does all actions and yet is akartā', i.e. is unaffected and unbound by those actions. In the same sermon as well as in Vac. Loyā.1 and Gaḍh. 2.10, he adds the following analogy: Just as all actions happen within space yet space is unaffected by them, similarly, God is totally 'untouched' or 'untainted' {nirlepa} by all these actions. His perfect nature is in no way damaged.[51] This being so, Parabrahman can justifiably be regarded as the pure all-doer of all that is.

[50] BS-SB 2.1.6, pp. 161–2.

[51] Two major objections still need to be contended with, which appear in consecutive adhikaraṇas in the second chapter of the Brahmasūtras. Firstly, regarding why Parabrahman would create the world in the first place and, secondly, if he did, why he would make it so that it is an intermixture of happiness and suffering. These have been saved for when we discuss the nature of the manifest world in the chapter on māyā, allowing, also, a fuller appreciation of the argumentation after having covered a description of jīvas and īśvaras. See Section 'Purpose of Creation and the Irreproachability of its Creator' in Chapter 10.

Parabrahman as Support, Indweller, Controller, Karmic Dispenser, Inspirer and Permitter

Understanding Parabrahman as creator, sustainer and dissolver of the universe, by way of being its combined efficient and material cause, also helps explain all else he does as a part of and in addition to those roles. Some of these aspects of his nature have already been covered at length in earlier sections dealing with his supremacy, as the sovereign lord and inner-soul. Nevertheless, it will be necessary to revisit some of them here, albeit collectively and very briefly, in the context of Parabrahman's divine doership.

Firstly, let us acknowledge that our understanding of what Parabrahman does has not been limited to him being the ultimate creator of the infinite number of brahmāṇḍas. As is hopefully apparent from many of the excerpts quoted above, Swaminarayan stresses that Parabrahman is just as much *sustainer* of what he creates as well as its eventual *dissolver*. In other words, the work of God is not over after the initial phase. Each brahmāṇḍa needs to be sustained – indeed, it needs to actually function – and this calls upon Parabrahman with his ensemble of powers and providence to continue to play an 'active' role. Thus Parabrahman's work continues until the timely end of each cycle, and even thereafter, because each brahmāṇḍa is dissolved – not just destroyed – and 'returned' into māyā (which in turn becomes dormant within Akṣarabrahman). This same cycle occurs for each brahmāṇḍa, and there are 'countless millions' of such brahmāṇḍas.

Swaminarayan brings this incessant work of Parabrahman into focus, that is, how he continues to be active in the world, in sermons such as Vac. Gaḍh. 1.78. In it, Swaminarayan describes Puruṣottama Bhagavān as

> by whose wish countless millions of brahmāṇḍas are created[a]; who, by his powers, supports these brahmāṇḍas[b]; who is distinct, yet is immanently present within everything, and while being immanent, is still distinct from everything; who dwells within each and every atom in his antaryāmin form just as he is in his manifest form[c]; without whose wish not even a blade of grass is able to flutter[d]; who is responsible for creating, sustaining and dissolving countless millions of brahmāṇḍas[a] and for the pain and pleasure beings encounter therein[e]. All that God does is all that happens.

Swaminarayan is implying that, apart from (a) creating, sustaining and dissolving everything (by his mere wish), Parabrahman's doership incorporates him (b) supporting everything, (c) dwelling within everything (even while being distinct), (d) controlling everything, and (e) dispensing the fruits of the karmas of all beings. It reveals a God continuously and intimately involved with all that he creates, for he continuously and meticulously sustains it until and after its end.

A good hint of this intimate relationship between Parabrahman and his creation is given further by the phrase above, 'without whose wish not even a blade of grass is able to flutter'. Gunatitanand Swami similarly states:

> All that happens is the doing of my lord, but without him, no one is able to stir even a leaf. (SV 1.88)

Furthermore, in Vac. Gaḍh. 1.62 for example, Swaminarayan states that a person with the 'perfect conviction of the nature of God'

> realises that God is not like time, not like karma, not like nature, not like māyā, and not like Puruṣa. He realises God to be distinct from everything, as the controller of them all and the cause of them all.

Together, these statements point to Parabrahman as also the absolute *controller* over all he creates, from the most meagre of things, such as a leaf or blade of grass, to the otherwise most powerful and ubiquitous, including time, karma and māyā.

In another sermon, Swaminarayan makes an important addition to this understanding when he stresses the omniagency of Parabrahman by again placing him in direct relation to the very things which he has argued are not the independent agents of the world.

> It is God who is the inspirer of everything – of place, time, karma and māyā. It is he himself who allows the factors of place, time, etc. to be predominant. Thus, they are all dependent upon God . . . just as all the subjects of a kingdom are dependent on their king. Furthermore, in a kingdom, the minister and secretaries can only do as much as their king allows them to do; when the king does not allow it, they cannot do even the smallest of tasks. In the same way, the factors of place, time, karma and māyā can only do as much as God allows them to do; they cannot do a single thing against the wish of God.

What Swaminarayan accepts here is that place, time, karma, māyā and many other factors may all have some influence over our complex world. However, he maintains, it is Parabrahman who *inspires* them all and *permits* them to operate. They do so, always within his laws and wishes. In other words, as the analogy Swaminarayan used suggests, Parabrahman still retains his impassable sovereign rule over everything. 'Therefore', Swaminarayan concludes at the end of the sermon,

> only God is the all-doer. (Vac. Gaḍh. 2.21)

Inevitably, we are coming to find that many of the aspects of Parabrahman's supremacy – as sovereign lord, omnisoul, support, indwelling controller and more – are all re-emerging, meeting and overlapping in his omnidoership. Indeed, the two affirm each other: He who is the sole independent doer of everything is the supreme among them all; only the supreme among all can be the sole independent doer of everything.

We now proceed to understanding another aspect of Parabrahman, which, like his supremacy, is also inextricably tied with him being the omniagent and omnicause.

Sākāra: God as Having Form

In his many descriptions of the nature of Parabrahman, Swaminarayan has spoken repeatedly and decidedly about the actual form of God. He insists that Parabrahman is sākāra {literally, 'with form'}, that he has an *eternally divine human form*. Each of these four terms is important for him: God has a form, but while it is human in shape, that form is not composed of any māyic material; it is divine and bereft of any of the limitations, imperfections or impurities of māyā. This is always true for God, when he is forever present in his transcendental abode or immanent throughout the world, and even when he chooses to manifest on earth.

In this section, we shall be exploring each of these aspects of Parabrahman's form and how potential charges against this belief have been addressed. First, though, as before, we shall learn of Swaminarayan's emphatic advocacy of what he believes is an imperative theological doctrine.

Emphasis on Knowing Parabrahman as Having a Form

We saw at the opening of the previous section that Swaminarayan stressed the need to know Parabrahman as the all-doer by explaining it as a soteriological requirement; to know God as kartā is essential for finite beings to secure liberation. A similar emphasis is applied when speaking of Parabrahman as sākāra. Swaminarayan explains in Vac. Gaḍh. 3.36:

> The most extraordinary spiritual endeavour for liberation is to understand Puruṣottama Bhagavān, who is seated amidst the mass of brahmic light {brahmajyoti}, as eternally having a form.

We also saw at the very beginning of this chapter the importance Swaminarayan lays on 'upāsanā' (worship informed by correct theological knowledge), without which, he said, 'nothing can be accomplished' (Vac. Gaḍh. 1.56). In Vac. Gaḍh. 1.40, he defines upāsanā almost entirely in terms of understanding Parabrahman as having a form.

> Upāsanā can be defined as having a firm conviction that God eternally possesses a form. Even if a person becomes brahmarūpa {fully enlightened; 'like Brahman'}, that conviction would never subside. Moreover, even if he happens to listen to any other texts propounding the view that God is formless, he would still understand God to always have a form. Regardless of what is mentioned in the scriptures, he would only propound that God has a form, never allowing his upāsanā to be impaired. One who has such a firm understanding is considered to have upāsanā.

In further emphasising the power of knowing Parabrahman as having a form, Swaminarayan goes as far as to say in one sermon:

> If a person knows God to possess a form and is convinced of this, then even if he may happen to commit some sin, what is there to worry about? All those sins will be burnt by the grace of God and his jīva will attain God.

Conversely,

> to realise God as being formless is a sin far graver than even the five grave sins. There is no atonement for that sin. (Vac. Gaḍh. 2.39)

Swaminarayan similarly admonishes in Vac. Gaḍh. 1.71:

> Of all offences made against God, to denounce the form of God is a very grave offence. One should never commit this offence. One who does incurs more sin than committing the five grave sins.

Such an offence is so irredeemable, Swaminarayan explains, because it is tantamount to maligning God, something he has repeatedly warned against when working towards correct theological knowledge.

> The path of jñāna should be understood in such a way that one does not malign the form of God in any way. In fact, one should not worry if at some time or other one has transgressed God's commands, but one should never malign the form of God. If one does disobey God's commands, then one can still be freed from that sin by praying to God. However, there are no means of release for one who has maligned the form of God. (Vac. Gaḍh. 2.9)

In Vac. Var.2, as was cited in the previous section, Swaminarayan explains that to accept anything other than God as sole doer of the universe is to severely slander him. In the same sermon, he continues:

> To say that he [God] is . . . formless . . . is equivalent to maligning God.

What is the consequence of such a grave offence? Swaminarayan explains:

> A person may well be endowed with each and every virtue, but if he believes God to be formless – not possessing a definite form – then that is a grave flaw. So much so that, because of this flaw, all of his virtues become defective. (Vac. Loyā.16)

More seriously, according to Swaminarayan, not only does one who misunderstands God as formless 'not go to the abode of Puruṣottama Bhagavān' and instead 'go to dwell in the realms of other devatās' (Vac. Gaḍh. 2.9 and Gaḍh. 1.37), but such a person is 'consigned to brahma-su ṣupti', a state of impenetrable oblivion, 'from which he never returns'[52] (Vac. Gaḍh. 1.64). To this, Gunatitanand Swami adds, rather strongly, that such a misbeliever will 'endlessly suffer despair for countless eons but never be happy' (SV 3.16).

Parabrahman as Eternally Having a Form

Swaminarayan explains in over twenty sermons that Parabrahman is 'sākāra'. For example:

> God, who is Puruṣottama, forever presides with a divine form in his Akṣaradhāma. (Vac. Gaḍh. 1.71)
>
> In that Akṣaradhāma, Śrī Puruṣottama Bhagavān is present in an eternally divine form. (Vac. Var.12)
>
> How does a true devotee of God understand God's greatness? He believes, 'God, who possesses a definite form, forever presides in his luminous Akṣaradhāma'. (Vac. Gaḍh. 3.32)
>
> Therefore God indeed forever possesses a form . . . and is forever present in his Akṣaradhāma. (Vac. Gaḍh. 3.35)

What is important to note from such statements is that Swaminarayan invariably mentions Akṣaradhāma, the divine abode of God wherein he eternally resides, and includes the term 'sadā' {forever or eternally}. Both serve to dispel the misconception that Parabrahman assumes a form *only* when he manifests on earth, but that in actual fact he is formless at all other times. Swaminarayan describes this problem in Vac. Gaḍh. 1.66 as arising from a potential misreading of theological texts.

[52] This should not be confused with eternal damnation. Swaminarayan explains that, eventually, by God's extreme grace, such souls can still be redeemed in later lives if they seek the refuge of God and earn his or the Guru's favour (e.g. Vac. Gaḍh. 1.58, Gaḍh. 2.45, Var.6, Var.7 and Gaḍh. 3.35).

> The scriptures also state, 'A thorn is used to remove a thorn. Thereafter, both are discarded. Similarly, God assumes a physical body to relieve the earth of its burdens. Then, having relieved the earth of its burden, he discards that physical body.'[53] Hearing such words, the foolish are misled into the understanding that God is formless; they fail to realise the form of God as being divine.

Swaminarayan emphasises here that Parabrahman always has a form, even when resident in Akṣaradhāma, and since he is forever resident in his abode, he always has a form. This is true even during the causal state of the universe. He states:

> Even at the time of ātyantika-pralaya {final dissolution, i.e. before the beginning of a new cycle of creation}, God and his [liberated] devotees remain in Akṣaradhāma with a divine and definite form enjoying divine bliss. (Vac. Pan.7)

Parabrahman's Human-Shaped Form

It is not enough to know that God has a 'divine and definite form' (Vac. Pan.7). We need to – want to – know what that eternal form is like, for even objects such as pots and pans and creatures such as cows and horses have 'a form'. So what does God look like? This tantalisingly simple yet bold question is at the heart of many spiritual strivings and debates. Swaminarayan is unequivocal in his description: God is manuṣyākāra {human in shape}.

We saw earlier that to malign God was to deny him of this shape. Instead, Swaminarayan insisted,

> God is complete with all limbs, including hands, feet, etc.; there is not the slightest deformation in any of his limbs. He eternally possesses a definite form. So, to say that he is . . . formless . . . is itself maligning God. (Vac. Var.2)

In Vac. Gaḍh. 3.38 as well, Swaminarayan indicates a full normal human form by mentioning that God is two-armed {dvibhuja}. He states:

> The form of God in Akṣaradhāma and the form of the muktas – the attendants of God – are all real, divine and extremely luminous. Also, the form of that God and those muktas is two-armed like that of a human being. (Vac. Gaḍh. 3.38)

[53] Swaminarayan is drawing from BP 1.15.34.

He adds more detail about that form in Vac. Loyā.18, as if in answer to our very own question above.

> Then you may ask, 'What is the form of that God like?' I shall explain. God is characterised by eternal existence, consciousness and bliss {saccidānanda}, and possesses a form full of divine light. In every single pore of his body, there is light equivalent to millions and millions of suns. Moreover, that God is so handsome that he puts even millions of Kāmadevas to shame. He is the lord of countless millions of brahmāṇḍas, the king of kings, the controller of all, the indweller of all, and extremely blissful. Before his bliss, the pleasure of seeing countless beautiful women pales into insignificance. In fact, before the bliss of the form of that God, the sensorial pleasures of this realm and the higher realms pale into insignificance. Such is the form of God. That form always has two arms . . .

Anticipating a follow-up question about other extraordinary forms of God, he quickly clarifies: 'but by his wish, he may appear to have four arms, or sometimes to have eight arms, or he may even be seen as having a thousand arms' (Vac. Loyā.18).

In addition, Swaminarayan mentions in several other sermons the 'holy feet' {'caraṇārvinda', or simply 'caraṇa'} of God (Vac. Gaḍh. 1.71, Gaḍh. 1.74, Loyā.13, Loyā.17, Gaḍh. 3.4, Gaḍh. 3.7, Gaḍh. 3.9, Gaḍh. 3.11, Gaḍh. 3.13), often as being worshipped in Akṣaradhāma by 'countless millions of liberated souls' (Vac. Gaḍh. 3.31; also Vac. Gaḍh. 2.25, Gaḍh. 3.39). Swaminarayan also cites descriptions from the Upaniṣads that describe Parabrahman as 'seeing',[54] and thereby argues that God has eyes and indeed all sense organs (Vac. Gaḍh. 1.45, Pan.7).[55] Together, these statements create a strong, clear image of Parabrahman as having a fully formed human shape, with two arms, feet, eyes and other sense organs, etc.

Swaminarayan provides the most vivid vignette of all in Vac. Gaḍh. 2.13, where he describes the 'extremely luminous form of God' present within the 'extremely luminous divine light' of his abode.

> The form is dark, but due to the intensity of the light, it appears to be rather fair, not dark. The form has two arms and two legs, not four, eight or a thousand arms; and its appearance is very captivating. The form is extremely serene. It appears like a human in shape and is youthful. Sometimes that form in the divine light is seen standing, sometimes sitting, and at other times, it is seen walking around.

[54] E.g. AU 1.1, BU 1.2.5 and CU 6.2.3.

[55] See also this argument in BS-SB 1.1.5, pp. 30–31.

Swaminarayan furthermore iterates that this human-shaped form is eternal; Parabrahman looks like a human when he manifests on earth, just as he does in Akṣaradhāma, even at the time of final dissolution.

> [A true devotee] understands that the manifest form of God which resides on this earth, and the devotees of God who remain in the vicinity of God, remain exactly as they are even during ātyantika-pralaya. (Vac. Gaḍh. 1.37)

Swaminarayan therefore describes this in Vac. Kār.8 as Parabrahman's 'original form' {mūḷ svarūp}. In this sermon, he first explains Parabrahman's nirguṇa form as being 'subtler than that which is subtle', because he ensouls and indwells all of the material elements and spiritual beings, including Akṣarabrahman. He then describes Parabrahman's saguṇa aspect as being 'extremely vast'; so vast, in fact, that

> before the vastness of Puruṣottama Bhagavān, countless millions of brahmāṇḍas, which are encircled by the eight barriers [i.e. earth, water, etc.], appear extremely minute, like mere atoms. Those brahmāṇḍas do not become smaller, but before the vastness of God they appear small. In this way, the extreme vastness of the form of God is the saguṇa aspect of God.

This leads Swaminarayan to anticipate a natural question:

> Then someone may doubt, 'In his nirguṇa form, God is subtler than the extremely subtle, and in his saguṇa form, he is more vast than the extremely vast. What, then, is the original form of God – who assumes both of these forms – like?'

He continues:

> The answer to that is that the manifest form of God visible in a human form is the eternal and original form of God. His nirguṇa and saguṇa aspects are the special, divine powers of that form.[56]

Dispelling Some Doubts about Parabrahman's Human-Shaped Form

As should be apparent from the statements cited above, a term that repeatedly features when Swaminarayan talks about the eternally human-shaped form of God is divine {divya}. This is to dispel the doubt that if Parabrahman has a human form, then it will necessarily be flawed, sullied

[56] Many of these points and earlier arguments are brought together by Bhadreshdas in the conclusion of the Antasdharmādhikaraṇa; see BS-SB 1.1.21, pp. 45–6. See also MuU-SB 3.1.3, pp. 283–4 and BU-SB 2.3.6, pp. 116–19 where 'Puruṣa' denotes Parabrahman, and also IU-SB 16, p. 24 for the elaboration of 'rūpam'.

and limited by all the imperfections, impurities and limitations of human corporeality. By adding 'divine' in his descriptions, Swaminarayan is effectively saying: Parabrahman's form is certainly human in shape (anthropomorphic), but it is by no means human in nature (anthropophysitic) or substance (anthrosubstantic). So while ordinarily human bodies are composed of māyā, God's form is not.

> God's form is not like any other form that has been created out of Prakṛti [i.e. māyā], like that of other devas or humans. (Vac. Gaḍh. 3.37)

> [Puruṣottama Bhagavān] eternally possesses a definite form, which is not an ordinary, worldly {prākṛta} form. (Vac. Gaḍh. 1.66)

In fact, Swaminarayan makes it a point to stress that God's form is totally unlike any other form. He explains this at considerable length in Vac. Pan.4. To cite two passages from that sermon:

> The Vedas, the Purāṇas, the Mahābhārata, the Smṛtis and other scriptures proclaim that the original form of God, which is eternal, without beginning and divine, resides in his Akṣaradhāma. What is that God like? His form is not like any form that can be seen by the eyes. His sound is not like any sound that can be heard by the ears. His touch is not like any touch that can be felt by the skin. His smell is not like any smell that can be smelt by the nose. Nor is God like anything that can be described by the tongue . . .
>
> The form of that God is such that it cannot be compared to the form of anyone in this brahmāṇḍa. Why? Because all of the forms in this brahmāṇḍa that have evolved from Prakṛti-Puruṣa are māyic, whereas God is divine, not māyic. So, since the two are totally different, how can they possibly be compared?

One reason for this stark difference is that God's body is not formed, as human or even devic bodies are, as a consequence of karmas accrued over numerous lives by way of their ignorance and association with māyā. Parabrahman, rather, is absolutely and eternally free of māyā, transcending it and controlling it instead. His form is thus never defiled by māyā in the slightest.

> In no way does even a hint of māyā taint the form of God. (Vac. Gaḍh. 2.4)

In fact, Parabrahman is wholly 'untouched by māyā' (Vac. Loyā.13) and

> does not have any māyic qualities {guṇas}. He is forever guṇātīta {transcending māyic qualities} and divine in form {divyamūrti}. (Vac. Kār.7)

Again, this is eternally so for Parabrahman, as the 'forever' in the above statement indicates. Swaminarayan stressed this while commenting on the first verse of the Bhāgavata-Purāṇa – 'Janmādyasya yataḥ . . .' – as it was being read in one of his assemblies. He explained that 'yatra trisargo mṛṣā' from that verse should be understood as meaning

> that the entities evolved out of the three qualities {guṇas} of māyā – namely the five material elements, the senses, the mind, etc. and their presiding devatās – are never at all present in God at any time, past, present or future. (Vac. Pan.7)

This point is used to refute one of the objections in BS 2.1.32, which draws from CU 6.2.1 and the same verse we saw earlier when discussing God as the combined efficient and material cause:

> Dear Son, in the beginning, there was verily only this Being {sat}.

Citing this, the objectors ask how it can be possible for Parabrahman to have eyes, ears, hands, feet, life-breath, mind, etc. when there was absolutely nothing apart from Being to make them from. Bhadreshdas effectively retorts: Precisely! They are not *made* from anything but are Being itself.[57]

This helps explain how God's eyes, ears and other 'sense organs' (as we would call them) are not like the organs of a human. As we learned when expounding upon Parabrahman's unlimited knowledge, he does not need any senses or organs or mental faculty to know. He knows everything independently and directly. This is because he is infinitely full of knowledge, and his mind, senses and organs are all divine and unlimited.

Continuing further, this non-material composition of God also helps explain why he is not ascribed a particular gender. As we shall see in more detail in the chapter on jīva, Swaminarayan describes even the finite soul as 'neither male nor female'. 'It is', like Parabrahman, 'characterised by pure existence and consciousness' (Vac. Gaḍh. 3.22). We receive another clue about the non-genderedness of God's form from the new, divine body that the jīvas and īśvaras receive during the state of post-mortem liberation when dwelling in the transcendental abode with God. Swaminarayan explains in Vac. Gaḍh. 3.38 and Loyā.18 that this body is like God's two-armed human-shaped form, but adds elsewhere that it is

> different from the two genders of the world. It is neither female in shape nor male in shape. It has a wholly brahmic body, which is neither feminine nor masculine. (SV 7.2)

Yet, in applying some sort of name or identity to God, the limitations of human language and imagination force us to use nouns, pronouns and

[57] BS-SB 2.1.32, pp. 181–3.

imagery that inevitably have gender connotations. For example, 'Bhagavān', the most commonly used term for God in the Vacanāmrut, is masculine, as is 'king', an analogy we have found being employed often. This, though, is not to discount the fact that God is equally identified by other names and images throughout Hindu texts, such as Puruṣottama (male), Paramātman (male), Parabrahman (neuter), Devatā (female) and many others. Thus, to attribute any particular gender to God would be incorrect.

To be clear, throughout this discussion, it needs to be remembered that Swaminarayan's emphasis is on Parabrahman being 'manuṣy*ākāra*' – human in *shape* or *form* – not on him having a human *body*. Not understanding this will lead to another false assumption: that like ordinary humans, Parabrahman's form must also be subject to change and decay – growing from that of a child, a youth and an adult, to eventually becoming old and infirm. But as Swaminarayan explained in Vac. Gaḍh. 2.13, the form of God 'appears youthful {kiśora}' and is unchanging. He adds in Vac. Kār.7:

> God remains as one form at all times during the creation, sustenance and dissolution of the universe, but does not undergo any changes as māyic objects do. He always maintains a divine form.

This is because

> time devours everything except God; that is to say, time's powers are incapable of affecting God's form. (Vac. Gaḍh. 3.37)

The same is true for space. One could question how God could have any form, let alone one that is human in shape, and not be limited to being within a certain spatial boundary. But as we saw earlier, Swaminarayan insists that Parabrahman is already unbound by space; there is no place where one can say that God is not. He is omnipresent, even while having a definite form, because of his divine, yogic powers. The point being made to any proponents of a formless God is this: If you resort to calling God formless simply to avoid him being limited by space, well, Parabrahman for us is already unbound by space. He is everywhere at all times. So there is no question of avoiding any undesirable but inescapable limitations. Besides, it is not possible to 'measure' him by any physical measurements, simply because he transcends all physicality and eludes all measurements. Swaminarayan stated in Vac. Kār.8 that God is 'subtler than the extremely subtle, and ... vaster than the extremely vast'. The Upaniṣads similarly proclaim that Parabrahman is

> smaller than a grain of rice, a barley corn, a mustard seed, a grain of millet or a kernel of a grain of millet.

And yet equally he is

> larger than the earth, larger than the intermediate region, larger than the sky, larger than these worlds. (CU 3.14.3)

Quite simply, God is

> Smaller than the smallest, larger than the largest. (SU 3.20, KaU 2.20)

What the Upaniṣads and Swaminarayan are trying to say, in effect, is that such physical measurements or boundaries do not apply to God. He is beyond all limitations of space, even as he remains in his 'original' human form (Vac. Kār.8). According to Swaminarayan, then, Parabrahman has an eternal human form that is wholly unique, uniquely pure and purely divine.

From Parabrahman possessing a divine human form in his transcendental abode, we move now to Parabrahman manifesting in divine human form on earth.

Pragaṭa: God as Manifest

We opened this chapter on Parabrahman by summarising Swaminarayan's formulation of 'jñāna' from Vac. Loyā.7. It told us about the four aspects of God that constitute true theological knowledge. So far, we have covered three of these aspects – God as sarvopari (transcending everything, even māyā and Akṣarabrahman), as kartā (being the doer and cause of all) and as sākāra (eternally having a divine form which is human in shape). In this final and all-important aspect, we shall expound upon Parabrahman as pragaṭa (manifesting on earth among humans).

While some of the specifics might differ, in the generalities, the description so far of a supreme, almighty, all-knowing, all-pervasive creator God is what one might expect, especially in a Hindu theist religious tradition. But perhaps what dramatically sets apart the Swaminarayan theological understanding of God from other systems is its emphasis that that supremely transcendental God can be, and indeed is, wholly present and personable among us, in human form, here and now.

Of course, that God descends upon earth in human (or any other freely chosen) form at a particular time is a concept that is familiar to many Hindu theologies, especially of the Vaiṣṇava kind. There are, however, two primary differences in this corresponding doctrine in the Swaminarayan tradition. Firstly, Parabrahman as pragaṭa is the descent of the avatārin himself, not an avatāra. Swaminarayan explains, for example, in Vac. Gaḍh. 2.9:

> One should realise the manifest God that one has met to forever possess a divine form and to be the avatārin, the cause of all avatāras.

In various Vaiṣṇava schools, these numerous avatāras have differing significance. Some are regarded as 'aṃśa avatāras' or 'kalā avatāras' (in whom only a partial manifestation of Viṣṇu has occurred, i.e. in whom Viṣṇu has manifested his powers, knowledge, etc. partially), while some – variously, for example, either exclusively Kṛṣṇa; or just Rāma, Kṛṣṇa and Nṛsiṃha; or the ten principal forms, including Matsya, Varāha, etc. – are regarded as the 'pūrṇa avatāra' (in whom a complete manifestation of Viṣṇu has occurred, with all his powers, knowledge, etc.). With respect to the latter, the Śrī Vaiṣṇava School, for example, accepts all ten descended forms as the direct vibhava, or manifestation, of Vāsudeva or Nārāyaṇa. As another example, the Gauḍīya Vaiṣṇava School believes Kṛṣṇa to be the source of all other avatāras and as 'Mahā-Viṣṇu' himself. In this respect, it is similar to the Swaminarayan doctrine that Parabrahman is the cause of all other avatāras and he himself also descends in human form. However, the significant difference is that in Swaminarayan Hindu theology, as we noted when understanding the absolute supremacy of Parabrahman, the other avatāras (Rāma, Kṛṣṇa, etc.) are metaphysically *different* entities from Parabrahman, i.e. they are īśvaras. They are certainly endowed by Parabrahman's special divinising and empowering presence during their time on earth, but they are *not* Parabrahman in being. In the other Vaiṣṇava schools, the cause of the other avatāras and the pūrṇa avatāra or vibhava, whoever and however many they may be, are ontologically the same. Thus, in Swaminarayan Hindu theology, the coming of Parabrahman *himself*, the highest existential reality, is realised as especially unique, gracious and powerfully liberative.

Secondly, after first manifesting and carrying out his desired plan on earth, Parabrahman continues to remain fully present even after returning to his abode upon completing a typical human lifespan. He does this by living on through Akṣarabrahman, whom, as we shall later see, he invariably brings with him in human form (Vac. Gaḍh. 1.71) and who takes the role of the Brahmasvarūpa Guru. This sets in motion the Guru Paramparā, an unbroken succession of enlightened Gurus through whom Parabrahman continues his liberative work. So even while the Guru is metaphysically Akṣarabrahman in entity and thus ontologically distinct from Parabrahman, he serves as the complete and perfect medium for God's love, bliss, blessings and grace, and, importantly, functions as the means to securing eternal communion with God in final liberation.

As we carefully unpack these ideas in the exposition ahead, we shall also need to address some important questions and challenges to this key Swaminarayan doctrine in order to understand it more fully. First, though, as has become the set pattern, we shall learn the significance of this doctrine in Swaminarayan Hindu theology as emphasised in Swaminarayan's own teachings from the primary revelatory text of the tradition.

Importance of Pragaṭa/Pratyakṣa Parabrahman in Swaminarayan Hindu Theology

Of all the aspects of Parabrahman discussed so far, Swaminarayan lays special stress on the importance of God being manifest {pragaṭa} and realising him as such. As we shall repeatedly encounter in his sermons, Swaminarayan often brings this belief into even sharper focus by referring to that God as being 'pratyakṣa' – literally, before the eyes. This is in direct contrast to God being 'parokṣa', i.e. beyond the eyes, as is Parabrahman's distinct, transcendental form in Akṣaradhāma and his immanent form pervading throughout the universe. And yet the two are dramatically brought together in sermons such as Vac. Loyā.7, which, as we have been seeing from the beginning of this exposition, includes an important epistemological discussion about what constitutes 'jñāna'. In fact, Swaminarayan defines 'paripūrṇa jñāna {perfect or complete theological knowledge}' in that discussion as

> to know and see with such an understanding of greatness that the God who dwells within all [material and spiritual realities] as their inner-controller and as their cause is the very God who is *manifest before the eyes*. (emphasis added)

What is also interesting here, especially when offering a definition of 'perfect theological *knowledge*', is the equal emphasis laid by Swaminarayan on 'knowing' and 'seeing'. It is not enough, then, to merely *know* God as being manifest 'before the eyes', but it is equally necessary to *see* him, that is, to be among him, allowing a direct and personal relationship with him.[58] It is therefore unsurprising that the statement used in our formulation of theological knowledge at the start of this chapter follows the excerpt above and includes a further hint about that relationship by

[58] Very soon below we shall also learn the converse, that merely *seeing* God in manifest form is insufficient; one must perfectly *know* him as well.

mentioning to 'singularly serve' {ananyapaṇe seve} that visible form. As a reminder, it reads:

> Such a jñānin is one who singularly serves God manifest before the eyes – who eternally has a form – realising him as transcending Prakṛti-Puruṣa and Akṣara, and as being the cause and support of all. Such understanding constitutes jñāna, and such jñāna leads to ultimate liberation.

If in Vac. Loyā.7 Swaminarayan urges that the parokṣa form of Parabrahman, which is immanent and pervasive, is the same as the one manifest before the eyes (i.e. pratyakṣa), in Vac. Pan.7 he stresses that that pratyakṣa form is the same as the parokṣa form of Parabrahman, which is distinct and transcendental in Akṣaradhāma.

> Those who realise this esoteric truth understand the human form of God on this earth as being exactly the same as the form of God residing in Akṣaradhāma; they do not feel that there is even a slight difference between that form and this form. One who has known God in this way can be said to have known God perfectly.

Wishing to emphasise the worth of this realisation still more, Swaminarayan adds:

> If, by chance, a person possessing such firm upāsanā of the manifest form of God before the eyes – never doubting any māyā to be present in that form of God – were to behave unbecomingly due to the influence of bad company or due to the influence of his own past karmas, even then he would attain liberation. (Vac. Pan.7)

In both Vac. Pan.7 and Vac. Loyā.7, Swaminarayan uses the soteriological imperative to emphasise the essentiality and primacy of such 'perfect' and 'ultimate' theological knowledge. This becomes a recurrent theme throughout the Vacanāmrut, where Swaminarayan reiterates the need to know, serve and engage with the manifest form of God:

- to overcome māyā (e.g. Vac. Gaḍh. 1.24, Gaḍh. 1.71, Kār.9, Gaḍh. 2.8, Gaḍh. 2.13, Var.5, Jet.1);
- to purify the self (e.g. Vac. Gaḍh. 1.38, Gaḍh. 2.13);
- to realise the self (e.g. Vac. Var.11);
- to realise Parabrahman (e.g. Vac. Kār.12, Gaḍh. 2.13, Var.11);
- and to secure ultimate liberation (e.g. Vac. Gaḍh. 1.3, Kār.7, Gaḍh. 2.8, Gaḍh. 2.21, Gaḍh. 2.32, Gaḍh. 2.35, Var.10, Var.12, Gaḍh. 3.2, Gaḍh. 3.7, Gaḍh. 3.36, Jet.4).

In fact, Swaminarayan invariably mentions both God and Guru alongside each other in important soteriological statements, referring variously to the latter by such terms as 'Sant', 'Sādhu', 'Satpuruṣa' and 'Bhakta', and usually qualified as 'God's Sant', 'God's Sādhu', 'Parama-Bhāgavata Sant', 'Ekāntika Sant', 'Ekāntika Bhakta', 'Uttama {Highest} Bhakta', 'Perfect Bhakta' and similar modifiers, depending also on the context.[59] For example, in Vac. Gaḍh. 2.21 – traditionally titled 'The Main Principle' – Swaminarayan begins by asserting that the form of God and his Bhakta before one's eyes {pratyakṣa} should be realised as being equally great as the past (i.e. parokṣa) avatāras of God, i.e. Rāma, Kṛṣṇa, etc.,[60] and his past sādhus, i.e. Hanumāna, Uddhava, etc.[61] 'If a person realises [this], then nothing remains to be understood on the path of liberation.' To stress this further, Swaminarayan immediately goes on to say:

> Whether this principle is understood after being told once, or after being told a thousand times; whether it is understood today, or after a thousand years, there is no option but to understand it.

Swaminarayan then explains the fruit of understanding this key principle.

> A person who has such a firm conviction has grasped all of the fundamental principles. What is more, he will never fall from the path of liberation.

Swaminarayan concludes the sermon with the yet more emphatic statement:

> Thus, the essence of all of the scriptures is this very fact. (Vac. Gaḍh. 2.21)

We shall be developing this topic and the role of the Brahmasvarūpa Guru with more soteriological context at its proper place in Chapter 11 on liberation. Here, we can briefly mention that liberation can take not only a post-mortem form, of eternal communion with Parabrahman in Akṣaradhāma, but can also be a state of enlightened living while still inhabiting the mortal body. Related to this latter state, Swaminarayan indicates in other sermons that knowing and developing resolute faith in God in human form here on earth leads to a sense of complete spiritual fulfilment and a feeling of heightened bliss. Devotees rejoice in the

59 To help with this identification, I also capitalise the terms related to the Brahmasvarūpa Guru, in keeping with terminology used for, for example, Christ and Buddha.

60 Swaminarayan clarifies and adds to this in Vac. Gaḍh. 2.9, as cited earlier, by saying that 'one should realise the manifest God that one has met' to be not a form of the past avatāras, but 'to be the avatārin, the cause of all avatāras'.

61 As we shall see later in this section, Swaminarayan explains the 'Sant' is actually Akṣarabrahman.

assurance that they have nothing left to accomplish and that their ultimate liberation is secured – indeed, it is already actuated – for the God they will meet and reside with after death in Akṣaradhāma they are seeing here, now, while alive. They thus feel extremely blessed and thankful for the grace bestowed upon them in meeting and serving God in human form. Swaminarayan describes this experience as accompanied by 'extreme elation' (Vac. Gaḍh. 1.63) and continuous 'awe all day and night', such that a devotee 'will sway in an ocean of bliss throughout the day' (Vac. Gaḍh. 1.78) and 'continuously experience wonder in his heart' (Vac. Kār.8).

Such overwhelming joy is the result of not some fanciful optimism but a deep-seated internal conviction that Swaminarayan narrates in sermons such as Vac. Loyā.2. A devotee who has developed absolute faith in the manifest form of God

> does not harbour any fear of death and believes, 'I have attained before my eyes the manifest form of Puruṣottama Bhagavān, and so I am fulfilled.'

In Vac. Gaḍh. 1.63, he adds more about what that mortal fear is replaced with.

> A person with perfect faith feels within, 'I have attained all there is to attain; and wherever the manifest form of God resides, that itself is the highest abode . . . Now I have nothing more to achieve. I have attained Goloka, Vaikuṇṭha and Brahmapura.'

In this same sermon, Swaminarayan states again that after perfectly knowing God in the manifest form, one is left with 'nothing more to realise' and 'nothing more to achieve'. Elsewhere he reiterates that such a person has 'nothing left to accomplish; he is fulfilled' because 'he has reached the culmination of all spiritual endeavours' (Vac. Gaḍh. 2.13). The overriding feeling that Swaminarayan is describing is one of absolute fulfilment. It is not to be mistaken with contentment, where one is satisfied with one's lot, however meagre it may be. Rather, it is when one becomes 'pūrṇakāma' {having all desires fulfilled} and 'kṛtārtha' {having all things accomplished} because such a person has attained the highest goal possible {paramapada}, here and now (Vac. Gaḍh. 1.72, Var.12).

In stark contrast, one who has not been blessed with such a relationship with the manifest form of God, or one who has been so blessed but does not have a true understanding of him as such, is left reeling in confusion, apprehension and a gnawing feeling of insufficiency, especially tormented by misgivings about his fate after death.

> A person who has not been graced with the presence of the Sant nor graced even with the presence of the form of God will feel in his mind, 'I am ignorant, and I will not be liberated.' As is his understanding, so will be his fate after death. (Vac. Gaḍh. 1.14)

But as explained earlier from Vac. Loyā.7, it is not enough to merely *see* God in manifest form; one has to *know* and realise him perfectly for what he is. Otherwise, Swaminarayan warns in Vac. Gaḍh. 1.72, one will doubt:

> Although I have met God, will I be liberated or not?

He adds to this in Vac. Var.12 that one who has a weak understanding of God in this regard, despite being within the religious community, 'still doubts',

> Who knows whether I will be liberated or not? When I die, will I become a devatā? Or will I become a king? Or will I become a ghost?

Gunatitanand Swami therefore explains that even if one has God manifest before one's eyes (i.e. as pratyakṣa), but if one cannot recognise him and appreciate his full, unbounded glory, then that God is as good as being parokṣa {beyond the eyes} (SV 5.392).

Such a person, Swaminarayan adds, is not a perfect jñānin and will therefore not 'overcome [the cycle of] births and deaths' (Vac. Loyā.7). Even if he be 'a perfect celibate of the highest order and a great renunciant', securing liberation for him will be 'extremely difficult' (Vac. Pan.7). In fact, even if such a person 'is a sincere renunciant' and 'is vigilantly striving to eradicate lust, anger, avarice, etc.', these impurities will not be 'eradicate[d] . . . by his efforts alone'. Instead, 'ultimately, he will become impure and be consigned to naraka' (Vac. Gaḍh. 2.14). At the very most, by virtue of their other spiritual endeavours, such persons may enter the paradisiacal realms of other devas, but they will certainly not be eligible to enter the highest abode of Parabrahman (Vac. Gaḍh. 2.9, Gaḍh. 2.13). 'Therefore', Swaminarayan urges,

> one should attempt to understand this profound principle by any means within this lifetime.

Otherwise, he warns,

> in no way will one ever be redeemable. (Vac. Gaḍh. 2.13)

It might have been noticed that some of these sermons are the very same ones – often using the same excerpts with greater detail – from those cited at the beginning of this chapter when highlighting the essentiality of correct theological knowledge within Swaminarayan Hindu theology.[62] What this means is that all those statements, when read in full and with their correct semantic context, actually refer to knowing the *manifest* form of God. So, if perfectly knowing the nature of God is foundational, central and apical to Swaminarayan Hindu theology, and that nature of God is crucially of the *manifest* form of God, it therefore follows that perfectly knowing the nature of the *manifest* form of God is foundational, central and apical to Swaminarayan Hindu theology. In other words, while this doctrine is not the whole of Swaminarayan Hindu theology, it is by what all other doctrines are illumined and consummated.

Parabrahman as Manifest

But what does it mean that Parabrahman is 'manifest before the eyes'? What does understanding Parabrahman as pragaṭa or pratyakṣa involve? Here we shall unpack this essential theological doctrine and understand its various facets while, along the way, considering some of the questions and challenges that arise from accepting God as being manifest in human form.

As an initial overview, to aid and guide our progress through the rest of this section, Parabrahman as pragaṭa involves the following:

- The manifest human form of Parabrahman is the very same transcendental form resident in Akṣaradhāma, complete with all his lordship and powers
- In his human form, Parabrahman is still totally divine and unaffected by māyā
  - yet he generally conceals his divinity, out of compassion, to be accessible to his devotees
  - furthermore, he often exhibits human traits and tendencies, to be relatable to his human devotees
- Parabrahman assumes a human form out of his free, loving and gracious will
- Parabrahman manifests in human form to fulfil the wishes of his beloved, loving devotees, to liberate innumerable souls, and to establish Ekāntika Dharma, the system of praxis for devotees to secure liberation

[62] See Section 'Absolute Essentiality of Knowing God' in this chapter.

- Parabrahman is Swaminarayan, who personally descended on earth in 1781 CE
- Parabrahman remains present on earth through his Sant (the Brahmasvarūpa Guru), who is the living form of Akṣarabrahman

We now address these aspects of Parabrahman's manifestation more fully below.

Divine Embodiment of the Transcendental Form

Swaminarayan makes it abundantly clear that the form of God 'manifest before the eyes' is the very same transcendental form that eternally presides over Akṣaradhāma. Should there be any lingering doubts, he explicitly and repeatedly stresses that 'both are one', with 'no difference at all' between the two. For example:

> There is no difference at all between the manifest form of Puruṣottama Bhagavān before your eyes and the form of God residing in Akṣaradhāma; both are one. (Vac. Gaḍh. 3.38; see also Vac. Gaḍh. 3.31)

Swaminarayan adds to this by often describing the manifest form in the same terms as the transcendental form, such as being replete with all his divine light, powers and lordship. Phrases such as '*that* God', 'that *very* God' and intensifiers such as '*himself*' serve to further enunciate the identity between the two. For example:

> God, who is Puruṣottama, forever resides with a divine form in his Akṣaradhāma, whose divine light is comparable to that of millions of suns and moons. Countless millions of brahmarūpa muktas serve the holy feet of that God. *That* God, Parabrahman Puruṣottama, *himself* manifests on earth.
>
> When *that* God manifests, he is indeed accompanied by . . . all of his divine lordly powers {sarve aiśvarya}. (Vac. Gaḍh. 1.71; emphasis added)

> That God, possessing countless divine powers, *himself* becomes like a human. (Vac. Gaḍh. 3.37; emphasis added)

To cite again from Vac. Pan.7, Swaminarayan states in one part:

> One should realise the manifest form of God before the eyes to be exactly the same as the form of God resplendent with infinite lordly powers and divine light in Akṣaradhāma at the end of final dissolution.

He then immediately follows with the familiar declaration:

> One who realises this is said to have known God perfectly.

Even the excerpt from this sermon cited earlier, emphasising 'knowing God perfectly', is preceded as follows:

> That God, who has a luminous and divine form, becomes like a human . . . always doing so with all of his strength, divine powers and attendants. Those who realise this esoteric truth . . . can be said to have known God perfectly. (Vac. Pan.7)

This again helps to contextualise 'perfect theological knowledge' in Swaminarayan Hindu theology as knowledge of the *manifest* form of God before the eyes.

As we near the end of our exposition of Parabrahman, many of the descriptive statements of his nature excerpted elsewhere will resurface, as can be noticed above. This is because, in their full, they actually go on to climax by stating that that very same God – one without second, the lord of all lords who impassably reigns supreme, who is the cause of all avatāras and who transcends even Akṣarabrahman, who is the supersoul residing within all, controlling, pervading, supporting, empowering the whole universe, who is its ultimate creator, sustainer and dissolver, indeed, the doer and cause of all, and who, unbound by time and space, is replete with unlimited divine glory, knowledge, power, splendour, bliss and auspicious virtues – is he who manifests in human form on earth. This will mean that while many of these statements have already been cited elsewhere in this chapter, it will be worth revisiting some of them – even at the risk of some repetition – to see the force and clarity of this point as well as how these earlier aspects come together in providing a fuller, clearer image of the nature of Parabrahman.

For example, when discussing the all-doership of Parabrahman and his role as both the efficient cause and the material cause of the universe, we cited excerpts from Vac. Gaḍh. I.51. In the build-up to those statements, Swaminarayan carefully and sequentially delineates each of the material elements and metaphysical entities involved in the creation process, every time highlighting the causality, subtlety and pervasiveness, and therefore the superiority, of each succeeding element. After describing Akṣarabrahman, the highest among all those realities, he states:

> Beyond that Akṣara is Akṣarātīta Puruṣottama Bhagavān, who is the all-doer – responsible for the creation, sustenance and dissolution of everything – and the cause of all . . . It is this very God who . . .[63] gives darshan in a manifested form to all of the people on earth. (Vac. Gaḍh. I.51)

[63] A small phrase has been elided here (and in similar excerpts in this discussion) so to not prematurely reveal the answer to a question we shall be asking very soon hereafter.

In another discourse, Swaminarayan wishes to state simply that 'Puruṣottama Bhagavān manifests on earth'. How he explains this at length perfectly demonstrates the point being made here. He says:

> Puruṣottama Bhagavān transcends Akṣara. By his wish, countless millions of brahmāṇḍas are created, and by his powers, these brahmāṇḍas are supported. That God is distinct, yet is immanently present within everything, and while being immanent, is still distinct from everything. He dwells within each and every atom in his antaryāmin form just as he is in his manifest form before the eyes. Without that God's wish, not even a blade of grass is able to flutter. He is responsible for creating, sustaining and dissolving countless millions of brahmāṇḍas and for all the pain and pleasure the beings encounter therein. All that God does is all that happens. It is *this* God who manifests on earth. (Vac. Gaḍh. 1.78; emphasis added)

When in Vac. Loyā.18 Swaminarayan asks the fundamental question,

> What is the form of that God like?

he answers with an extensive description of Parabrahman's divine, exceedingly brilliant and incomparably blissful form. After various examples and counter-examples to accentuate his point, he returns to the idea of that very same God manifesting in human form, confirming that

> even though God appears to be like a human, that form still has the aforementioned luminosity and bliss. Those who are adept in the [yogic] practices of meditation {dhyāna}, concentration {dhāraṇā} and contemplative absorption {samādhi} see that very form as having the light of millions and millions of suns. (Vac. Loyā.18)

In Vac. Gaḍh. 3.38, Swaminarayan reverses the order of his statements while still maintaining the tenor of his point. This sermon has already been mentioned earlier in this section, but it is noteworthy in its fuller context for the additionally important clarification it provides about the manifest form of God as not an avatāra but the avatārin.

> There is no difference at all between the manifest form of Puruṣottama Bhagavān before your eyes and the form of God residing in Akṣaradhāma; both are one. Moreover, this manifest form of Puruṣottama Bhagavān before your eyes is the controller of all, including Akṣara. He is the lord of all lords and the cause of all causes. He reigns supreme, and he is the avatārin of all avatāras. (Vac. Gaḍh. 3.38)

Amid these emphatic statements, it is important to not lose sight of the fact that Parabrahman still never vacates his place in Akṣaradhāma; he does not *move* from there to be manifest on earth. That distinct form remains as it is, eternally presiding over the highest abode where innumerable liberated souls continue to enjoy his divine communion. Even more so, then, this serves to underscore the enormity and uniqueness of Parabrahman's manifestation on earth, among bound beings, where his form is real and full, and diminished not in the slightest by human corporeality. It is to this aspect of Parabrahman's manifest form, and the associated questions, that we now turn.

Absolute Divinity of the Embodied Form

Parabrahman's manifestation on earth is real and full. The very same transcendental God of Akṣaradhāma is he who manifests on earth in human form. An important clarification that Swaminarayan makes with regard to this is that Parabrahman does not *become* human *per se*, but *assumes* a human form, or, as he says, 'becomes like a human' (e.g. Vac. Gaḍh. 1.72). By doing so, Parabrahman does not forfeit any part of his inherent nature. He remains, as he is in his abode, absolutely divine and untouched, unsullied by māyā.

Indeed, if it is the 'very same' transcendental Parabrahman of Akṣaradhāma who manifests himself on earth, replete with all his divine powers, light and lordship – 'without the slightest difference' – it should evidently follow that he is as divine and untouched by māyā on earth as he is in his abode. Swaminarayan makes this point clear in Vac. Gaḍh. 3.31.

> The same form that is in Akṣaradhāma – which transcends the qualities of māyā [i.e. is gunātīta] – is manifest before the eyes. There is no difference between the two. Just as the form in the abode is gunātīta, the human form is also gunātīta. (Vac. Gaḍh. 3.31)

That is to say, both forms are equally divine, equally transcendental of māyā.

Yet it is also true that Parabrahman at least *assumes* a human form. What is one to make of that? Is his 'body' of flesh and bones like that of any other human being? Is it to be considered material? Swaminarayan explains in Vac. Gaḍh. 1.71 that it is not, because 'when Puruṣottama Bhagavān manifests on earth, all entities that he accepts become divine' by his own overwhelming divine nature. Therefore, he adds, 'the three bodies, i.e. gross, subtle and causal; the three states, i.e. waking, dream and deep sleep; the ten senses; the five life-breaths; etc.' may all be *apparent* in the manifest form, and 'although all of them appear to be like those of ordinary humans', in reality, they are all divine, 'not māyic'. Swaminarayan's point is that there can be no material-spiritual dichotomy to be found in

God's human form; it is *all* 'Parabrahman'. It is, he explains analogously, 'like an image made of pure sugar crystals'; it is entirely sweet, 'with no scope for any part being worthy of disposal' (Vac. Pan.7, Gaḍh. 2.17; see also Vac. Var.7).

This effectively answers the charge that if Parabrahman has a human form then he will necessarily be sullied and limited by all the imperfections and limitations of human corporeality. As Swaminarayan has explained, a human form for God is not detrimental to his perfect nature because even the material elements of that body are divinised and subsumed within God's complete, eternally divine being. It is for this reason also that I have avoided using the term 'incarnation' for the manifestation of Parabrahman in human form, because, strictly speaking, it is not 'God become flesh'.

It may also have been noticed at the other junctures where Parabrahman's perfect nature has been challenged – when he is immanent within māyā and the whole universe as their inner soul or material cause, or as the doer of all actions, or even in his distinct human-shaped form in Akṣaradhāma – Swaminarayan has repeatedly stated that Parabrahman is 'sadā divya', i.e. *eternally* divine, and immutable and the very same at all times (e.g. Vac. Kār.7, Kār.8, Gaḍh. 2.10, Gaḍh. 2.17). This necessarily includes Parabrahman's time on earth.

In Vac. Gaḍh. 2.49, Swaminarayan more specifically addresses the divinity of this human form by contrasting it with other forms.

> There is a great difference between the form of God manifest before the eyes and other, māyic forms. However, those who are ignorant and those who are utter fools consider God's form and māyic forms to be the same.

This expectedly leads to two difficult questions: If Parabrahman is indeed fully divine in his manifest form – complete with all his powers, light and lordship – why is that divinity not (always and fully) visible? And if he is not really human like other beings, why, then, are human features and traits visible in him?

Swaminarayan answers both questions in an extensive sermon he delivers in Vac. Pan.4. It is worth working through that sermon and following his line of explanation. Swaminarayan begins by stating:

> When that [transcendental] God assumes the form of a human being, he behaves exactly like a human.

He elaborates on this by explaining that God assumes the same lifespan, strength and all the outer appearances of a normal human being passing through the phases of life, from birth, childhood, youth and old age, to eventually death. These outer similarities are accompanied by inner human tendencies, which Swaminarayan describes extensively, including in a list of twenty-eight human traits that incorporates such shortcomings as lust, anger, avarice, arrogance and jealousy. He clarifies, though, that despite God's human appearance and behaviour, his inherent divinity is not totally indiscernible. 'One who is intelligent', he explains, can discern that even though such human tendencies are apparent in God,

> they certainly are not like those possessed by other humans. An intelligent person realises that there is something divine about that God, and with this understanding, he develops the conviction of him being God.

If that is the case, Swaminarayan anticipates a query from his audience.

> Then you may say, 'If someone develops the conviction of God on noticing something divine, then if he were to display much divinity, many people would develop such conviction.'

Swaminarayan is effectively asking our first question: Why does God not display his full divinity if it helps in people realising him as God?

He answers this most directly when he draws upon two famous incidents, one from the Mahābhārata and the other from the Bhāgavata-Purāṇa. He firstly narrates:

> When Kuntājī invoked Sūrya [the deity of the sun] using the mantra given by Durvāsā, Sūrya came to Kuntājī in a human form just like Kuntājī's own form. As a result, she was able to enjoy his intimacy and thus conceived Karṇa.[64] In actuality, Sūrya is extremely luminous; if he had come with all of his light, Kuntājī would have been burnt to death, and she would not have been able to enjoy his intimacy. Also, when Sūrya used to come to Satrājīta Yādava, he came as a human.[65] But when he came to Kuntājī and came to Satrājīta, did he leave his place in the sky? In reality, he did remain in the sky; but assuming another form, that very same Sūrya came to Kuntājī and Satrājīta. Moreover, there was just as much luminosity in that form as there is in the sun, but he suppressed that luminosity and came as a human.

Then moving on to the point at hand he explains:

> In the same way, if God were to present himself to beings with all of his divinity, then humans would not find it suitable, and they would wonder, 'Is this a ghost, or what?' Therefore, God suppresses his own divine powers and presents himself exactly like a human. But at the same time, he still

[64] See Mahābhārata, Vana Parva 290–1. [65] See BP 10.56.3.

> remains present in his own abode. Only when God manifests as a human are people able to see him, touch him, and offer the nine types of devotion to him. If God does not become like a human and instead behaves with complete divinity, then people would not be able to develop affection or feelings of affinity for him.

Swaminarayan explains very clearly here that God does not abandon his original divine form, but, deliberately, and only temporarily, conceals his full divinity. He has good reason to, he explains. It is so that he can become accessible and adorable to ordinary beings and they in turn can relate to him, developing that personal, intimate relationship that we have learned is an essential aspect of 'perfect theological knowledge'. To reiterate this vital point, Swaminarayan explains the reasoning further.

> Those belonging to the same category {sajātīya} develop affection towards each other, but not towards those belonging to different categories {vijātīya}. Similarly, God suppresses his divinity and becomes exactly like a human so that his devotees can develop affection for him. He does not exhibit his divinity. His exhibiting divinity would place him in a different category, and as a result, devotees would not be able to develop affection and affinity towards him. It is for this reason that when God appears in human form, he remains extremely mindful of ensuring his own divinity is concealed.

Swaminarayan then cites the famous example of Arjuna when Kṛṣṇa revealed to him his 'universal form' {viṣvarūpa}, as narrated in the eleventh canto of the Bhagavad-Gītā. Arjuna did not enjoy seeing the divinely magnificent form, and became agitated instead. Only when Kṛṣṇa presented himself in a human form again was Arjuna appeased and 'returned to his senses' (BG 11.51). Swaminarayan thus concludes:

> Therefore, only when God behaves like a human does a person find it suitable; otherwise he would not. (Vac. Pan.4; see also Vac. Gaḍh. 1.72)

Swaminarayan makes it decidedly clear, then, that it is the conscious and supremely loving and compassionate choice of God to become as human-like as possible – while remaining exactly as he is – so that humans can relate to him and love him, which would otherwise be impossible. It seems it is more important to God that humans can grow to love him than be impressed by his lordly powers. We shall elaborate upon the nature and efficacy of this choice in the following section, but here we can say that in order to become so relatable and endearing, Parabrahman must necessarily conceal his transcendental powers (Vac. Gaḍh. 1.78) and positively 'exhibit' all the same outer appearances and inner tendencies – flaws, failings, foibles and all – of a typical human being (Vac. Gaḍh. 1.72),[66] even at the very real risk of being perceived by the ignorant as being 'just like any other human' (Vac. Gaḍh. 1.58, Loyā.18, Vac. Gaḍh. 2.65, Vac. Amd.4). This is why the (full) divinity of God when he is manifest before the eyes is not (always) perceivable, but the humanity is.

If we return to our two questions, the above explanation provides the answer from God's side as to why *he* does not reveal his divinity and exhibits human traits instead. There is an equally important and useful answer to be yielded when we reframe the questions to lay the burden of responsibility on humans: why is it that *humans* cannot see that divinity in the manifest form of God and instead see only the human traits?

Swaminarayan provides answers for this in Vac. Pan.7, another extensive sermon rich in imagery and an extended analogy, which, again, we shall follow in detail corroborated with excerpts from other sermons.

He begins with a familiar statement:

> One should realise the manifest form of God before the eyes to be exactly the same as the form of God resplendent with infinite lordly powers and divine light in Akṣaradhāma at the end of final dissolution. One who realises this is said to have known God perfectly.

It is true, though, that not everyone has such a realisation of the manifest form of God. Swaminarayan therefore explains:

> However, when an ignorant person looks at that manifest form of God before the eyes with a māyic vision, he perceives a human like himself. Just as he himself is born, becomes a child, becomes a youth, becomes old and dies, in the same way, he believes God to undergo the same process. But when one sincerely worships God having faith in the words of the Ekāntika Sant of God, one's māyic vision is resolved. Thereafter, one realises that same form of God as being the supreme conscious being, characterised by eternal existence, consciousness and bliss.

Here Swaminarayan has clearly distinguished those who are ignorant, whose perception of God's fully divine reality is clouded by their māyic vision, and the devotees who have learned from the Brahmasvarūpa Guru how to correctly see and serve that God.

Swaminarayan then goes on to explain these two types of audiences using an elaborate version of the 'classical Indian rope trick' as an analogy.

[66] Swaminarayan adds in several other sermons (e.g. Vac. Gaḍh. 1.3, Gaḍh. 1.47, Gaḍh. 1.78, Loyā.9, Gaḍh. 2.10, Gaḍh. 2.17, Gaḍh. 2.35, Gaḍh. 2.39, Gaḍh. 2.58) that for the discerning devotees, even these 'weaknesses' and the apparently human behaviour of God become worthy of narrating, extolling and remembering, for they are just as auspicious and carry just as much liberative force.

> For example, an adept magician arms himself with weapons and ascends to the sky to fight against the warriors of the demons, the enemies of Indra. Then, having been cut to pieces, he falls to the ground. Thereafter, the magician's wife gathers those pieces together and burns herself on his funeral pyre. After a short while, the magician appears out of the sky, armed with weapons, exactly as he appeared before. He then asks the king for a reward and requests, 'Please return my wife.' Having seen such an astonishing performance, if one is unable to comprehend the 'māyā' [i.e. mystery or amazing powers] of even a magician, how, then, can the yogic powers {yogamāyā} of God possibly be comprehended? One who does comprehend the 'māyā' of the magician realises: 'That magician has not died, nor has he been burnt; in reality, he is exactly the same as he was before.' In a similar manner, one who is said to have perfectly realised the nature of God understands God to be immutable[67] and imperishable, absolutely unchanging. (Vac. Pan.7)

This idea is taken up again in Vac. Amd.4, where Swaminarayan explains the seemingly incomprehensible mystery of God's human manifestation further. He firstly describes the 'mystification' or 'confusion' {bhrahma} of those who are not devotees and who, having an unfavourable or atheistic intelligence {nāstika mati}, allege that God, too, passes through birth and death, just like themselves, and his body is the result of an accruement of karmas, just like their own. They thus 'superimpose' their own māyic transformations onto God. To this, Swaminarayan contrasts the devotees who, with their favourable, theistic intelligence {āstika mati},

> realise the understanding of the atheists to be wrong. They know the body of God to be eternal, and that the birth, childhood, youth, old age and death of God, as well as whatever other bodily traits he may display, are his līlā {intended sport}. This is because time and māyā are not powerful enough to have any sort of influence on God's body. In fact, all transformations that do appear to occur in God's body are all due to his yogic powers. (Vac. Amd.4)

Swaminarayan also rebuts here the non-believers' challenges about Parabrahman's human form. Ordinarily, a human body is necessitated by, and its nature and development are governed by, the good and bad deeds performed over previous lives. But Swaminarayan clarifies that Parabrahman's manifestation is not compelled or determined by karma,

[67] The original term here is 'akhaṇḍa'. Considering the context and how it is used more widely throughout the Vacanāmrut, the more consistent translation here would not be 'indivisible' but 'eternal' or 'immutable'. I have chosen the latter since 'avināśī' {imperishable or indestructible} follows immediately.

nor is his human form detrimental to his perfect nature. He manifests independently, by his own free will, or 'līlā' as he calls it.

Returning to Vac. Pan.7, Swaminarayan similarly concludes:

> One who has such an understanding is not confused about God in any way.

Throughout both sermons, Swaminarayan's use of the magician's astonishing and mystifying act points to the wondrous and otherwise incomprehensible mystery of that transcendental, wholly divine, immutable and eternal Parabrahman manifesting in human form, apparently being born, changing and eventually dying. He explains this is possible by God's freely willed application of his 'yogamāyā' {yogic powers}, which he juxtaposes with the magician's own 'māyā' or amazing powers. 'If one is unable to comprehend the "māyā" of even a magician, how, then, can the yogamāyā of God possibly be comprehended?' However, moving on to the audience now, Swaminarayan qualifies that those 'who are aware of the magician's techniques' – such as his wife, children and assistants – are not at all 'bewildered' and realise that the magician has neither been severed nor died; 'in reality, he is exactly the same as he was before'. Similarly, those devotees with the correct theological understanding of Parabrahman's divine, eternal and immutable nature realise him to be 'exactly the same as the form of God resplendent with infinite lordly powers and divine light in Akṣaradhāma'.

Here, it is important to note, Swaminarayan is also positioning the erroneous perception {ayathārtha jñāna} of God, born of the seer's own ignorance {māyā}, against correct and complete theological knowledge {yathārtha paripūrṇa jñāna} made possible by the Ekāntika Sant, the Brahmasvarūpa Guru. The 'māyā' therefore referred to in the magician's act is not to be misconstrued as suggesting that God's 'show' of human traits is somehow illusory, in the sense of being a deception or a falsehood. Rather, it is explaining the seer's veil of ignorance that obstructs or distorts the reality that God is unborn, unchanging and undying, divine, unlimited and transcendental. Those who are freed of this veil have the unhindered vision to see the reality as it is.[68]

Properly understood, then, both sets of answers to our pair of questions combine to explain that Parabrahman manifests in his human form concealing his divine powers and instead, by his yogic powers, exhibits human

[68] This is the form of revelation discussed in Section 'Revelation as Unveiling of the Soul' in Chapter 3, where the soul is 'de-veiled' of its ignorance to behold God fully. See also the passage from Vac. Loyā.18 cited earlier in this section.

traits. Those who have the correct theological knowledge can appreciate the absolute divinity of that manifest human form, while others cannot.

Divine Embodiment by Free Will and Loving Compassion

Parabrahman chooses to manifest on earth ontologically unchanged, to offer no less an experience to his human devotees, but in a form that makes him accessible, appreciable and adorable. Having learned this much from the previous section, we proceed now to understand that fully divine manifestation in human form as a freely willed act of God's loving compassion.

We begin by referring to a question asked to Swaminarayan in Vac. Gaḍh. 1.78, a sermon in which he calls upon his younger, student-sādhus to pose various questions to him. One such student asks:

> God transcends Akṣara; he is beyond mind and speech; and he is imperceptible to all. Why, then, can everyone see him as manifest before the eyes?

It is a natural question, especially when Swaminarayan has previously extolled the absolute transcendental nature of Parabrahman. Underlying the question seems to be the query that if Parabrahman is so divine, transcendental and imperceptible to the mind and senses, and it is that same eminently distinct form which manifests on earth, then that too should be similarly imperceptible. Otherwise, if it is perceptible, it cannot be the same transcendental form.

Swaminarayan duly replies:

> God – who transcends Akṣara, who is beyond mind and speech, and who is imperceptible – himself, out of compassion, resolves: 'May all the enlightened and unenlightened people on earth behold me.' Having resolved in this manner, God – whose will always prevails – becomes perceivable to all people on earth out of compassion. (Vac. Gaḍh. 1.78)

Swaminarayan thus explains that Parabrahman is indeed how you describe him – transcendental and truly beyond the full grasp of the mind and senses – yet it is by his own free, compassionate will {saṅkalpa} that he makes himself perceptible to the people on earth.

Another similar question triggered the discussion in Vac. Gaḍh. 1.51. Swaminarayan was asked:

> All of the senses and inner faculties are māyic. God, however, transcends māyā. How, then, can one cultivate the conviction of God through the māyic faculties? Also, how can one perceive God with one's māyic eyes and other senses?

Swaminarayan first sought to clarify and corroborate the question by asking:

> Māyic objects can be realised by māyic means, and if one has realised God through the same māyic faculties and senses, then it implies that God must also be māyic. That is your question, is it not?

The audience confirmed:

> Yes Mahārāj, that is precisely our question. You have clarified it for us.

Swaminarayan then embarked on an extensive elucidation of the utter supremacy of Puruṣottama with respect to the other elements and entities within the creative process (which we touched upon earlier). He then concludes:

> It is this very God who, out of compassion, for the liberation of the jīvas, gives darshan in a manifested form to all of the people on earth.

Again, we see a conscious, compassionate act by Parabrahman to present himself to all those on earth. What is especially striking, again, is that Swaminarayan emphasises it is 'this very' supremely transcendent Parabrahman who has made himself available to those who are incapable of availing him, 'out of compassion', 'for the[ir] liberation'. They could in no way rise up to reach him, and so he 'stoops down' to uplift them.

Parabrahman's manifestation on earth as an act of supreme grace is made clearer when we recall from Vac. Pan.4 the earnest supplication of 'all of the Brahmās, Viṣṇus and Maheśas' who beseech Parabrahman to grace them with his audience. Even as the great lords of the brahmāṇḍas, Swaminarayan describes them as 'utterly insignificant' before Parabrahman (Vac. Gaḍh. 3.39). And yet, rather than visit these lords in their higher realms, that supremely transcendental God chooses to manifest on earth among humans.

The climax of God's loving compassion is that before such 'utterly insignificant' souls, Parabrahman, too, makes himself equally insignificant in order to be accessible to them. Swaminarayan continues in Vac. Gaḍh. 1.78 to emphasise this dramatic contrast between Parabrahman's inherent powers and the 'modest' form he graciously assumes. After listing the transcendental features of Puruṣottama Bhagavān's nature – he transcends Akṣara, by whose mere wish countless millions of brahmāṇḍas are created, without whose wish not even a blade of grass is able to flutter, etc. – and clarifying that it is '*this* God who manifests on earth' (emphasis added), he immediately says:

> Yet, when that very God mounts a horse, it appears that the horse is carrying him; though, in reality, it is God who is the upholder of the horse. Furthermore, when God sits on the earth, it seems that the earth is supporting God; yet, in reality, it is God who supports the entire earth along with its mobile and immobile forms of life. Moreover, at night, the light of the moon, an oil lamp or a torch allow one to see God; or during the day, the light of the sun allows one to see God. In reality, however, it is that God who provides light to the sun, the moon and the flames of fire. Such are the magnificent powers of God. Despite this, though, God has become like a human for the sake of the liberation of the jīvas. (Vac. Gaḍh. 1.78)

Swaminarayan thus impresses upon his audience the magnanimity and utter graciousness of Parabrahman in manifesting on earth in so modest a human form. It is an act, he explains, born of God's free, loving and supremely compassionate will.

Purpose of Divine Embodiment

Parabrahman's love, compassion and grace become even more appreciable by understanding the reasons for his manifestation, for the important question of 'Why?' still remains to be answered. Why does Parabrahman so manifest in human form on earth and continue to remain present? Even if he can – without injury to his perfect nature – why should he? What is his purpose {prayojana} in making himself so relatable and endearing?

Three objectives are discernible from Swaminarayan's sermons.

Firstly, as the many afore-cited excerpts have already iterated, Parabrahman manifests on earth to grant ultimate liberation to countless souls. To add one more statement:

> It is that same supreme Puruṣottama Bhagavān who manifests on this earth out of compassion, for the purpose of granting liberation to the jīvas. (Vac. Gaḍh. 3.38)

Related to this is the second reason for Parabrahman's manifestation on earth: to establish dharma. Swaminarayan clarifies that this is not merely the moral injunctions codified in the śāstras enjoining people of various classes {varṇa} and stages {āśrama}. Rather, the purpose of God's manifestation is to establish the more comprehensive Ekāntika Dharma (Vac. Gaḍh. 2.46, Gaḍh. 3.21), of which the aforementioned is only a part.

Ekāntika Dharma, also known as Bhāgavata Dharma, is a fourfold system of theological praxis defined by Swaminarayan that individuals need to observe to please God and thereby secure their liberation. It comprises (1) dharma – leading a righteous life by observing the moral codes of the śāstras;

(2) jñāna – realising oneself to be the ātman, distinct from the body; (3) vairāgya – being dispassionate towards worldly pleasures; and (4) bhakti – offering selfless devotion to God while realising his greatness.

The third reason why Parabrahman personally manifests on earth is so that he can personally fulfil the wishes of his beloved, loving devotees. Swaminarayan reveals this in Vac. Kār.5 when he asks:

> God assumes a form on earth to grant liberation to the jīvas, but is he not capable of granting liberation while remaining in his abode, without assuming a form? After all, God can grant liberation in any manner he wishes. What, then, is the purpose of him assuming a form on earth? Furthermore, if God can only grant liberation when he assumes a form, and he is incapable of granting liberation otherwise, it would suggest that much of a weakness in God. But in reality, God is capable of granting liberation to the jīvas by assuming a form, and he is also capable of granting liberation to the jīvas without assuming a form. So, then, what is the purpose of God assuming a form on earth? That is the question.

The question itself is a classical interrogation related to God's descent or manifestation on earth. The Vacanāmrut notes that many senior sādhus in the assembly answered Swaminarayan's question according to their understanding but none to his complete satisfaction. An interactive discourse ensued, wherein Swaminarayan raised doubts to their answers and ultimately refuted them. The sādhus then 'folded their hands and requested, "O Mahārāj, only you are capable of answering this question"'. Swaminarayan thereafter explained:

> The very purpose for which God assumes a form is this: Having surrendered himself to the loving devotion of those devotees who have intense love for him, God assumes whichever form the devotees wish for in order to grant them bliss. Whatever wishes those devotees may then have, he fulfils all of them. Since the devotees are physical and have bodies, God also assumes physicality and becomes like a person with a body, and showers affection upon those devotees. In addition to this, he hides his powers and behaves with the devotees as a son, or as an intimate companion, or as a friend, or as a relative. Because of this, the devotee may not maintain much protocol with God. Nonetheless, God showers his affection upon the devotee in whichever manner he desires.

'Thus', Swaminarayan concludes,

> the very purpose God assumes a form is to fulfil the desires of his loving devotees. Along with this, he grants liberation to innumerable other jīvas and also establishes dharma. (Vac. Kār.5)

While Swaminarayan includes the other aforementioned two reasons at the end of this sermon, he seems to be giving primacy to the third by twice referring to it as the 'very purpose'. This may be due to the vital importance he lays on the personal relationship between Parabrahman and individuals. As we shall see later, it this intimate loving relationship with the manifest form of God before the eyes that is central in the practice of Ekāntika Dharma and by which liberation of the soul is possible. In this sense, then, all three reasons are inextricably tied together.

What is also striking from this sermon is that while Parabrahman manifests for the benefit and uplift of everyone, it is for his loving devotees that he offers himself most unreservedly. Swaminarayan uses the phrase 'ādhīn thaine' to describe how Parabrahman surrenders himself or, literally 'becomes supported by', the devotion of those devotees who love him intensely. Within the tradition, this is regarded as an especially significant aspect of this doctrine: He, who is the grand support and ontic ground of all {sarvādhāra}, willingly becomes 'supported' {ādhīna} by the love of his otherwise feeble devotees. He, by whose mere wish countless millions of brahmāṇḍas are created, sustained and dissolved, and without whose wish not even a single blade of grass is able to stir, readily submits to the wishes of his mortal devotees, surrendering his wishes and actions to them in order to fulfil *their* will, not his. He, who is supremely divine and characterised by pure existence, consciousness and bliss, and who is replete with unlimited lordly powers, deliberately conceals that divinity and instead assumes a modest, physical form, just like that of his devotees, so that they can relate to him as *they* prefer. He is aware that this may – and often does – result in a breach of proper decorum with him. But that is insignificant to him. What *is* vitally important to him is that he, personally, is present on earth to receive their love and reciprocate it, personally.

Parabrahman Manifest in Human Form as Swaminarayan

The exposition of Parabrahman as found in the Swaminarayan tradition comes to its full culmination and concreteness in the person of Swaminarayan. The first and best way to examine this is to consider Swaminarayan's own words from the Vacanāmrut where he reveals himself as such. This revelation is confirmed, clarified and consolidated by Gunatitanand Swami in the Svāmīnī Vāto, and attested to by many others in the scores of voluminous texts and diaries and thousands of kīrtanas {hymns} from the tradition's corpus. The limited nature of this exposition will not permit a study of all of these sources. In any case, it is certainly not the remit of this introduction to prove or disprove Swaminarayan's claim to Godhood. Here, we are concerned only with the theological nature of Parabrahman in Swaminarayan Hindu theology, and need only to draw from our already established theological texts.

It needs to be acknowledged first, though, that Swaminarayan spoke of himself in varying ways, reportedly in accordance to the receptivity and spiritual maturity of his varying audiences.[69] These and other factors would need to be properly understood in their full contexts before a complete and accurate theological picture can emerge about Swaminarayan from these texts or any one text or statement alone. He was, nevertheless, unequivocal in his most profoundly revelatory statements. For example, from many of the statements cited in this chapter discussing the various aspects of Parabrahman, it may have been noticed that they invariably contained references to Parabrahman as 'this manifest form' or 'manifest before the eyes' or, even more directly, 'manifest before *your* eyes', and similar. Swaminarayan is evidently referring to himself as he spoke these words to his audience at the time. Some of these important statements include the following:

> God eternally possesses a form. He is the creator, sustainer and dissolver of countless brahmāṇḍas; he is forever present in his Akṣaradhāma; he is the lord of all lords; and it is *he* who is *this manifest form before the eyes*. (Vac. Gaḍh. 3.35; emphasis added)

> He [Puruṣottama Bhagavān] transcends both kṣara [i.e. māyā, jīvas and īśvaras][70] and Akṣara; he is the cause of all causes; and countless millions of akṣararūpa muktas worship his holy feet. Out of compassion, *that very same God* is manifest *now* and *visibly present before your very eyes* for the purpose of granting ultimate liberation to jīvas. (Vac. Gaḍh. 3.31; emphasis added)

> It is the same master of that [Brahmapura] abode – the lord of Akṣara and the muktas, Parabrahman Puruṣottama – who is present *here* in *this Satsaṅga fellowship*. (Vac. Amd.6; emphasis added)

If the above statements identify Swaminarayan with the distinct, luminous and supremely sovereign Parabrahman resident in Akṣaradhāma (i.e. vyatireka), the following identify him with that same transcendental being who is also immanent {anvaya} within every being and thing.

[69] Brahmadarshandas offers an extensive analysis of these statements in his *Vacanāmrut Rahasya*, vol. II, pp. 257–333. To this, Shrutiprakashdas adds a useful historical perspective and contextualises several other sampradāyic sources in another in-depth interrogation in *Svāminārāyaṇ Sampradāymā Avatār-Avatārī Nirūpaṇ*, pp. 241–451.

[70] See note 99 in Section 'Soul of All Beings and Things', this chapter.

> [Puruṣottama Bhagavān] dwells within each and every atom in his antaryāmin form just as he is in his manifest form *before the eyes*. (Vac. Gaḍh. 1.78; emphasis added)

> One should think of the greatness of God in the following way: 'I am the ātman, while the manifest form of God *before the eyes* whom *I* have met is Paramātman . . . That Paramātman forever resides in my ātman'. (Vac. Sār.1; emphasis added)

Here he reveals himself as the omniagent and omnicause:

> God fully resides in the heart of a person who possesses the following understanding: 'The earth remains stable and trembles; the stars remain steady in the sky; the rains fall; the sun rises and sets; the moon appears and disappears, waxes and wanes; the vast oceans remain constrained within their boundaries; a drop of liquid develops into a human possessing hands, feet, a nose, ears and the rest of the ten senses; the clouds, through which lightning strikes, float unsupported in the sky – these and a countless variety of other wonders are due only to the form of God that *I* have attained.' With this understanding, he has the conviction that no one except the manifest form of God is the cause of these wonders. He realises, 'The countless wonders which have occurred in the past, those which are currently taking place, and those which will occur in the future are all only due to the manifest form of God that *I have met before my eyes*.' (Vac. Gaḍh. 1.27; emphasis added)

In the following statements, Swaminarayan identifies himself as the avatārin, the cause of all of the avatāras.

> One should realise the visible {sākṣāt} form of God that one has met to forever possess a divine form and to be the avatārin, the cause of all avatāras. (Vac. Gaḍh. 2.9)

> It is this Puruṣottama [residing within the divine light of Akṣaradhāma] who transcends Akṣara and who is the cause of all avatāras . . . Realise that the form amidst the divine light is indeed *this Mahārāj visible before you*. (Vac. Gaḍh. 2.13; emphasis added)

> All of the avatāras of God manifest from the very God who is present in *this Satsaṅga fellowship*. That is to say, he is the cause of all of the avatāras and is the indwelling controller of all. (Vac. Amd.6; emphasis added)

Swaminarayan brings many of these aspects together in Vac. Gaḍh. 3.38. After describing God as true, divine and extremely luminous, as characterised by eternal existence, consciousness and bliss, and as resident in Akṣaradhāma in a two-armed human-like form where he is served by the liberated souls upon whom he bestows his supreme bliss, he goes on to conclude, speaking directly to his audience:

It is *that* same supreme Puruṣottama Bhagavān who manifests on this earth out of compassion, for the purpose of granting liberation to the jīvas. He is *presently visible before everyone*, he is your chosen deity {iṣṭadeva}, and he accepts your service. In fact, there is no difference at all between the manifest form of Puruṣottama Bhagavān before your eyes and the form of God residing in Akṣaradhāma; both are one. Moreover, this manifest form of Puruṣottama Bhagavān before your eyes is the controller of all, including Akṣara. He is the lord of all īśvaras and the cause of all causes. He reigns supreme, and he is the avatārin of all the avatāras. He is worthy of being worshipped single-mindedly by all of you. The many previous avatāras of this God are also worthy of being paid obeisance and are worthy of reverence. (Vac. Gaḍh. 3.38; emphasis added)

Swaminarayan also spoke explicitly about himself in the first person. For example, in Vac. Amd.7, he reveals the following by way of describing his yogic journey through various realms and abodes:

I went alone to the abode of Śrī Puruṣottama Nārāyaṇa, which transcends everything. There, I saw that it was I who am Puruṣottama; I did not see anyone eminent apart from myself. In this manner, I travelled to these places [the various realms and abodes] and finally returned to my body.

Then, when I looked within again, I realised that I am the creator, sustainer and dissolver of all of the brahmāṇḍas. In those countless brahmāṇḍas, it is by my divine light that countless Śivas, countless Brahmās, countless Kailāsas, countless Vaikuṇṭhas and Golokas, Brahmapuras, as well as countless millions of other realms are all radiant.

And what am I like? Well, if I were to shake the earth with the toe of my foot, the earths of countless brahmāṇḍas would begin to shake. It is also by my light that the sun, the moon, the stars, etc. are radiant.

Several texts of the tradition also carry a statement from Swaminarayan found in old manuscripts. In it, he is believed to reveal his ontological identity and the liberative purpose of his manifestation on earth in human form. It reads:

While other avatāras had manifested to fulfil a particular task, my manifestation is to make souls brahmarūpa and grant them ultimate liberation. That is why I, Puruṣottama who transcends even Akṣara, have become like a human.[71]

As we saw in the previous section, this is outlined as one of the three purposes of Parabrahman's divine embodiment on earth.

[71] Nandkishor Swami, *Ātyantika Kalyāṇa* (Bhuj, India: the author, 1958), p. 76. A very similar statement can be found in one of Swaminarayan's few extant letters written to his lay and monastic devotees. See Madhavlal Dalsukhram Kothari (ed.), *Śrījīnī Prasādīnā Patro* (Ahmedabad: the editor, 1978), 7.

Throughout this section, I have relied on simply presenting the statements from the Swaminarayan tradition's principal theological text with little or no commentary, hoping that the statements themselves, already of quite considerable length, would adequately elucidate the point being made about the revelation of Swaminarayan as Parabrahman. All that needs to be said in conclusion is that based on these and other such statements and sources, those of the Swaminarayan religious community confess their faith in Swaminarayan as being the human form of Parabrahman manifest on earth during the relatively recent and short period of time between 1781 and 1830 CE. 'Swaminarayan' therefore becomes the name of choice for followers of the tradition by which to identify and worship Parabrahman, hence the name of the tradition itself.[72]

Continued Presence of Parabrahman through Akṣarabrahman

Our chapter on Parabrahman, especially the aspect of his manifestation on earth, is not quite complete. We earlier established that one of the distinguishing features of Swaminarayan Hindu theology was that Parabrahman – distinct from and the cause of all avatāras – himself manifests on earth in human form and, vitally, that he chooses to remain present ever thereafter.

How does he do this? If Swaminarayan was only present on earth from 1781 to 1830, how does Parabrahman remain present to continue his liberative work after that period? Crucially, to whom do the evocative words of 'God manifest before your eyes' apply now, today?

These tantalising questions can only be properly answered after our exposition of Akṣarabrahman is complete, so it is to this which we now promptly turn.

[72] Bhadreshdas elucidates upon the nomenclature of the 'Swaminarayan' School, or Svāminārāyaṇa Darśana, in MuU-SB 3.2.11, p. 306.

CHAPTER 7

Akṣarabrahman

When we began Part II with an overview of the Swaminarayan tradition's metaphysics, we noted that an immediately distinguishing feature of the system is its *five* eternal entities (or realities) – Parabrahman, Akṣarabrahman, māyā, īśvara and jīva – in contrast to other systems, which generally have one, two or three. One of the metaphysical entities of Swaminarayan Hindu theology with which readers might be unfamiliar is Akṣarabrahman, known also as Akṣara and Brahman. Specifically, we noted that it raised a number of important and difficult questions of the system, such as:

1. Is the 'Brahman' of the Swaminarayan School the same 'highest reality' as that of the other schools?
2. If so, then what/who is 'Parabrahman'?
3. If not – and 'Parabrahman' is the name simply applied to what others call Brahman – then what/who is this other 'Brahman'?
4. Are there *two* 'highest realities' in the Swaminarayan School? Clearly not, for this, by definition of the superlative, is implausible. But then how are 'Brahman' and 'Parabrahman' related? Indeed, how are the two distinct?

During the process of our exposition of Akṣarabrahman in this chapter, we shall be answering all of these questions in some detail. We shall begin with the last question, which, in many ways, will help answer the rest as well as others about the nature, function and significance of Akṣarabrahman. While it will not be possible to raise and address all of the debates here concerning Akṣarabrahman, especially when introducing it for the first time in such a theological context, all of the major themes shall nonetheless be covered using the key textual sources of Swaminarayan Hinduism. As before, though, it will be helpful to our progress through this chapter if we first have an initial outline.

Akṣarabrahman is ontologically the second-highest entity, transcendent to everything, including māyā, except Parabrahman. It serves in the following four forms:

- As the abode of Parabrahman – the divine, luminous realm called Akṣaradhāma,[1] which is presided over by Parabrahman in his distinct transcendental form, and which also holds the innumerable liberated souls {akṣara-muktas} who enjoy there the eternal unlimited bliss of Parabrahman.
- As a sevaka in Akṣaradhāma – the ideal devotee, human in form, forever residing in Akṣaradhāma as an exemplar to all other liberated souls.
- As Cidākāśa – the all-pervading conscious space supporting countless millions of brahmāṇḍas.
- As the Brahmasvarūpa Guru – the human form on earth whom Parabrahman brings with him when he manifests in person and through whom Parabrahman lives on and continues his work of liberation. The Guru leads jīvas and īśvaras to the liberated state of brahmarūpa (or akṣararūpa), wherein they experience the undisturbed bliss of Parabrahman.

Akṣarabrahman as Ontologically Distinct from Parabrahman

Our first task will be to establish Akṣarabrahman as a metaphysical entity ontologically distinct from Parabrahman. Why does Swaminarayan Hindu theology feel the need to have another, discrete entity – apart from the highest entity Parabrahman – when other schools of Vedānta have managed without it? Crucially, is there scriptural support for such an entity within the Vedānta canon?

To adequately answer these very important questions, we shall need to conduct a focussed study of the three primary Vedānta texts – the Brahmasūtras, Upaniṣads and Bhagavad-Gītā – and their Swaminarayan readings. As we learned in the Prolegomenon and when introducing the sources of Swaminarayan Hindu theology, all doctrines of the tradition must conform to a valid interpretation of these canonical texts if they are to be deemed authentic. Any deviation from this sacred revelation would render the doctrines invalid.

[1] Swaminarayan occasionally refers to Akṣaradhāma by various other names, including Brahmadhāma, Brahmapura, Brahmaloka and Brahmamahola.

For this limited inquiry, I have chosen to examine three passages from the Vedānta canon that are rich in content about 'Akṣara' and 'Brahman', offering ample opportunity for exegetical analysis and debate. These passages are the following:

1. 'akṣarāt parataḥ paraḥ' from the Muṇḍaka Upaniṣad (2.1.12), which invites a discussion from the Brahmasūtras (1.2.21–24);
2. the eighth chapter of the Bhagavad-Gītā, beginning with Arjuna's question at verse 8.3, 'What is that Brahman?'; and
3. verses 15.16–18 of the Bhagavad-Gītā, which discuss 'kṣara', 'akṣara' and 'uttama puruṣa'.

To test the validity of these passages as they are understood within the Swaminarayan tradition, each interpretation will need to meet the rigorous hermeneutical rules developed within the Vedānta system itself. Chief among these hermeneutical devices is a set of six tools which are collectively known as the ṣaḍ-liṅga, or 'six clues'. These are famously presented in a Sanskrit verse that reads:

Upakramopasaṃhārāvabhyāso'pūrvatā phalam |
Arthavādopapattī ca liṅgam tātparyanirṇaye ||[2]

That is, to determine the import {tātparyanirṇaya} of a text treated within a particular section {prakaraṇa}, one must check for

1. opening {upakrama} and ending {upasaṃhāra} – consistency between what is stated in the introduction and at the conclusion;
2. repetition {abhyāsa} – what is stated repeatedly;
3. novelty {apūrvatā} – what is novel or stated in a novel way as compared to other sections;
4. fruit {phala} – what the fruits stated relate to;
5. commendation {arthavāda} – what is commended (or condemned); and
6. reasoning {upapatti} – what is logically argued for or against.

Of these six tools, the first, relating to semantic consistency, is considered of prime importance and especially inviolable in determining the sense and coherence of a text.[3] By employing these long-established and widely used

[2] Sāyaṇa Mādhava, *Sarvadarśanasaṅgraha* (Pune: The Bhandarkar Oriental Research Institute, 1924), pp. 405–6.

[3] Van Buitenen asserts in his notes to Rāmānuja's *Vedārthasaṃgrah* that of the six 'canons of exegesis ... by which the right interpretation is determined', 'the most important are upakrama and upasaṃhāra: the latter may never be in conflict with the former in order to establish the ekavākyatā [i.e. consistency, literally "one-statementness"] of a context'. Van Buitenen, *Rāmānuja's*

tools,[4] particularly semantic consistency, to scrutinise our three chosen passages, we shall be able to determine the validity of their readings in the Swaminarayan tradition and thereby the scriptural basis for the ontological distinction between Parabrahman and Akṣarabrahman. Thus conducted, this study offers a valuable opportunity to classically test a doctrine that is central to Swaminarayan Hindu theology.

Muṇḍaka Upaniṣad 2.1.2: akṣarāt parataḥ paraḥ

The Muṇḍaka Upaniṣad belongs to the Atharva Veda and is considered one of the principal Upaniṣads in Brahmanical discussion.[5] It comprises sixty-four verses over three chapters, themselves called muṇḍakas, with each muṇḍaka being further divided into two parts, called khaṇḍas.

The first part of Chapter One introduces brahmavidyā, 'the knowledge that is the basis of all forms of knowledge' (MuU 1.1.1), by tracing its transmission from Brahmā (not to be confused with Brahman) to his eldest son Atharvan, then successively on to Aṅgir, Bhāradvāja Satyavāha, Aṅgiras and, finally, Śaunaka, 'the wealthy householder'. In the ensuing dialogue between the last two, Śaunaka asks:

> O venerable [Aṅgiras], by knowing what can all else be known? (MuU 1.1.3)

Vedārthasaṅgraḥ, annotated trans. and critical edn (Poona: Deccan College Postgraduate and Research Institute, 1956), p. 200 n134.

Richard De Smet in his pioneering work *The Theological Method of Śaṃkara* elucidates upon each of the six exegetical tools in helping to determine the meaning of a text. In elaborating upon the first tool, he cites chapter six of the Chāndogya Upaniṣad as an example. He then concludes: 'Such clear beginnings and ends are the best sign of the intention of the śruti [Vedic verse or text]'. Richard de Smet, *The Theological Method of Śaṃkara* (Rome: Pontifical Gregorian University, 1953), pp. 207–08 cited in Julius Lipner, *The Face of Truth* (Albany: State University of New York, 1993), p. 150 n38.

[4] Sāyaṇa Mādhava mentions that this set of tools was 'demonstrated by the earlier ācāryas' (Mādhava, *Sarvadarśanasaṅgraha*, p. 405). Indeed, exponents of each of the major schools are known to have applied these tools to advance their arguments. Rāmānuja, for example, cites them repeatedly in his *Vedārthasaṅgraha*. Śaṅkarite commentators such as Akhaṇḍānanda (fourteenth century), Vidyāraṇya (fourteenth century) and Govindānanda (sixteenth century) have also used them, as has the Bengali scholar of the Svābhāvikabhedābheda School, Mādhava Mukundadeva (sixteenth century). As a result, the verse has since found its place in several encyclopaedic glosses of the Vedānta system. For example, see: Tārānātha Bhaṭṭācārya, ed., *Vācaspatyam*, 7 vols (Varanasi: Chaukhamba, 1962), vol. II, p. 1199; Bhīmācārya, ed., *Nyāyakośa*, 4th edn (Pune: Bhandarkar Oriental Research Institute, 1973), p. 158; and *Viśiṣṭādvaitakośa*, ed. by Lakṣmītātācārya, 6 vols (Melukoṭe: Saṃskṛta Saṃśodhana Saṃsat, 1983), vol. III (1989), pp. 211–12.

[5] Three of the twenty-eight adhikaraṇas in the Brahmasūtras that directly discuss Brahman are devoted to the Muṇḍaka Upaniṣad. Śaṅkara alone cites it 129 times in his *Brahmasūtrabhāṣyam*. Paul Deussen, *Sixty Upaniṣads of the Veda*, trans. by V.M. Bedekar and G.B. Palsule, 2 vols (Delhi: Motilal Banarsidass, 1980), vol. II, p. 569.

In reply, Aṅgiras defines two types of knowledge {vidyā} – lower {aparā} and higher {parā}. The lower knowledge, he explains, includes learning of the four Vedas and their auxiliary disciplines: phonetics, metrics, grammar, etymology, astronomy and ritual science. In contrast:

> The higher knowledge is that by which 'akṣara'[6] can be realised. (MuU 1.1.5)

The immediately following verse describes 'akṣara' as

> invisible, intangible, without lineage and without caste, without eyes or ears, and without hands or feet; eternal, pervading, omnipresent and exceedingly subtle.

It then concludes:

> That which is immutable, the wise perceive as the source of all beings. (MuU 1.1.6)

The remaining verses in this first part of the Muṇḍaka Upaniṣad continue to describe that 'akṣara'.

In the second part of the first chapter, a comparison unfolds between the two knowledge-types, specifically describing the transient fruits of purely ritualistic Vedic karma. It ends with another mention of the higher brahmavidyā. Thus, the first chapter serves as a foreword to the continuing elucidation of brahmavidyā.

The second chapter opens with a descriptive verse narrating the process of creation and dissolution in relation to 'akṣara':

> This is the truth: As from a blazing fire, sparks of like form issue forth by the thousands, similarly, O dear [Śaunaka], beings of various forms issue forth from akṣara and return to it only. (MuU 2.1.1)

Immediately thereafter, we find a turn in subject. With the following verse begins the description of [Parama]Puruṣa, the supreme person:

> Divine and formless is Puruṣa; residing without and within, unborn. Without breath and without mind, pure, he is. (MuU 2.1.2)

The remaining portion of this verse reads in Sanskrit:

> **akṣarāt parataḥ paraḥ |**

6 We shall leave the term 'akṣara' un-translated since its interpretation is the very core of this discussion.

This seemingly simple phrase, Bhadreshdas argues, holds the key to unlocking a correct, consistent reading of the entire Muṇḍaka Upaniṣad and perhaps other texts too.

While it is clear that 'paraḥ', an adjective qualifying Puruṣa, means 'high' and that 'parataḥ', an indeclinable adjective also meaning 'high', is following akṣara in the ablative case, at the core of our discussion lies this unresolved term 'akṣara'.

Etymologically, 'akṣara' is derived from the verb 'kṣiṇ', meaning 'to wane' or 'to perish'. The negating 'a' prefix thus relates 'akṣara' to 'imperishable'.[7] But even so, the term can equally serve as an adjectival noun, an adjective and a proper noun, just as 'brown', for example, in English can refer to the actual colour brown, the quality describing something of brown colour and Mr Brown, respectively. Which of these applies to 'akṣara' in the phrase above?

We find a major clue to the answer in Vac. Gaḍh. 1.64, where Swaminarayan states:

> Puruṣottama is greater even than Akṣara who is greater than all else.

This appears to be a direct translation of the phrase in MuU 2.1.2. Swaminarayan's statement gains meaning as an interpretation, however, when we realise from its surrounding context that 'akṣara' here is being used as a proper noun – not an adjective or adjectival noun – thus implying a distinct and unique metaphysical entity called 'Akṣara'. This would be a 'conventional' {rūḍha} use of the term, as opposed to an etymologically derived {vyutpanna} one, since its significance as meaning 'imperishable' is rendered secondary. But if this is so, and – crucially – semantic consistency is to be maintained, then that would mean that this same Akṣara is also the 'akṣara' described in the preceding verses as 'the source of all beings' (MuU 1.1.6), and from what all things spring forth and (ultimately) return (MuU 2.1.1). This is indeed the case within Swaminarayan Hindu theology. At least twice in the Vacanāmrut Swaminarayan describes Akṣara as 'the cause of all' (Vac. Gaḍh. 1.63 and Gaḍh. 2.3) and a further three times as wherein all things return at the time of dissolution (Vac. Gaḍh. 1.12, Kār.7 and Bhūgoḷ-Khagoḷ).

[7] Van Buitenen, in tracing 'the career of *akṣara*' through Vedic texts, emphasises its meaning as 'syllable', and later as relating to the creative syllable 'aum'. He rejects its literal meaning as 'imperishable', but accepts that it becomes a descriptor of another being or entity – an adjectival noun. 'Akṣara', *Journal of the American Oriental Society*, 79.3 (1959), 176–87.

Furthermore, in the opening section of the Vedaras, his long, doctrinally rich letter to his monastic disciples, Swaminarayan's description of Akṣara matches MuU 1.1.6 virtually verbatim. It reads:

> And that [Akṣarabrahman] is invisible, ungraspable, and intangible; it is without lineage, without eyes, without ears, without hands and without feet; it is eternal, pervading, omnipresent, exceedingly subtle and immutable; and that Brahman is the cause for the creation of all living beings. (VR 17)

Thereafter at the very end of the Vedaras, Swaminarayan reiterates:

> And the creator and dissolver of the whole world ... is Akṣarabrahman. (VR 213)

But this raises an inevitable question: If Akṣara is the cause of all and to what all returns, does this not undermine the supremacy and ultimate causality of Parabrahman? Apparently not. In line with MuU 2.1.2, Swaminarayan explains in Vac. Gaḍh. 2.3:

> Parabrahman, that is Puruṣottama Nārāyaṇa, is distinct from Brahman, and is also the cause, support and inspirer of Brahman.

Parabrahman is therefore still superior to Brahman, and the ultimate cause of all, including Brahman.

Swaminarayan emphasises the supremacy of Parabrahman/Puruṣottama over Brahman/Akṣara on several other occasions also. We noted a few of these in the section on Parabrahman as Akṣarātīta.[8] As a reminder, here is one such statement:

> This manifest form of Puruṣottama Bhagavān before your eyes is the controller of all, including Akṣara. He is the lord of all iśvaras and the cause of all causes. He reigns supreme. (Vac. Gaḍh. 3.38)

Thus, despite Akṣara having such an exalted status, the supremacy and ultimate causality of Puruṣottama are in no way diminished or challenged. If anything, Puruṣottama's supremacy is raised even higher, for he is, as the MuU phrase explains, 'greater even than Akṣara, the greatest'.

It is this ontologically distinct-yet-connected relationship between Brahman and Parabrahman within Swaminarayan Hindu theology that helps in consistently interpreting the Muṇḍaka Upaniṣad from beginning

[8] See Section 'Transcendent to Akṣara' in Chapter 6.

to end. MuU 1.1.5, for example, begins with a definition of the lower knowledge. The verse then states

> And now the higher [knowledge],

which initiates an extended description that continues until MuU 1.2.11. These verses describe both Akṣara and the higher Puruṣa, i.e. Puruṣottama. After urging the aspirant to seek a Brahmasvarūpa Guru in MuU 1.2.12 –

> To realise that [higher knowledge], imperatively surrender, with sacrificial wood in hand, to only that Guru . . . who is Brahman[9]

– MuU 1.2.13 then brings the two together as pertaining to brahmavidyā:

> And that enlightened [Guru] comprehensively reveals that brahmavidyā . . . by which Akṣara and Puruṣa are truly known.[10]

That is, for the Swaminarayan tradition, both Akṣara (Brahman) *and* Puruṣottama (Parabrahman) are the subjects of brahmavidyā, the highest knowledge. (We shall return to this conceptualisation of brahmavidyā in the next section when elaborating upon BS 1.1.1.)

This is reiterated at the end of the Muṇḍaka Upaniṣad with an interestingly novel concept being introduced. Verse 3.2.1 states:

> The wise and desire-free who know that highest abode Brahman – which is resplendent with light and wherein all resides – and offer upāsanā to Puruṣa, transcend the seed of this [transmigratory life].

Brahman is described here as the 'abode'. As we have initially learned and shall discuss at greater length soon,[11] in the Swaminarayan tradition, Akṣarabrahman also serves as the transcendental abode of Parabrahman. Moreover, this verse corresponds to arguably the central doctrine of Swaminarayan Hindu theology: realising oneself as Akṣara and worshipping Puruṣottama. Swaminarayan brings both of these points together in

[9] This verse is explained in full according to MuU-SB 1.2.12, pp. 253–6 further on in this chapter when discussing Akṣarabrahman as the Brahmasvarūpa Guru. See Section 'Akṣarabrahman as Brahmasvarūpa Guru' in this chapter.

[10] This passage in Sanskrit reads:

> Yenākṣaram puruṣam veda satyam provāca tām tattvato brahmavidyām |

It will be noticed that there is no explicit term for 'and', such as 'ca' or 'tathā'. However, since 'akṣara' here is not an adjective or adjectival noun – but, as we have seen, is evidently denoting the *distinct* Akṣarabrahman – the subjects of brahmavidyā delineated in this verse are both 'akṣara' *and* 'puruṣa'. Hence, 'and' becomes a natural and necessary part of the articulation of this verse. See MuU-SB 1.2.13, pp. 256–7.

[11] See Section 'Akṣarabrahman as Parabrahman's Abode' in this chapter.

many discourses that closely agree with the aforementioned MuU 3.2.1. For example, in Vac. Loyā.12 he explains:

> Countless millions of brahmāṇḍas, each encircled by the eight barriers,[12] appear like mere atoms in Akṣara. Such is the greatness of Akṣara, the abode of Puruṣottama Nārāyaṇa. One who offers upāsanā to Puruṣottama realising oneself as this Akṣara can be said to have attained the highest level of resolute faith.

This faith, Swaminarayan explains, leads to 'ultimate liberation' from the cycle of births and deaths (e.g. Vac. Kār.7, Loyā.7). And this liberation is the fruit of brahmavidyā commended and described in further detail in the subsequent, final verses of the Muṇḍaka Upaniṣad (3.2.9–10). This provides a neat conclusion {upasaṃhāra} to the topic of brahmavidyā that saw its introduction {upakrama} in MuU 1.1.1.

We thus notice here in the Muṇḍaka Upaniṣad all six tools, or 'clues', of exegetical analysis coming into play: repetition, novelty, fruit, commendation, reasoning and, most significantly, consistency throughout the beginning and end.

Each of these tools is also employed by Bhadreshdas in his concluding comment at the end of the Adṛśyatvādhikaraṇa (BS 1.2.21–24), which takes its cue from the opening of MuU 1.1.6. Initially, as his prima facie viewpoint, he offers pradhāna of the Sāṃkhya School, the individual soul, Akṣarabrahman and Parabrahman as possible contenders for that which is qualified by invisibility, etc. (MuU 1.1.6), i.e. 'akṣara'. He quickly rejects the first two options, arguing that the qualities of omniscience, etc. and world-causality mentioned later, in MuU 1.1.9, could not possibly apply to the insentient pradhāna or the limited soul. After explaining over the three sūtras how it can apply to Akṣarabrahman, he finally asks: But why can 'akṣara' not be denotive of Parabrahman? Surely all the qualities apply to him, as he is invisible, etc., omniscient, and also the cause of the world. Furthermore, 'akṣara' can simply be an adjective to Parabrahman, for he is, of course, imperishable. So why the need to introduce another entity distinct from Parabrahman?

Bhadreshdas firstly acknowledges that this is a natural question for 'those who are unaware of the entity of Akṣarabrahman' and therefore 'have an impoverished understanding of the actual denotation of revealed words'. He then goes on to demonstrate by employing the six

[12] The eight barriers {aṣṭāvaraṇa} are (1) pṛthvi, (2) jala, (3) tejas, (4) vāyu, (5) ākāśa, (6) mahattattva, (7) Pradhāna-Puruṣa and (8) Prakṛti-Puruṣa.

hermeneutical tools that it is necessary and proper to accept Akṣarabrahman as the subject of MuU 1.1.6 because only then will the integrity of the entire Muṇḍaka Upaniṣad text be possible, especially with the explicit reference in MuU 2.1.2 to the higher-than-highest Puruṣa transcending this Akṣara – the superiority {paratva} of the former over the latter itself confirming the distinction between the two.[13]

If a semantically consistent interpretation throughout the Muṇḍaka Upaniṣad is possible in the Swaminarayan tradition, it is because of this belief that Akṣarabrahman is a unique metaphysical entity ontologically distinct from Parabrahman and subordinate to him. In turn, for the Swaminarayan tradition, the Muṇḍaka Upaniṣad helps canonically validate this distinction between Akṣarabrahman and Parabrahman.

Bhagavad-Gītā 8.3: kim tad brahma

The eighth chapter of the Bhagavad-Gītā is an especially fitting text for examination in this study of Akṣarabrahman for two primary reasons: firstly, the Bhagavad-Gītā has brahmavidyā as its running theme;[14] and secondly, the eighth chapter is focussed on Akṣarabrahman, hence titled 'Akṣarabrahmayoga'.

The chapter begins with a string of seven questions posed by Arjuna that have arisen from the terminology and teachings offered by Kṛṣṇa at the end of the previous chapter (BG 7.29–30). The first of Arjuna's questions is: What is 'Brahman' {kim tad brahma}?[15]

The answer begins with a brief reply in BG 8.3. The relevant portion of the verse reads in Sanskrit:

> Akṣaraṃ brahma paramaṃ |

With 'parama' the superlative meaning 'highest' or 'greatest', we are left with a number of options for interpreting 'akṣara' depending on its connection with 'brahma'. The term also appears elsewhere in the chapter. In particular, we are interested in how it is interpreted towards its end.

[13] BS-SB 1.2.24, pp. 78–9. See also MuU-SB 2.1.2, pp. 260–1.

[14] The colophon at the end of each chapter of the Bhagavad-Gītā includes 'brahmavidyāyām yogaśāstre', revealing the dialogue between Kṛṣṇa and Arjuna as a yogic text dealing with brahmavidyā.

[15] The term 'brahma', derivatives of 'brahma' (e.g. brāhmī) and compounds involving 'brahma' (e.g. brahmabhūta and brahmanirvāṇa) appear in several verses in the Bhagavad-Gītā prior to this point, i.e. in 2.72, 4.24, 4.25, 4.31, 5.6, 5.10, 5.11, 5.20, 5.21, 5.24, 5.25, 5.26, 5.27, 5.28 and 7.29. This also seems to have triggered Arjuna's curiosity for this term.

In BG 8.21, 'akṣara' is described as 'paramā gati' {highest goal or place}, and the following:

> It is my highest abode {dhāma} from which, having attained, none revert.

The last verse of the eighth chapter (8.28) also mentions reaching the 'highest place' {param sthānam}.

In the Swaminarayan tradition, where 'Akṣara' and 'Brahman' are synonymous,[16] the following excerpt from the Vedaras reads like a gloss on BG 8.3:

> Now to expound upon the term 'Brahman'. That Brahman is entwined in everything . . . and is called Akṣarabrahman. (VR 152)

Earlier in the letter, another statement links this with BG 8.21 and 8.28. Swaminarayan writes:

> And that abode {dhāma} in the form of Akṣara is higher than the high {parāt-para}. (VR 146)

In the Vacanāmrut, too, Swaminarayan makes several references to Akṣara as the abode of Puruṣottama, for example,

> That Akṣara is the abode of Puruṣottama Bhagavān (Vac. Gaḍh. 1.63),

and as the highest abode or ultimate goal (Vac. Gaḍh. 1.21, Gaḍh. 3.21 and Amd.7), a place from where there is no return to the cycle of births and deaths (Vac. Sār.14). This thus confirms that, according to the Swaminarayan reading, 'Akṣara' in BG 8.3 refers to Akṣarabrahman, which does indeed serve as the abode of God,[17] as stated in BG 8.21 and is semantically consistent until the end of that chapter. Importantly for our study here, since Parabrahman presides over Akṣaradhama, *his* abode, this verifies Parabrahman and Akṣarabrahman as two distinct entities, and that the former is superior to the latter.

In his extensive comment on this opening phrase of BG 8.3, Bhadreshdas firstly explains why etymologically 'Akṣara' is a fitting name or defining term for Brahman, before going on to argue why it cannot be applicable to any other entity or sentient being. Since he draws heavily upon BG 15.16–18, which forms the third passage of our study, we shall consider those arguments there in the immediately following section.

[16] According to Bhadreshdas, the synonymy of 'Akṣara' and 'Brahman' is confirmed by BG 8.3 itself, and can also be found in the Upaniṣads, e.g. in MuU 2.2.2 and KaU 2.16 and 3.2.

[17] See Section 'Akṣarabrahman as Parabrahman's Abode' in this chapter.

What is worth mentioning here is the interesting observation Bhadreshdas makes at the very end of the eighth chapter of the Bhagavad-Gītā. He notes that the entire text can in fact be conceived as being of two distinguishable parts, with the first eight chapters speaking predominantly of Brahman, and the latter ten chapters focussing predominantly on Parabrahman. To substantiate his categorisation, he provides a summary with sample verses of each of the first eight chapters and alludes to what is to come in the remainder. He then concludes with the statement: 'Thus, this entire Gītā is imbued with [the siddhānta of] Brahman and Parabrahman.'[18]

Bhagavad-Gītā 15.16–18: kṣara, akṣara and uttama puruṣa

From 'Akṣarabrahmayoga' we move on to 'Puruṣottamayoga', the fifteenth chapter of the Bhagavad-Gītā. A relatively short chapter – comprising only twenty verses – it is nonetheless exegetically one of the more intricate because it refers so explicitly not only to the highest person, Puruṣottama (i.e. Parabrahman), from which the chapter receives its title, but also to that entity's juxtaposition with all other beings.

Three verses lie at the heart of the chapter – 15.16, 15.17 and 15.18 – and form the focus of this, the last section of our investigation. In all, the three verses discuss three types of beings – 'kṣara', 'akṣara' and 'uttama puruṣa'– as follows:

- there are two types of persons {puruṣa} in this world – 'kṣara' and 'akṣara'
- all beings are kṣara {literally, 'perishable'}
- [whereas] 'akṣara' is said to be immutable {kūṭastha; literally immovable, as if braced on or like an anvil}
- the uttama puruṣa {highest person} is different [from the above two]. He
  - is God, known also as Paramātman and Puruṣottama
  - is immutable
  - supports the whole world having entered it
  - is the highest; higher than both 'kṣara' and 'akṣara'

Again, we find sermons in the Vacanāmrut that closely agree with the metaphysical juxtaposition and description from the BG verses above. For example:

[18] BG-SB 8.28, pp. 198–9.

> And what is God like? He transcends both kṣara and Akṣara. (Vac. Gaḍh. 3.31)

> Nevertheless, when that Puruṣottama Bhagavān, who transcends both kṣara and Akṣara, assumes a human form . . . He supports both kṣara and Akṣara by his powers while he himself is different from both kṣara and Akṣara. (Vac. Gaḍh. 1.72)

More specifically, the following statement clarifies what we are to understand as 'kṣara'.

> That form of Puruṣottama – which transcends jīvas, īśvaras and Akṣara – should be understood as his transcendental form. (Vac. Sār.5)

By simple elimination, 'kṣara' thus represents all jīvas (individual souls) and īśvaras (empowered super-souls).[19]

Moving on to Akṣara, Swaminarayan calls it 'kūṭastha', just as in BG 15.16, in several of his sermons. For example, he writes:

> That Akṣara is the seer of all, the witness of all, and worthy of being known by all of the Vedas . . . It is kūṭastha and devoid of any insentience. (VR 213)[20]

Swaminarayan also emphasises the singularity of Akṣara, which corresponds with the use of 'akṣara' in singular form in BG 15.16 in contrast to the plural used for other beings. He states:

> There are many who, having realised Akṣara to be their ātman, have attained qualities similar to that of Akṣara. That Akṣara, however, is one. (VR 213–4)[21]

And finally, as in BG 15.17 and 15.18, Puruṣottama is described as different from and higher than the others. Towards the end of the Vedaras, Swaminarayan writes:

> Puruṣottama is distinct from Akṣara, is the highest person {uttama Puruṣa}, and is [known as] Paramātman, Parabrahman and Parameśvara. (VR 214)

Bhadreshdas's extensive comment on BG 15.16 actually comes in BG 8.3 when he cites the former in support of his identification of 'akṣara' in 'Akṣaraṃ brahma paramaṃ' with the entity Akṣarabrahman. There he

[19] Etymologically, 'kṣara' means 'perishable'. However, jīvas and īśvaras are eternal entities and so their classification as 'kṣara' is due to their physical embodiments, composed of māyā, which are indeed subject to birth, change and death. This is how other ācāryas have also explained this classification. See also BS-SB 1.1.2, p. 15.

[20] See also VR 171, and similarly 144, 151 and 152.

[21] See also VR 144 and 146, and Vac. Loyā.17.

suggests a number of alternative readings for 'kṣara' and 'akṣara'. After presenting their case as convincingly as possible, he rejects all of them one after the other using the qualifier 'kūṭastha' – which he explains as involving eternal and complete immutability – to assert that it cannot tenably apply to individual souls, liberated souls or any other sentient form except Akṣarabrahman.

But why can it not also apply to Parabrahman, for surely he is also entirely and eternally immutable? Bhadreshdas argues simply that the Bhagavad-Gītā itself explicitly mentions in 15.17 and 15.18 that Puruṣottama is 'different {anya}' from and 'higher {uttama}' than or 'transcendent {atīta}' to both kṣara and Akṣara, and also calls the latter Puruṣottama's 'highest abode' in 15.6 and 8.21. And since Parabrahman is explicitly distinguished from Akṣara in 15.17 and 15.18, neither can Parabrahman be accepted in 8.3, that is, 'akṣara' is not merely an adjective qualifying the imperishable (Para)Brahman. Thus, Bhadreshdas concludes, since 'akṣara' in 15.16 applies to Akṣarabrahman, it must also apply to Akṣarabrahman in 8.3 where the same topic is being discussed, thereby preserving coherency and continuity throughout the Bhagavad-Gītā text.[22]

Conclusion

Our study of the selected passages[23] from the Muṇḍaka Upaniṣad, Brahmasūtras and Bhagavad-Gītā has allowed us to scrutinise how the term 'akṣara' has been interpreted in each of these passages and if indeed by properly adhering to the classical rules of Vedāntic hermeneutics. The result of this examination has been that, according to Swaminarayan readings at least, these three passages provide canonical validation for the ontological distinction between Brahman and Parabrahman (or Akṣara and Puruṣottama) as understood within Swaminarayan Hindu theology.

In examining and understanding this distinction, we have also found much to answer many of the questions with which we began this chapter. To return to the questions briefly (in a slightly modified order to aid logical flow), we can now summarise:

[22] BG-SB 8.3, pp. 173–8. See also BG-SB 15.16–18, pp. 314–16.

[23] A similar survey of other Upaniṣadic and Gītā statements – such as 'So'śnute sarvān kāmān saha brahmaṇā vipaścitā' (TU 2.1.1), 'Anāndi mat-paraṃ brahma' (BG 13.12), 'Brahmaṇo hi pratiṣṭhā'ham' (BG 14.27), etc. – has been found to lead to the same conclusion.

4. There is only one 'highest reality' in the Swaminarayan School, not two.
1. & 2. This is known as 'Parabrahman' (or Puruṣottama).
1. & 3. The 'Brahman' (or Akṣara) of the Swaminarayan School is distinct from and subordinate to 'Parabrahman'.
3. & 4. 'Brahman' has many roles and functions. One of them is to serve as the transcendental abode of Parabrahman.

Members and proponents of Swaminarayan Hinduism will feel that theological inquiries such as these prove the tradition as being both distinctive from other Vedāntic schools yet still authentic within the Vedānta system as a whole. For us, it has provided a useful insight into the deep exegetical discussions that can ensue in Swaminarayan Hindu theology when difficult questions are raised and answered from within the tradition.

Essentiality and Centrality of Akṣarabrahman in Swaminarayan Hindu Theology

Having established Akṣarabrahman as an ontologically distinct metaphysical entity apart from and subordinate to Parabrahman, we can now move on to further understanding its role within Swaminarayan Hindu theology.

If we can briefly return to our formulation of jñāna from Vac. Loyā.7 that guided our exposition of Parabrahman, we will recall that one of the key aspects of correct theological knowledge is that Parabrahman transcends Akṣarabrahman. We noted when discussing Parabrahman as sarvopari and briefly in the previous section that Swaminarayan frequently juxtaposes Parabrahman's supremacy against the greatness of Akṣarabrahman (e.g. Vac. Kār.8, Loyā.13, Gaḍh. 2.13, Gaḍh. 3.38 and Amd.6). In summary, we learned that Parabrahman is

- greater even than Akṣarabrahman
- the cause of all, even Akṣarabrahman
- the support of all, even Akṣarabrahman
- the inspirer of all, even Akṣarabrahman
- the controller of all, even Akṣarabrahman
- pervasive within all, even Akṣarabrahman
- the soul of all, even Akṣarabrahman
- independent from all, even Akṣarabrahman

We observed that while this unequivocally stresses the impassable supremacy of Parabrahman, it also serves to highlight Akṣarabrahman's own position as being exceedingly great – indeed, as being impassable by all except Parabrahman. We can add here that this greatness is due entirely to Akṣarabrahman's relationship with and subordination to Parabrahman, and if the above summary also indicates Akṣarabrahman as one who also causes, supports, inspires, controls, pervades, ensouls and is independent, it is only by the full will and calling of Parabrahman himself (e.g. Vac. Loyā.13).

Akṣarabrahman thus provides the touchstone for knowing Parabrahman (Vac. Gaḍh. 1.63). If, then, the most accurate description of Parabrahman's limitless, unfathomable greatness is that he is simply greater than Akṣara – he is Akṣarātīta – our understanding of Parabrahman cannot have begun in earnest without having first fully understood Akṣarabrahman. In this sense, as we progress along our exposition of Akṣarabrahman, our journey to learn about God is only just beginning. Indeed, if knowing Parabrahman is absolutely essential, and the best that can be said about him is that he transcends Akṣarabrahman, it follows that knowing Akṣarabrahman is also absolutely essential – for all the reasons it is necessary to know Parabrahman, primary of which, as we learned, is for ultimate liberation.

We shall be addressing the many aspects of liberation in our final chapter in this part, but it is relevant to include here that Swaminarayan explains such liberation, both pre- and post-mortem, as a state of perfect spiritual purity and maturity, which he calls being akṣararūpa or brahmarūpa {literally, 'like Akṣarabrahman'}. Thus, liberation not only entails eradicating māyic impurities born of an ignorant, material self-understanding but, more positively, acquiring the qualities of Akṣarabrahman. Swaminarayan explains how both are made possible for a finite being in Vac. Gaḍh. 2.31.

> The jīva remains continuously attached to māyā . . . Only when one continuously associates with Brahman, one's inspirer, through contemplation – as previously described – is that attachment broken . . .
>
> If one associates with Brahman through continuous contemplation in this manner, the jīva acquires the virtues of Brahman. (Vac. Gaḍh. 2.31)

It is this constant association and spiritual connection with Akṣarabrahman, in the form of the living Guru, that we shall discuss in more detail further on.[24] For our purposes here, the above points to the essential soteriological role of Akṣarabrahman in helping devotees overcome māyā and become

[24] See Sections 'Realising Brahmavidyā by Serving the Brahmasvarūpa Guru' and 'Serving and Associating with the Brahmasvarūpa Guru by Deed, Word and Thought' in Chapter 11.

brahmarūpa. This is reiterated even more clearly in the Vedaras where Swaminarayan simply states:

> There is no path to liberation without knowing Brahman. (VR 18)

We should also recall here the soteriological purpose of Parabrahman's manifestation on earth as described by Swaminarayan himself:

> While other avatāras had manifested to fulfil a particular task, my manifestation is to make souls brahmarūpa and grant them ultimate liberation. That is why I, Puruṣottama who transcends even Akṣara, have become like a human.[25]

Swaminarayan notably brings together here the description of Parabrahman's being as transcendent to Akṣarabrahman, and his function as making souls Akṣarabrahman-like.

Swaminarayan further stresses the need for Akṣarabrahman by stressing the need to become brahmarūpa. Only then, he asserts, can one develop the highest level of resolute faith (Vac. Loyā.12) and spiritual experience (Vac. Gaḍh. 1.40), and enjoy unhindered devotion to God (Vac. Gaḍh. 1.23, Loyā.13, Gaḍh. 2.35); otherwise, all of one's spiritual understanding is rendered futile (Vac. Gaḍh. 1.44) and the result will be incessant internal turmoil (Vac. Sār.15, Gaḍh. 3.1, Gaḍh. 3.21, Gaḍh. 3.39) and certain uncertainty on the path of devotion (Vac. Sār.1, Sār.15, Loyā.17, Gaḍh. 2.30). In fact, Swaminarayan goes as far as to say in Vac. Loyā.7:

> Only one who is brahmarūpa is worthy of offering devotion to Puruṣottama.

Conversely, he reiterates in the same sermon:

> One who does not offer devotion to Parabrahman after becoming brahmarūpa cannot be said to have attained ultimate liberation.

This statement needs to be read in two ways: to secure ultimate liberation, one must offer devotion to God even *after* becoming brahmarūpa; and equally, to offer devotion to Parabrahman in order to secure ultimate liberation, one must *first* become brahmarūpa. Thus both are essential – becoming brahmarūpa *and* offering devotion to Parabrahman. As we have seen before, this is arguably the central doctrine of Swaminarayan Hindu theology: to offer devotion to Parabrahman having become brahmarūpa.

Swaminarayan and Gunatitanand Swami call a person who observes such a method of devotion a definitive (Vac. Gaḍh. 3.39), perfect (Vac. Gaḍh. 1.11)

[25] Nandkishor Swami, *Ātyantika Kalyāṇa*, p. 76.

and complete devotee (SV 3.9, 5.88), with Swaminarayan adding in Vac. Amd.2:

> He who worships God having discarded all māyic influences and become brahmarūpa is the best devotee . . . Only he who worships Parabrahman having become brahmarūpa is the best.

Drawing upon this last sermon and four others – Vac. Gaḍh. 1.23, Amd.3, Gaḍh. 2.30 and Gaḍh. 2.45 – Gunatitanand Swami further stresses that no matter how eminent one may be, 'there is no alternative in millions of eons' but to become brahmarūpa and offer devotion to Parabrahman, because 'this is the principle of Swaminarayan' (SV 3.13). In another sermon he succinctly states:

> Believing oneself as brahmarūpa and offering devotion – this is *the* conclusive principle {siddhānta}. (SV 1.59)

Thus, becoming Akṣarabrahman-like is essential, for which knowing and serving Akṣarabrahman is essential.

This essentiality and centrality of Akṣarabrahman in Swaminarayan Hindu theology is also iterated by Bhadreshdas in a way that would be useful to cover here in some detail.

In the preface to each of the volumes of his Svāminārāyaṇa-Bhāṣya, Bhadreshdas opens with a statement about the central topic of these revealed texts. He asserts that it is brahmavidyā, the knowledge of 'Brahman'. Citing the Īśā Upaniṣad and Kena Upaniṣad, he firstly explains that it is only by such 'vidyā' that ultimate liberation from the incessant cycle of births and deaths can be secured.

> By knowledge {vidyā}, one enjoys the immortal state. (IU 11)

> By knowledge {vidyā}, one attains the immortal state. (KeU 2.4)

However, Bhadreshdas observes from the Muṇḍaka Upaniṣad, as we also did in our earlier study, that there are two types of knowledge: higher and lower. It is the higher knowledge – synonymous with 'brahmavidyā' – which leads to ultimate liberation. The subject of this ultimate knowledge, as we saw, is both Parabrahman and Akṣarabrahman (or Puruṣottama and Akṣara). An important way in which this dual subjectivity is substantiated is through the exegesis of the crucial opening aphorism of the Brahmasūtras:

> Athā'to brahmajijñāsā |

> Next, therefore, the desire to know 'Brahman'. (1.1.1)

After confirming continuity from the Purva Mīmāṃsā {Former Inquiry} to the Uttara Mīmāṃsā {Latter Inquiry} by the word 'atha' {next}, and explaining the consequential import of the term 'ataḥ' {therefore}, Bhadreshdas begins to carefully dismantle the 'brahmajijñāsā' compound.

He firstly explains the genitive relationship between 'jijñāsā' {literally, 'knowledge-desire'} and 'Brahman'; i.e. it is the 'knowledge-desire of Brahman', or, more plainly, the desire to know 'Brahman'. He then continues to unpack the term 'brahma' in 'brahmajijñāsā' by stating that the latter is a type of coordinative or copulative compound {dvandva samāsa} called the ekaśesa, often translated as residual or elliptical. Such a compound allows two (or more) related words to be conjoined in the sense of 'addition' while taking the dual (or plural) form of only its final constitutive member, for example: mātā {mother} + pitā {father} = pitarau {two parents}. The morphological similarity of the two terms 'Akṣarabrahman' and 'Parabrahman' allows both to be called collectively by their common element 'brahman', also making them suitable candidates for the residual compound. Examples of this grammatical device abound in Hindu texts. For example, Rāma and Balarāma (the elder brother of Kṛṣṇa) are often referred together as simply 'Rāmau' {the two Rāmas}. Another common example, drawing on not philological similarities of the words themselves but extending to the affinity of the characters, leads Arjuna and Kṛṣṇa to sometimes be collectively known as 'Kṛṣṇau' (e.g. Mahābhārata, Ādi Parva 221.33). In the same way, 'brahmaṇī' is the conjugated form denoting Akṣarabrahman and Parabrahman. The correct grammatical resolution thus takes the form: brahma [i.e. Akṣarabrahman] + brahma [i.e. Parabrahman] = brahmaṇī {the two Brahmans, i.e. Akṣarabrahman and Parabrahman}. It is this term when inflected in the genitive case that becomes 'brahmaṇoḥ', which in turn conjoins with 'jijñāsā' to provide the full meaning of the 'brahmajijñāsā' compound: the desire to know Akṣarabrahman and Parabrahman.

Bhadreshdas adds, since Akṣarabrahman and Parabrahman are eternally by their very nature greater than all jīvas and īśvaras (even when liberated) and māyā, the name 'Brahman' {literally, 'great' or 'vast'} is wholly befitting for both.[26]

[26] When the topic first arises in the Svāminārāyaṇa-Bhāṣya of the Upaniṣads, in KaU 2.16, Bhadreshdas also explains why, etymologically, 'Akṣara' and 'Brahman' are appropriate names for Akṣarabrahman. He goes on to provide a useful overview of all four forms and the nature of Akṣarabrahman. See KaU-SB 2.16, pp. 103–11.

In support of the two types of Brahman, Bhadreshdas cites from the fifth chapter of the Praśna Upaniṣad. Here, in reply to the question posed by Satyakāma pertaining to the after-life, Pippalāda states:

> That which is the sound of 'Aum', O Satyakāma, is verily the higher and lower Brahman. (PU 5.2)

The dual classification of 'higher' and 'lower' confirms the distinction between Parabrahman and (Akṣara)Brahman, especially when the fruit of meditating on 'Aum' is described as attaining 'either' {ekatara} of them.

However, Bhadreshdas is quick to warn against carelessly ascribing either or both Akṣarabrahman and Parabrahman to wherever the term 'Brahman' appears in Vedānta texts. Rather, he insists, as always, the import of a word must be determined by carefully considering the topic of a text (whether a passage, chapter or entire work) from beginning to end, looking out also for such important hermeneutical clues as repetition, novelty, commendation, reasoning, etc. For example, just as the Sanskrit word 'saindhava' can denote both 'salt' and 'horse', its intended meaning in each instance must be ascertained by the context within which it is being used.[27] Hence, in some cases, 'Brahman' might exclusively refer to Parabrahman (e.g. TU 3.1.1) or exclusively to Akṣarabrahman (e.g. KaU 2.16), or, in some cases, it might refer to both Parabrahman *and* Akṣarabrahman (e.g. CU 3.14.1).

To corroborate his position, Bhadreshdas raises a challenge from a would-be resister. Why, he asks, cannot 'brahma' in 'brahmajijñāsā' denote Parabrahman alone? Why are you insisting on both Akṣarabrahman and Parabrahman being the subject of knowledge? Bhadreshdas defends: It is not our insistence at all, but rather the insistence of the sacred revealed texts that brahmavidyā constitutes the knowledge of both Akṣarabrahman and Parabrahman, the fact of which the Sūtrakāra is supremely aware.

At this, Bhadreshdas enters into an extensive defence of this interpretation based on the entire Muṇḍaka Upaniṣad text, employing all six of the hermeneutical tools mentioned earlier, to conclusively demonstrate how brahmavidyā must necessarily comprise both Parabrahman *and* Akṣarabrahman. After citing a total of twenty-eight verses in sequence from the Muṇḍaka Upaniṣad, each time bringing them into the context of brahmavidyā, Bhadreshdas concludes:

[27] Another example, in English, would be the word 'bat'. Whether it was being used by a zoologist or a cricketer, and in which context, would help determine what it was denoting.

> Thus, accepting both entities is certainly in consonance with revelation {śruti} and reasoning {yukti} as well as with the opinion of the Sūtrakāra. In so interpreting the texts, we are saved from maligning the letter [i.e. spirit] of the revealed texts [i.e. Upaniṣads], the letter of the sūtras and also the letter of Brahman [or Akṣarabrahman[28]].[29]

If this interpretation of 'Brahman' denoting both Akṣarabrahman and Parabrahman in BS 1.1.1 is to be valid, though, it must also hold for BS 1.1.2–4 to then be applicable for the whole of the Brahmasūtra text. These first four aphorisms, known collectively as the 'catuḥsūtrī', are effectively a text in themselves, which also set the parameters for the analysis of all subsequent sūtras. Bhadreshdas duly continues this interpretation throughout the catuḥsūtrī and the complete Brahmasūtras, and indeed the Upaniṣads and Bhagavad-Gītā as well. In BS 1.1.2, he cites several Upaniṣadic verses that point to Akṣarabrahman as well as Parabrahman being both the efficient and material cause of the universe (which we shall explore below when discussing Akṣarabrahman's nature and his role in creation, etc.).[30] Similarly, in BS 1.1.3, he cites several verses to show that, like Parabrahman, Akṣarabrahman too can only be known by scriptural testimony.[31] And in BS 1.1.4, he confirms that Akṣarabrahman, along with Parabrahman, is also the consistent subject of Vedānta, and therefore the texts need to be harmonised accordingly to bring opposing and incoherent interpretations into line.[32] Continuing with this line of interpretation until the very end, Bhadreshdas explains the final sūtra (BS 4.4.22) as proclaiming that those who realise this brahmavidyā, i.e. who know both Akṣarabrahman and Parabrahman, attain an eternal place in the abode of God, from which there is no reversion {anāvṛtti}.[33]

To conclude, the dialogue between Yājñavalkya and Gārgī in the Bṛhadāraṇyaka Upaniṣad succinctly summarises both affirmatively and negatively the result (or 'fruit') of including and excluding Akṣarabrahman from brahmavidyā. Yājñavalkya warns his fellow sage:

> In this world, O Gārgī, he whosoever without knowing Akṣara worships, makes offerings or performs austerities for many thousands of years, the fruit of all his [endeavours] will indeed be impermanent.
>
> O Gārgī, whosoever leaves this world without having known Akṣara, he is pitiful {kṛpaṇa}.

[28] This also serves as a play on words since 'akṣara' also means 'letter' in Sanskrit.
[29] BS-SB 1.1.1, pp. 4–8. [30] BS-SB 1.1.2, pp. 13–16. [31] BS-SB 1.1.3, pp. 18–19.
[32] BS-SB 1.1.4, pp. 25–9. [33] BS-SB 4.4.22, pp. 431–2.

Whereas,

> O Gārgī, whosoever leaves this world having known Akṣara, he is a brāhmaṇa [a perfect knower of Brahman, i.e. brahmarūpa]. (BU 3.8.10)

Thus, according to Swaminarayan revelatory texts and the Svāminārāyaṇa-Bhāṣya commentary upon the Vedānta canon, Akṣarabrahman has a central and indispensable role in Swaminarayan Hindu theology in helping devotees to fully know Parabrahman and reach the highest Brahman-like spiritual state for liberation here and forever after.

Nature of Akṣarabrahman

Our initial textual inquiry and subsequent study of the essential role of Akṣarabrahman in Swaminarayan Hindu theology have necessitated and therefore already resulted in the introduction of some important aspects of Akṣarabrahman's nature. These and other aspects will be developed yet further as we expound upon each of the four forms of Akṣarabrahman in the following section. However, still more needs to be said about the nature of Akṣarabrahman in a way that will lead to a more complete elucidation of this central metaphysical entity. We therefore turn our attention here to see more closely what Swaminarayan texts and the Vedānta canon have to say about the nature of Akṣarabrahman.

What is noticeable in these śāstric descriptions of Akṣarabrahman is that they are not always found in neat categories ready for easy presentation in systematic expositions. Even while listing some of Akṣarabrahman's many inherent qualities, a discussion may suddenly mention his role in creation or as the support of the world, for example. This need not hinder us particularly. Indeed, it will allow us to traverse more freely through the many passages, picking up important aspects as and when they are presented, thereby gradually building the complete theological image of Akṣarabrahman. However, it will mean that this and the following section will need to be read together to fully understand Akṣarabrahman's nature – reminding us readers again of the abiding patience necessary when attempting to grasp a complex system of ideas. Not until the very end after such long, patient and diligent reading do all the parts fit together, and our learning and satisfaction then is all the richer for it.

One Without Second

There is only one Akṣarabrahman. Swaminarayan affirms this by using the singular pronoun when referring to it in his sermons. For example, when explaining how one can develop an aversion for worldly pleasures, Swaminarayan states that part of the solution is to realise the greatness of God. A person who has such a realisation also has a fair assessment of the entire world. 'He knows', Swaminarayan explains, that

> God is like this, and these are the rewards of engaging in the worship of God and listening to religious discourses. Akṣara is like this, and the bliss associated with *him* is like this. (Vac. Loyā.17; emphasis added)

In the Vedaras, too, Swaminarayan uses the same singular personal pronoun in Gujarati ('evo') when discussing Akṣarabrahman.[34] In the last of these statements, Swaminarayan explicitly writes:

> There are many who, having realised Akṣara to be their soul, have attained qualities similar to that of Akṣara. That Akṣara, however, is one. (VR 213–4)

Gunatitanand Swami similarly states:

> Akṣara in the form of [God's] abode is only one while there are countless millions of akṣara-muktas {liberated souls in Akṣaradhāma}. (SV 5.177)

This singularity was also noted in the Bhagavad-Gītā in 15.16 for example, where 'kūṭasthaḥ' used to define Akṣara is in the singular case whereas 'all [other] beings' {sarvāṇi bhūtāni} is in the plural.

More explicitly, the Bṛhadāraṇyaka Upaniṣad proclaims Akṣara (in the form of Brahmaloka) as being simply 'eka' and 'advaita' (4.3.32), i.e. one without second. Bhadreshdas explains that this is because no other being or thing is capable of eternally holding Parabrahman and countless millions of liberated souls.[35]

Transcendent to All (Except Parabrahman)

We noted during our study of the Muṇḍaka Upaniṣad passage 'akṣarāt parataḥ paraḥ' that an almost identical statement can be found in Vac. Gaḍh. 1.64. Swaminarayan said:

> Puruṣottama is greater even than Akṣara, who is greater than all else.

[34] See, for example, VR 144, 146 and 213–4. [35] BU-SB 4.3.32, p. 258.

While this affirms Parabrahman's outright supremacy, it just as much describes Akṣarabrahman's greatness above all other entities. In his comment in MuU 2.1.2, Bhadreshdas firstly explains how 'parataḥ' can indeed qualify 'akṣarāt', 'because [Akṣara] is greater than all jīvas, īśvaras, māyā and brahmarūpa liberated souls'. He then goes on to elucidate individually how Akṣarabrahman is superior to each of these, beginning with the insentient māyā.

Akṣarabrahman is superior to māyā because he is 'the cause of the origination, etc. of the world', for which māyā is the base material. As we shall see further on in this very section, Akṣarabrahman is both the material and efficient cause of the world, controlling, inspiring and using māyā for the purpose of creation.

In relation to jīvas and īśvaras, 'who fall into the category of "kṣara"', Akṣarabrahman is superior because he

> pervades them and is their indwelling controller {antaryāmin}, support and governor; grants the fruits of their karmas . . . and creates the places, bodies, etc. of these souls whereby they can experience these fruits; serves as the bridge for those of them seeking liberation, helping them cross the ocean of misery associated with the cycle of births and deaths, and being extremely instrumental in their attaining the natural, superlative bliss of Paramātman; and makes brahmarūpa those who associate with him so that they are able to offer the highest devotion to Paramātman.

This leaves the muktas. Akṣarabrahman is superior to them because, though they have already reached this highest state, even they are 'not eternally devoid of any contact with māyā'. In fact, it is Akṣarabrahman who 'grants the liberated state to the jīvas' and, 'as the divine Akṣaradhāma', also 'serves as the support of all muktas even now [in their final, liberated state] by way of being their śarīrin, etc.'.

Bhadreshdas then goes on to provide a string of śāstric references supporting each of these ways in which Akṣarabrahman is superior to jīvas, īśvaras, māyā and liberated souls.[36]

He similarly comments on the adjective 'paramam' of BG 8.3 (also discussed in our study earlier) by explaining that Akṣarabrahman 'transcends everything except Parabrahman, i.e. all jīvas, īśvaras, māyā and all its work, and all liberated souls'. In other words, Bhadreshdas stresses, Akṣarabrahman is 'the best {śreṣṭa}'. Again, this 'eternal transcendence' over all these entities is attributed to Akṣarabrahman pervading, controlling, supporting and illuminating them, by being their cause and soul, and

[36] MuU-SB 2.1.2, p. 259–60.

because of other such qualities of excellence. Here, again, he cites several references supporting each of these points.[37]

What needs to be added here is that Bhadreshdas also uses the 'paraḥ' in MuU 2.1.2 to describe how, despite all this greatness, Akṣarabrahman is still subordinate to Parabrahman, 'because that highest Being is the governor, master, inspirer, support, śarīrin, etc. of even that great Akṣara'. Thus, Bhadreshdas adds, the name for God as 'Parabrahman' {literally, 'greater-Brahman'} is wholly appropriate, since he is greater {para} even than Brahman. Moreover, he stresses, the fact that Akṣarabrahman is greater than all else besides Parabrahman is also only because of the wish of Parabrahman, but not otherwise.[38] In support of this, he cites KaU 3.11, KaU 6.8 and TU 2.1.1, as well as such verses from the Bhagavad-Gītā as

> Brahman is eternal and transcended only by me (13.12),

and

> I am the support of Brahman. (14.27)

Together, not only do these statements serve to further establish the ontological distinction between Parabrahman and Akṣarabrahman, but they also reveal the impassable greatness of Akṣarabrahman – impassable, that is, by all except Parabrahman.

Immutable

In describing the transcendence of Akṣarabrahman, it is especially stressed by Swaminarayan that it transcends māyā. This is to be absolutely clear that Akṣarabrahman is beyond the reach of māyā's defiling and destructive influence.

One way that Swaminarayan does this is to explain Akṣarabrahman's immutability and completeness. While we had touched upon Akṣara as 'kūṭastha' in our study of BG 15.16 earlier, the topic warrants a little more attention here where we can provide further statements from sampradāyic texts that use other terms corresponding to this important concept. Swaminarayan states, for example, in Vac. Gaḍh. 2.3:

> Brahman is immutable {nirvikāra} and indivisible {niraṃśa}, that is, it does not suffer from any alterations nor can it ever be fragmented.

He similarly writes in the Vedaras:

[37] BG-SB 8.3, pp. 173–8. [38] MuU-SB 2.1.2, p. 260.

> That Akṣara is immutable {nirvikāra} and does not falter from or change its extraordinary form by way of this immutability. Therefore, that Akṣara is unfaltering {acaḷa} and constant {dhruva}. That Akṣara is eternal {nitya}. (VR 171)

This is all true despite Akṣarabrahman being immanent throughout all of māyā's work. Swaminarayan explains:

> And what is that Brahman like? Well, it is immanently present within all, from māyā to . . . the entire individuality and collectivity of the world. [Yet] it is devoid of the world's qualities and flaws; it is untainted {nirlepa}. It cannot be cut, pierced, burnt, wet or dried. It is pure {śuddha} like space. It dwells within all things, yet it remains untouched by anything. It is pure {nirmala, literally 'unsullied'}. (VR 151)

Earlier in the letter, Swaminarayan writes about the immutability or constancy of Akṣarabrahman by highlighting its power over time (an aspect of māyā).

> That Akṣara is without the states of creation, sustenance and destruction. By its light, even time can be destroyed. Akṣara is stable {sthira} and eternal {sanātana}. (VR 144)

Like Parabrahman, this is also due to Akṣarabrahman having a distinct form of its own, as we shall see further on in this section. Moreover, Akṣarabrahman's transcendence over māyā will especially be brought into focus when we discuss in this chapter its soteriological role in the form of the Brahmasvarūpa Guru.

Satyam, Jñānam, Anantam

An important description of Akṣarabrahman can be found in the opening passage of the Taittirīya Upaniṣad's Ānandavallī. It reads:

> Satyam jñānam anantam brahma | (2.1.1)[39]

[39] Bhadreshdas argues that this description can only be of Akṣarabrahman, not Parabrahman. In the opening phrase of the same mantra,

> Brahmavid-āpnoti param
>
> He who knows Brahman attains the highest (2.1.1),

the term 'Brahma' relates to Akṣarabrahman, and 'param' {highest} refers to Parabrahman, since this latter relative term must denote something that transcends even Akṣarabrahman. It is wholly correct according to Swaminarayan theology that he who perfectly knows Brahman (i.e. is brahmarūpa) attains Parabrahman (Vac. Gaḍh. 1.21, Gaḍh. 2.8, Gaḍh. 2.62). Furthermore, since the description immediately following 'satyam jñānam anantam brahma' in the very same verse clearly refers to

Bhadreshdas expands each of these three important definers to explain that, firstly, Akṣarabrahman's existence is real, meaning that it is eternally divine and immutable in form and nature.

Secondly, Akṣarabrahman is eternally of the form of knowledge. This knowledge is devoid of even the slightest contact of māyā, saving it from any form of corruption or compromise. Furthermore, not only is Akṣarabrahman *made* of knowledge, it also *has* knowledge as a quality, because only then would it be able to know. This knowledge, again, is eternal and unlimited.

Lastly, 'ananta'. This is defined in two ways: without end, as in without destruction, to explain that Akṣarabrahman is imperishable; and without end, as in without limit, since Akṣarabrahman is also unlimited. On the latter, this infiniteness is to be further understood in three ways, as being unbound by space, time and object, which, Bhadreshdas explains, means it cannot be said that Akṣarabrahman is 'here but not there', 'now but not then', 'this but not that'. This is because Akṣarabrahman is omnipresent (in its Cidākāśa form), eternal, and the omni-soul pervading everything (except Parabrahman).[40]

Role in the Origination, Sustenance and Dissolution of the Universe

In our discussion about the essential role of Akṣarabrahman in Swaminarayan Hindu theology, we came across the notable interpretation of the first aphorism of the Brahmasūtras, where 'brahma' in 'brahmajijñāsā' denotes both Parabrahman and Akṣarabrahman.

By its very function, however, the second aphorism of the Brahmasūtras,

> Janmādyasya yataḥ (BS. 1.1.2),

is what defines the 'Brahman' of BS 1.1.1, i.e. it is 'that from which [occurs] the creation, etc. of this [world]'. In other words, we can only accept Akṣarabrahman to also be the subject of the desirable knowledge if it can be proven to be the cause of the world's origination, sustenance and dissolution.

Bhadreshdas endeavours to prove this is indeed the case by citing śāstric statements. For example, as we saw earlier, the Muṇḍaka Upaniṣad states:

Akṣarabrahman as the 'highest abode {parame vyoman}', the portion in-between them must also relate to Akṣarabrahman. It is untenable that a denotation of a word would change so rapidly within the same verse or that God be called 'the highest abode'. TU-SB 2.1.1, pp. 361–3.

40 TU-SB 2.1.1, pp. 362–3.

> This is the truth: As from a blazing fire, sparks of like form issue forth by the thousands, similarly, O dear [Śaunaka], beings of various forms issue forth from Akṣara and return to it only. (MuU 2.1.1)

Akṣarabrahman's causality is also confirmed by an earlier verse from the Muṇḍaka Upaniṣad (1.1.6) where it is described as 'bhūtayoni', the cause of all beings. The text goes on to explicitly state:

> This world is created from Akṣara. (1.1.7)

Three similes are provided in this verse to consolidate the point, which, Bhadreshdas explains, provide useful insights about how exactly Akṣarabrahman is the cause. The world is created from Akṣara:

1. 'as a spider spins out and draws in' its thread. This firstly points to Akṣarabrahman as the material cause of the world, since he creates the world from his own 'body', i.e. māyā, and māyā, too, at the time of dissolution, returns into him, just like the silk thread extruded and then retracted by a spider. Moreover, Bhadreshdas stresses, this simile also importantly indicates that Akṣarabrahman does not change its form or nature in any way while being the cause of the world; it remains immutable throughout. Using a counter-example, Bhadreshdas explains that Akṣarabrahman's causality is not like that of milk, which, as the material cause of yoghurt, turns *into* its effect; the milk ceases to exist in its original state after it has become the yoghurt. Akṣarabrahman, on the other hand, has an eternal existence, and remains exactly as it is throughout the process of creation, sustenance and dissolution.
2. 'as plants sprout from the earth'. Here Bhadreshdas highlights that various plants, shrubs and trees all grow from the soil – some bear thorns; some are lush with fragrant flowers; and some abound with fruits, sweet, sour, bitter or pungent – but each one only according to the qualities inherent in its own seed. Similarly, while Akṣarabrahman makes possible the origination of the world and all its inhabitants, they all 'grow' only according to their own 'seed' of karma which contains the code – the combined impressions of all their past deeds, good and bad – that in turn determines the body and conditions they receive during that particular lifetime. This exonerates Akṣarabrahman from the double-charge of partiality {vaiṣamya} and cruelty {nairghṛṇya} often associated with 'the problem of evil', just as the unbiased earth is blameless for the disparate flora that sprouts from it. (We shall be

taking up this topic in more detail in the chapter on māyā, when discussing the nature and process of creation.[41])

3. 'as hair [grows] on a living person's head and body'. This shows, Bhadreshdas explains, that the world is created from Akṣarabrahman effortlessly, without exertion or labour, just as facial and other types of androgenic hair grow naturally on a person.[42]

Akṣarabrahman is thus the cause of the origination, sustenance and dissolution of the world, and it is so immutably, blamelessly and effortlessly.

Sometimes, Bhadreshdas explains, Akṣarabrahman's role is mentioned in texts conjointly with that of Parabrahman, when generic terms such as 'Brahman' or 'Sat' (Being) are employed. This can be confirmed when the import of the entire text is examined, as we did with the Muṇḍaka Upaniṣad. Examples of such texts include the following:

> All this [visible world] is verily Brahman, from which it comes forth, in which it is dissolved, and by which it lives {taj-jalān[43]}. This is how, tranquil, one should offer upāsanā to it. (CU-SB 3.14.1)

> In the beginning, there was only this Brahman ... From that, all that was created. (BU 1.4.10)

> O dear [Śvetaketu], all these beings have 'Sat' as their source, 'Sat' as their support, and 'Sat' as their resting place. (CU-SB 6.8.4)

What thus begins in BS 1.1.2 to define 'Brahman', confirming both Parabrahman and Akṣarabrahman as causes of the world and therefore worthy of being known (BS 1.1.1), continues throughout the first chapter of the Brahmasūtras where causality is a key tool in harmonising equivocal śāstric statements. In the last full adhikaraṇa of that chapter, before the final colophonic sūtra, we see the arguments against the Sāṃkhya School drawing to an end, confirming that Pradhāna (i.e. Prakṛti or māyā) is not the independent cause of the world but rather, its inner soul, i.e. Parabrahman and Akṣarabrahman, are in fact the cause. Why?

> Because both {ubhaya} have been explicitly proclaimed. (1.4.26)

41 See Section 'Purpose of Creation and the Irreproachability of Its Creator' in Chapter 10.

42 MuU-SB 1.1.7, pp. 239–40.

43 'jalān' is a hapax legomenon, which requires the commentary to provide its full meaning. Bhadreshdas explains that it is an acronym composed of 'ja' from 'jāyate', meaning 'to be born'; 'la' from 'līyate', meaning 'to be dissolved'; and 'an' from 'aniti', meaning 'to live'. The term therefore becomes 'jalān', and together with 'tat', the demonstrative pronoun referring back to 'Brahman', provides the extricated meaning given above. CU-SB 3.14.1, pp. 131–2.

Here again Bhadreshdas cites several verses from the Upaniṣads confirming Parabrahman and Akṣarabrahman as the material and efficient cause of the world, as indicated by the Sūtrakāra himself.

Like Parabrahman, though, Akṣarabrahman's cosmological role is not limited to the origination and dissolution of the world but extends also to its sustenance in various ways. Swaminarayan states, for example:

> Brahman, who is the witness, enters the brahmāṇḍa ... and makes it conscious, giving it the powers to perform all activities. The nature of that Brahman is such that when it enters an object that is as inert as wood or stone, that object becomes such that it can move. (Vac. Gaḍh. 2.20)

It is Akṣarabrahman, then, which also enlivens and empowers the created world by entering within it. If we recall, this is similar to the description of Parabrahman being the 'śarīrin' of the universe, and indeed, Akṣarabrahman is thus the embodied soul of all things and beings (except Parabrahman) in the same way. This is why we see the Muṇḍaka Upaniṣad talk of Parabrahman and Akṣarabrahman in almost identical terms. For example, in 2.1.10, Parabrahman (or Puruṣottama, the highest person) is 'verily' {eva} identified with 'this world' {idam viśvam} on account of his omnisoulship:

> Puruṣa evedam viśvam |

Just a few mantras later, the very same phrase is used for Akṣarabrahman, 'verily' identifying him also with 'this world' on account of *his* omnisoulship:

> Brahmaivedam viśvam | (2.2.11)[44]

This omnisoulship is further confirmed when we learn of Akṣarabrahman as also being the ontic ground supporting the material and spiritual world, and controlling it by dwelling within it. While some of the statements above have mentioned this already, both these aspects can be seen more clearly, for example, in the dialogue between Yājñavalkya and Gārgī in the Bṛhadāraṇyaka Upaniṣad symposium. After seeking permission from the assembled scholars and Yājñavalkya himself, Gārgī asks:

[44] According to Bhadreshdas, 'Brahman' throughout the Muṇḍaka Upaniṣad refers only to Akṣarabrahman, but never Parabrahman. See also his note in MuU-SB 1.1.8, p. 249 where he asserts that 'Akṣara' and 'Brahman' are synonyms, citing several instances where they have been used interchangeably, e.g. MuU 2.2.2, KaU 2.16, KaU 3.2 and BG 8.3.

> O Yājñavalkya, what is that which is above the sky and beneath the earth, and between both the sky and earth, and that which is called the past, the present and the future? Upon what is all this woven back and forth? (BU 3.8.3)

In response to her question, Yājñavalkya firstly replies that it is 'ākāśa'. Pressing further, Gārgī asks:

> Upon what is 'ākāśa' woven back and forth? (BU 3.8.7)

It is then that Yājñavalkya states:

> That, O Gārgī, is indeed what the knowers of Brahman proclaim as Akṣara. (BU 3.8.8)[45]

Akṣarabrahman is thus the ontic ground upon which all of existence – past, present and future – subsists, just as the warp is upon which the weaver's shuttle moves back and forth.

After describing Akṣarabrahman with a string of apophatic and sometimes contrastive terms – 'it is neither gross nor subtle, neither short nor long', etc. – Yājñavalkya then goes on to repetitively state Akṣarabrahman's governance {praśāsana} over all aspects of the universe that it also upholds {vidhṛta}.

> Within the governance of this Akṣara, O Gārgī, do the upheld sun and moon verily stand.
>
> Within the governance of this Akṣara, O Gārgī, do the upheld sky and earth verily stand.
>
> Within the governance of this Akṣara, O Gārgī, do the upheld moments, hours, days and nights, half-months, months, seasons and years verily stand.
>
> Within the governance of this Akṣara, O Gārgī, do the rivers flow – some to the east from the white [snowy] mountains, others to the west in their own directions.
>
> Within the governance of this Akṣara, O Gārgī, do recipient men praise donors, deities [praise] the patron, and forefathers [praise] the ancestral offering. (BU 3.8.9)

Bhadreshdas explains that these are just a few indicative features of the entire universe; it should thereby be understood that Akṣarabrahman supports and governs all beings and things.

It should be stressed again that here and wherever else the causality and governance of Akṣarabrahman are mentioned, Bhadreshdas keenly points

45 This verse is the subject of the Akṣarādhikaraṇa in BS 1.3.10–13. Bhadreshdas explains here why the term 'akṣara' is indeed denotive of Akṣarabrahman and not Pradhāna or the individual soul, whether jīva or īśvara. See BS-SB 1.3.10–13, pp. 97–101.

out that it is only possible by the 'eternal wish of Paramātman'.[46] As we saw earlier, Swaminarayan explains:

> Brahman is the cause and support of all, including Prakṛti-Puruṣa, etc., and pervades everything by its antaryāmin powers ... Parabrahman, that is, Puruṣottama Nārāyaṇa, is distinct from that Brahman and also the cause, support and inspirer of Brahman. (Vac. Gaḍh. 2.3)

Like Parabrahman, then, and only by his will, Akṣarabrahman is the material and efficient cause of the world, its support and also its indwelling controller by virtue of pervading everything as its soul.

Anvaya-Vyatireka, Saguṇa-Nirguṇa and Sākāra-Nirākāra

Before we go on to further explore the nature and function of Akṣarabrahman, let us briefly touch upon three pairs of terms by which Swaminarayan describes Akṣarabrahman in the Vacanāmrut. We shall explore these with a little more detail when looking at each of the four forms of Akṣarabrahman in the following section, but it is useful nonetheless to see Swaminarayan's description of Akṣarabrahman's nature based on these statements alone. The three pairs are:

- Anvaya and vyatireka
- Saguṇa and nirguṇa
- Sākāra and nirākāra

As we learned when expounding upon Parabrahman, the two contrastive terms of 'anvaya' and 'vyatireka' essentially refer to immanence and transcendence, respectively. Swaminarayan applies them both to Akṣarabrahman in two sermons, Vac. Gaḍh. 1.7 and Vac. Sār.5. In the former, he describes Akṣarabrahman's immanent form as when it

> pervades māyā and the entities evolved from māyā, the countless millions of brahmāṇḍas.

To this, he adds in Vac. Sār.5:

> That which is the inspirer of Prakṛti-Puruṣa and all of the devatās, such as Sūrya, Candra, etc., should be known as the immanent form of Akṣara.

As for Akṣarabrahman's distinct, transcendental form, that is

[46] E.g. MuU-SB 1.1.7, pp. 240, 241.

> when it is distinct from everything and has the attributes of eternal existence, consciousness and bliss. (Vac. Gaḍh. 1.7)

This is the form

> in which there is not even a trace of the influence of Prakṛti-Puruṣa, etc. and in which only Puruṣottama Bhagavān resides. (Vac. Sār.5)

Together, these statements emphasise Akṣarabrahman's absolute purity, transcendence (especially above māyā) and independence, except, of course, from Parabrahman.

When describing Akṣarabrahman as both saguṇa and nirguṇa, Swaminarayan mainly refers to size. He explains in Vac. Gaḍh. 2.42 that Akṣarabrahman has an extremely subtle form, smaller even than an atom. This is its nirguṇa form. Conversely, the saguṇa form is much larger than even the largest of objects. In describing this further, Swaminarayan explains:

> Countless millions of brahmāṇḍas dwell like mere atoms around each and every hair of that Akṣara. It is not that those brahmāṇḍas become small compared to Akṣara; they still remain encircled by the eight barriers. Rather, it is because of the extreme vastness of Akṣara that those brahmāṇḍas appear so small. (Vac. Gaḍh. 2.42)

It would be correct to add here that, like Parabrahman, Akṣarabrahman is devoid of any defiling māyic qualities, hence also 'nirguṇa', and is replete with countless superlatively excellent auspicious qualities, hence also 'saguṇa'.

In Vac. Gaḍh. 1.21, Swaminarayan alludes to two types of Akṣarabrahman's forms.

> One, which is formless {nirākāra} and pure consciousness {caitanya}, is known as Cidākāśa.

In contrast, the other type is when Akṣarabrahman has a form {sākāra}. This relates to Akṣarabrahman as the abode of Parabrahman, the servant resident within that abode, and the Brahmasvarūpa Guru on earth. We shall be expounding upon all four of these forms in more detail in the section following the summary below.

In Relation to Parabrahman

A useful conclusion to this section on the nature of Akṣarabrahman can be provided by the following summary, listing the similarities and differences between Akṣarabrahman and Parabrahman gleaned from both chapters (including the section to come).

Similarities between Akṣarabrahman and Parabrahman

- Both eternally transcend māyā.
- Both are one without second.
- Both have a definite human-like shape in their distinct transcendental form.
- Both are replete with divine virtues and devoid of māyic impurities.
- Both have a causal role in the origination, sustenance and dissolution of the world, though neither engage actively; their mere will activates the process.
- Both support, empower, inspire, pervade and control by dwelling within all other beings and things, i.e. both are their embodied soul {śarīrin}.
- Both, even while eternally residing in Akṣaradhāma in human form, manifest in various brahmāṇḍas in human form for the liberation of countless souls. Yet, even then, they are both divine and unsullied by māyā.
- Both need to be known to attain brahmavidyā, which is essential for securing ultimate liberation.

Differences between Akṣarabrahman and Parabrahman

- Parabrahman supports, empowers, inspires, pervades and controls from within even Akṣarabrahman, whereas Akṣarabrahman does not support, empower, inspire, pervade or control Parabrahman.
- Parabrahman is the soul of Akṣarabrahman, whereas Akṣarabrahman is a part of the body of Parabrahman.
- Parabrahman is the extremely powerful owner and master {svāmin} of Akṣarabrahman, whereas Akṣarabrahman is the extremely subservient servant {sevaka} of Parabrahman.
- Parabrahman is eminently worshippable {upāsya}, whereas Akṣarabrahman is the perfectly devout and humble worshipper {upāsaka}.
- Parabrahman, with all his unlimited powers, splendour, knowledge, bliss, virtues, etc., is totally independent, even of Akṣarabrahman, whereas Akṣarabrahman and his unlimited powers, splendour, knowledge, bliss, virtues, etc. are all totally dependent on Parabrahman.
- As Akṣaradhāma, Akṣarabrahman is the abode of Parabrahman, where Parabrahman and countless liberated souls reside. Parabrahman is the

Lord of Akṣaradhāma, presiding over it as its sovereign ruler and owner.[47]

Four Forms of Akṣarabrahman

Akṣarabrahman is 'one without second'. Yet as one entity, it functions in four different ways and so can be seen in the following four forms:

- As Cidākāśa, the all-pervading conscious space
- As Akṣaradhāma, the abode of Parabrahman
- As the ideal sevaka in Akṣaradhāma
- As the Brahmasvarūpa Guru on earth

Before we turn to expound upon each, it is necessary to reiterate that in being of one substance, there is no internal relationship between the four forms; they are all ontologically the one and same Akṣarabrahman entity. This is made all the more clear in the Muṇḍaka Upaniṣad, where all four forms are mentioned in one mantra:

> Āviḥ sannihitam guhācaram nāma mahat padam atraitat samarpitam |
> Ejat prāṇan nimiṣac ca tad etaj jānatha sadasadvareṇyam param vijñānād yad variṣṭam prajānām || (MuU 2.2.1)

As a Swaminarayan reading of the verse, Bhadreshdas explains that the first two terms point to the two types of Akṣarabrahman: āvis, meaning 'manifest', is Akṣarabrahman as the abode, sevaka and Guru, all of which have a definite form; whereas sannihitam, or 'concomitant', is Akṣarabrahman in its all-pervading form, i.e. Cidākāśa. These four are then individually referred to in the verse, as shown in Table 3.

The verse concludes with the instruction:

> Know that Akṣara, which is both gross and subtle, the most desirable, the highest because of its extraordinary knowledge, and what people most desire. (MuU 2.2.1)[48]

We ourselves can now move on to understanding each of these four forms of Akṣarabrahman in more detail.

[47] For a more detailed discussion about the relationship between Parabrahman and Akṣarabrahman, and the supremacy of the former over the latter, see the Svāminārāyaṇa-Bhāṣya commentary on the Ubhayavyapadeśādhikaraṇa (BS-SB 3.2.26–29, pp. 302–4) and especially the Parādhikaraṇa (BS-SB 3.2.30–35, pp. 304–10).

[48] See also MuU-SB 2.2.7, pp. 276–7 and MuU-SB 3.1.7, p. 288 for other instances, according to Bhadreshdas, where all four forms of Akṣarabrahman are indicated in one verse.

Table 3 *Four forms of Akṣarabrahman mentioned in MuU 2.2.1*

Akṣarabrahman Form	Term/Phrase	Meaning
Cidākāśa	guhācaram	dwelling within the cave [of the heart]
Abode	mahat padam	great place
Sevaka in Abode	atraitat samarpitam	dedicated here [in the great place]
Guru	ejat prāṇan nimiṣat	moving, breathing, blinking

Akṣarabrahman as Cidākāśa

Of the four forms of Akṣarabrahman, the only one without a definite shape is Cidākāśa. As quoted earlier, Swaminarayan states in Vac. Gaḍh. 1.21 that Akṣara, when

> formless {nirākāra} and pure consciousness {caitanya}, is known as Cidākāśa.

This is also the anvaya {immanent} form of Akṣarabrahman described in Vac. Gaḍh. 1.7 and the nirguṇa {subtle} form described in Vac. Gaḍh. 2.42, which we also saw earlier. In both these senses, Cidākāśa is described as being all-pervading. The Muṇḍaka Upaniṣad, too, explains:

> This immortal Brahman is verily in front. Brahman is behind. Brahman is to the right and to the left. It is below and above. This Brahman verily pervades the whole world. (2.2.11)

Furthermore, as the name suggests, Cidākāśa is a form of space {ākāśa}, but it is wholly different from material space; it is spiritual and sentient, i.e. composed of consciousness {cit}. Swaminarayan explains this difference at great length in Vac. Gaḍh. 1.46 when he is questioned by a Vedāntin about the assimilation {līnatā} of 'ākāśa' during the state of samādhi (spiritual absorption). Swaminarayan clarifies that the two types of ākāśa – one which is full of consciousness and the other which is one of the five material elements (alongside earth, water, fire and air) – are different and should not be confused. The gist of Swaminarayan's explanation on how they differ is as follows:

- Cidākāśa is never assimilated; it is eternal, i.e. it is not created or dissolved, unlike material space which originates during the creative process of each brahmāṇḍa.

- Cidākāśa is immutable and infinite; it has no states of contraction or expansion like material space.
- Cidākāśa is extremely bright, whereas material space is marked by the absence of light.
- Cidākāśa is immanently present everywhere, within the smallest part of an atom and around the vast brahmāṇḍas; countless millions of brahmāṇḍas are 'within' Cidākāśa.
- Cidākāśa is the omni-support {sarvādhāra}; it supports everything, including māyā and its work, i.e. countless millions of brahmāṇḍas.

A similar description of Akṣarabrahman can be found in the Muṇḍaka Upaniṣad in 2.2.2. It reads:

> That which is subtler than the subtle and within which the realms and their inhabitants rest, that is this Akṣarabrahman.

The Kaṭha Upaniṣad similarly mentions that 'all realms are supported by it [which is called Brahman]' (5.8), while the Bhagavad-Gītā simply calls Akṣarabrahman 'the supporter of all beings {bhūtabhartṛ}' (13.16) and 'the supporter of all' {sarvabhṛt} (13.14).

If we also recall Yājñavalkya's answer to Gārgī in BU 3.8, it is this Akṣara upon which the whole world is 'woven back and forth' and 'within the governance of this Akṣara' that all is upheld in its proper place, functioning as it should. A similar proclamation can be found in the Chāndogya Upaniṣad:

> As far as this [material] space extends, so extends the [dahara {literally 'subtle'}, i.e. spiritual] space within the heart. Within it rests both the sky and the earth, both fire and air, both the sun and the moon, lightning and the stars. Whatever of this [world] is here and whatever is not – it all rests within this [spiritual space]. (CU 8.1.3)

This forms the topic of discussion for the Daharādhikaraṇa in BS 1.3.14–23, which Swaminarayan points to at the end of his explanation in Vac. Gaḍh. 1.46 by referring to the knowledge of Cidākāśa as 'daharavidyā'. In much the same vein as Swaminarayan's explanation noted above, Bhadreshdas argues in the Daharādhikaraṇa that the 'subtle space' {dahara ākāśa} within the heart mentioned in CU 8.1.1 should refer to Akṣarabrahman dwelling in the form of Cidākāśa, not the material space of the worldly sort {bhautika ākāśa}, because it is Akṣarabrahman that is full of higher consciousness and the all-pervading support of the world.[49]

[49] BS-SB 1.3.14–23, pp. 101–09.

Akṣarabrahman as Parabrahman's Abode

The sākāra {having a definite shape} and saguṇa {vast} form of Akṣarabrahman described by Swaminarayan in Vac. Gaḍh. 1.21 and Gaḍh. 2.42, respectively, relates to Akṣarabrahman as the abode of Parabrahman. Called Akṣaradhāma (and occasionally Brahmadhāma, Brahmaloka, Brahmapura and Brahmamahola), it is the transcendental divine realm where Parabrahman and innumerable liberated souls eternally reside. It is the place where earthly souls aspire to transcend upon death, to forever enjoy the undisturbed, unlimited bliss of God. It is their place of final rest, the ultimate destination, the highest goal.

As we already saw in our study of the Muṇḍaka Upaniṣad and Bhagavad-Gītā passages at the beginning of this chapter, Swaminarayan explicitly states in sermons such as Vac. Pan.1 that

> Akṣarabrahman is the abode wherein God resides.

In his comment on the Kaṭha Upaniṣad phrase,

> That place which all the Vedas extol . . . (2.15),

and a similar phrase in BG 8.11,

> Which Akṣara, the knowers of the Vedas proclaim,

Bhadreshdas provides scores of references from the Vedas, Upaniṣads and Bhagavad-Gītā confirming Akṣarabrahman as the home of God as well as various aspects of its nature.[50] We now have occasion to learn more about these aspects.

Undoubtedly the most important feature of Akṣaradhāma is that at its centre sits the distinct, transcendental, human-shaped form of Parabrahman in all his divine and resplendent glory. In our extensive discussions in the previous chapter about the immanently pervading {anvaya} yet eternally distinct {vyatireka} form of Parabrahman, we noted Swaminarayan explaining that this was possible by way of Parabrahman's extraordinary yogic powers. What he was stressing was that God, even while revealing himself throughout the universe,

> Nevertheless, he himself is still always present in his Akṣaradhāma. (Vac. Gaḍh. 2.64)

[50] KaU-SB 2.15, pp. 99–102 and BG-SB 8.21, pp. 189–93.

Swaminarayan adds that this is also true when Parabrahman manifests in human form on earth. He never abandons his place in Akṣaradhāma; he does not 'move' from there to be on earth.

Gunatitanand Swami provides a description of this eternally resident form in one of his sermons. He states:

> He who is unborn even though taking birth; whose form is unfaltering and eternal; who has a divine form even while having a human-shaped form, and who has a human-shaped form which is divine; who is in Akṣaradhāma yet here and here yet certainly in Akṣaradhāma; in fact, wherever he is, is indeed the centre of Akṣaradhāma; who is complete with magnanimity, profundity, sweetness, loving compassion, integrity, knowledge, strength, splendour, taste, smell and other similarly extremely wondrous divine qualities – that is Puruṣottama, the supreme Shri Sahajanand Swami [Swaminarayan] who forever resides in his Akṣaradhāma being served by countless liberated souls and divine powers, where he is blissful in and of himself but out of sheer compassion, accepts the service of Akṣara and all others. (SV 7.27)

Swaminarayan also describes the majestic form of Parabrahman in Akṣaradhāma, giving special reference to the abode's extreme luminance.

> There is an all-transcendent mass of divine light which cannot be measured from above, below or in any of the four directions; that is to say, it is endless. Amid this mass of light lies a large, ornate throne upon which presides the divine form of Śrī Nārāyaṇa Puruṣottama Bhagavān. Countless millions of liberated souls are seated around that throne and enjoy the darshan of God. (Vac. Loyā.14)

Swaminarayan describes the divine and intense light of Akṣaradhāma in other sermons also, calling the abode 'replete with light {tejomaya}' (Vac. Gaḍh. 1.71, Gaḍh. 2.39, Gaḍh. 2.50, Gaḍh. 3.31, Gaḍh. 3.32), 'a mass of light {tejno rāśi or tejno samūh}' (Vac. Loyā 14, Gaḍh. 3.31), 'a mass of Brahmic light {Brahmajoytino samūh}' (Vac. Gaḍh. 3.36) and the 'realm of light {tejnu maṇḍaḷ}' (Vac. Gaḍh. 3.33). In Vac. Var.12 he adds that it is 'luminous {prakāśamān} like countless millions of suns, moons and fires'.

As bright as this may sound, this light is also described as extremely cool, pleasant and beautiful. Swaminarayan begins describing this transcendental beauty in Vac. Gaḍh. 1.12 with the following terms:

> The abode of God is without a beginning and without an end; it is divine {aprākṛta, i.e. non-māyic or not of this world}, infinite and indivisible; and it is characterised by eternal existence, consciousness and bliss.

Seeking to provide some sort of visual representation after these abstract terms, Swaminarayan then continues:

> I shall describe it using an analogy. Imagine that this whole world, with all of its mountains, trees, humans, animals and all other forms, is made of glass. Also imagine that all of the stars in the sky are as bright as the sun. Then, just as this glass world would glow with extreme beauty amid this radiance, the abode of God is similarly beautiful. Devotees of God see this in samādhi and attain that luminous abode after death.

Similar descriptions of the luminous abode of God can be found in MuU 2.2.10, KaU 5.15, SU 6.14, BG. 15.6 and CU 3.11.1–3. They all refer to it as 'beyond the reach of the sun and moon', i.e. worldly light, with the first three identically proclaiming that it is Akṣarabrahman's light by which all else is illumined.

> There shines not the sun. There shines not the moon or stars, nor does shine this lightning. How, then, can this fire [shine there]? By it alone, being luminous, is all else reflected. By its light is all this [world] illumined. (KaU 5.15, MuU 2.2.10, SU 6.14)

That the sun, etc. do not shine in Akṣaradhāma further points to the abode's transcendence beyond all earthly and celestial regions. With the sun and moon also symbolic of the passage of time, it reiterates Akṣaradhāma as being eternal and beyond temporal measure. As we saw earlier:

> That Akṣara is without the states of creation, sustenance and destruction. By its light, even time can be destroyed. Akṣara is stable, eternal and the place of residence of Parameśvara. (VR 144)

The Chāndogya Upaniṣad also describes it as a place where 'neither days nor nights, age nor death' can enter, adding,

> nor sorrow, nor good or bad deeds. All impurities retreat from here. This is the pure Brahmaloka. (8.4.1)

Such transcendence above time and impurities explains that Akṣaradhāma is beyond the destructive and defiling influence of māyā. This is the distinct form of Akṣarabrahman Swaminarayan describes in Vac. Sār.5,

> in which there is not even a trace of the influence of Prakṛti-Puruṣa, etc. and in which only Puruṣottama Bhagavān resides.

One way in which Swaminarayan reiterates Akṣaradhāma's transcendence beyond all other realms, even those of other devas, is by describing it as absolutely unique and incomparable to them. He states in Vac. Pan.4:

> The abode of God is such that it cannot be compared to any other place in this brahmāṇḍa. Specifically, out of all of the various places . . . [including]

> the realms of Indra, Varuṇa, Kubera, Śiva and Brahmā, and many other places, not one can compare to the abode of God.

This is why the Bṛhadāraṇyaka Upaniṣad in 4.3.32 describes Brahmaloka as 'unique' and the 'highest goal', the 'highest place', the 'highest realm', with KaU 2.17 calling it simply 'the best {śreṣṭa}'. Similarly, as we saw in our study earlier, the Bhagavad-Gītā extols it as the 'highest goal' (8.13, 8.21), 'highest place' (8.28) and 'highest abode' (8.21, 15.6).

In Vac. Gaḍh. 2.24, Swaminarayan provides a reason for why Akṣaradhāma is unique and transcends other realms. He explains:

> With the exception of God's Akṣaradhāma, the form of God in that Akṣaradhāma and his [liberated] devotees in that Akṣaradhāma, all realms, the devas inhabiting those realms, and the opulence of the devas – everything – is perishable.

Another important aspect of Akṣaradhāma further establishing its eminence is the highest, unparalleled bliss experienced there because of Parabrahman's unconcealed presence. When describing in ascending order the relative happiness of various realms and then the superiority of God's bliss, Swaminarayan states in Vac. Pan.1:

> The happiness of humans exceeds the happiness of animals; and the happiness of a king exceeds that; and the happiness of devatās exceeds that; and the happiness of Indra exceeds that; then Bṛhaspati's happiness, then Brahmā's, then Vaikuṇṭha's [abode of Viṣṇu]. Beyond that, the happiness of Goloka [abode of Kṛṣṇa] is superior, and finally, the bliss of God's Akṣaradhāma is vastly superior.

Reminiscent of the Taittirīya Upaniṣad's Ānanadavallī, this is also similar to BU 4.3.33 where Yājñavalkya describes to King Janaka the happiness of the various realms in ascending order, each a hundredfold greater than the previous, climaxing finally with the supreme bliss of Brahmaloka.

So superior is this bliss of God's abode compared to the pleasures of the other paradisiacal realms that, Swaminarayan adds,

> it is said in [the Mahābhārata's] Mokṣadharma[51] that the realms of the other devatās are like naraka [i.e. hell] compared to the Akṣaradhāma of God. (Vac. Sār.1)

What, then, can be said of this bliss in relation to the pleasures of the earthly realm?

[51] Mahābhārata, Śānti Parva 191.6.

> Compared to the bliss of the abode of God, the māyic sensorial pleasures are like excreta. Only worms that live in excreta feel that there is profound bliss in excreta; a human would realise excreta to be nothing but utter misery. (Vac. Var.19)

In reality, though, the bliss in Akṣaradhāma is simply incomparable.

> The bliss experienced by the devotees of God residing in that abode is such that it cannot be compared to any other type of bliss in this brahmāṇḍa. (Vac. Pan.4)

It is by a mere 'trace' of this 'supreme bliss', explains the Bṛhadāraṇyaka Upaniṣad, that 'all other creatures survive' (4.3.32).

Furthermore, not only is Akṣaradhāma the only place where this highest bliss is available, it is available there forever, for this is a place from which there is no return to a transient, worldly existence (Vac. Sār.14, BU 6.2.15, CU 4.15.6, BG 8.21, BG 15.6, BS 4.2.2). Entry, though, is only possible to those who have reached the highest enlightened state of being brahmarūpa (Vac. Pan.7).[52] Both of these points affirm Akṣaradhāma as the transcendental abode.

Another way of understanding Akṣaradhāma's greatness is by its size. Swaminarayan describes the immense vastness of Akṣaradhāma in Vac. Gaḍh. 1.63 and Gaḍh. 2.42, stating that 'countless millions of brahmāṇḍas float like mere atoms' around it. 'It is not that those brahmāṇḍas become small compared to Akṣara', he clarifies, because 'they still remain encircled by the eight barriers'.

> Rather, it is because of the extreme vastness of Akṣara that those brahmāṇḍas appear so small. (Vac. Gaḍh. 2.42)

It is clear that Swaminarayan is talking here about Akṣarabrahman as the abode, and not the all-pervading Cidākāśa,[53] because he goes on to mention in the same sermon:

> Moreover, God – who is Puruṣottama – forever remains present in that Akṣaradhāma.

[52] Akṣaradhāma is the final place of rest after death for liberated souls. We shall therefore be revisiting some of these ideas when discussing liberation, as we deal also with such topics as the type of body that liberated souls assume in Akṣaradhāma and the 'service' they perform there. See Section 'Videha Mukti: Post-Mortem Liberation' in Chapter 11.

[53] For a detailed discussion of the problems that would arise were Akṣaradhāma not considered to be an actual place and simply like the all-pervading Cidākāśa, see Brahmadarshandas, *Vacanāmrut Rahasya*, vol. III, pp. 94–101. He also addresses questions arising from considering Akṣaradhāma as an actual place; ibid, pp. 87–93. See also BG-SB 8.21, pp. 190–1.

Thus, by its size, bliss, finality, exclusivity, timelessness, imperishability, purity, luminance and other qualities, we have attempted to understand the nature of Akṣaradhāma and its transcendence. Of course, being the singular home of Parabrahman – the impassably supreme entity, the creator and controller of all beings and things, the cause of all avatāras, etc. – is itself sufficient in establishing it as the supreme abode, beyond all other abodes, realms and regions in the countless millions of brahmāṇḍas.

Akṣarabrahman as Sevaka in Akṣaradhāma

We have already noted from Vac. Gaḍh. 1.21 that Swaminarayan talks about the two types of forms of Akṣarabrahman: one which is formless, i.e. Cidākāśa, and the others which have a definite form. In that sermon, Swaminarayan specifically mentions:

> In its other form, that Akṣara remains in the service of Puruṣottama Nārāyaṇa.

Swaminarayan is referring to the human-shaped form of Akṣarabrahman that resides within Akṣaradhāma, itself another of its forms. As a sevaka {literally 'servant'} there, he is the supreme devotee of Parabrahman, serving as an exemplar for all the liberated souls who are also resident within the divine realm. Together, they enjoy the bliss of Parabrahman. This is mentioned as a part of the description of the superlative, matchless bliss which forms the central theme of the Taittirīya Upaniṣad's Ānandavallī. The long opening verse begins with a statement confirming the distinction between Brahman and the 'highest', i.e. Parabrahman, and the three terms we saw earlier describing Brahman – satyam, jñānam and anantam. It then states:

> Who knows [that Brahman] dwelling in the cavity [of the heart] and in the highest abode, he enjoys all pleasures with the omniscient {vipaścita[54]} Brahman. (2.1.1)

Bhadreshdas explains that the person who knows the various forms of Akṣarabrahman, as including the all-pervading Cidākāśa and the abode of

[54] This is another hapax legomenon. Bhadreshdas explains that term in the instrumental case qualifying the neuter 'brahmaṇ' is composed of parts from three terms: 'vi' from 'viśeṣa', meaning 'especially'; 'paś' from 'paśyat', meaning 'seeing' or 'knowing'; and 'cit', meaning consciousness. Together they provide the full meaning relating to Brahman's extraordinary capacity to know all things on account of his supreme consciousness, which I have shortened in the translation to 'omniscient'.

God, becomes liberated. Upon death, he reaches that abode of God and experiences the highest bliss along with Akṣarabrahman, who is also present there with other liberated souls.[55] This verse therefore points to the form of Akṣarabrahman resident within Akṣaradhāma.

The Muṇḍaka Upaniṣad further describes this Akṣarabrahman 'firmly residing' in that 'divine Brahmapura abode' in terms suggesting a divine human-shaped form (2.2.7), which is pure, beautiful and resplendent (2.2.9).

As we also saw at the beginning of this section, MuU 2.2.1 describes this form as being 'dedicated' or totally devoted {samarpita}. This further reiterates that Akṣarabrahman, in *all* its forms, is first, foremost and always a devotee of Parabrahman, serving him variously in four different forms. This servitude and devotion is perhaps most distinguishable in this human-shaped form within Akṣaradhāma.

Akṣarabrahman as Brahmasvarūpa Guru

If we recall, we left our chapter on Parabrahman with a somewhat incomplete ending. We had already established that a cardinal and distinguishing doctrine of Swaminarayan Hindu theology, by which all others are illumined and consummated, is that Parabrahman – distinct from and the cause of all avatāras – himself manifests on earth in human form and, vitally, that he chooses to remain present on earth ever thereafter. Our subsequent question was: How does he do this? If Swaminarayan was only present on earth from 1781 to 1830, how does Parabrahman continue to remain present to continue his work after that period? That is, to whom do the evocative words 'God manifest before your eyes' – which Swaminarayan uses so profusely – apply today?

We can now answer these questions about Parabrahman in this section on Akṣarabrahman as the Brahmasvarūpa Guru.

From a careful study of the Vacanāmrut, it becomes clear that Swaminarayan did not intend those words about 'God manifest before the eyes' to remain restricted to his own limited time of embodiment on earth. He makes the profoundly important revelation in Vac. Gaḍh. 1.71:

> When God manifests for the purpose of granting liberation to the jīvas, he is always accompanied by his Akṣaradhāma.

Parabrahman, then, is never alone on earth; he is *always* accompanied by Akṣarabrahman. It is this Akṣarabrahman – in another form, the abode of

[55] TU-SB 2.1.1, p. 363.

God – that is the Brahmasvarūpa Guru on earth. Just as in his eternally distinct form Parabrahman is fully manifest in his abode called Akṣaradhāma; on earth, he chooses to similarly reside in his 'human-abode', the same Akṣarabrahman who assumes the form of the Guru.

Swaminarayan provides two analogies in Vac. Pan.7 to help explain how this presence of Parabrahman within Akṣarabrahman can be understood. The first is of a red-hot piece of iron. Having fully 'entered' the metal, fire 'suppresses the quality of coldness and the black colour of the iron' and instead 'exhibits its own quality' of heat and redness. Similarly, 'when the sun rises, the light from all of the stars, the moon, etc. merges into the sun's own light, and only the sun's light remains'. In the same way, Swaminarayan explains, when God 'enters' into the Guru, 'he overpowers [Akṣarabrahman's] light and exhibits his own divine light to a greater degree'. In this way, Swaminarayan extends the full substantial presence[56] of Parabrahman to the Brahmasvarūpa Guru.

Swaminarayan reiterates this throughout his sermons in various ways, referring to the Guru variously (and sometimes interchangeably in the same statement) as the 'Sant', 'Satpuruṣa', 'Sādhu', 'Bhakta', etc. In Vac. Sār.10, for example, he unequivocally reveals:

> When one has the darshan of such a Sant, one should realise, 'I have had the darshan of God himself'.

These remarkable words epitomise the doctrine that God is present in and functions through the Guru. As we learnt in 'Parabrahman as Pragaṭa' in the previous chapter and in the chapter on revelation, 'seeing' within such theological contexts is indicative of the face-to-face meeting with God, a personal, intimate encounter and relationship with him. While the Guru neither is nor ever becomes God, God is revealed in and by the Guru. Quite simply, according to Swaminarayan, to have seen the Guru is to have seen God; to have met the Guru is to have met God.

This also has an equally powerful implication from God's side. If the devotees see and relate to God through the Guru, it is just as true that God reciprocates by meeting and relating with his devotees through the Guru as well. The Guru is thus the mediator between humans and God, making possible the personal encounter that Swaminarayan stressed was the reason for Parabrahman's manifestation on earth (Vac. Kār.5). Equally, then, to

[56] Of course, Parabrahman has a presence in all beings and things. However, his *substantial* presence in Akṣarabrahman is like in no other entity or element. In Vac. Gaḍh. 1.41, an extensive sermon in which he lists the various constituents of the creative process, Swaminarayan states that 'Puruṣottama Bhagavān . . . does not manifest' in any of these entities 'to the extent he manifests in Akṣara'. Thus, Swaminarayan explains, Parabrahman resides most fully in Akṣarabrahman.

have been seen by the Guru is to have been seen by God; to have been blessed by the Guru is to have been blessed by God.

Such emphatic statements are validated by the Upaniṣads (which we shall consider shortly) and by Swaminarayan when he reveals the full presence of God in the Guru. For example, in explaining in Vac. Gaḍh. 1.27 the 'countless types of powers' of the Guru, he adds:

> Since it is God who sees through his [the Sant's] eyes, he empowers the eyes of all the beings in the brahmāṇḍa; and since it is God who walks through his legs, he is also capable of endowing the strength to walk to the legs of all the beings in the brahmāṇḍa.

He goes on to conclude:

> Thus, since it is God who resides in all of the senses and limbs of such a Sant, that Sant is able to empower the senses and limbs of all the beings in the brahmāṇḍa. Therefore, such a Sant is the support {ādhāra} of the world.[57]

Swaminarayan relates here both the Guru's cognitive sense-organs {jñāna indriya} and his conative sense-organs {karma indriya} – indicated by the specific examples of the eyes and feet, respectively – as being inhabited by God. He then expands this by mentioning 'sarva indriya', implying that all parts of the Guru's being are imbued with God's presence. This leads to the belief that God perceives and functions through the Guru.

This also explains what Swaminarayan means when he says 'such a Sant has a direct relationship {sākṣāt saṃbandh} with God' (Vac. Gaḍh. 3.27). It is a direct, complete and substantive relationship. Gunatitanand Swami reinforces this in his sermon in SV 5.392 when he states:

> The association of the Sādhu is a direct relationship with God and leads to the bliss of God. Why? Because God fully resides in the Sādhu.

Further along in the same sermon, Gunatitanand Swami is posed with an important question that we also need to address as a part of this elucidation on the Guru and the continued manifestation of God. A member from the assembly asked him:

> Is not God manifest before the eyes through the mūrtis?

It is a valid question born of theological reflection and practice since mūrtis (sacred images ritually infused with the presence of the deity) hold a key role in the daily worship of God. The presence of God in them is undeniable for

[57] This also resonates with the Bṛhadāraṇyaka Upaniṣad statements of Yājñavalkya, which talk of Akṣara as upholding the whole universe. See BU-SB 3.8.9, pp. 193–5.

the faithful, with Swaminarayan himself mentioning in Vac. Gaḍh. 1.68, drawing also from BP 11.27.12, that God resides in the various types of mūrtis as well as in the Sant. However, is God's presence in the mūrtis the same as it is in the Guru? Gunatitanand Swami provides an extensive answer based on other Vacanāmrut sermons (primarily Vac. Var.12), before concluding:

> Therefore, only the walking-talking form of God should be understood as the manifest form before the eyes. Indeed, it is the great Sant who infuses the mūrti with the presence of God. Mūrtis, scriptures and places of pilgrimage cannot together form a Sādhu, but it is the great Sant who forms all three. Therefore, only the Sant in whom God fully resides is the manifest form of God before the eyes.

To iterate this unique theological status of the Guru, Swaminarayan extols him in his sermons in the highest possible manner, often in the first person. For example, in Vac. Gaḍh. 1.37 he goes as far as to say:

> Even I place the dust of his feet on my head. In my mind, I am afraid of hurting him, and I also long to have his darshan . . . The darshan of such a perfect Bhakta of God is equivalent to the darshan of God himself. He is so great that his [mere] darshan redeems countless fallen souls. (Vac. Gaḍh. 1.37)

As he lauds the Guru, Swaminarayan also firmly and repeatedly warns against hurting or maligning him, often showing dire and irreparable spiritual consequences if one does (Vac. Gaḍh. 1.1, Gaḍh. 1.35, Gaḍh. 1.53, Gaḍh. 1.58, Gaḍh. 1.73, Sār.18, Loyā.1, Gaḍh. 2.46, Gaḍh. 3.12). In this regard, Vac. Var.14 is especially noteworthy for its mention of 'seeking the refuge of the Satpuruṣa' and the pre-eminence of this above all other forms of dharmic living.

> Thus, by seeking the refuge of the Satpuruṣa, regardless of how terrible a sinner a person may be, he becomes extremely pure and attains samādhi. On the other hand, a person who maligns the Satpuruṣa is still a terrible sinner, regardless of how sincere he may seem to be in abiding by dharma. Moreover, he can never have the realisation of God in his heart.

Conversely, Swaminarayan stresses that serving the Guru and earning his favour is tantamount to serving God and earning God's favour. He explains in Vac. Gaḍh. 3.26:

> Such a Sant should not be thought to be like a human nor should he be thought to be like even a deva . . . Such a Sant, even though he is human [in form], is worthy of being served like God.

Swaminarayan elaborates on how to serve the Guru 'like God' in Vac. Var.5 by instructing 'equal service' of both, further establishing the full presence of God in the Guru. He states:

> Just as one performs the mānsi pūjā [worship by mental visualisation] of God, if one also performs the mānsi pūjā of the highest Bhakta along with God; and just as one prepares an offering of food for God, similarly, if one also prepares an offering for God's highest Bhakta and serves it to him; and just as one donates five rupees to God, similarly, if one also donates money to the great Sant – then, by performing with extreme affection such equal service of God and the Sant who possesses the highest qualities, even if such a person is a devotee of the lowest calibre and was destined to become a devotee of the highest calibre after two lives, or after four lives, or after ten lives, or after a hundred lives, he will become a devotee of the highest calibre in this very life. Such are the fruits of the equal service of God and God's Bhakta. (Vac. Var.5)

Serving the Guru is thus serving God, the fruit of which can accelerate one spiritually a hundred-fold.

Swaminarayan substantiates the service of the Guru in Vac. Gaḍh. 2.28 by adding his personal example again. He says:

> Even I am the devotee of such a perfect Bhakta of God and offer my devotion to the Bhakta of God.

Equally remarkable statements continue throughout the rest of this sermon, in which Swaminarayan reiterates in various ways the influential theological role of the Guru.

> Those who have perceived flaws in the Bhakta of God, even though they were very great, have fallen from their status of eminence. Those who progress do so only by serving the Bhakta of God, and those who regress do so only by maligning the Bhakta of God.

'In fact', Swaminarayan declares, such is the direct relationship between God and Guru that

> the only method for a person to please God is to serve the Bhakta of God by thought, word and deed. The only method to displease God is to malign the Bhakta of God.

Perhaps feeling that he had still not sufficiently emphasised the theological significance of the Guru, Swaminarayan completes his address with the following emphatic addendum:

> What is this sermon like that I have delivered before you? Well, I have delivered it having heard and having extracted the essence from the Vedas,

the Śāstras, the Purāṇas and all other words on this earth pertaining to liberation. This is the most profound and fundamental principle; it is the essence of all essences. For all those who have previously attained liberation, for all those who will attain it in the future, and for all those who are presently treading the path of liberation, this discourse is like a lifeline.

In another sermon, Swaminarayan draws upon the 'king' analogy that we saw being used several times throughout the exposition of Parabrahman. Here, Swaminarayan still reserves the kingship for God, but includes the Guru as his 'queen'. He explains:

> For example, in a kingdom, the queen reigns over the same land the king reigns over, and the queen has the same authority as the king's authority.[58] In the same way, that Sādhu has the very same influence as God's influence. (Vac. Gaḍh. 2.22)

What is especially remarkable about all these statements is that they are being made by Swaminarayan, who has already revealed himself as Parabrahman.[59] He evidently felt that revealing the Guru as bearing the full substantial presence of God would in no way undermine or compete with his own position as being Parabrahman in person. What this tells us about God in Swaminarayan Hindu theology is that Parabrahman remains Parabrahman – the one without second; impassable and unchallengeable. Yet his full glory and work is fulfilled through the Guru when Parabrahman is not personally present. Thus the cognate doctrines of Parabrahman as Pragaṭa and Akṣarabrahman as Guru point to a continued presence of Parabrahman not limited to Swaminarayan's own time on earth.

Here, we should pause for some theological reflection to clarify and confirm the important issue about the metaphysical identity of the Guru.

Cannot the 'Sant' or 'Sādhu' from these many statements refer to any ordained monk of the Swaminarayan order, or the 'Bhakta' refer to any devotee of the fellowship, or the 'Satpuruṣa' refer to any noble person? How can we be certain that he is Akṣarabrahman?

The answer to this critical question about the *being* of the Guru lies in his *function* revealed by Swaminarayan in these very statements. Throughout, he identifies the Guru with the work of liberation. For example, in Vac. Var.10, Swaminarayan states:

[58] This of course relates to a particular Indian conception of monarchy from the early nineteenth century.

[59] See Section 'Parabrahman Manifest in Human Form as Swaminarayan' in Chapter 6.

> One who aspires for liberation should recognise God through these characteristics and seek the refuge of that God ... However, when God is not manifest on this earth before the eyes, one should seek the refuge of the Sant who is absorbed with that God, because the jīva can also secure liberation through him.

As another example, in Vac. Jet.1 Swaminarayan firstly describes the insurmountability of māyā and how 'no jīva can conquer it' alone. Then in explaining 'the means to transcend[ing] māyā', he states:

> When the jīva meets the manifest form of Śrī Puruṣottama Bhagavān – who is beyond māyā and who is the destroyer of māyā and all karmas – or the Sant who is absorbed with that God, then, by accepting their refuge, the jīva can transcend māyā.

As we learnt at the very opening of Part II, there are five metaphysical entities in the Swaminarayan theological system. Of these five, only two – Parabrahman and Akṣarabrahman – transcend māyā, and so only they can possibly liberate others from it. Yet Swaminarayan mentions above that both 'Śrī Puruṣottama Bhagavān' and 'the Sant' can do this. What does this tell us about the metaphysical identity of the Guru? He is not Parabrahman, who, as we know, is one without second. But if the Guru is capable of functioning as liberator, then he must be Akṣarabrahman.

The Upaniṣads similarly reveal the Guru's metaphysical credentials as well as the absolute need for such a Guru in order to transcend māyā and realise the highest, brahmic state of enlightenment. For example, as part of the continuing elucidation of brahmavidyā in the Muṇḍaka Upaniṣad, each seeker is instructed thus:

> To realise that [higher knowledge of Akṣara (also known as Brahman) and Puruṣa (also known as Parabrahman), i.e. brahmavidyā], imperatively surrender, with sacrificial wood in hand, to only that guru who has the realisation of revealed texts {śrotriyam}, who is Brahman {brahma} and who is ever steadfast {niṣṭham} [in God]. (MuU 1.2.12)

By splitting 'brahma' and 'niṣṭham' normally considered as a single compounded term, Bhadreshdas provides the crucial distinction here that the Guru is one not just 'established in Brahman' {brahmaṇi niṣṭhaḥ} but 'the very form of Brahman' {brahmasvarūpa eva}. Hence, the correct qualifier for the Guru is 'brahmasvarūpa', the form of Brahman (or Akṣarabrahman).

This means the Guru is further qualified by two adjectives: niṣṭha, which reveals that he is 'entirely and eternally established {nitāntam nityam tiṣṭhati} in Parabrahman'; and śrotriya, which has the richly multifarious meaning of one who not only is well-versed in the true meaning of the revealed texts, but has a direct and full realisation {sākṣātkāra} of them, which means that he has effortlessly applied their principles in his life and who, by his own exemplary life {ācāra} and teachings {upadeśa}, can adeptly convey those principles to those seeking liberation.

Bhadreshdas also makes clear what this list of essential credentials does *not* include. He emphasises this by way of the accentuating 'eva' used in the instruction. Not only, he explains, does it mean that it is *essential* to seek the refuge of such a guru in order to gain brahmavidyā, i.e. there is absolutely no other way to assimilate the highest theological knowledge, but also that one should seek the refuge of *only* such a guru. That is, one should not surrender to any other person who may bear some semblance to a guru by way of his ochre robes, erudition, oratory skills, institutional power, large following, etc. but who in fact does not have a complete realisation of the revealed texts and is not metaphysically Akṣarabrahman in being.[60]

When expanding upon KaU 2.8–9, Bhadreshdas again draws a particularly sharp contrast between the essential bona fide Guru, who must above all be Akṣarabrahman, and the 'inferior' {avara} teachers of brahmavidyā. Those who fall under this latter category are, he explains, they who worship merely the words of scriptures (rather than their meaning or practice), who are interested in mere debates about the Vedas (but not understanding their true meanings), who determine meanings of words independently (without appeal to revelation), who have not sought the refuge of a Guru themselves, who are unbelievers, who have imperfect knowledge, whose intellect on the spiritual path has been afflicted by unbridled reason, who are of weak faith, who identify with the body (rather than the soul) and who do not have a direct realisation of the 'Akṣara-Puruṣottama-siddhānta'.[61]

The Upaniṣads provide further evidence of the Guru being Akṣarabrahman by using a term that also elucidates his role in connecting humans to God. He is repeatedly described as the 'setu', or bridge.

> The bridge for those who offer sacrifices is Akṣarabrahman, the highest. (KaU 3.2)
>
> This is the bridge to the immortal. (MuU 2.2.5)
>
> Now, the Soul [of all] is the bridge . . . (CU 8.4.1)
>
> The best bridge to immortality . . . (SU 6.19)[62]

[60] MuU-SB 1.2.12, pp. 253–6. [61] KaU-SB 2.8, p. 91.

[62] See also the other analogy used in SU 2.8, of Akṣarabrahman being a boat {uḍupa} used by the wise to cross the frightful forces of māyā.

In all four instances, Bhadreshdas describes Akṣarabrahman as the bridge spanning across the incessantly gushing 'great river of saṃsāra' (perpetual transmigration from birth to death and rebirth brought on by ignorance, which is māyā), allowing one to cross from this side of a worldly, transient and sorrow-mixed existence over to a divine, eternal and purely blissful communion with God. Bhadreshdas adds that the Guru thus serves as a 'mādhyama' {literally, 'medium'} so that devotees can 'reach' God and personally experience him – know him and love him – here and now on earth.

Interestingly, in extrapolating the analogy in MuU 2.2.5, Bhadreshdas explains that it also reiterates the distinction between the five metaphysical entities of Swaminarayan Hindu theology: if the bridge is Akṣarabrahman and the 'other side' is Parabrahman, what the bridge spans over is māyā and those who need the bridge to cross over are jīvas and īśvaras.[63] What this also tells us, importantly, is that even while the Guru's position can hardly be overstated, he remains the bridge, the means; he never becomes the end, which is always and only Parabrahman. Worship – or 'upāsanā', more correctly – is always of Parabrahman (the upāsya, or worshippable), albeit in his most accessible form manifest through the Guru. Thus, whatever reverence or devotion or praise is offered to the Guru, it is with the good knowledge that Parabrahman is fully residing within him and is ultimately accepting the devotion. To recall the cup and water analogy introduced in Chapter 3 when discussing revelation in and by the Guru, consider now that the water is from a holy river. The river itself is distant and inaccessible. Yet in hoping to offer pūjā {acts of devotional reverence} to the river, one does so to the cup that contains the same river water. Similarly, if one serves the Guru it is because he is the vessel containing Parabrahman, who is otherwise inaccessible in his transcendental abode. Thus, despite all of the Guru's glory mentioned above, upāsanā – loving worship informed by correct theological knowledge – is exclusively of Parabrahman. Akṣarabrahman himself is the perfect, eternal devotee of Parabrahman. And as great as he may be in relation to all other entities, the Brahmasvarūpa Guru is infinitely subordinate to Parabrahman himself (Vac. Gaḍh. 1.64, Loyā.13).

In balance, then, the Guru is metaphysically Akṣarabrahman in entity and eternally and ontologically distinct from and subordinate to Parabrahman, yet he serves as the complete and perfect medium for God's presence – his love, bliss, grace, blessings and more – and,

[63] MuU-SB 2.2.5, p. 274.

importantly, functions as the means to securing eternal communion with God in final liberation.

There are other vital connections to be made here with liberation, and we shall clarify at the appropriate point how exactly the Guru facilitates it.[64] Now, it is important to simply affirm that because of his role in liberating souls from māyā and leading them to Parabrahman, the 'Sant', 'Sādhu', 'Bhakta', 'Satpuruṣa', etc. mentioned in all such statements denote only the māyā-transcending Akṣarabrahman Guru.

As we draw this section to a close, and with it the chapter on Akṣarabrahman – and indeed now, also the chapter on Parabrahman – it should be evident that the doctrine which Swaminarayan was most prolific about and for which he reserved some of his most emphatic statements was the doctrine of Pragaṭa, i.e. Parabrahman living on and working through Akṣarabrahman in the form of the Guru – a principle he feels is so essential that 'there is no option but to understand it', whether 'after being told once, or after being told a thousand times', whether 'today, or after a thousand years'; it is the crux of 'all the fundamental principles' and 'the essence of all of the scriptures' (Vac. Gaḍh. 2.21); the 'one central principle' of all śruti and smṛti texts (Vac. Gaḍh. 2.59); indeed, this is 'the most profound and fundamental principle', 'the essence of all essences', 'the essence' of all words 'on this earth pertaining to liberation', and the very 'lifeline' of all those on the path to liberation – past, present and future (Vac. Gaḍh. 2.28). This is because Parabrahman fully resides in the Guru (Vac. Gaḍh. 1.27). So complete and substantive is this presence that seeing him is seeing God (Vac. Sār.10, Gaḍh. 1.37); serving him is serving God; maligning him is maligning God (Vac. Gaḍh. 2.28, Gaḍh. 3.26, Var.5, Var.14, Gaḍh. 3.35). Thus, having attained him *or* God, 'then, apart from this, there is no other liberation for the self; this itself is ultimate liberation' (Vac. Gaḍh. 2.59).

In this way, Parabrahman is entirely present and graciously active through the Brahmasvarūpa Guru, who accompanied him on earth and through whom Parabrahman remains forever present, continuing his liberative work among the people and allowing them a direct and personal relationship with him. Thus, though not God himself, all statements containing the words 'God manifest before the eyes' now refer forthrightly and exclusively to the Brahmasvarūpa Guru.

[64] See especially Section 'Liberation by Brahmavidyā' in Chapter 11.

CHAPTER 8

Jīva

This is a good juncture to briefly pause and consult our roadmap, to reflect upon the ground we have covered so far and assess the path ahead in this introductory exposition of the major themes of Swaminarayan Hindu theology.

At the opening of this part, we had been introduced to the five eternal metaphysical entities of the Swaminarayan Vedāntic system: Parabrahman, Akṣarabrahman, māyā, īśvara and jīva. As an initial overview, we learned that the entities were contrasted in their natures by virtue of their sentiency; the first two and last two are sentient, spiritual entities, whereas māyā is essentially insentient and material. Another way of categorising them, we observed, was that Parabrahman and Akṣarabrahman transcend and are free of māyā, whereas jīvas and īśvaras are bound by māyā.

Having completed extensive expositions of Parabrahman and Akṣarabrahman, the two highest entities, we now move on in the subsequent, smaller chapters to expounding upon the remaining three entities – jīva, īśvara and māyā – ending finally with some elucidation on the topic of mukti {liberation}.

A brief explanation of the ensuing sequence will be helpful as we move forward. After Parabrahman and Akṣarabrahman, both of which are sentient and beyond māyā, we shall next expound upon jīva and īśvara, which are also sentient but within māyā. This will mean that we will be covering all four of the spiritual entities first, before progressing on to māyā, the only material entity. Of the two – jīvas and īśvaras – ontologically, īśvaras transcend jīvas. However, with īśvaras being so similar to jīvas, and with more to say about jīvas, it makes sense to cover the lesser souls first before looking at the distinguishing features of īśvaras thereafter. The reason for dealing with these sentient entities first and holding back on expounding upon māyā is that the chapter on māyā will contain discussions about creation (how jīvas receive their bodies and the role of īśvaras in each brahmāṇḍa, for which a primary understanding of jīvas and īśvaras will be necessary) and about ignorance (which forms the bondage of jīvas and īśvaras, therefore also serving as a better link to the final chapter on mukti, i.e. liberation from that māyic bondage). And so we proceed, firstly, to expositing the jīva.

Nature of Jīva

Every living being (human, animal, insect, plant, fungus, etc.) is ensouled by – indeed, *is*, in its truest form – a spiritual entity.[1] Swaminarayan calls it the jīva – from the Sanskrit verb-root 'jīv', to breathe or to live – sometimes also referring to it as the ātman or jīvātman.

When once asked in an assembly by a devotee,

> Mahārāj, what is the nature of the jīva? Please reveal it to me as it is,

his reply was a succinct exposition that provides for us a useful introductory overview before we subsequently enter into the specifics. Swaminarayan explained:

> The jīva is uncuttable, unpierceable, immortal, formed of consciousness, and the size of an atom[2] {aṇu}. You may also ask, 'Where does the jīva reside?' Well, it resides within the space of the heart, and while staying there, it performs different functions. From there, when it wants to see, it does so through the eyes; when it wants to hear sounds, it does so through the ears; it smells all types of smells through the nose; it tastes through the tongue; and through the skin, it experiences the pleasures of all sensations. In addition, it thinks through the mind, contemplates through the citta [one of the inner faculties] and forms convictions through the intelligence {buddhi}. In this manner, through the ten senses and the four inner faculties, it perceives all of the sense-objects [i.e. objects of sensorial perception]. It pervades the entire body from head to toe, yet is distinct from it. Such is the nature of the jīva. (Vac. Jet.2)

In what follows, we look more closely at each of the aspects mentioned in this sermon.

Distinct from the Body, Senses and Inner Faculties

A good place to start in expounding upon the jīva is where Swaminarayan ends in the summary above, to discount what the jīva is *not*. In being the

[1] We shall see in the following chapter how īśvaras may also embody a human form on earth in order to secure their liberation.

[2] As mentioned in an earlier note in Section 'Sarvopari: God as Supreme' in Chapter 6, 'atom' is used in translation for 'aṇu' in its pre-modern or philosophical sense, meaning an infinitesimally minute particle.

conscious spirit which is the actual subject of a person's sense of 'I'-ness – the very being of one's self, indeed, the 'self' itself – it is largely misidentified with the somatic body and its associated components, i.e. the senses, mind, intellect, etc. Swaminarayan therefore repeatedly and firmly instructs spiritual aspirants to realise their true self to be the soul within, not the external body (Vac. Gaḍh. 1.16, Gaḍh. 1.21, Gaḍh. 1.38, Gaḍh. 1.44, Gaḍh. 1.61, Gaḍh. 1.72, Gaḍh. 1.73, Sār.1, Sār.4, Sār.9, Sār.10, Sār.12, Loyā.17, Pan.3, Gaḍh. 2.1, Gaḍh. 2.2, Gaḍh. 2.6, Gaḍh. 2.33, Gaḍh. 2.57, Var.8, Gaḍh. 3.19, Gaḍh. 3.24, Gaḍh. 3.26, Gaḍh. 3.33, Jet.3). As an example, Swaminarayan urges and describes a correct self-understanding in Vac. Gaḍh. 2.2 thus:

> In this body resides the jīva, and the senses and inner faculties have attached themselves to that jīva. They have also attached themselves externally to the sense-objects. However, out of ignorance, the jīva believes those senses and the inner faculties to be its own form, whereas in actual fact, it is distinct from them . . . One should think, 'I am the ātman, and the senses and inner faculties are absolutely unrelated to me.'

In attempting to emphasise the complete disassociation between the jīva and the physical body, Swaminarayan often describes both by their sharply contradistinctive qualities.

> One should realise the ātman as follows: 'I am sentient, while the body is insentient. I am pure, whereas the body is full of naraka [i.e. hellish defilement]. I am imperishable, while the body is perishable. I am blissful, whereas the body is full of misery.' (Vac. Sār.1)

In another sermon, in response to the question,

> How should one think of one's ātman?

Swaminarayan similarly replies:

> One should ascribe the attributes of the body unto the body and the attributes of the seer [soul] – the conscious spirit – unto the spirit. Also, childhood, youth, old age, stoutness, thinness, birth and death are all aspects of the body; they should never be thought of as belonging to the ātman. Conversely, being uncuttable, unpierceable, unaging, immortal, formed of consciousness, formed of bliss and formed of existence are all aspects of the ātman; they should in no way be considered to belong to the body. Instead, those attributes should be understood to belong to the ātman. (Vac. Sār.12)[3]

[3] See also Vac. Gaḍh. 1.72 and Sār.4.

The differentiation emphasised here by Swaminarayan is one of mutual exclusion, where not only are the jīva's desirable qualities not to be found in and attributed to the body but, equally, neither should the body's flaws and deficiencies be ascribed to or found in the jīva. In addition to providing a correct spiritual self-understanding, what Swaminarayan seems to be guarding against is an unhealthy preoccupation with the physical body which would detract one from spiritual praxis.

Continuing, Swaminarayan adds that an inevitable corollary of a false understanding of the self as the body is a false and detracting attachment to whatever is associated with that body, such as the body's biological parents or its place of birth and social rank, and also its wealth and possessions. For example, he explains:

> The jīva has a misconception in that it does not believe itself to be the jivātman, i.e. distinct from the body. Instead, it believes itself to be the body. To illustrate how the body clings to the jivātman, consider a person who wears a shirt after having it sewn by a tailor. That person then begins to believe, 'The tailor is my father and the tailor's wife is my mother.' Such a person would be considered a fool. In the same manner, the jivātman is given a shirt in the form of this body,[4] which is born sometimes to a Brāhmaṇa couple, sometimes to a couple of a lower social order, or in any of the 8.4 million life-forms. (Vac. Gaḍh. 1.44)

In Vac. Gaḍh. 1.21, Swaminarayan elaborates on the jīva's previous lives and why such a sense of '"I"-ness {ahaṃtā}' for the body and '"my"-ness {mamatā}' for its relatives and belongings is so utterly foolish.

> This body should not be believed to be one's true self. Nor should one's bodily relations be regarded as one's true relations. This is because the jīva has previously assumed 8.4 million bodies. In fact, the jīva has taken birth in the wombs of all females in this world; it has also taken birth numerous times in the wombs of all dogs, cats, monkeys, and all other types of life-forms in the cycle of 8.4 million life-forms. Moreover, of all the different types of females in this world, which has it not previously made its wife? All have been its wife at one time or another. Similarly, assuming numerous female bodies, that jīva has also made all of the different forms of males its husband. Hence, just as one does not believe the relations of those previous 8.4 million life-forms to be one's true relations, and just as one does not believe the bodies of those 8.4 million life-forms to be one's true body, similarly, one should not believe this present body to be one's true self, nor should one believe the relations of this body to be one's true relations. Why?

[4] The analogy of a shirt as a body for the soul closely resembles that used in BG 2.22. Here, Swaminarayan extends it to relate the tailor of the shirt to a person's parents.

> Because just as no relationship remains with bodies from the previous 8.4 million life-forms, similarly, the relationship with this body will not remain either.

Therefore, Swaminarayan adds:

> That ātman is neither a Brāhmaṇa, nor a Kṣatriya, nor a Kaṇbi.[5] It is no one's son and no one's father. It is of no social order and no community. (Vac. Gaḍh. 3.39)

Furthermore:

> The body – be it male or female – is material and perishable, but the jivātman, the worshipper, is neither male nor female. It is characterised by pure existence and consciousness. (Vac. Gaḍh. 3.22)

This important doctrine clearly has wide-reaching implications in a number of critical ways, least not socially and politically, and in fields such as medical ethics, human rights, gender studies, etc. It also raises important questions about how such a spiritual understanding of the self can, for example, be reconciled with maintaining one's physical health, or how such an understanding of one's relatives can accommodate a healthy family life or meaningful relationships with anyone. While it will not be possible to explore the full gamut of all these topics and questions in this introductory theological study, we shall, however, touch upon some of them at their proper points over the course of our discussions in subsequent sections.

The Three Bodies of the Jīva

In distinguishing the jīva from all that is not the self, it is apparent from Swaminarayan's statements above that he not only means the visible somatic body but also the non-visible senses and psychological self. Swaminarayan often refers to the non-self collectively as the jīva's 'three bodies' (Vac. Gaḍh. 1.7, Gaḍh. 1.12, Gaḍh. 1.23, Gaḍh. 1.46, Gaḍh. 1.56, Gaḍh. 1.78, Sār.10, Pan.3, Gaḍh. 2.32, Gaḍh. 2.66, Var.2, Var.8). These are as follows:

1. **sthūla deha**: the 'gross body' composed of the five material elements, i.e. earth {pṛthvī}, water {jala}, light {tejas}, air {vāyu} and space {ākāśa}. This provides the physical support system for the senses, mind, etc. of the subtle body to function (Vac. Gaḍh. 1.12, Sār.14).

[5] A sub-division of the Vaiśya order of communities, traditionally engaged in trade and commerce.

2. **sukṣma deha**: the 'subtle body' (referred to by some as the 'astral body') comprising of the following nineteen elements:

   - five cognitive senses {jñānendriya}, i.e. sight {cakṣus}, hearing {śrotra}, touch {tvak}, taste {rasanā or jihvā} and smell {ghrāṇa}. These should not be confused with their corresponding sense organs, which are parts of the gross body and by which the subtle senses inextricably operate, i.e. sight allows the eyes to see, hearing allows the ears to hear, etc.
   - five conative senses {karmendriya}, i.e. speech {vāk}, dexterity {pāṇi}, locomotion {pāda}, excretion {pāyu} and generation {upastha}. These, too, are subtle powers, operating through their respective external organs, i.e. the mouth, hands, feet, anus and genitals.
   - five quintessential elements {tanmātrā}, i.e. sound {śabda}, touch {sparśa}, sight {rūpa}, taste {rasa} and smell {gandha}. These are extremely subtle elements related to the five material elements mentioned above, which we shall cover in a little more detail in the chapter on māyā and creation.
   - four inner faculties {antaḥkaraṇa}, i.e. manas, buddhi, citta and ahaṃkāra, by which a person can think, reason, contemplate and affirm identity, respectively (Vac. Gaḍh. 1.12, Sār.14). These are sometimes collectively referred to as the 'manas', or mind – the 'eleventh sense' – which is one but functions in four ways, hence the four names.

Together, these twenty-four elements – all products of māyā – create the psychosomatic body of the jīva (Vac. Gaḍh. 2.34).

3. **kāraṇa deha**: the 'causal body' which stores the jīva's karmas and is the form of ignorance, therefore the 'cause' of rebirth (Vac. Sār.11, Kār.12, Gaḍh. 2.66, Var.6).

Swaminarayan provides more information about the causal body and the interrelationship between all three in Vac. Kār.12.

> The causal body is the māyā [i.e. ignorance] of the jīva. That same causal body evolves into the gross and subtle bodies. Thus, all three – the gross, subtle and causal bodies – can be said to be the māyā [or ignorance] of the jīva.

We shall be exploring māyā as ignorance in a later chapter, seeing also the causal body's determinant role in assigning the jīva its gross and subtle bodies. It should be noted, however, that all three bodies – including the subtle and causal – are considered a part of the material order, with the twenty-four elements from which the gross and subtle bodies are composed especially constitutive of each brahmāṇḍa, which shall also be made apparent in that chapter.[6]

Here, we can add that Swaminarayan explains in reference to these three bodies that when falsely identified with them (Vac. Gaḍh. 1.7), thereby assuming their joys and sufferings (Vac. Gaḍh. 1.78) – including birth and death (Vac. Sār.5) – as its own, the jīva is said to be known to be in its concomitant {anvaya} form. Conversely, when it realises itself as distinct from the three bodies, as purely consciousness (Vac. Gaḍh. 1.7), separate from the bodies' joys and sufferings (Vac. Gaḍh. 1.78), as uncuttable, impierceable, indestructible, etc. (Vac. Sār.5), that is the distinct {vyatireka} form of the jīva. In other words, the anvaya form is the jīva in its state of ajñāna (ignorance or false self-understanding), whereas the vyatireka form is the jīva in its state of jñāna (enlightenment or correct self-realisation).

But while the jīva is not the body, mind and senses, what relationship do they hold with the jīva?

One way in which this relationship has been described is like that of a king (the jīva) ruling over the subjects (the mind and senses) living within his kingdom (the body). Swaminarayan presents this analogy at length in Vac. Gaḍh. 2.12, firstly explaining the potential ramifications of a lax soul not controlling its mind and senses, which then go on to 'usurping kingship' over the body. He concludes by teaching 'the art of statecraft' whereby 'no one can overthrow [the soul's] authority in the kingdom that is its body'.

We find a clue to another understanding of the body–soul's integral relationship in the term 'karaṇa', meaning 'instrument'. In opposition to the senses and mind (the inner faculties, or antaḥkaraṇa), the physical body is often called the 'bāhyakaraṇa', or outer faculty. Instructively, this tells us they are all *instruments* of the self, which the jīva can wield to know, act and enjoy (as we shall soon see).

The three bodies could also be described as *mere* instruments, for what can a chisel do without a carpenter? But the opposite is also true. No matter how humanly strong a carpenter may be, he/she requires a chisel to accomplish his/her task. Similarly, as sentient as the jīva is, without the physical body, senses and mind, it cannot perceive the sensory world nor

6 See Sections 'Ignorance' and 'Creative Process' in Chapter 10.

make sense of it. Notably, both the gross and subtle bodies are necessary for this; the physical body alone cannot perceive or cognise, while the senses and mind cannot survive outside of the bodily substratum. Swaminarayan describes the intricate interdependence at play here using another analogy:

> Just as a flame cannot remain aloft in space on its own without the combination of oil, a wick-holder and a wick, similarly, without associating with the disc of flesh [in the body] – which is a transformation of the five material elements – the jīva cannot remain alone. (Vac. Gaḍh. 3.4)

More importantly, as we shall see further in the chapters on māyā and mukti, the body, senses and mind are all essential and powerfully efficacious instruments, provided by God not just for personal enjoyment but for performing the necessary religious endeavours to secure ultimate liberation. This is not fully possible outside of human embodiment. The paradox worth noting here is that while the bodies are not the true self, to realise this – that is, to progress from a state of ignorance to a state of enlightenment – they are indispensable. This being so, the physical body is not intrinsically evil and certainly warrants care. One should therefore endeavour to keep it as healthy and functioning as possible to optimally facilitate theological praxis. Properly understood, then, a deeply religious life and a healthy physical lifestyle are not contradictory but in fact finely compatible, if not also complementary.

The Three States of the Jīva

Alongside the three bodies, Swaminarayan also refers to the three 'states' {avasthā} that the jīva experiences but from which it is also distinct (Vac. Gaḍh. 1.23, Gaḍh. 1.65, Gaḍh. 1.77, Pan.3, Gaḍh. 2.31, Gaḍh. 2.51, Amd.2, Jet.3). It is within these three states of varying awareness that it experiences the fruits of its karmas (Vac. Gaḍh. 1.56, Sār.6). The three states are as follows:

- jāgrata avasthā: the 'waking state', in which the body, senses and mind are all alert and active
- svapna avasthā: the 'dream state', in which the body and senses are dormant and inactive; only the mind is alert and active
- suṣupti avasthā: the 'deep or dreamless sleep state', in which even the mind is dormant; it is characterised by total inertness and self-unawareness/unconsciousness

These three states are born of māyā, with each state predominantly the cause of one of the three māyic qualities: sattvaguṇa, rajoguṇa and tamoguṇa.

Table 4 *Three states of jīva*

State of Jīva	Predominant Māyic Quality	Predominant Awareness	Title of Jīva
Waking	Sattvaguṇa	Gross Body	Viśva
Dream	Rajoguṇa	Subtle Body	Taijasa
Deep Sleep	Tamoguṇa	Causal Body	Prājña

Furthermore, while in each state, the jīva is said to be more aware of and functioning in one of the three bodies than the others, lending it a specific technical title in that state: Viśva, Taijasa and Prājña.[7]

This information has been succinctly collated in Table 4.

Pure

In distinguishing the jīva from its three māyic bodies and the its three states born of the three māyic qualities, Swaminarayan wishes to emphasise the jīva, in its most pristine form, as being devoid of all māyic flaws and impurities. Indeed, an important and striking characteristic of the jīva is that, in its very essence, it is pure. Swaminarayan thus calls the jīva 'śuddha' in three sermons (Vac. Sār.1, Kār.8, Loyā.10), using 'atiśuddha' {extremely pure} in Vac. Pan.3. Swaminarayan elaborates on this spiritual purity in several more sermons, including most emphatically in Vac. Gaḍh. 2.12 where he calls believing anything to the contrary nothing less than foolishness.

> The jīva, which resides in the body, feels, 'Lust, anger and other vicious natures are attached to my jīva.' In this manner, depending on which of the vicious natures, i.e. lust, anger, avarice, etc. is predominant in a person, he believes his jīva to be full of that nature due to his association with it. But, in fact, not a single one of these vicious natures lies within the jīva; the jīva has merely believed itself to possess them out of its own foolishness.

As true as this is, though, the jīva's ignorance or perverse knowledge {viparīta jñāna} about its true nature is equally real and problematic. Thus, despite being essentially pure in nature, this māyā (as the form of ignorance) propels the jīva through the incessant cycle of births and deaths,

[7] See also MāU 2.1–3 for more on these three states and three titles for the jīva.

necessitating it to be enlightened and liberated. We shall pick up on this in subsequent chapters after further elucidating the nature of the jīva.[8]

Sat-Cit-Ānanda

If the jīva is not to be identified with the somatic body made of material elements or the senses and mind made of similarly subtle elements, what *is* it composed of? What constitutes the jīva most fundamentally and essentially?

Swaminarayan answers this question in Vac. Gaḍh. 1.73, again, juxtaposing the soul with that which it is not. He explains:

> After developing knowledge of the ātman and the thorough knowledge of God's nature, one should think, 'I am the ātman, characterised by eternal existence {sat}, consciousness {cit} and bliss {ānanda}, whereas the body and the brahmāṇḍa are māyic and perishable. How can they compare to me?'

Swaminarayan also iterates the jīva as being 'sat', 'cit' and 'ānanda' by using these terms (and their synonyms) separately in several other sermons:

- 'satya' and 'sattārūpa': Vac. Gaḍh. 1.7, Gaḍh. 1.14, Gaḍh. 1.16, Gaḍh. 1.47, Loyā.17, Gaḍh. 2.57, Gaḍh. 2.66, Gaḍh. 3.3, Gaḍh. 3.22, Gaḍh. 3.33, Gaḍh. 3.39
- 'caityana' and 'caitanyarūpa': Vac. Gaḍh. 1.23, Sār.1, Sār.4, Sār.10, Sār.12, Loyā.7, Loyā.18, Pan.3, Gaḍh. 2.2, Gaḍh. 2.17, Gaḍh. 2.20, Gaḍh. 2.22, Gaḍh. 2.55, Gaḍh. 2.60, Gaḍh. 2.66, Var.4, Gaḍh. 3.2, Gaḍh. 3.3, Gaḍh. 3.19, Gaḍh. 3.22, Gaḍh. 3.27, Jet.2, Jet.3
- 'ānandarūpa' and 'sukharūpa': Vac. Sār.1, Sār.12, Kār.3, Loyā.10

What is striking here are the clear points of similitude between the nature of the jīva and the nature of Parabrahman and Akṣarabrahman. While much is often made of their differences, we should also note that jīvas – characterised as they are by sat-cit-ānanda as well – share in the infinite nature of God and Guru, if only to an infinitesimally minute extent. That is, by nature, jīvas are qualitatively similar to Parabrahman and Akṣarabrahman, yet metaphysically distinct from and infinitely inferior to them.

Knower

As is evident from the string of references above, Swaminarayan especially emphasises the soul as consciousness. He adds that the jīva is not just

[8] See Sections 'Ignorance' in Chapter 10 and 'Nature and Cause of Bondage in Chapter 11.

formed of or *is* consciousness {caitanya} but also *has* consciousness as a quality. He thus calls it 'cetana' {conscious, i.e. having the quality of caitanya} in Vac. Loyā.10 and Pan.3. This allows the jīva to also be a 'knower' {jñātā}. This is essential if it is to be aware of (and be able to choose) its own actions and perceive the sensory world, including its own body, while also being able to acquire the necessary theological knowledge to secure its liberation.

Swaminarayan often presents the jīva as the 'knower', again, usually in relation to the body and world around it, which are the 'knowable' or objects of knowledge {jñeya}. For example, in Vac. Gaḍh. 1.16, Swaminarayan explains that a wise devotee

> accepts whatever teachings God and the Sant offer as the highest truth but does not doubt their words.

He then lists their teachings as follows:

> You are distinct from the mind, body, senses and vital breaths. You are real. You are the knower of the body, senses and vital breaths, which are all non-real.

Swaminarayan similarly describes in Vac. Gaḍh. 1.61 how one should reinforce one's true, spiritual identity:

> I am not the body. I am the ātman, distinct from the body, and the knower of all [the body, senses, mind, etc.].

In calling 'the three bodies – gross, subtle and causal – and the three states – waking, dream and deep sleep' the 'field' {kṣetra}, he goes on in Vac. Pan.3 to say:

> [A jñānin] realises his ātman to be distinct from the 'field', and believes, 'They can never be a part of me. I am their knower.'

He thus calls the jīva 'kṣetrajña' {literally, 'knower of the field'} in this and four other sermons (Vac. Gaḍh. 1.57, Kār.12, Gaḍh. 2.1, Gaḍh. 2.17).

This topic forms the subject of the Jñādhikaraṇa in BS 2.3.19–32, in which the opening sūtra straightforwardly confirms on the basis of śāstric revelation that the jīva (and īśvara) is not only 'of the form of knowledge {jñānamātram}' but a 'knower also {jñātā'pi}'. Bhadreshdas also makes the important clarification here that this quality of knowledge is an intrinsic and natural, therefore consistent, attribute of the jīva, but not adscititiously arising in the intellect or outside of the jīva, as is asserted by some schools.[9]

[9] BS-SB 2.3.19, pp. 232–3.

As the adhikaraṇa proceeds beyond this relatively brief first sūtra, the focus of the debate shifts to the size of the jīva, because this will affect how much the jīva can know and how. We can therefore continue this discussion in the following two sections, where we firstly see what Swaminarayan has to say about the size of the jīva and how he resolves the epistemological difficulty that arises from it, and thereafter as we discuss the jīva as the continuing subject of actions and experiences.

Atomicity

Various schools of Vedānta have traditionally propounded and defended one of three sizes for the individual soul. It can either be extremely minute, 'like an atom'[10] {aṇu-parimāṇa}, or assume the size of the body it inhabits {madhyama-parimāṇa; literally, 'mid-sized'}, or be spatially limitless and all-pervading {vibhu}.

Swaminarayan is unequivocal that the jīva is 'atomic in size {aṇu-mātra}' (Vac. Jet.2), describing it analogously in Vac. Kār.1 'as fine as the tip of a spear'. In both cases, he is referring to its extreme subtlety, i.e. being immeasurably small in size.

The Upaniṣads are similarly definitive in their descriptions. For example, the Muṇḍaka Upaniṣad states:

> Know by thought this atomic ātman, in which the vital breath enters fivefold. (MuU 3.1.9)

And like Swaminarayan in Vac. Kār.2, the Śvetāśvatara Upaniṣad analogises:

> It is as fine as the tip of a goad. (SU 5.8)[11]

Swaminarayan adds that the eminently subtle soul resides primarily within the heart of the physical body (Vac. Kār.12, Gaḍh. 2.34, Gaḍh. 3.4, Loyā.15), as also described by the Upaniṣads:

> This ātman resides within the heart. (PU 3.6)

> That [ātman] is full of consciousness within the vital breaths[12] and is the inner light within the heart. (BU 4.3.7)

[10] See earlier notes 36 and 211 on the use of 'atom' for 'aṇu'.

[11] Bhadreshdas cites these verses in his commentary of BS 2.3.23 to prove the ātman's atomicity. This follows from BS 2.3.22 where he argues that the all-pervasive 'ātman' stated in CU 3.14.2–3 and BU 4.4.25 refers to Parabrahman, not the individual soul. See SB-BS 2.3.22–23, pp. 234–5.

[12] By extension, Bhadreshdas takes the plural term for 'prāṇa' here to include all of the senses and faculties. See BU-SB 4.3.7, p. 241.

But this then leads at once to the question of how there can be sentiency throughout the body if the jīva is limited in size and located only within the heart. It is in fact a question that Swaminarayan himself asks his audience in Vac. Gaḍh. 3.4.

> Please describe how the jīva, which resides within the body, is present in one location and how it pervades the entire body.

Not fully satisfied with any of the answers he receives, he answers his own question with the following analogy:

> If an oil lamp is placed at one location in a mandīra {temple}, its flame predominantly pervades the wick, and secondarily, it also pervades the entire building. In the same manner, the jivātman also predominantly resides in and pervades the disc of flesh [in the heart] that is a product of the five material elements; and secondarily, it resides in and pervades the entire body. This is how the jīva resides within the body.

Thus, Swaminarayan makes clear that

> the jīva actually resides in the disc of flesh [in the heart], and by its consciousness pervades the entire body. Therefore, regardless of where pain is felt in the body, it is the jīva itself that feels the pain. (Vac. Gaḍh. 3.4)

What this tells us about the jīva – as consciousness in its very form and also having consciousness as an inherent quality – is that, like the flame and its light, while both are self-illuminating (i.e. they do not require another source of consciousness to make them known), both differ somewhat in their function of illuminating others. The jīva, like the flame, is limited in its form and place, thereby unable to make known anything apart from itself, whereas its consciousness, the light, can radiate out to illuminate other objects within its vicinity.

The Sūtrakāra offers the very same flame-light analogy in BS 2.3.26, and yet another analogy – of sandalwood ointment and its diffusive fragrance – in BS 2.3.24. Using these, Bhadreshdas goes on to confirm with support from various Upaniṣadic and Bhagavad-Gītā statements that the jīva and its consciousness are indeed distinct even if inseparable, as are the odorous and its odour (BS 2.3.27–28).

The Jñādhikaraṇa which we began in the previous section thus concludes in BS 2.3.32, arguing, firstly, that if the soul were hypothetically considered to be all-pervasive (rather than atomic), then the perverse result would be that every soul would be continuously experiencing everything. Secondly, if the soul were merely formed of consciousness (but not having consciousness as a quality), then it would not experience anything at all (apart from itself). Both outcomes are contrary to general perception. Therefore, the soul must be atomic in size and have the inherent quality of consciousness. This consciousness pervades the body even while the jīva resides in the heart, thus allowing the jīva to be the consistent subject of its personal experiences, i.e. 'the knower'.[13]

Agent and Enjoyer

A direct corollary of the jīva as knower {jñatā} is the jīva as doer {kartā} and enjoyer {bhoktā} (or one who experiences). This is no less evidenced in the Brahmasūtras, where the Jñādhikaraṇa is immediately followed by the Kartrādhikaraṇa (BS 2.3.33–40). Here, the very thrust of the first sūtra's argument is that if the jīva is not accepted as the intelligent agent (and enjoyer), all teachings and injunctions of the scriptures will be rendered meaningless, for to whom would they otherwise be addressed? It is implausible to claim such calls to action as

> Always performing works here, one should wish to live a hundred years (IU 2)

and

> With inner tranquillity, one should offer upāsanā (CU 3.14.1)

are made to an inert, insentient entity which is incapable of any action or even conceiving of it. Since the words of the scriptures are always meaningful, and they enjoin action on only that which is able to act and experience the fruits of that action, i.e. reap its consequences, it therefore follows that that which is addressed is the sentient agent and enjoyer.[14]

This also has much significance to the free will of the jīva, as debated in the final sūtra of the Kartrādhikaraṇa, which we shall examine at the end of this chapter when discussing the jīva's relationship with Parabrahman.[15] Here, let us briefly restate the above with some of our earlier points.

The body, composed of gross matter, is inherently inert. It cannot in and of itself know or act or experience. It must be vivified by a sentient entity, which is thus the true agent of all actions and the real subject of all experiences, even though it is by means of the body, the senses and other faculties that it can be so. As in the chisel and carpenter example upon which we drew earlier, the chisel is necessary for a carpenter to create his/her furniture or toy, but on its own, the chisel being inert is utterly

[13] See BS-SB 2.3.19–32, pp. 232–9. [14] BS-SB 2.3.33, pp. 240–1.
[15] See Section 'Relationship with Parabrahman: Dependent and Free' in this chapter.

ineffective. In the hands of an expert carpenter, though, it is as if the chisel springs to life, carving wood with consummate ease. Going further, since it is the carpenter who chooses how to use the chisel and when to use it (or not use it), it is he/she who deservedly receives the payment for his/her labours – not the chisel. Similarly, as the intelligent agent, it is the soul that is held accountable for its actions, good and bad, and to whom the deserts are accordingly conferred, not to the body.

As we saw in the introductory overview from Vac. Jet.2, Swaminarayan stresses that it is the jīva – using its bodily instruments – that knows, acts and perceives. Notably, Swaminarayan frames the knowing and experiencing there as 'functions' – the *act* of seeing, hearing, tasting … even thinking – confirming the coherency and unity of the jīva as jñatā {knower}, kartā {doer} and bhoktā {enjoyer}. This statement also closely resonates with the following Chāndogya Upaniṣad passage:

> Now, when this sight here gazes into the sky, that is the seeing self; the faculty of sight allows it to see. That which knows 'Let me smell this', is the ātman; the faculty of smell allows it to smell. That which knows 'Let me say this', is the ātman; the faculty of speech allows it to speak. That which knows 'Let me hear this', is the ātman; the faculty of hearing allows it to hear. That which knows 'Let me think about this', is the ātman; the mind is its divine faculty of [inner] sight. (CU 8.12.4–5)

The Praśna Upaniṣad states more straightforwardly:

> This intelligent self … is verily the one that sees, feels, hears, smells, tastes, thinks, understands and acts. (PU 4.9)

An important clarification that needs to be made here is that the jīva's ability to act and experience is not wholly independent. As the 'body' of Parabrahman (and Akṣarabrahman), it is supported, empowered and also governed by them. This is debated in the very next adhikaraṇa of the Brahmasūtras, which, too, we shall discuss in the section about the jīva's relationship with Parabrahman, attempting, as aforementioned, to also resolve how this doctrine can accommodate the jīva's freedom of will.

Imperishability, Eternality, Individuality and Immutability

A number of characteristics of the jīva were already mentioned in the opening section of this chapter as we looked to see how the jīva differs from the body. A few of these characteristics deserve further elucidation, and can be treated together.

One point that Swaminarayan makes repeatedly, for example in Vac. Sār.12, is that it is the body that undergoes 'birth and death', passing through phases such as 'childhood, youth [and] old age', whereas the jīva is 'uncuttable, unpierceable, unaging, immortal'. Thus, the jīva is described as unborn {aja}, unaging {ajara} and undying {amara}. It is imperishable and immutable. It is eternal.

Swaminarayan iterates the jīva's imperishability by making an interesting point in Vac. Gaḍh. 3.39. He explains:

> The ātman has passed through countless life-forms. In fact, it is said that a person has drunk as much milk from his mothers as there is water in the ocean. In those lives, the ātman has experienced death in countless ways, yet it has not perished. It has remained as it is. So, if it did not perish in that state of ignorance when it regarded itself as the body, how shall it perish now that we have knowledge of it?

The jīva's insusceptibility to death and deterioration is thus a matter of fact. Whether one knows this or not is immaterial to reality.

Continuing the analogy of the oil lamp's flame from Vac. Gaḍh. 3.4, Swaminarayan further explains:

> Just as fire – which is distinct from the container, the oil and the wick – cannot be destroyed by breaking just the container, in the same way, the jīva, even though it pervades the disc of flesh [in the heart] and the body, does not die with the death of the body. (Vac. Gaḍh. 3.4)

Those familiar with Vedāntic texts will be aware of numerous statements in the Upaniṣads and Bhagavad-Gītā supporting this point. As one example, a popular phrase found almost identically in the Bhagavad-Gītā and Kaṭha Upaniṣad proclaims:

> This [soul] is unborn and eternal, everlasting and primeval. It is not slain by the slaying of the body. (BG 2.20, KaU 2.18)

Swaminarayan also iterates the beginninglessness of the jīva, tracing its existence back to beyond the re-origination of each brahmāṇḍa after the state of dissolution. Using another analogy, he explains in Vac. Gaḍh. 3.10 that even during this state of primeval dormancy, the jīvas continue to exist within māyā.

> Just as seeds in the soil sprout by the association of rainwater, similarly, the jīvas, which are eternal, arise from within māyā; but new jīvas are not created. Therefore, . . . the jīvas residing in māyā are also eternal, and they are not components {aṃśa} of God; they are always jīvas.

Swaminarayan adds here an important point at the end, clarifying that the jīvas do not have an aṃśa-aṃśin {component-composite} relationship with Parabrahman. This predictably becomes the topic of discussion in the Aṃśādhikaraṇa between BS 2.3.43 and 2.3.53, where Bhadreshdas argues that to believe sentient beings to be fragmented parts of God contradicts śāstric texts revealing Parabrahman to be indivisible {akhaṇḍa}, non-fragmentary {niraṃśa} and without parts {niravayava}. Those texts which do mention the jīvas as being the 'aṃśa' of Parabrahman should be understood as describing them as *devotees* of God, inseparable from him by virtue of their intense love and total dependency on him, as they are, of course, a 'part' of his body which is the entire universe.[16] This is indeed the exegesis Swaminarayan provides for BG 15.7 –

> My 'aṃśa' alone in this living realm, of the form of the eternal jīva

– when he cites the verse in Vac. Gaḍh. 2.8.

During the pre-origination stage of each brahmāṇḍa that Swaminarayan mentions above in Vac. Gaḍh. 3.10, it should be noted that each jīva is dormant within māyā with only its causal body. When, by the will of Parabrahman, the creative process is initiated, each jīva receives its composite body (gross and subtle) according to the karmas encoded within its individual causal sheath. During the sustenance stage of the brahmāṇḍa, each jīva will continue to transmigrate – until securing final liberation – from one such body to another as and when the lifetime of each body expires, again, always according to the jīva's own karmic blueprint, which continues to evolve and be transferred from one life to another. To reiterate, the birth, development, decay and eventual death are of the body only; the jīva is distinct from the body and unaffected by its corporeal deterioration and death. Finally, at the time of that particular brahmāṇḍa's dissolution, the jīva discards its body (gross and subtle) and returns with its remaining causal body to a state of dormancy within māyā – until the next cycle of creation. This continues for the jīva until it can eradicate its causal body, i.e. māyā in the form of ignorance, and become brahmarūpa by acquiring the qualities of Akṣarabrahman, thereby making it eligible for eternal communion with Parabrahman in Akṣaradhāma.

All throughout this time – while in a state of bondage within māyā, when liberated from it in Akṣaradhāma, and during the origination, sustenance and dissolution stages of the world – the jīvas exist *as* jīvas,

[16] See BS-SB 2.3.43–53, pp. 246–53 and BG-SB 15.7, p. 310.

with each jīva retaining its distinct individuality; it neither merges into māyā during dissolution, nor into Parabrahman upon liberation.

Some of these points are also clarified in the single-sūtra Ātmādhikaraṇa in BS 2.3.18. In the continuing debate about the omnicausality of Parabrahman and Akṣarabrahman (BS 1.1.2), and therefore whether they can be the subject of the desire to know 'Brahman' (BS 1.1.1), the contention raised by the objector is that jīvas (and īśvaras) are unborn and therefore outside the purview of 'creation'. Hence, the sentient beings should not be said to have Parabrahman and Akṣarabrahman as their cause. In support of his case, the objector cites verses describing them as unborn {aja}, i.e. KaU 2.18 and SU 1.9. In response, Bhadreshdas goes on to cite other verses proclaiming the 'creation' of all beings. For example:

> That from which these beings are born . . . (TU 3.1.1)

> From that all these being are born . . . (PU 1.14)

> That which the wise perceive as the source of all beings . . . (MuU 1.1.6)

But how should these verses and others like them be reconciled with those proclaiming sentient beings as unborn and eternal? For example:

> This [soul] is never born nor does it ever die. (KaU 2.18, BG 2.20)

> This soul within the body is eternal and cannot be killed. (BG 2.30)

> He [Akṣarabrahman] is the one eternal soul among many eternal souls. (SU 6.13)

Bhadreshdas explains that the 'creation' of souls should be understood as a figurative description; it refers to the *body* a jīva receives in every new life-event. Similarly, 'death' is simply the falling of that body, not of the jīva itself. In this way, the jīva is eternal, and yet its bodies are created, allowing it to still be a part of the universal effect caused by Parabrahman and Akṣarabrahman. Furthermore, Bhadreshdas adds, since there is no alteration in the essential form of the jīva {svarūpā'nyathābhāva} at any time throughout this process, it can still be said to be immutable. Nevertheless, it may undergo other forms of change, such as the ceaseless contraction and expansion of its knowledge on account of it pervading its changing bodies.[17] Since, as we learned earlier, this knowledge or consciousness is an inherent but distinct quality of the jīva ('the light of the flame' in Swaminarayan's analogy in Vac. Gaḍh. 3.4), this does not result in any distortion in the essential form of the jīva ('the flame' itself).

[17] BS-SB 2.3.18, pp. 231–2.

Multiplicity

A small but nonetheless important point about the nature of the jīva remains to be made. It relates to the soul's individuality mentioned above.

Even while all jīvas are ontologically the same, they are not one. The multiplicity of jīvas (and īśvaras) is shown by the plural nouns and pronouns used in verses such as the following:

> He [Akṣarabrahman] is the one eternal soul among many eternal souls . . . (SU 6.13)

> That from which these beings are born . . . (TU 3.1.1)

> From that all these being are born . . . (PU 1.14)

> . . . whereas all beings are 'kṣara'. (BG 15.16)

Swaminarayan also refers to the jīvas in the plural (Vac. Var.6, Gaḍh. 3.10, Gaḍh. 3.39), sometimes even adding such telling qualifiers as 'all' and 'each'. For example:

> In addition, when all of those brahmāṇḍas are destroyed, all other jīvas lie dormant within māyā. (Vac. Gaḍh. 1.12)

> That [God] . . . resides as the indwelling controller {antaryāmin} in all jīvas and grants each jīva a body according to its past karmas. (Vac. Gaḍh. 1.13)

> God dwells within all jīvas, but his form is different from the jīvas. (Vac. Gaḍh. 3.37)

Swaminarayan also talks explicitly of 'countless millions of liberated souls' (Vac. Gaḍh. 1.21, Gaḍh. 1.63, Loyā.14).

Because the jīvas' individuality is preserved at all times – while in a state of bondage within māyā, when liberated from it in Akṣaradhāma, and during the origination, sustenance and dissolution stages of the world – so is their multiplicity. Just as jīvas do not merge into māyā or Parabrahman, nor do they ever merge into themselves to form one 'super-jīva'; the inter-differentiation between them is real and eternal. Nor, as we saw, are the many jīvas fragments of one super-being, for, like Parabrahman and Akṣarabrahman, the jīvas (and īśvaras) are indivisible and non-fragmental.

This multiplicity is also evidenced by the many differing personal experiences jīvas have simultaneously. While one may feel happy, another will feel sad. While one may be in a state of bondage, another will be liberated. And while all jīvas are identical in essence and form, each bound jīva differs from another by its own individual code of karma, leading to differences in body and circumstances for each individual jīva. All this would be untenable were it not for multiple jīvas.

This completes the elucidation of the jīva's nature introduced at the beginning of this chapter from Vac. Jet.2. We now turn to a vital aspect of understanding the soul within Swaminarayan Hindu theology – its relationship with God.

Relationship with Parabrahman: Dependent and Free

A consistent feature of Swaminarayan Hindu theology, as probably with most theological systems, is that every discussion has God at its centre and as its ultimate goal. We saw this during the extensive chapter on Akṣarabrahman, and it remains true for the jīva. We thus conclude this chapter on the jīva by expounding what its relationship with Parabrahman entails, reconciling both the jīva's dependency on Parabrahman and its own freedom of will and action.

In an earlier chapter, we made an effort to understand Parabrahman's overall supremacy by looking at his relationship with other entities. We learned there that Parabrahman is the king of all kings {rājādhirāj} and the lord of all lords {īśvarnā paṇ īśvar}, ruling over his dominion, which has jīvas and īśvaras as subjects. His reign is eminently right and appropriate, for God has not usurped his vast realm from any other rival lord; he is the one without second, and its very creator and cause. That is why he is also the owner of the entire cosmos, giving him an especially personal interest in his subjects; the jīvas rightfully *belong* to him. For the jīvas' part, they find their greatest joy and fulfilment in being so owned and ruled by him, feeling privileged and exalted to have been accepted as such. They thus devoutly serve their master in joyful duty, because God reigns not by coercion or tyranny but by loving providence.

In this sense, Parabrahman is also the 'pati' of the world, like the lord of an estate or head of a household, providing for and protecting his extensive family who are eminently grateful and indebted to him, as adoring children to their doting father whom they worship.

We also learned that Parabrahman is the śarīrin {embodied soul}, who has as his śarīra {body} the spiritual world comprising all jīvas, īśvaras and Akṣarabrahman, as well as the material world of māyā and all things evolved from it. As the soul of all souls, he supports them, empowers them and controls them from within (Vac. Gaḍh. 1.64, Kār.8, et al.). To paraphrase from that section, he is their very life-source – the cause for their existence and the ontic ground {ādhāra} upon which they can function. Just as a physical body perishes once separated from its soul, so, too, the jīvas (and īśvaras) cannot survive even momentarily without Parabrahman. And as the body is wholly incapable of doing anything without the will, knowledge and strength of the inner self, similarly, all jīvas (and īśvaras) are totally dependent on Parabrahman to inspire them and bring them to action. Swaminarayan explains in Vac. Gaḍh. 1.65:

> When a jīva enters the state of deep sleep, it becomes inert like a slab of stone and retains no type of consciousness . . . When a jīva enters such a state, God awakens it from unconsciousness through his 'jñānaśakti' and makes it aware of its actions. This is known as 'jñānaśakti', the faculty of cognition. Furthermore, whatever action a jīva engages in, it does so with the support of what is known as God's 'kriyāśakti', the faculty of conation. Finally, whatever object a jīva desires, it acquires with the help of what is known as God's 'icchāśakti', the faculty of volition. (Vac. Gaḍh. 1.65)

Bhadreshdas cites the above passage in his comment of KeU 1.2, which describes Parabrahman as

> the ear of the ear, the mind of the mind, the tongue of the tongue, the vital breath of the vital breath, the eye of the eye.

The ears can only hear because it is God who has empowered them with the ability of hearing. The mind can only think and perceive because God has infused it with the power of thinking and perception. The body is enlivened not by the breath alone, but by God who breathes life into that vital breath. In all, Bhadreshdas explains, Parabrahman is 'the provider of the power by which the inner and outer faculties can engage in all their respective functions . . . making them instruments for the jīva' by which to know, enjoy, act and live.[18]

So, even as the jīva is the knower, doer and enjoyer, it does not know, do or enjoy independently. It is always enabled by God. 'Indeed', Swaminarayan emphatically states,

> God is the very life of all jīvas. Without him, those jīvas are incapable of doing anything or enjoying anything. (Vac. Gaḍh. 3.37)

This leads us to the natural and necessary question: Is the jīva, then, simply an automaton or puppet in the hands of an almighty God, absolutely dictated by *his* will but with no freedom of its own to act and enjoy? Without this free will, all that the jīva does is rendered inauthentic, meaningless – including its so-called devotion and obedience to God.

[18] KeU-SB 1.2, pp. 33–5. See also AU-SB 3.1, pp.437–9.

So how can one make sense of the jīva as knower, agent and enjoyer as well as of God's omniscience, omniagency and omnicausality?

For this, we must turn to the Paratantrādhikaraṇa of BS 2.3.41–42.

Having established the sentiency and agency of the jīva in the preceding Jñādhikaraṇa (BS 2.3.19–32) and Kartrādhikaraṇa (BS 2.3.33–40), respectively, the Sūtrakāra immediately moves to qualify both in this two-sūtra debate.

The first sūtra is preluded by Bhadreshdas with the following prima facie view.

> At that, there is a doubt. Is the agency of the ātman exclusively self-supported {svamātrādhīna}, or is it dependent on anything else {paratantra}? What is appropriate? Self-supported is [appropriate]. Why? Because otherwise, if the dependent view is taken, that would undermine {literally, 'damage'} [the ātman's] independence, which would in turn fail to confirm its agency.

To this, Bhadreshdas retorts 'no', and states that the jīva is indeed dependent {tantra} on the highest {para[19]} entities because that is what the śrutis proclaim {parāt-tu tacchruteḥ} (BS 2.3.41). In support, he cites statements from the Upaniṣads and Bhagavad-Gītā confirming, firstly, Parabrahman and Akṣarabrahman as the 'highest', and then how they both support and control all jīvas (and īśvaras). For example:

> [Parabrahman,] the soul of all, having entered within, is the controller of all beings. (Taittirīya Āraṇyaka 1.3.21)

> Within the governance of this Akṣara, O Gārgī, do recipient men praise donors, deities [praise] the patron, and forefathers [praise] the ancestral offering. (BU 3.8.9)

But if the jīva is not considered independent, the fictive objector contends, the moral injunctions of the śāstras – enjoining humans to do some things and prohibiting them from doing others – and the extolled fruits of observing such injunctions would all be rendered meaningless, for they would be addressing those which are incapable of acting or enjoying freely. This being so, it would disarray the whole system of praxis and moral deserts. Moreover, if God is deemed the sole agent of all actions, then he

[19] Bhadreshdas is clear here that the 'para' within the compounded word 'paratantra' should be taken to mean not just 'other' but 'higher'. While both translations are correct lexically, the latter ascribes the jīvas' (and īśvaras') dependency not generally, on any or all others, but specifically on Parabrahman and Akṣarabrahman.

will have to be held accountable for all the wrongdoings in the world. How can this apparent conflict be resolved?

Bhadreshdas explains, in effect, that there is no conflict to resolve as soon as one appreciates that dependency and free will are not incompatible. The jīvas (and īśvaras) are indeed free to decide what to desire, what to know and what to do. But since this freedom has been lovingly and graciously granted – permitted – by Parabrahman, and it is he who empowers them with the *ability* to desire, know and do (as seen above), they are still very much dependent on him.

To elucidate, Bhadreshdas extends a familiar analogy. Just as a sovereign king[20] bestows upon a subject from his realm some powers of authority and gives him or her the permission to exercise that authority in whatever tasks he or she sees fit, saying, 'Here, use this as you wish', in the same way, Parabrahman gives his permission {anumati} to the jīvas and īśvaras to endeavour as they wish. Bhadreshdas clarifies that this endeavour {prayatna} can take the form of both dharmic and non-dharmic acts.

In BG 13.22 also, when Parabrahman is described as the 'anumantā' {permitter}, Bhadreshdas explains it in reference to allowing jīvas and īśvaras the freedom to perform their own actions, of which Parabrahman is the 'upadraṣṭā' {close witness} dwelling within their bodies.[21]

Continuing the analogy in BS 2.3.42, Bhadreshdas adds that as the authorised subject exercises his or her sovereign-granted powers in various tasks, the king observes those tasks, rewarding him or her when pleased by good accomplishments and penalising when displeased with bad accomplishments. So it is with the endeavours of the jīvas and īśvaras. Parabrahman is pleased with those endeavours that are dharmic (in accordance to scriptural prescriptions) and displeased with those that are adharmic (contrary to scriptural prescriptions), administering the fruits of those endeavours accordingly. To be clear, while the fruits of the jīvas' karmas are dispensed by God as an expression of his pleasure and displeasure, it is strictly according to the karmas freely accrued by the jīvas themselves.[22] In this way, Bhadreshdas concludes, the meaningfulness of scriptural injunctions is preserved and God is acquitted of any charge of partiality

[20] Bhadreshdas appropriately includes in the analogy the 'king's secretary' who, by royal decree, can also bestow, permit and pay or penalise the authorised subject. This refers to Akṣarabrahman, upon whom the jīvas and īśvaras are also dependent.

[21] BG-SB 13.22, p. 286.

[22] More on the Hindu doctrine of karma and God as karmaphalapradātā will be explored in Section 'Purpose of Creation and the Irreproachability of Its Creator' in Chapter 10, in relation to the diversity found within creation.

and cruelty, even while confirming both the jīva's dependency on God and its own free will.[23]

On this point, we should also refer to the final sūtra of the Kartrādhikaraṇa (immediately preceding the Paratantrādhikaraṇa) which likewise relates to the free will of the jīva to act. The objection there is that if the jīva is the conscious agent, and consciousness is its intrinsic, inseparable quality, why is it that the jīva is not continuously acting? The Sūtrakāra replies analogously that, 'like the carpenter {yathā ca takṣā}', it can do 'both {ubhayathā}' – act as well as not act. Just because a carpenter has tools at his/her disposal does not mean that he/she is forced to always be at work. He/she works and rests as he/she pleases. In the same way, while the jīva has the body and its senses, etc. – its tools for cognition, action and enjoyment – they do not compel it to always act. The jīva will act when it wishes to act and not act when it wishes not to.[24]

Crucially, then, the jīva has the option to *not* act, making its actions all the more meaningful. There is now choice and, to make that choice, the intelligent being can weigh up the consequences for both acting and not acting; so, howsoever it eventually does choose to act, it is the jīva that is exclusively responsible for those actions, making also their consequences fully deserved for the jīva.

This free choice is also precisely why, as is so obviously evident, that all souls are *not* engrossed in joyful devotion to God nor totally subservient and obedient to him. Some do exercise their God-given freedom to not only disobey and disrespect him but to outrightly deny him. Only then do the devotion and obedience of the faithful carry such force and value.

In this way, the apparent tension between ascribing all actions to God at the expense of the freedom and responsibility of individual souls, and compromising the omniagency of God by allowing some autonomy to human activity, is relieved. Both are respected and kept intact. The jīva is not totally independent though not enslaved either. And while God is still the omnipotent, omniscient cause and agent of all, he has, out of his loving grace, granted and empowered the jīvas with the tools, options and judgement to act freely.

[23] BS-SB 2.3.41–2, pp. 244–6. [24] BS-SB 2.3.40, pp. 243–4.

Here Bhadreshdas confirms the being of the Vairāja Puruṣa (also known as Virāṭa Puruṣa) as an īśvara. He then describes how, like the jīva, it is bound by māyā but has a considerably longer lifespan of about two parārdhas, i.e. 2×10^{17} human years. Like the jīva's gross, subtle and causal bodies, it has its own three bodies known as virāṭa, sūtrātman and avyākṛta. These are encircled by the eight sheaths (i.e. constituents of the creative process), and are evolved from mahattattva {literally, 'the great element', which is itself originally evolved from māyā}. And like the jīva's three states of waking, dream and deep sleep, so, too, the īśvara has the states of creation, sustenance and dissolution.[1]

These three states are born of māyā, with each state predominantly the cause of one of the three māyic qualities: sattvaguṇa, rajoguṇa and tamoguṇa.

While in each state, the īśvara is said to be more aware of and functioning in one of the three bodies than the others, lending it a specific technical title in that state: Vairāja, Hiranyagarbha and Īśvara.

As we did for the jīva, this information can be succinctly tabulated (Table 5).

When placed alongside the same information about the jīva, we have another useful comparative summary (Table 6).

Like the jīvas, when an īśvara falsely identifies with its three bodies, that is known as its anvaya {concomitant} form, whereas when it correctly self-identifies itself as distinct from all its bodies and as characterised by pure eternal existence, consciousness and bliss, that is its vyatireka {distinct} form (Vac. Gaḍh. 1.7, Sār.5).

Since īśvaras suffer from ignorance, it is evident that they, too, are in need of correct knowledge. But are they eligible for brahmavidyā just as

Table 5 *Three states of īśvara*

State of Īśvara	Predominant Māyic Quality	Predominant Body	Title of Īśvara
Creation	Sattvaguṇa	Virāṭa	Vairāja
Sustenance	Rajoguṇa	Sūtrātman	Hiranyagarbha
Dissolution	Tamoguṇa	Avyākṛta	Īśvara

[1] AU-SB 1.1.2, pp. 418–19.

Table 6 *Comparative summary of the three states of jīva and īśvara*

Body		State		Title	
Jīva	Īśvara	Jīva	Īśvara	Jīva	Īśvara
Sthūla (Gross)	Virāṭa	Jāgrata (Wakefulness)	Uttpati (Creation)	Viṣva	Vairāja
Sūkṣma (Subtle)	Sūtrātman	Svapna (Dream)	Sthiti (Sustenance)	Taijasa	Hiranyagarbha
Kāraṇa (Causal)	Avyākṛta	Suṣupti (Deep Sleep)	Pralaya (Dissolution)	Prājña	Īśvara

humans are? This question forms the topic of debate in BS 1.3.26. After a prima facie view rejecting their eligibility, the Sūtrakāra, as interpreted by Bhadreshdas, emphatically asserts that they are indeed eligible, as evidenced by such śruti statements as the opening verse of the Muṇḍaka Upaniṣad where Brahmā, an īśvara, is noted as the first preacher of brahmavidyā, having taught it to his eldest son, Atharvaṇ.[2]

Swaminarayan mentions explicitly in Vac. Gaḍh. 2.31 that 'like the jīva, that Virāṭa Puruṣa is also bound', adding that it can transcend māyā and become brahmarūpa only when it worships God (whom he calls there 'Puruṣottama' and 'Vāsudeva Bhagavān'). Importantly, this is only possible for īśvaras on earth in human embodiment, which they receive when their karmas sufficiently ripen. Here on earth, an īśvara would need to perform the same praxis as a jīva, by devoutly serving with correct theological knowledge the manifest form of Parabrahman, i.e. the Brahmasvarūpa Guru. Interestingly, then, when in human form, an īśvara would appear visibly indistinguishable from a jīva.

As similar as they are, though, Swaminarayan warns against the mistake of equating jīvas and īśvaras. In Vac. Pan.2, he firstly states that such an identification

> would suggest that the gross body is the same as virāṭa, the subtle body is the same as sūtrātman, and the causal body is the same as avyākṛta. It also suggests that the waking state is the same as that of sustenance, the dream state is the same as that of creation, and the deep sleep state is the same as

[2] BS-SB 1.3.26, pp. 111–12.

> that of dissolution. Moreover, Viśva, Taijasa and Prājña would be considered equal to Viṣṇu, Brahmā and Śiva, respectively.[3]

This understanding is incorrect, he stresses, and encourages that it be rectified by learning the following distinction from a wise person:

> The five material elements residing in the body of īśvara are known as mahābhūtas {literally, 'great elements'}, and those elements sustain the bodies of all jīvas. On the other hand, the five material elements in the body of the jīva are minor and are incapable of sustaining others. Also, a jīva possesses limited knowledge compared to an īśvara, who is [relatively] all-knowing.

Īśvaras are thus distinct and superior to jīvas by way of their composition, knowledge and Parabrahman-endowed authority. Therefore, Swaminarayan concludes:

> One should learn such a method of interpretation so that jīva and īśvara are not misunderstood to be equal. (Vac. Pan.2)

Roles and Functions of Īśvaras

Who are these īśvaras? And what do they do?

By its very nature, this topic is inextricably tied with creation, and so can only really be treated satisfactorily by returning to it after a description of the creative process, which we shall be turning to shortly in the next chapter. There, a simple but complete classification of beings in a chart of the cosmic order shall hopefully elucidate the matter sufficiently. Here, we can introduce īśvaras collectively as all those sentient beings involved in the creative and governing processes of a brahmāṇḍa (e.g. Pradhāna Puruṣa, Virāṭa Puruṣa, Aniṛddha, Saṅkarṣaṇa, Pradyumna, etc.), including the Hindu triad (Brahmā, Viṣṇu, Śiva), those divinities who enliven the various forces of nature (Sūrya, Candra, Varuṇa, etc.) and all avatāras, albeit with the special re-entering of Parabrahman (Matsya, Varāha, Nṛsiṃha, Rāma, Kṛṣṇa, etc.).

To briefly elaborate, Swaminarayan points to a set of īśvaras in Vac. Gaḍh. 2.22 as 'the lords of countless millions of brahmāṇḍas'. There he explicitly mentions 'Brahmā' (not to be confused with Brahman) before simply adding

[3] This prima facie view seems to be gleaned from the Mokṣadharma, chapters 289–306, particularly 289.3–6 and 306.75–7, found in the Mahābhārata's Śānti Parva.

'ādika {etcetera}'. Similarly, in the immediately previous sermon when talking about the visceral world of dreams, he states:

> In the same way as jīvas, īśvaras such as Brahmā, etc. also experience creations during their dream state. (Vac. Gaḍh. 2.21)

Swaminarayan is referring, firstly, to the familiar Hindu triad of Brahmā, Viṣṇu and Śiva, the 'gods' assigned the tasks of origination, sustenance and dissolution within each brahmāṇḍa. Alongside them are other beings in the protological process up to and including the countless pairs of Pradhāna-Puruṣa, who are first evolved from the converging of māyā (known in the creative process as Mūla-Prakṛti) and a liberated soul (given the designation 'Mūla-Puruṣa'), and who together go on to create each individual brahmāṇḍa. This set of beings includes Virāṭa Puruṣa, who is the inner soul of each brahmāṇḍa and therefore has the physical brahmāṇḍa as its gross body (Vac. Kār.12, Gaḍh. 2.10, Gaḍh. 2.31). Its subtle body, like the subtle body of a jīva, comprises its own senses and inner faculties. These are presided over by various divinities of nature who are said to facilitate each function. For example, Sūrya, the sentient being of the sun, facilitates the sense of sight. These divinities also preside over the senses and faculties of each jīva, as listed in Table 7.

As explained, these divinities include the sentient beings enlivening the various forces of nature (Table 8), reiterating the important Hindu belief of a living world infused with energy and emotion.

Some of these as well as a few other divinities are mentioned in AU 1.1.3 as 'hatching' from the various organs and senses of Vairāja Puruṣa, who is the 'guardian of the world' (AU 1.1.2). The world is depicted there as a massive cosmic egg.[4]

As aforementioned, more about this topic will be covered in the following chapter on māyā when we discuss the order of creation for each brahmāṇḍa. A brief explanation can nonetheless be provided here analogously using the following downscaled model adapted from Swaminarayan's own sermons.

Consider a country comprising many cities. Each city is assigned a minister to oversee its smooth and efficient running. Furthermore, each minister is assisted by junior ministers, secretaries and council members, each with a specific portfolio of duties. All these people are just like the citizens they serve, only with more power and authority. Similarly, each world ('city') is under the 'local' authority of Vairāja Puruṣa ('minister'), who is the soul of the living brahmāṇḍa and who has other divinities

[4] See AU-SB 1.1.3, pp. 419–20.

Table 7 *Presiding divinities of the ten senses and four inner faculties of each jīva*

Sense/Faculty			Presiding Divinity
Four Inner Faculties (Antaḥkaraṇa)	Manas	Thinking	Aniṛddha/Candra
	Buddhi	Reasoning	Pradyumna/Brahmā
	Citta	Contemplating	Vāsudeva
	Ahaṃkāra	Self-Identifying	Saṅkarṣaṇa/Rudra
Five Cognitive Senses (Jñānendriya)	Cakṣus	Sight	Sūrya
	Śrotra	Hearing	Diśā
	Ghrāṇa	Smelling	Aśvinīkumāra
	Rasanā	Taste	Varuṇa
	Tvak	Touch	Vāyu
Five Conative Senses (Karmendriya)	Vāk	Speech	Agni
	Pāṇi	Dexterity	Indra
	Pāda	Locomotion	Viṣṇu
	Pāyu	Excretion	Mitra
	Upastha	Generation	Prajāpati

Table 8 *Divinities presiding over aspects of nature*

Sentient Divinity	Aspect of Nature
Sūrya	Sun
Candra	Moon
Pṛthvī	Earth
Ākāśa	Space
Diśā	Directions
Varuṇa	Water
Vāyu	Wind
Agni	Fire
Indra	Rain

('junior ministers') – such as Sūrya (of the sun), Pṛthvī (the earth), Varuṇa (water), etc. – working under him in various assigned duties to ensure its ordered functioning. All these beings are metaphysically īśvara; they are distinct from, superior and yet similar to the jīvas of each brahmāṇḍa, i.e. bound by māyā but with more power and authority.

A natural progression of this analogy would be to extend it up to the 'national' level, relating the prime minster or king of the land to Parabrahman, who holds overall power and control for the workings of each city, i.e. brahmāṇḍa, though he may not always exercise it directly. That leader devolves some of that authority to each of his/her appointed ministers to allow them to fulfil their duties, who, all the while, remain answerable and subordinate to him/her. Importantly, however, one needs to remember that while the leader of the land is another human just like his/her ministers and deputies, Parabrahman is metaphysically distinct from all īśvaras. This leads us neatly on to the following section, where we further explore this distinction and relationship between the two.

Distinction from and Relation to Parabrahman

A conventional Hindu understanding of God as the creator and governor of the world would seem to fit precisely with īśvara. By their name, too, etymologically meaning 'lord' or 'powerful', one can be forgiven for mistaking 'īśvara' to denote God, a personal deity. Īśvaras are in fact ontologically distinct entities, metaphysically different from Parabrahman as well as infinitely inferior to him.

Swaminarayan emphasises this repeatedly in various ways. For example, when narrating a correct form of theological reflection, he states in Vac. Sār.1:

> One should think of the greatness of God in the following way: '. . . I have attained Śrī Puruṣottama Bhagavān in person, the very Puruṣottama Bhagavān who is . . . the master of Brahmā and the other devas, who themselves are the lords of countless millions of brahmāṇḍas.'

Swaminarayan reiterates this relationship through his familiar analogy of Parabrahman as a world-emperor in which the countless īśvaras are mere village chiefs. This is most vividly presented in Vac. Pan.4, as was cited at length when discussing Parabrahman's outright supremacy over even Brahmā, Viṣṇu and Maheśa (Śiva), who pray with sheer supplication, beseeching Parabrahman to grace them with his audience.[5] To be clear, they are still the mighty lords of each brahmāṇḍa, exercising phenomenal power and commanding the veneration and obedience of humans and even lesser divinities. But as powerful, venerable and dominating as they may be, they are of utter lowly rank before the Lord of all lords – like 'poor' 'village chiefs' to the 'Great King of all kings'. Even their mention in the plural – 'Brahmās, Viṣṇus and Maheśas', each of the countless brahmāṇḍas – further attests to their relative powerlessness; together, they are reigned over by only the one supreme Parabrahman.

This master–subordinate or ruler–ruled relationship between Parabrahman and īśvaras is especially reinforced by the evocative phrase 'īśvarnā paṇ īśvar', meaning that Parabrahman is the Īśvara (Lord) of all īśvaras (lords). It highlights Parabrahman as being at least as superior to the īśvaras as they themselves are over others. Whatever power or control they wield over their individual world, it is Parabrahman the Great Lord who reigns over all such lesser lords in all worlds. Swaminarayan uses the phrase in Vac. Gaḍh. 3.38, framing it, importantly, within the doctrine of Pragaṭa. He proclaims:

> This manifest form of Puruṣottama Bhagavān before your eyes is . . . the Lord of all lords {īśvarnā paṇ īśvar}. (Vac. Gaḍh. 3.38)

The Śvetāśvatara Upaniṣad similarly states:

> He who is the Supreme Great Lord {paramam maheśvaram} of all the lords {īśvarāṇām}. (SU 6.7)

Likewise, when the term 'maheśvara' appears in the Bhagavad-Gītā, Bhadreshdas relates it to Parabrahman as the 'Lord of all īśvaras', i.e. their controller (5.29, 10.3, 13.22).

As powerful as the īśvaras are, though, their powers are delegated to them and ultimately regulated by Parabrahman. Indeed, Swaminarayan emphasises, the īśvaras are able to function at all only by the enlivening and empowering presence of Parabrahman within them, just as he dwells in all other beings and things as their embodied soul.

> The inspirer of both the īśvara known as Virāṭa Puruṣa and of this jīva is Puruṣottama. (Vac. Gaḍh. 2.31)

Further on in this sermon, Swaminarayan expands upon what he means by the 'inspirer' of Virāṭa Puruṣa. He describes in detail how 'the senses, inner

[5] See Section 'Lord of All Beings and Realms' in Chapter 6.

faculties and their presiding divinities' had all 'entered that Virāṭa' and 'attempted to awaken him'. Yet, 'despite Virāṭa's soul being inside his body, Virāṭa still did not rise'. It was only when Parabrahman, the Soul of all souls, 'entered him ... did the body of Virāṭa rise' and 'only then did Virāṭa Puruṣa become capable of performing all his activities' (Vac. Gaḍh. 2.31).[6]

Swaminarayan extends this discussion into the avatāra–avatārin doctrine, an important and distinguishing feature of Swaminarayan Hindu theology. As we learned when understanding the supremacy of Parabrahman, he is described as the avatārin, the cause of all avatāras, whereas these avatāras themselves are metaphysically īśvara and thus ontologically distinct from Parabrahman. It is only by Parabrahman's special 're-entering' {anu-praveśa} that the īśvaras are empowered to fulfil their task on earth and become worthy of human veneration (Vac. Gaḍh. 2.31, Pan.7).

This concept of Parabrahman inspiring and mobilising the gods is also presented anecdotally in KeU 3–4, where Indra, Vāyu, Agni and the other divinities are seen arrogantly celebrating their victory over the asuras and congratulating each other on their greatness. They are summarily made to realise how powerless they actually are and that their triumph was due only to the gracious empowerment of Parabrahman, without whom they would not be able to function at all.

Apart from their functioning in general, īśvaras also cannot experience anything independently of Parabrahman, for he is the omniscient, omnipresent grantor of the fruits of their karmas, just as he is for the jīvas (Vac. Gaḍh. 1.45), since the īśvaras, too, are still subject to karmas, just like the jīvas. This is also true of karmas that sometimes express themselves in the dream state (Vac. Gaḍh. 2.21). In Vac. Kār.1, Swaminarayan extends Parabrahman's inspiration to the state of 'deep sleep' at the time of final dissolution, when the īśvaras (and jīvas) are dormant within māyā without name or form. Only when Parabrahman wills and inspires do those īśvaras assume a name and form.

In all ways and in every state, then, the īśvaras are absolutely dependent on Parabrahman, for their functioning and experiences, and for their very existence.[7]

Swaminarayan is sure to add, though, that the relationship between Parabrahman and the īśvaras is a devout and loving one. While it is true that

[6] See also Vac. Gaḍh. 2.10.

[7] See also the Jyotirādyadhiṣṭhānādhikaraṇa at BS-SB 2.4.14–15, pp. 261–2.

> God is very powerful; even the devas such as Brahmā and others live under his command (Vac. Gaḍh. 2.66),

it is not a fearful compliance. Rather, as mentioned in the sovereign king–village chief analogy in Vac. Pan.4,

> Brahmā, Viṣṇu and Śiva in turn worship Puruṣottama Bhagavān and follow his command,

even though they themselves are worshipped and obeyed in their respective worlds. This is because Parabrahman is eminently worthy of their highest reverence, adoration and humility, which the īśvaras so readily accord him.

> Even the great such as Brahmā, Śiva . . . apply the dust of God's holy feet upon their heads. They put aside all of their self-importance and constantly offer devotion to him. (Vac. Gaḍh. 3.39)

The Bṛhadāraṇyaka Upaniṣad, too, states:

> The devas worship that immortal [Parabrahman]. (BU 4.4.16)

This best summarises and concludes the relationship īśvaras enjoy with Parabrahman.

CHAPTER 10

Māyā

Having expounded upon the four sentient eternal entities of the Swaminarayan metaphysical quintet, we now move on to the final and only non-sentient entity, māyā. Known variously as māyā, mūla-māyā and mahā-māyā, as well as Prakṛti[1] and Mūla-Prakṛti, it is the root or universal material source of the world, the cosmic material principle. Often depicted as feminine in nature, juxtaposed against Puruṣa, its masculine counterpart in the creative process, it represents matter complementing – not necessarily opposing – the spirit {caitanya} of the other entities. While irreconcilably different from each other, together, they form and enliven all that there is.

Also known as avidyā, because it is antithetical to vidyā {knowledge}, māyā is also the ignorance that shrouds intelligent beings. It is the root cause of the soul's incessant transmigration through various life-forms, attended to by suffering, sorrow and disappointment. Māyā thus has to be transcended in order to secure final liberation.

It is this dual form and function of māyā as primordial matter and ignorance that we shall be exploring in this chapter.

Nature of Māyā

Swaminarayan provides a succinct definition of māyā, calling it Prakṛti, in Vac. Gaḍh. I.12. He states:

> Prakṛti is characterised by the three guṇas, and by both insentience and sentiency. It is eternal, indistinct, the 'field' of all beings and all elements including mahattattva, and also the divine power of God.

[1] The term 'Prakṛti' will be recognised by those familiar with the Sāṃkhya School, and indeed the conceptualisation of māyā in Swaminarayan Hindu theology is similar, except that whereas Prakṛti in the Sāṃkhya system is considered wholly independent to initiate creation, in Swaminarayan Hindu theology, māyā is dependent on and controlled by Parabrahman, as is explained further on. For more on this comparison between the two schools in their understanding of Prakṛti, see Shrutiprakashdas, 'Sāṅkhyadarśanāntargata Prakṛtipuruṣa Śrī Svāminārāyaṇa Darśana ke Sandarbha meiṅ', *Dārśanika Traimāsika: Journal of Akhila Bhāratīya Darśana Pariṣad*, 36.1 (1990), 60–71.

Our exposition of māyā can be guided by this compact elucidation. As we unpack each of these terms and aspects, we should eventually arrive at a fuller understanding of its nature.

Characterised by the Three Guṇas

Māyā has three fundamental qualities, or guṇas, known as sattva {literally, 'goodness'}, rajas {'passion'} and tamas {'darkness'}. While literally meaning 'threads', these guṇas are not the constitutive components of māyā but its essential *characteristics*. This is evidenced from the Bhagavad-Gītā, where the guṇas are described as being 'born of Prakṛti' (3.5, 13.19, 13.21, 14.5, 18.40) and otherwise distinct from it (3.27, 13.23). Swaminarayan, too, talks of them as 'aris[ing] from māyā' (Vac. Loyā.10).

Each of the guṇas lends its own specific 'personality' to māyā. Respectively, sattvaguṇa, rajoguṇa and tamoguṇa lead to calmness and clarity, activity and creativity, inertia and obscurity. Naturally, each is found to be at work more sharply than the others in one of the three stages of creation: rajas is employed for and leads to generation, sattva for sustenance, tamas for destruction. As we shall see shortly in the description of the creative process, the delicate balance of these forces, and their disturbance, is what triggers generation. Here, we should note that in all three phases of the world – generation, sustenance and dissolution – māyā retains all three of its qualities.

In everyday life, these three primary qualities mix in differing proportions to create an infinitely diverse palette of propensities which colours everything created of māyā. The Śvetāśvatara Upaniṣad even describes māyā as 'red, white and black' (4.5), referring to rajoguṇa, sattvaguṇa and tamoguṇa, respectively. This helps explain why certain places or objects or foods are said to be predominantly sāttvic or rājasic or tāmasic. Since the mind and body are also products of māyā – the soul's causal body is itself māyā – the three guṇas also deeply affect individuals. With all three qualities being in constant flux, the mood and attitude of each individual are accordingly fluid or unstable, influencing a person's ever-changing actions and responses. When sattvaguṇa is predominant, one is more inclined to observe restraint, discretion and tolerance, to be humble and self-content (without indulging in sensorial pleasures), to engage in charity and other uplifting or enlightening activities, and to generally be at peace with one's self and in harmony with others. Under the influence of rajoguṇa, however, one finds a predomination of desire, impulse, indulgence, self-interest, arrogance, bravado but also industry and intent. Most dangerously, tamoguṇa is what leads to avarice, anger, fear, quarrelsomeness, violence, infatuation, connivance, dejection, delusion, indolence, indecision and the like.[2] Importantly, however, no one guṇa works in isolation; there is always a triadic combination at play, though one can have a greater prevalence over the other two.

Those who are uninfluenced by or have risen above the influence of these māyic qualities are called nirguṇa {without the guṇas} or guṇātīta {beyond the guṇas}.

Characterised by Insentience and Sentiency

Māyā is essentially and eternally material, i.e. insentient, or without consciousness {jaḍa}. It can never become sentient {cetana} like Parabrahman, Akṣarabrahman, īśvaras and jīvas.

However, it is sometimes referred to as being jaḍacidātmikā – characterised by both insentience and sentiency – because countless sentient beings (jīvas and īśvaras) lie dormant within mūla-māyā after final dissolution, giving the notion that it is 'ensouled' by them, just as, indeed, the physical body composed of māyā is ensouled by the jīva. Similarly, mūla-māyā's concomitance with the sentient Mūla-Puruṣa (a liberated soul in Akṣaradhāma) when initiating the process of creation also helps explain why māyā can be called cidātmikā, if only by association.

Eternal (Yet Mutable)

Like Parabrahman, Akṣarabrahman, īśvaras and jīvas, māyā is eternal – without beginning and without end. It was never created, nor will it ever be destroyed.[3] One may overcome it to secure liberation, but it can never be eliminated.

But unlike the other four entities, māyā is not immutable. As we saw in the opening chapter of this part, māyā is set apart from those sentient entities, which are immutably eternal {kūṭastha nitya}, by having mutable eternality {pariṇāmī nityatā}. Though never being obliterated, it nonetheless undergoes various transformations during the process of creation and sustenance. Upon final dissolution, however, it is not destroyed; it simply dissolves into a minutely compact or indistinguishably subtle form within one part of Akṣarabrahman's light.

[2] See also, for example, BP 11.25.2–5; Mahābhārata, Aśvamedha Parva, 36–9; and BG 17.

[3] See, for example, SU 1.9, 4.5 and BG 13.11.

It is this aspect of māyā's mutability that allows its products – the material body, objects and all the features that comprise the world – to be changing and perishable, explaining how beings can be born and can die and how things are said to be created and destroyed. Thus, all things evolved from mūla-māyā, including the elements of mahat-tattva, etc., are indeed generated and dissolved in each cycle of creation.

Indistinct

During the period of complete rest after final dissolution, māyā is said to be non-distinct {nirviśeṣa}, because all its creations with name and form have been dissolved within it. It, too, dissolves into a subtle, unmanifest {avyakta} form within Akṣarabrahman.

In contrast, when called into action for the process of creation, māyā becomes especially gross and manifest through its myriad creations, each with a distinctive name and form inspired by Parabrahman and Akṣarabrahman.

Material Substratum of All Beings and Things

Māyā as matter is not necessarily opposed to spirit. In fact, as we shall see further on, it can be complementary and positively useful, especially in attempting to understand God's purpose in creating the world. As we also learned earlier, the psychosomatic body is a necessary and powerful tool for the intelligent soul by which to know, act and enjoy, and to eventually secure liberation.

As the material from which the bodies of all jīvas and īśvaras are composed and from which all objects are made, māyā serves as their substratum. This is often termed as māyā being the 'field' or kṣetra (with the intelligent beings called the 'field-knowers', or kṣetrajña). This idea is also useful in analogously explaining the creative process. At the time of rest after final dissolution, the jīvas and īśvaras lie dormant like un-germinated seeds in the 'field' (i.e. soil) of māyā. Upon raining, i.e. Puruṣa associating with Prakṛti (as māyā is known then), those beings 'sprout' forth from māyā into forms with names and identity. Swaminarayan employs this analogy in Vac. Gaḍh. 3.10, cited earlier, affirming māyā as the 'field' or material substratum of all beings and things.

Power (or Means) of God

Since māyā is insentient, it can only be effective in creation when 'crafted' by an intelligent creator, as clay is in the hands of a potter. In other words, while māyā is the basic raw material of the world – the very 'stuff' from which all things are made – it is by the will and 'skill' (powers) of Parabrahman that creation is made possible. In this sense, māyā is described as the 'power' of God[4] or the means by which he creates. This should not, however, be confused as implying māyā to be an inherent quality or consort of God; his nature in no way entertains māyā nor is he affiliated to it in person. For God, māyā is a tool or means for his creative ends. Swaminarayan makes this clear in Vac. Gaḍh. 1.13 and Loyā.17, where he refers to māyā as well as kāla {time}, Puruṣa and even Akṣarabrahman as 'God's powers', all of which have a role in the process of creation.

The possessive case in the phrase 'God's power' or, as Swaminarayan repeatedly uses, 'God's māyā' (e.g. Vac. Gaḍh. 1.34, Pan.3, Gaḍh. 2.65) also alludes to māyā *belonging* to God and being under his authority and dependence. As we have already learned earlier, māyā is a part of Parabrahman's vast universal body, which he indwells, supports, mobilises and controls (e.g. Vac. Gaḍh. 1.64, Kār.8). Thus, even if māyā is the immediate material cause of the world, it is not so independently of Parabrahman, making him the ultimate material cause of everything as well as its efficient cause.[5]

At the disposal of and empowered by Parabrahman, māyā becomes a powerful and mystifying force. Though singular in its causal state, it goes forth to transform into myriad effects, producing a world – worlds, in fact – of unimaginable and bewildering diversity, filled with all things bright and beautiful, all things great and small, all things weird and wonderful, bringing joy and sorrow to all.

Ignorance

Apart from its role in creation as the primordial material reality, on the personal plane, māyā is also avidyā or ignorance. It is therefore framed in terms of darkness, because it is seen as directly antithetical to knowledge (analogously presented as light) and all that is enlightening. It is this māyā that enshrouds the essentially pure, radiant, conscious and blissful soul,

4 See also SU 6.8.

5 For a fuller discussion of this, see Section 'Parabrahman as Creator, Sustainer and Dissolver and Both Efficient and Material Cause' in Chapter 6.

What is interesting here is that Swaminarayan is subjectifying the positive or negative impact of māyā on the strength of the individual's faith in God; māyā itself is neither intrinsically evil nor good. Since māyā belongs to God and functions only under his authority, why indeed would it harm anyone who also belongs to God and is similarly acting under his authority? In fact, māyā exists to facilitate devotion of God for fellow dependants. What Swaminarayan is emphasising, it seems, is the need to fully and exclusively submit oneself to God, and thereby not only escape the detractive effects of māyā but, more positively, take full advantage of its potential usefulness in worshipping him. For us, this provides a more holistic understanding of the nature of māyā in the Swaminarayan tradition.

Māyā as Jagat

While māyā in its state of rest is unmanifest and indistinguishably subtle, it becomes most distinctively manifest and gross as it transforms into the created world visible around us, including the bodies that each individual receives. It is to this world that we now turn to understand the workings of māyā, attempting to make sense as far as possible of how it was created, why it was created, why it was created in the way that it is and what happens to it hereafter.

The first thing that needs to be said about this world is that it is real, not illusory. This is made patently clear by Swaminarayan in Vac. Gaḍh. I.39, when he challenges an adherent and scholar of Advaita Vedānta who was sitting in the assembly at that time. As a good example of a theological discussion grounded in textual exegesis, it is worth recounting the sermon here in part.

First, Swaminarayan pointedly addresses the Advaitin regarding the central doctrine of strict monism. He says to him:

> You claim that in reality only Brahman exists. Furthermore, you say that with the exception of that Brahman, jīvas, īśvaras, māyā, the world, the Vedas, the Śāstras and the Purāṇas are all illusory. I can neither understand this concept of yours, nor can I accept it.

Swaminarayan invites the scholar to defend the Advaitin position, but is clear about the terms upon which this theological discussion ought to proceed. The scholar should respond by citing only the Vedas, the Śāstras, the Purāṇas, the Smṛtis or the Itihāsa scriptures. If, however, you reply quoting the words of some inauthentic scripture, then I will not accept your answer. But, since I have absolute faith in the words of Vyāsjī, I will be able to accept your reply if you reply quoting his words.

The Advaitin offered his defence using various arguments, but each time, the Vacanāmrut notes, Swaminarayan raised doubts to the Advaitin's response leaving the query unresolved. Thereupon Swaminarayan began to resolve the query himself. He explained that there are in fact 'two different states' of spiritual experience, what he calls 'savikalpa samādhi' and 'nirvikalpa samādhi'. Those who attain the former state 'see jīvas, īśvaras, māyā, and their supporter, Brahman, as being distinct from each other', just as a person standing atop a mountain sees everything in the vicinity – 'other mountains, trees, as well as the ground that supports the mountains and the trees' – as distinct. In contrast, a person looking down from a cosmic vantage 'sees everything in the vicinity ... as being one with the ground, but he does not see them as being distinct'.

> Similarly, those great liberated souls who have attained nirvikalpa samādhi see jīvas, īśvaras and māyā as being one with Brahman – but they do not see them as distinct entities.

It is due to these differing experiential states of the seers whose visions have been shared in the scriptures that we find seemingly contradictory or inconsistent statements.

> The words of those who have attained the savikalpa state noted in the Vedas, the Śāstras, the Purāṇas, etc. describe all of those entities as being satya {real}. However, the words of those who have attained the nirvikalpa state describe all of those entities as being asatya {non-real}. In reality, however, they are not asatya {non-real}. They are only described as being asatya {non-real} because they cannot be seen due to the influence of the nirvikalpa state.

Swaminarayan goes on to explain how both descriptions can be correct – given that they are coming from different positions – thereby avoiding confusion and ensuring an essential congruency and harmony among all revelatory statements, since, crucially, they are all true. He concludes:

> So, if one interprets 'Brahman' in this manner, then there will never be any contextual inconsistencies in the statements of the scriptures, but if one does not, then inconsistencies will arise.

Swaminarayan then ends the sermon with a stern warning against a lopsided reading of the scriptures – privileging those statements which propound the existence of Brahman alone and deny the existence of the world – without the contextual exegesis explained above, calling it 'extremely foolish' and spiritually perilous.

Thus, for all its mutations and transience, the world is nonetheless real and not some illusory figment of an inconceivable ignorance that will dematerialise upon self-realisation. Even in the liberated state, Swaminarayan asserts, the world or māyā is not obliterated for the individual; it is merely transcended so as to become inconsequential. This means that if ever the world, the physical body or any of māyā's other creations are described as 'mithyā' {false} (e.g. Vac. Gaḍh. 1.14, Gaḍh. 1.70, Sār.14, Pan.2, Gaḍh. 3.38) or 'asatya' {non-real} (e.g. Vac. Gaḍh. 1.16, Gaḍh. 1.21, Gaḍh. 2.30), it is simply to underscore their perishability and māyā's own mutability, especially in relation to the immutable eternality of Parabrahman and the other sentient beings. Swaminarayan makes this clear with his definition of 'satya' and 'asatya' in Vac. Gaḍh. 3.38:

> All forms that are the result of the entities evolved from māyā are asatya. Why? Because all those forms will be destroyed in time. Conversely, the form of God in Akṣaradhāma and the form of the muktas – the [liberated] attendants of God – are all satya.

Bringing this together with the earlier point that māyā can indeed be useful, we can arrive at an interesting theological and practical insight. Swaminarayan seems to advocate neither a world-negating nor world-affirming *Weltanschauung* (or world view), but what might be called a world-*contextualising* view. The world is not illusory; it is real, and therefore cannot be dismissed. Yet, being composed of māyā, it can (without a firm refuge in God) distract the jīva away from God, and so cannot be foolhardily advocated either. Nevertheless, the world plays an essential role in providing a platform and set of tools with which the jīva can transcend māyā and reach God. What is required is for the world to be properly understood in its correct context, as a tool in the service of God. Those striving for liberation from māyā therefore find themselves straddling two realms: diligently fulfilling their duties in the material world yet using that as a form of praxis {sādhanā} to achieving a higher spiritual realisation of themselves and their creator and cause.

Parabrahman as Creator and Cause

Theologically, the most important thing that can be said about the world is that Parabrahman is its creator and cause. While this has been extensively discussed in our chapter on Parabrahman, it warrants some recapitulation and further reflection here in the context of our attempt to understand the māyic world.

We had earlier raised an important question on this topic: How justifiable is it that God be called the creator when māyā, the primordial substance from which the material world is composed, is coeternal with God? If māyā already exists, what exactly has God 'created'?

The question becomes even sharper when we recall the satkāryavāda view of causality adopted by Swaminarayan and most other Vedāntins. It maintains that nothing new is ever created; substances merely change state, from a causal state of being to an effected state. Just as an earthen pot is not a new substance apart from the clump of clay from which it was crafted, so, too, the world always existed, albeit without distinguishable names and forms, in the causal state of primordial dormant matter.

This common Hindu doctrine of *creatio ex materia* (creation from matter) differs radically from the *creatio ex nihilo* (creation from nothing) doctrine of other theological systems, particularly the Abrahamic faiths, making the question all the more intriguing and worth exploring. A clue to its answer lies in the metaphor used to define the question itself. Firstly, the Vedāntins argue, the familiar clay-pot metaphor of the Nyāya system actually reveals the need for an intelligent creator. Just as a clump of clay cannot be moulded into a pot by itself, but in the hands of an adept potter, it can be transformed into numerous vessels and artefacts, similarly, māyā may be the primordial material reality, but it is insentient, like the clay; it cannot of its own accord create the world. It needs a sentient world-maker to bring it to action, transformation, generation.

If we now modify and develop this analogy, we can find new ways of understanding the world-maker and the world he makes. Can God insomuch be the creator of the world as a sculptor who creates a statue from a boulder of stone, a painter who creates a masterpiece with paints or a musician who creates a symphony from musical notes? The stone, paints and notes all pre-exist, albeit indistinctively, but it is the creativity and mastery of the artiste that brings to life something wholly new from them yet not distinctly apart from what each was before. The creation is at once both new and the same. Similarly, it can be said, God inspires from the preexistent, indistinguishable māyā innumerable masterpieces each with their own name and form and all still intrinsically māyic.

This model of creation as art (as opposed to mere manufacturing) also helps in explaining how the 'work' of God might better be described as 'play' – joyful and expressive. It is not the necessary, laborious, mostly unpleasant routine that is often associated with work, but that which occurs freely, willingly and lovingly for the sheer joy of it by its creator. In this sense of artistic expression, Parabrahman can still be properly conceived as 'creator' of the world even though māyā always exists.

Swaminarayan responds by firstly establishing the 'intimate relationship' between the gross and subtle bodies with the causal body, 'in the same way that a tree is intimately related to its seed'.

> Just as seeds that are planted in the earth sprout forth after coming into contact with rainwater, similarly, during the period of creation, the jīvas, which had resided within māyā together with their causal bodies, attain various types of bodies according to their individual karmas by the will of God, the grantor of the fruits of karmas.

Swaminarayan is effectively explaining that although rain allows the seeds to grow, it is inconsequential in *what* they grow into. That is determined entirely by each seed's own latent potentiality. Sugarcane seeds will grow only into sugarcane, and pepper seeds only into peppers. Equally, only sugarcane grows from sugarcane seeds, and only peppers from pepper seeds. Why is one sweet and the other hot? The difference is due to the genetic encoding within the respective seeds themselves, not due to the rain that indiscriminately falls for both. Thus, Swaminarayan maintains, the different conditions of individual beings are due to their own karmic 'DNA' stored in the causal body of each soul. This provides the decisive information according to which subsequent bodies will be composed and life-circumstances (place of birth, parents, etc.) determined. 'That is why it is called the "causal" body {kāraṇa śarīra}', Swaminarayan clarifies, adding that it is 'without beginning'. For each undying soul, this ensures two things: (1) an essential unity between lives, and (2) consistent fairness; he/she who sows the seed (in a past life) is the one who reaps the fruit (in a subsequent life). The souls can thus neither complain about their lot nor blame it upon God.

But this then raises another complaint against God, as presented in the first part of the double-binding question in Vac. Var.6. If each soul is enjoying and suffering the consequences of its own karmas, where is there room in all of this for God or his compassion? How can creation still be regarded as an act of his benevolence, when it can neither fully be called 'his' nor is it fully 'benevolent'? If anything, he is merely an automated dispenser, the last cog in the universal workings of karmic determinism. Impartial, yes. But apathetic, too.

Not so, Bhadreshdas retorts. While the body, senses, faculties, sense-objects and physical realm that the soul deserves are its own earnings, they are nonetheless created for it by God, for who else has the power to activate māyā and has the knowledge of what exactly needs to be made from it? Moreover, the dispensation of karmic fruits is not at all divorced from God's pleasure and displeasure, just as a noble king metes out reward and retribution upon deserving subjects only after being pleased or displeased by their acts. You also forget, Bhadreshdas reminds the objector, that it is God who graciously endows each soul with the means to act, know and enjoy in the first place. Along with that, he allows them the freedom to act and grants the capacity to discriminate between good and bad deeds, each having their own inescapable consequences. With their highest welfare at heart, God has thus given finite beings the opportunity to use their God-granted material bodies and material things to secure liberation from their transmigratory existence, to enjoy eternal, blissful communion with him. How can God be so quickly dismissed from this system? And how can his compassion be denied? He is the very soul of the souls, empowering, indwelling and supporting them, without whom they would not be able to do anything at all.

In that case, does this not make God at least partially or indirectly responsible for the souls' suffering or their inequality, for without him they would not have accumulated the karmas which they are now experiencing? No, the answer must be, for that would be tantamount to blaming the rain or soil for what the seeds grow into.[10]

A marked feature of this Hindu theodicy, presented here in only a condensed and truncated form, is that it not only attempts to defend the goodness of God and ensure justice for individual beings, but it also seeks to preserve God's indispensability and intimate relationship with those beings. God is not accountable for the inequity or suffering among the souls of the world because it is determined by the karmas that they themselves have accrued and therefore deserve. But nor does this make God redundant or detached, for the doctrine of karma is not simply an inert law of cause and effect. It requires to be presided over or mediated by God, because only an all-knowing, all-pervading, all-loving being can know all the actions and thoughts happening in all places at all times and then dispense with the fruits accordingly.[11] As we saw, Swaminarayan was clear to add at the end of the passage above that it was 'by the will of God' that the karmic fruits are dispensed and therefore the world created.[12]

10 Based on BS-SB 2.1.35–36, pp. 184–7, with additional reflection.

11 It should be added that as the supreme power, Parabrahman can always veto karma and provide for souls independently, solely according to his own will and judgement.

12 See also the Phalādhikaraṇa – the last debate of BS 3.2 – that argues for Parabrahman as the grantor of karmic fruits to souls. BS-SB 3.2.36–9; pp. 310–12.

For a more detailed discussion on the topic of karma, including how endeavour, charity, sympathy, etc. can still be reconciled, see Brahmadarshandas's *Karmasiddhānta ane Punarjanma*, 2 vols (Ahmedabad: Swaminarayan Aksharpith, 2002).

Other aspects of the so-called problem of evil still require attention and further reflection, but the limited discussion here should nonetheless provide an idea of the scripturally grounded and reasonably argued attempt to reconcile the presence of suffering in a world created by a compassionate God. It also allows us to retrace the argumentation for the world's creatorship introduced at the beginning of this section: God is not responsible for the inequality and suffering in the world, therefore his impartiality and compassion remain intact. So he *is* benevolent, creating the world for the benefit of others. Because this amounts to a definite purpose for creating the world, it means God can indeed be its creator.

Creative Process

Swaminarayan describes the process of creation in various sermons (Vac. Gaḍh. 1.12, Gaḍh. 1.13, Gaḍh. 1.41), mentioning it still further in many others (e.g. Vac. Gaḍh. 1.51, Gaḍh. 2.31). What follows is an account of that protological process {utpatti-sarga} based on these sermons.[13]

Our starting point is the pre-creation state of final dissolution, when all matter – sentient (jīvas and īśvaras) and insentient (māyā) – is resting condensed within the being of Parabrahman and Akṣarabrahman (both residing with the liberated souls in Akṣaradhāma). This is why CU 6.2.1 and AU 1.1.1, for example, speak of nothing existing 'in the beginning' except pure 'Being' or the 'Soul'. While according to the satkāryavāda view of causality it is true that the variegated world exists in all its potentiality during this causal state, it is indistinguishable by name and form from Parabrahman and Akṣarabrahman, even though their distinction is real. Bringing this unmanifest world to its manifest, effected state is itself the very act of 'creation'.

The process for this creation is initiated when Parabrahman 'sees' (CU 6.1.3, BU 2.1.5, AU 1.1.1) or looks with intent, i.e. inspires Akṣarabrahman with a resolve to create the manifest world for the benefit of the souls that they may seek liberation and redeem their karmic accruement. Upon perfectly receiving Parabrahman's will, Akṣarabrahman selects a liberated soul (akṣara-mukta) from the countless millions in Akṣaradhāma and inspires it to engage with māyā, better known here as Prakṛti. Because of its primal role in this process, the akṣara-mukta is given the designation of 'Mūla-Puruṣa' (sometimes also called 'Mahā-Puruṣa' or 'Akṣara-Puruṣa'),

[13] Bhadreshdas also presents the same account, for example, in MuU-SB 1.1.7, pp. 240–1. It largely follows the process described in the Vāsudeva-Māhātmya of the Skanda-Purāṇa (Chapter 24) and in the Bhāgavata-Purāṇa's Kapila-Gītā (3.26).

and the Prakṛti it engages with is similarly referred to as 'Mūla-Prakṛti' (or 'Mahā-Prakṛti'). Together, they are called simply 'Prakṛti-Puraṣa'. Parabrahman 're-enters' this pair for the special task ahead, empowering both to continue forth the order of creation (e.g. TU 2.6.3).

Despite Mūla-Prakṛti being conceived of as feminine in nature, it is of course insentient. Moreover, the liberated soul, though termed in the masculine 'Puruṣa', is genderless and desireless. Hence the 'coming together' of Mūla-Prakṛti and Mūla-Puruṣa is not to be misconstrued as copulative, even though creation is sometimes metaphorically described in terms of human procreation (Vac. Gaḍh. 1.12, BG 14.3, BP 3.5.26). Rather, by its mere Parabrahman-empowered presence, Mūla-Puruṣa causes Mūla-Prakṛti to be stirred from its dormant state. Up until that point, the three fundamental qualities of Prakṛti – sattva, rajas and tamas – had been in perfect equilibrium. Once that delicate balance is disturbed, Mūla-Prakṛti produces countless parts from itself – rather like mini-versions of Prakṛti – each called Pradhāna-Prakṛti. Īśvaras (previously dormant within māyā) are called to individually join with each Pradhāna-Prakṛti, making countless pairs of what are each called 'Pradhāna-Puruṣa'. To briefly recap to this point, the primeval Mūla-Prakṛti and Mūla-Puruṣa – known jointly as Prakṛti-Puruṣa – produce countless pairs of Pradhāna-Puruṣas.

From each pair of Pradhāna-Puruṣa is produced a brahmāṇḍa (what we have loosely been calling 'world'), which itself comprises fourteen lokas {realms}. Since there are countless Pradhāna-Puruṣas, countless such brahmāṇḍas are created, all as originally willed by Parabrahman and inspired by Akṣarabrahman.

Focussing now on a single brahmāṇḍa, a series of elements evolve from Pradhāna-Puruṣa that forms the 'body' of the world as we see it and beyond what is visible. We have to remember that this brahmāṇḍa is a living entity, which has an īśvara – called Vairāja Puruṣa (or Virāṭa Puruṣa) – as its soul.

First to evolve from Pradhāna-Puruṣa is mahattattva. As the name might suggest {literally, 'great element'}, it is the fundamental material source from which the other elements of the world-body will evolve. It also represents the citta {contemplative mind} of the world.

From mahattattva evolve three types of Ahaṃkāra, a form of cosmic ego, each formed predominantly from one of the three qualities of Prakṛti. From Sāttvic Ahaṃkāra evolve the (cosmic) mind and the deities who preside over the (cosmic) senses; from Rājasic Ahaṃkāra evolve the (cosmic) senses, intellect and vital breaths; and from Tāmasic Ahaṃkāra evolve the five gross elements {mahābhūta} and the five subtle elements, called tanmātrā.

Actual Dissolution Actual, final dissolution occurs when Parabrahman decides.

> This is when countless millions of brahmāṇḍas are destroyed. At that time, even Prakṛti-Puruṣa – the cause of Pradhāna-Puruṣas – draws countless brahmāṇḍas within itself, and is then eclipsed by the light of Akṣara-Puruṣa [who in turn is absorbed into Akṣarabrahman]. This, the fourth type of dissolution, is called Ātyantika Pralaya. (Bhūgoḷ-Khagoḷ)

Swaminarayan similarly describes it in Vac. Kār.7:

> During the dissolution of the brahmāṇḍas, the twenty-four elements that have evolved from Prakṛti are assimilated into Prakṛti. Then Prakṛti-Puruṣa also disappear into the divine light of Akṣarabrahman.

Thus everything, including Mahā-Māyā, 'is absorbed into the divine light of Akṣarabrahman – as night merges into day' (Vac. Gaḍh. 1.12).

Quite simply, then:

> During final dissolution, nothing remains of anything that has evolved from Prakṛti-Puruṣa. (Vac. Gaḍh. 3.10)

That would mean that everything that transcends māyā continues to exist beyond final dissolution. Swaminarayan thus explains in Vac. Gaḍh. 2.24 that during this 'end time', nothing remains except the divine form of Parabrahman in Akṣaradhāma, Akṣaradhāma itself (i.e. Akṣarabrahman) and the akṣara-muktas (liberated souls) in Akṣaradhāma.

Jñāna Pralaya Jñāna Pralaya is subjective dissolution. It is an elevated individual state of understanding induced by theological knowledge {jñāna} whereby Prakṛti-Puruṣa and the entities evolved thereof do not come into view. Instead, one sees only pure consciousness within which only the form of God resides, but no other forms remain. In other words, all māyic influences are dissolved, as if a complete dissolution of the entire created world has taken place for that particular individual. Swaminarayan explains:

> In Ātyantika Pralaya, which is Jñāna Pralaya, everything up to and including Prakṛti is eclipsed by the light of Brahman. (Vac. Amd.2)

Elaborating upon this as a state of enlightened being, Swaminarayan firstly explains in Vac. Gaḍh. 1.24 that jñāna 'transcends Prakṛti-Puruṣa'. He then adds:

> When an elevated spiritual state is attained by this jñāna, Prakṛti-Puruṣa and the entities evolved from them do not come into view. This is known as Jñāna Pralaya.

Gunatitanand Swami relates this to the state of being brahmarūpa, where all forms of māyā are transcended. He explains:

> What is Jñāna Pralaya? It is to eradicate every single work of Prakṛti from one's heart and become brahmarūpa. Then nothing else remains to be done. This was the very principle of Swaminarayan. (SV 5.195)

What is also clear from this is that during this subjective state of enlightenment, the brahmāṇḍas still remain in existence for everyone else; after all, they are real, not illusory. They simply cease to have an influence on that particular enlightened being. This fittingly leads us closer to the *end* of this book and the final chapter in this part, where we expound upon this liberated spiritual state.

CHAPTER II

Mukti

We began this part with Swaminarayan's formulation of theological knowledge:

> A jñānin is one who singularly serves God manifest before the eyes – who eternally has a form – realising him as transcending Prakṛti-Puruṣa and Akṣara, and as being the cause and support of all. Such understanding constitutes jñāna, and such jñāna leads to ultimate liberation. (Vac. Loyā.7)

It served to structure our exposition on Parabrahman into the four themes of Sarvopari, Kartā, Sākāra and Pragaṭa. It also helped explain how, even though knowing Parabrahman is of primary importance in Swaminarayan Hindu theology, a complete understanding of his nature necessarily requires understanding Akṣarabrahman, Prakṛti (māyā), as well as jīva and īśvara. What is also striking about the formulation is that it immediately and unequivocally ties knowledge with liberation. Swaminarayan is clear: the goal, culmination and fruit of all theology is final release from the incessant cycle of births and deaths, to enjoy eternal fellowship with God.

We have touched upon this and many other aspects of mukti along our way in the chapters on Parabrahman, Akṣarabrahman, jīva, īśvara and māyā. This in itself is telling, reinforcing liberation as what permeates all theological reflection and to what it must ultimately lead. Here, we have occasion now to bind those points together and add further details to allow for a more complete, though still very introductory, understanding of liberation within Swaminarayan Hindu theology.

Nature and Cause of Bondage

Before we can move on to understanding liberation, we must first remind ourselves from what one is to be liberated and why. We should therefore begin with a brief review of the nature of spiritual bondage {bandhana} and its cause.

Earlier we learned that jīvas and īśvaras are essentially pure (devoid of any māyic traits) and have existence, consciousness and bliss as their most fundamental characteristics. So why, then, do they experience sorrow when they should be intrinsically and eternally blissful? Swaminarayan explains that it is the body which encounters pain and (worldly) pleasure. However, if the soul falsely self-identifies with the three bodies, it will also experience that same pain and pleasure. Only when it realises itself to be distinct from them can it experience the transcendental, continuous bliss of its own self and the God within (e.g. Vac. Gaḍh. 1.78, Gaḍh. 1.20). In other words, it is the soul's ajñāna or ignorance – better understood as 'anti-knowledge' {viparīta jñāna}, i.e. that which *opposes* true knowledge, rather than simply the lack of knowledge – which is the root cause of pain and suffering.

This ignorance, we now know from the previous chapter, is of the form of māyā. Swaminarayan identifies it in Vac. Kār.12 with the soul's causal body, making the connection even more explicit in Vac. Gaḍh. 2.66.

> The jīva also possesses the causal body, which is the embodiment of eternal ignorance.

Linking this ignorance back to māyā, Swaminarayan defines māyā as

> nothing but the sense of I-ness towards the body and my-ness towards anything related to the body. (Vac. Gaḍh. 3.39)

Interestingly, then, ignorance {ajñāna, avidyā}, māyā and the causal body are essentially the same in this soteriological context and are indeed often seen being used interchangeably. All three are charged as the very reason – as the name 'causal' suggests (Vac. Var.6) – why the soul has to transmigrate from one gross and subtle body to another in each subsequent life.

But how exactly is one's ignorance instrumental in perpetuating transmigration? This connection requires further elucidation.

Firstly, any actions performed while in a state of ignorance (i.e. self-identification with the bodies) accrue karmas which are then stored in the causal body. As these karmas fully 'ripen', they cling to the soul, as if becoming a part of it. Swaminarayan explains in Vac. Kār.12:

> This māyā of the jīva, i.e. the causal body, is attached so firmly to the jīva that they cannot be separated by any means whatsoever . . . [just as] the shell of a tamarind seed is extremely firmly attached to the seed.[1]

Those ripened karmas, so closely and firmly attached to the soul, manifest themselves as desires for even more māyic pleasures (Vac. Gaḍh. 3.20). To fulfil these desires, i.e. to expend those stored karmas, the soul has

[1] See also Vac. Var.6, where Swaminarayan repeats the seed-shell analogy for the soul and its causal body.

to assume another body in another life. If in that subsequent life those karmas are not fully expended and if, by the soul's continuing ignorance, still more karmas are accrued, the surviving stock in the causal body will again need to be lived out in yet more lives. Swaminarayan explains this in Vac. Amd.3 using the example of a banyan tree and its roots.

> Everyone knows that the roots of a banyan tree keep the tree green. Even if all of its roots, except for a few minor roots, are uprooted, the banyan tree will still remain green. In the same way, one may have outwardly renounced the sense-objects, but if thoughts of them are entertained, then those thoughts become a cause of births and deaths.

And so desires {vasanā}, born of ignorance, become the root cause of more and more lives in the perpetual transmigratory cycle.

What needs to be noted apropos is that even in a state of ignorance there is no change in the essential nature of the soul – just as the seed's shell does not affect the seed. To believe otherwise is the very form of ignorance – or 'foolishness' – that Swaminarayan had so emphatically admonished in Vac. Gaḍh. 2.12, cited earlier. Going even further, Swaminarayan explains:

> Even before one had been graced with the attainment of God, kāla {time} – a power of God – was unable to destroy the jīva; karmas were unable to destroy the jīva; not even māyā was able to assimilate the jīva into itself. (Vac. Gaḍh. 2.50)

Nevertheless, māyā/ignorance/the causal body still enshrouds the soul, obstructing and obscuring a full realisation of its pure, conscious, blissful self and of the limitlessly blissful God who dwells therein and all around. Instead, that ignorance holds the soul captive to the never-ending needs of the body and the insatiable desires of the mind, entrapping it ever more into a transmigratory existence with all its limitations and sufferings of birth, decay, disease, disappointment and death. This is what the Vedānta texts promise liberation from, and what aspirers of liberation {mumukṣus} so earnestly endeavour towards.

Nature of Liberation

Mukti or mokṣa – from the Sanskrit verb-root 'muc' {to free} – relates in theological terms to freedom, liberation or release from the captivity and oppression of māyā and the incessant cycle of births and deaths it enforces. The first thing, therefore, we can say about mukti in Swaminarayan Hindu soteriology is that it is a state of immortality, where death and rebirth are no more, because their very cause, māyā or ignorance, is no more.

> Just like a grain of rice that has had its outer chaff removed does not grow, one who . . . is freed from eternal ignorance in the form of māyā becomes free of birth and death. (Vac. Sār.11)

This is explicitly and repeatedly corroborated by such important adjectives as 'amṛta' {literally, 'immortal'} found to describe the liberated soul in the Upaniṣads (IU 11, 14; KeU 1.2, 2.4, 2.5; KaU 1.28, 6.2, 6.9, 6.14, 6.15; PU 1.10, 3.11, 3.12; MuU 3.2.9; TU 1.10.1; AU 3.4; CU 1.4.4, 1.4.5; BU 1.3.28, 2.4.2, 2.4.3, 4.4.7, 4.4.14, 4.4.17, 4.5.4, 5.14.8) and the Bhagavad-Gītā (13.12, 14.20). We also learned in the chapter on Akṣarabrahman that Akṣaradhāma, the abode of Parabrahman where liberated souls eternally rest in communion with him, is a place from where there is no return to a transmigratory existence (Vac. Sār.14; CU 4.15.6, BU 6.2.15, BG 8.21, 15.6, BS 4.4.22).

Of course, as we learned in the chapters on jīva and īśvara, the finite soul is by its very nature immortal and pure. However, liberation in Swaminarayan Hindu theology is more than just a return to an original state of being for the soul. It is a new, higher spiritual state – indeed, the highest, perfect spiritual state – that is enriched by the direct realisation of Parabrahman. It is not just release from the pain and limitations of transmigration but an eternal, overwhelming experience of the limitless and unending bliss of God. It entails not merely the dispelling of ignorance but the positive receiving of Akṣarabrahman's qualities. In other words, this is the pre-eminent brahmic state, what Swaminarayan calls the state of being brahmarūpa or akṣararūpa, and described in the Bhagavad-Gītā as 'brāhmī sthiti' (2.72) or being 'brahmabhūta' (18.54). It is so called because the liberated soul becomes 'like Brahman', that is, it receives many of the qualities of Akṣarabrahman. As Swaminarayan explains in Vac. Gaḍh. 2.20:

> When the jīva attains a likeness to that Brahman . . ., then that jīva can also be said to be brahmarūpa.

This is made clear, for example, by the identical descriptions found in CU 8.1.5 and then in CU 8.7.1, which relate, according to Bhadreshdas, to the universal soul Akṣarabrahman and the liberated soul, respectively. The verses describe both as being 'without evil, free from old age and

This place in Akṣaradhāma, Swaminarayan clarifies, is the state of liberation achieved after death, upon leaving the material body behind. For this reason, it is called 'videha mukti' {incorporeal liberation}. He states, for example:

> After such an enlightened devotee {ekāntika bhakta} leaves his body and becomes free of all influences of māyā, he attains Akṣaradhāma. (Vac. Gaḍh. 1.21)[5]

Upon death, however, having shed its material body, the soul does not forever thereafter remain formless in Akṣaradhāma, as some sort of unbodied spirit or phantom. Swaminarayan explains in Vac. Gaḍh. 3.7 that, like God who possesses a definite form there, the liberated devotees in his service also possess a form.

What is this form of the liberated souls in Akṣaradhāma? This is the question posed to Swaminarayan in Vac. Gaḍh. 2.66. He replies:

> When the jīva's ignorance is dispelled, its association with the three māyic bodies is broken. Thereafter, the jīva remains as pure consciousness and existence. Then, by God's will, the jīva receives a body composed of sentiency {caitanya prakṛti}, which is distinct from the eight inert elements {jaḍa prakṛti} of God, i.e. earth, water, etc. With that body, then, it resides in God's Akṣaradhāma.

In answer to a similar question in Vac. Gaḍh. 1.1 –

> What type of body does a devotee of God attain when he leaves his physical body, which is composed of the five material elements, and goes to the abode of God?

– Swaminarayan replies that such a devotee receives, 'by the will of God', a brahmic body, what he calls here a 'brahmamaya tanu'.

Bhadreshdas draws upon this when commenting on CU 8.12.2. He explains that when the soul leaves the body and reaches the supremely glorious form of Parabrahman in the divinely luminous Akṣaradhāma, it receives a divine, brahmic body {divyabrāhmavigraha; brāhmatanu} in which it continuously experiences the divine bliss of Parabrahman and Akṣaradhāma.[6]

This is analogously and even more explicitly stated in BU 4.4.4:

> As a goldsmith takes a piece of gold and turns it into another, newer, more beautiful form, in the same way, this soul, having discarded this body and

[5] See also Vac. Gaḍh. 1.1, Gaḍh. 1.12, Gaḍh. 2.67, Gaḍh. 3.22.
[6] CU-SB 8.12.2, pp. 386–7. See also the discussion based on this verse in BS-SB 4.4.1, p. 416.

> dispelled its ignorance, receives another, newer, more beautiful . . . brāhma form.[7]

Elaborating upon this new form in Vac. Gaḍh. 3.38, Swaminarayan speaks of it alongside God's form in the following way:

> The form of God in Akṣaradhāma and the form of the muktas – the attendants of God – are all real, divine and extremely luminous. Also, the form of that God and those muktas is two-armed like that of a human being, and it is characterised by eternal existence, consciousness and bliss. (Vac. Gaḍh. 3.38)

Going even further in likening the muktas' form with God's human-shaped form, Swaminarayan calls theirs a 'godly body', or 'bhāgavatī tanu' (Vac. Sār.14). The climax of this similarity is found in Vac. Kār.1, where Swaminarayan states that the liberated souls, 'due to their knowledge of God, assume a form like God's form'. That is, he explains, 'they become divine'.[8]

Being divine and composed solely of consciousness means that the liberated souls are without any of the distinctions of name and form possible only with māyic materiality. In other words, the forms in Akṣaradhāma of Parabrahman, Akṣarabrahman and all liberated souls are virtually identical, with the muktas themselves being visually indistinguishable from one another (even while retaining their ontological individuality).

Another reason for this is that the forms of the muktas are genderless, just as the souls themselves are (Vac. Gaḍh. 3.22). In a sermon recorded in SV 7.2, Swaminarayan explains:

> The form of a mukta is different from the two genders of the world. It is neither female in shape nor male in shape. It has a wholly brahmic body, which is neither feminine nor masculine.

This also helps explain that, even while having a human-*shaped* form – complete with senses, inner faculties, etc. – the fact that it is divine, brahmic and composed entirely of consciousness, the liberated souls are devoid of any human functions and urges. Having transcended māyā, they are beyond hunger, thirst, fatigue, etc. and free of all forms of mundane passions.

[7] See BU-SB 4.4.4, pp. 268–9 for a fuller explanation of this verse, where it relates the brahmarūpa mukta receiving a brāhmaśarīra for enjoying Parabrahman in Akṣaradhāma, whereas other, less-elevated souls will receive other types of bodies as they enjoy the pleasures of lesser abodes.

[8] Despite these similarities, the liberated souls remain ontologically distinct from Parabrahman and Akṣarabrahman, as explained earlier in note 291.

stock of *past* karmas (called prārabdha) which have been activated and need to be depleted. These are responsible for the current gross and subtle body. As soon as they are exhausted, no further reason remains for the body to exist, and the soul can then discard it and transcend to Akṣaradhāma. While alive, though, it must be stressed, the body carries no sway over the liberated soul within. Swaminarayan explains with various analogies that the soul 'rattles' distinctly separate from within the body, like a sword in its scabbard or a seed within a dried mango; the body is merely the old slough on a moulting snake to be shortly shed (VR 149; see also BU 4.4.7).

Way to Liberation

In many ways, the final portion of this chapter concluding our exposition of Swaminarayan Hindu theology is a recapitulation of many of the key doctrinal points already covered up till now. This is, again, revealing, reminding us of the nature of systematic theology, where the individual parts come together at the end and, when the final part is 'slotted in', the whole becomes properly functional and all the more appreciable. Of course, the task of theology is not simply the mechanical assembling of theoretical cogs and wheels, nor can we expect for an exposition of such a nature to function like clockwork, for neither is theology a machine nor God so simple or facilely reducible that he can be understood by a clever combination of doctrines. Nonetheless, the bringing together of many complex ideas within a coherently structured framework can indeed advance our always limited understanding of God. And as in assembling a still imperfect, intricate scale model, the endeavour of systematic theology duly demands a wholesome level of patience, application and cogency.

The subject of liberation as a whole perhaps more than any other doctrine also calls for a good degree of humility. The broad, hefty and exceptionally complex topic cannot possibly be covered with its full gamut of accompanying issues in a few thousand words. Indeed, any treatment within even a few hundred pages would still fall woefully short; a treatise similar to the preceding overview of the five eternal realities could provide only a similarly brief introduction. We must therefore content ourselves with the following sections, wherein we can touch upon only a handful of the most fundamental topics and questions within the field of soteriology and orthopraxy, and merely point at possible ways of addressing them based on the theological sources of the Swaminarayan tradition.

Grace and Effort

For our starting point in discussing the way to liberation, we should address the fundamental soteriological question of not *how* liberation can be achieved but whether it can be *achieved* at all. That is, is it a state that really comes as the fruition of one's endeavours – often termed 'sādhanā' {literally, 'means'}, also referred to as praxis – or is it purely an unearned gift from God? Framed another way, what roles do God's grace {kṛpā} and human effort {prayatna} play in securing liberation?

We have already seen in Part I from our discussion about the sources and tools of Swaminarayan Hindu theology how God can only truly be realised by revelation, itself a supreme act of his loving grace. To remind ourselves of the important Upaniṣadic verse we cited there:

> This Self [Paramātman] cannot be attained by instruction, nor by intellectual power, nor even through much hearing [i.e. learning]. He is attained only by the one whom the Self [Paramātman] chooses. To such a one, the Self [Paramātman] reveals his own form. (MuU 3.2.3, KaU 2.23)

When elaborating on the term 'chooses' {vṛnute}, Bhadreshdas explains this as the gracious and loving acceptance by Parabrahman – whom he variously describes as 'an ocean of great compassion' {paramadayāsāgara} and 'a treasure trove of grace' {kṛpānidhi} – of the worshipper who is dedicated solely to him {svaikaniṣṭha upāsaka}. Only to such a vessel of Parabrahman's grace {paramātmakṛpābhājana} does he become realisable {labhya} and reveal himself. [12]

Bhadreshdas adds at KaU 2.23 that instruction, intellectual power and scriptural learning are representative of all endeavours that can be performed in an attempt to reach God. They alone are inadequate. Parabrahman thus remains 'kṛpaikasādhya', attainable by grace alone. [13]

Swaminarayan, too, chides those who rely on their endeavours to achieve liberation while discounting the absolute need and power of God. Evoking the classical imagery of crossing the ocean of life and death, Swaminarayan explains in Vac. Gaḍh. 1.37:

> A person without such a [resolute] conviction [of God's nature] attempts to attain liberation using the strength of his own endeavours, but he does not strive for it by relying on the grace of God. Such a senseless person is as foolish as someone wishing to cross the ocean by his own efforts, without the aid of a ship. Conversely, one who wishes for liberation through the

[12] MuU-SB 3.2.3, p. 293; KaU-SB 2.23, pp. 118–19. [13] KaU-SB 2.23, pp. 118–19.

> grace of God is wise, like one who wishes to cross the ocean by travelling in a ship.[14]

Bhadreshdas is careful, however, of not being overly forceful in pitting human effort against divine grace. In adding the word 'kevala' {alone} in his comment above, he clarifies that while all endeavours are inadequate in realising God, they are inadequate *alone*, in and of themselves. They can still be effective in pleasing God, who will then bestow his liberating grace upon his beloved devotee. To be absolutely clear here: God is pleased with the seeker's devout, sincere and persistent *effort*, or striving, not necessarily the 'works' themselves. God himself remains infinitely beyond the reach of those actions. So God's grace is absolutely indispensable, but efforts are not totally useless either, even though they can only please God and never (fully or directly) earn his grace.

If there are any efforts that Bhadreshdas does dismiss as utterly futile, they are the 'self-imagined means' {svataḥkalpitasādhana} of a person who refuses to follow the authoritative teachings enjoined in revealed texts or by the Guru. These qualifications are necessary because of the immediately following verse in the Muṇḍaka Upaniṣad:

> This Self [Paramātman] cannot be attained by one who is weak, nor by inadvertency, nor by austerities marked without authoritative endorsement.

It then concludes:

> But the knower [of brahmavidyā] who strives by these means [i.e. learning, austerities, etc.] attains this Self [Paramātman] and enters Brahmadhāma. (MuU 3.2.4)

Thus, when these same efforts – including those mentioned in MuU 3.2.3 and all others – are informed by correct theological knowledge, practised according to the calling and guidance of the Guru and directed solely to pleasing God, they can indeed play some useful part in securing liberation by God's grace.[15]

Praxis, therefore, is not in total contradistinction to the idea of *sola gratia* (liberation by 'grace alone'). All efforts are directed to pleasing God and thereafter receiving his grace, which alone is capable of granting liberation. Liberation thus comes at the end of one's endeavours, but not as their fruit. With liberation being totally unattainable by human effort alone, it leaves no scope for finite souls to boast of it as their 'accomplishment'. What

[14] See also Vac. Gaḍh. 1.60 and Gaḍh. 2.35 for similar analogies and instructions.
[15] Based on MuU-SB 3.2.3–4, pp. 293–5. See also KaU-SB 2.23, pp. 118–19.

praxis does do, however, is to develop the aspirer of liberation into a 'vessel' ('pātra', or 'bhājana' as Bhadreshdas states) capable of effectively receiving and, importantly, retaining and responding to God's grace. Without in any sense diminishing the potency of God's grace, this also helps explain why God is not an unjust or capricious distributor, injudiciously doling out his favour. In so saying, however, nor does God relinquish his absolute prerogative to shower his grace upon whomsoever he pleases.

Thus, even if God's grace is regarded as absolutely free and un-earnable, yet available fully and equally for everyone, like the rain that showers upon earth, it is only those who are adequate 'vessels' who can receive that grace and make use of it. Swaminarayan elaborates on this in Vac. Sār.11. When Muktanand Swami asks,

> Personal endeavour is mentioned in the scriptures, but how much is actually achieved by personal endeavour and how much is achieved by God's grace?

Swaminarayan goes on to describe a worthy recipient of God's grace. Such a person, he explains, strictly observes dharmic disciplines such as non-violence and eightfold brahmacarya, has an absolutely firm realisation of him/herself as the ātman, is firmly detached from worldly pleasures and has an intense and enduring devotional faith. These four aspects of sādhanā correspond to what is traditionally termed within Swaminarayan texts as dharma {observance of scriptural injunctions}, jñāna {ātman-realisation} (not to be confused with the broader, more theological knowledge of Brahman and Parabrahman), vairāgya {detachment} and bhakti {devotion}. Collectively, they are called 'Ekāntika Dharma' or 'Bhāgavata Dharma', which we learned earlier is one of the reasons for God's manifestation on earth (Vac. Gaḍh. 2.46, Gaḍh. 3.21), and which features repeatedly in the Vacanāmrut and Svāmīnī Vāto as a matrix for pleasing God (e.g. Vac. Gaḍh. 1.21, SV 3.25). In Vac. Sār.11, Swaminarayan is sure to add that all of these endeavours should be enjoined 'by the words of a true Guru and the scriptures', before concluding:

> God's grace is only bestowed upon one who has such characteristics.

Perhaps sensing the enormity of the task of perfectly cultivating these characteristics, Nityanand Swami firstly acknowledges Swaminarayan's point but then immediately asks:

> But what becomes of one who has some deficiency in cultivating these characteristics?

Swaminarayan forthrightly answers:

> Then he does not attain ultimate liberation, i.e. God's Akṣaradhāma. Instead, he attains some other abode of God.

Swaminarayan refers here to the abodes of other avatāras and even the paradisiacal realms of the devas, which, in comparison to Akṣaradhāma, are as good as naraka, he states. After further elaboration Swaminarayan ends his answer by reiterating his earlier position, this time with added force.

> Hence, whether it takes one life or innumerable lives, only when one develops the previously described characteristics and becomes extremely free of worldly desires, does one become a worthy vessel of receiving God's grace, and only then will one attain ultimate liberation. Without it, one will definitely not attain it.

Swaminarayan is clear, then, that liberation is a result of God's grace only, and that spiritual praxis is necessary to receive and apply that liberative grace.

Another way this soteriological discussion is often framed is by asking the classical question of whether liberation is a gift or reward from God. Surely grace has to be unmerited for it to be meaningfully grace at all. So it can never be earned. But calling liberation a gift would implicate God as being unfair or whimsical, for can liberation be bestowed arbitrarily upon the completely undeserving? Some effort at least would seem warranted. Otherwise what will inspire people to do anything at all for God? Yet no matter how hard and long a seeker endeavours, so ultimately insignificant are his/her efforts in winning over the otherwise unattainable God, and God's blissful experience is so staggeringly disproportionate to those efforts, that it can neither be called a reward in any legitimate sense. We are left with an intractable dilemma.

Perhaps a more useful way within Swaminarayan Hindu theology to resolve this important soteriological conundrum is to understand liberation as neither gift nor reward, but with reference to the model of a jackpot prize and the lottery ticket that one buys for winning it. So negligible is the price of the ticket which leads to the jackpot that to call it as being 'earned' is ridiculous. Yet the prize is not totally arbitrary either, for only one who has bought a ticket is eligible to receive the prize. Of course, the analogy breaks down at the point where it is not sheer chance that provides the winner of the lucky draw but God himself who decisively *chooses* {vṛṇute} the recipient of his overwhelming favour. The means for liberation are thus insignificant but nevertheless necessary, utterly meagre but not totally worthless either. They are necessary and worthwhile for receiving the gracious favour of God, who graciously grants his blissful experience in liberation infinitely many times more intensely than it could ever be earned or fully deserved, if at all.

At this point we should ask the more pointed question: What form does this loving grace take?

Bhadreshdas answers when commentating on KaU 2.23, the same verse found in MuU 3.2.3 cited above.

> This is the form of his [Paramātman's] grace: Seeing his devotee earnestly endeavouring by several means to please him, God, the ocean of grace that he is, grants that devotee access to the profound association of the Akṣarabrahman Guru – who is his [Paramātman's] supreme worshipper, who has the greatest love for him, who eternally has a complete and perfect realisation of him, and who can be regarded as his own form – so that his devotee can easily realise him [Paramātman]. Then, by listening, reflecting, etc. upon the Guru's teachings, and serving him with the belief that he is the very form of God – as directed by such statements as 'Who has the highest devotion to God and, as he does to God, also to the Guru (SU 6.23)', etc. – that devotee, having developed a oneness with his self and Brahman and having received the grace of God, realises Paramātman.[16]

The following sections can now serve as an elaboration upon these means to liberation made possible by God's grace.

Liberation by Brahmavidyā

We learned at the beginning of this chapter about the soul's karmic predicament – incessantly journeying through the cycle of births and deaths – and its cause as ignorance in the form of māyā. To dispel this veil of ignorance and break free from this transmigratory cycle, the Vedāntic texts unequivocally state:

> By knowledge, one attains the immortal state. (KeU 2.4)

> By knowledge, one enjoys the immortal state. (IU 11)

The Vacanāmrut is similarly clear about the essential role of theological knowledge in leading to liberation from saṃsāra, both from śāstric statements cited in its sermons – such as

[16] KaU-SB 2.23, p. 119.

> There is no liberation without knowledge (Hiraṇyakeśīyaśākhāśruti[17])

and

> Only by knowing him [Parabrahman] does one pass beyond death; there is no other path for attaining [liberation] (SU 3.8)

– to statements from Swaminarayan himself:

> The knowledge of God's nature and the knowledge of God's greatness are the two extraordinary means to liberation. (Vac. Gaḍh. 1.57)

We learned in our elucidation of Parabrahman that as absolutely indispensable as this knowledge of God is, the most accurate description of his limitless, unfathomable greatness is that Parabrahman is greater than Akṣarabrahman (MuU 2.1.2). This being so, we cannot really begin to know Parabrahman without first fully knowing Akṣarabrahman, who also reveals Parabrahman. Equally, if knowing Parabrahman is absolutely essential for liberation, and the best that can be said about him is that he transcends Akṣarabrahman, it follows that knowing Akṣarabrahman is also absolutely essential to securing ultimate liberation. Swaminarayan thus writes in his doctrinal letter, the Vedaras:

> There is no path to liberation without knowing Brahman.[18] (VR 17–18)

This is why we find the Upaniṣads (e.g. MuU 1.2.13) configuring brahmavidyā – the highest form of knowledge, which leads to final liberation – as the knowledge of both Akṣara and Puruṣottama, i.e. Brahman and Parabrahman. Hence also, Bhadreshdas explains, the 'desire to know Brahman' {brahmajijñāsā} enjoined at the very beginning of the Brahmasūtras must necessarily comprise the knowledge of both Parabrahman *and* Akṣarabrahman if it is to effectively result in final liberation. Swaminarayan states the same in Vac. Gaḍh. 2.3, using the synonym 'brahmajñāna' for brahmavidyā:

> Brahman is the cause and support of all, including Prakṛti-Puruṣa, etc., and pervades everything by its antaryāmin powers ... Parabrahman, that is Puruṣottama Nārāyaṇa, is distinct from that Brahman, and also the cause, support and inspirer of Brahman. With such understanding, one should develop a oneness between one's jivātman and that Brahman and worship

[17] This is a non-extant Vaiṣṇava text, but the phrase is attributed to it in the *Setumālā* commentary on the *Śrīharivākyasudhāsindhu* in 115.7.

[18] Swaminarayan uses 'Brahman' and 'Akṣarabrahman' interchangeably in this passage of the Vedaras, making it explicit that 'Brahman' here refers to Akṣarabrahman, not Parabrahman or even both.

> Parabrahman while maintaining a master-servant relationship with him. With such understanding, 'brahmajñāna' also becomes an unobstructed path to attaining the highest state of enlightenment. (Vac. Gaḍh. 2.3)

In this key theological statement, Swaminarayan points to the cosmic role of Akṣarabrahman, its ontological distinction from and subordination to Parabrahman, and also the soul's need for Akṣarabrahman to properly worship Parabrahman (upon which we shall further elaborate shortly), all of which constitute brahmajñāna/brahmavidyā, or what we might call theological knowledge.

Realising Brahmavidyā by Serving the Brahmasvarūpa Guru

If the Vacanāmrut and Vedāntic texts are clear that brahmavidyā is essential to securing liberation, they are equally unequivocal about how to realise that highest, theological knowledge. The Muṇḍaka Upaniṣad immediately preceding the statement cited above states, according to Bhadreshdas:

> To realise that [brahmavidyā], imperatively surrender, with sacrificial wood in hand, to only that guru who has the realisation of revealed texts, who is Brahman and who is ever steadfast [in Parabrahman]. (MuU 1.2.12)

Bhadreshdas explains the instruction to 'imperatively go' as indicative of fully surrendering to the Brahmasvarūpa Guru. Alongside 'with sacrificial wood in hand', it implies a relationship of service, obedience and total dedication.[19]

In a specifically soteriological context, Swaminarayan, too, stresses the Sant, i.e. Brahmasvarūpa Guru, as the starting point for acquiring theological knowledge. He states in Vac. Kār.12:

> This māyā of the jīva, i.e. the causal body, is attached so inextricably to the jīva that it cannot be separated by any means whatsoever. However, if a person attains the association {samāgama} of the Sant, realises the nature of God through the words of that Sant, meditates on that nature of God and imbibes the words of God in his heart, then the causal body attached to his jīva is burnt asunder.

'However', Swaminarayan concludes in a particularly emphatic closing statement,

> even if one were to try a million other methods, one could not destroy the jīva's ignorance in the form of the causal body.

[19] See MU-SB 1.2.12, pp. 253–6.

The exceptional significance of this doctrine within Swaminarayan Hindu theology is reflected as a particularly emphatic and recurrent theme throughout the Vacanāmrut, where Swaminarayan reiterates the need to attain, know, serve, love, obey, trust and surrender to the Guru as the way to overcoming māyā and securing liberation when God is not personally present on earth. For example:

> One who aspires for liberation should recognise God through these characteristics and seek the refuge of that God . . . However, when God is not manifest on this earth before the eyes, one should seek the refuge of the Sant who is absorbed with that God, because the jīva can also secure liberation through him. (Vac. Var.10)[20]

What is especially noteworthy in these important soteriological statements is that both God and Guru are invariably mentioned in tandem. For example, in Vac. Gaḍh. 2.21, Swaminarayan stresses that all authoritative texts and wise seers reveal 'the manifest form of God before the eyes and the manifest form of the Sant before the eyes as being the only grantors of liberation'.

> Whether this principle is understood after being told once or after being told a thousand times, whether it is understood today or after a thousand years, there is no option but to understand it.

'A person' who *has* understood this

> has grasped all of the fundamental principles. What is more, he will never fall from the path of liberation.

Swaminarayan concludes this sermon with the yet more emphatic statement:

> Thus, this very fact is the essence of all of the scriptures. (Vac. Gaḍh. 2.21)

This final point is made even more explicit in Vac. Gaḍh. 2.59, where Swaminarayan begins:

> In the four Vedas, the Purāṇas and the Itihāsa scriptures, there is but one central principle, and that is that only God and his Sant can grant liberation.

He then goes on to conclude:

> So, when one attains God or his Sant, then, apart from this, there is no other liberation for the self; this itself is ultimate liberation. (Vac. Gaḍh. 2.59)

To reiterate the important clarification learned earlier, the soteriological function of the 'Sant', 'Sādhu', 'Bhakta', 'Satpuruṣa', 'great Puruṣa'

[20] Similarly, see Vac. Jet.1.

described in these and all such statements unequivocally confirms his personhood as that of māyā-transcending Akṣarabrahman in the earthly form of the Brahmasvarūpa Guru. As if corroborating this, Swaminarayan instructs in Vac. Gaḍh. 3.26:

> Those who are eager to secure their liberation should thus serve such a Sant.

Why? Because

> such a Sant should not be thought to be like a human nor should he be thought to be like even a deva . . . Such a Sant, even though he is human [in form], is worthy of being served like God.

Swaminarayan elaborates on how to serve the Guru 'like God' in Vac. Var.5 by instructing perfectly 'equal service' of both. This is evocative of the famous proclamation at the end of the Śvetāśvatara Upaniṣad cited by Bhadreshdas in his elaboration of KaU 2.23 above:

> All objectives declared [in the sacred texts] shine forth [i.e. become attainable] for the great soul who offers the highest devotion to God and, as he does to God, also to the Guru. (SU 6.23)

Swaminarayan substantiates such devotion to the Guru in Vac. Gaḍh. 2.28 by adding his personal example. He says:

> Even I am the devotee of such a perfect Bhakta of God and offer my devotion to the Bhakta of God.

In stressing this as a crucial soteriological principle, Swaminarayan concluded this sermon with the following emphatic epilogue:

> What is this sermon like which I have delivered before you? Well, I have delivered it having heard and having extracted the essence from the Vedas, the Śāstras, the Purāṇas and all other words on this earth pertaining to liberation. This is the most profound and fundamental principle; it is the essence of all essences. For all those who have previously attained liberation, for all those who will attain it in the future, and for all those who are presently treading the path of liberation, this discourse is like a lifeline. (Vac. Gaḍh. 2.28)

Thus, according to Swaminarayan, devoutly serving the Brahmasvarūpa Guru is essential to securing liberation.

Serving and Associating with the Brahmasvarūpa Guru by Deed, Word and Thought

If associating with or devoutly serving the Brahmasvarūpa Guru is essential to securing liberation, what form(s) should this service of the Guru take?

And what significance does this hold if all efforts for liberation should be directed to pleasing only God (in readiness for his essential grace)?

Swaminarayan provides a succinct answer to both these questions in the same sermon cited above before the emphatic ending.

> The only method for a person to please God is to serve the Bhakta of God by thought, deed and word. (Vac. Gaḍh. 2.28)

Again, this is a striking revelation by Swaminarayan, made all the more emphatic with the 'ja' in Gujarati, making serving the Guru the *only* means to truly pleasing God. The means of serving the Guru are noted as threefold. Swaminarayan calls upon the same three ways in Vac. Var.4, this time using the term 'saṅga' {association}, thereby clarifying the concept of 'service' as a holistic relationship[21] with the Guru. When Muktanand Swami asked the important soteriological question,

> For a devotee of God walking the path of devotion, which one spiritual endeavour incorporates all of the other endeavours for liberation?

Swaminarayan replied:

> All of the spiritual endeavours for attaining liberation are incorporated in keeping the association {saṅga} by thought, deed and word of a Sant who possesses the 30 attributes of a Sādhu.[22] (Vac. Var.4)

Gunatitanand Swami similarly states in SV 3.60:

> An aspirer of liberation becomes brahmarūpa if he faithfully associates with the Satpuruṣa by thought, deed and word.

This form of 'association' with the Guru – variously called 'saṅga', 'prasaṅga' and 'samāgama' in sampradāyic texts – warrants a little elaboration. Based on a collection of teachings from various theological sources of the Swaminarayan tradition, we can now unpack this relationship in an attempt to understand what it entails, even while appreciating that it cannot be compartmentalised into these three neat forms.

In the sermon just cited above, after Gunatitanand Swami offered this statement, a member from his audience asked him the same question we

[21] This is a broader rendering of the multivalent term 'sevā', with which we began in Vac. Loyā.7. In Gujarati, the term 'sevan' (present participle of the same verb) can also have connotations of 'relating to, receiving or partaking, and absorbing', for example, as one would with medicine or treatment.

[22] These are described in BP 11.11.29–33. Swaminarayan mentions in Vac. Var.13 that God adopts these virtues when he manifests upon earth as a sādhu. For a list, see Section 'Virtues' in Chapter 6.

ourselves are asking now: What does it mean to associate with the Guru by thought, deed and word? Gunatitanand Swami replied:

> [To associate] by deed is to do as the Satpuruṣa instructs; by word, is to extol the Satpuruṣa's infinite virtues; and by thought, is to not allow any disbelief towards the great Sādhu. (SV 3.60)

Briefly expanding upon each in turn now, to serve or associate with the Guru 'by deed' – through one's actions – is first and foremost to do as he instructs. Swaminarayan directly connects such obedience to liberation in Vac. Gaḍh. 1.78. When asked,

> What is the cause of the jīva's liberation?

he succinctly replies:

> To do exactly as the Sant says without harbouring any doubts is the very cause of the jīva's liberation.

Again, in a sermon emphasising the need to transcend māyic influences and realise the self in order to be eternally happy, Swaminarayan concludes:

> Only one who follows the commands of the Satpuruṣa is behaving as the ātman. (Vac. Gaḍh. 2.51)

This provides another example of the immediate connection Swaminarayan strikes between (external) actions and (internal) spiritual development, between outer behaviour {vartana} and inner state {sthiti}. As we shall see shortly, the instruction in Vac. Gaḍh. 2.51 is based on the practice of mentally 'joining' with the Brahmasvarūpa Guru and realising him as one's true self, thereby acquiring his brahmic qualities and becoming brahmarūpa. By doing as the liberating Guru instructs, and not succumbing to the whims and distractions of the māyic mind, the aspirer of liberation is overcoming the limitations of his/her own material self and acting as the ātman within, which he/she regards as assimilated with the Guru. In other words, he/she is emulating the Brahmasvarūpa Guru, the perfect devotee of God, and so acting as brahmarūpa (like Brahman) as he/she would in the state of living liberation. Understood this way, such obedience to the Guru becomes highly liberative, and his guidance can be appreciated as a gracious call to higher spiritual awareness and living. With this practice so inextricably tied with mentally (and spiritually) connecting with the Guru, we are already seeing how the three ways of associating with him tend to coalesce, supporting and enriching one another, confirming it as a holistic method of association.

Furthermore, as already mentioned earlier, Swaminarayan intends the devotee's encounter with the Guru to be wholly personal, as an intense and intimate relationship. This 'active' or 'physical' association thus includes being with him or near him in person – seeing him, listening to him, relating with him in ways that enhance a loving spiritual bond.

Also, as noted above, Swaminarayan instructs those aspiring for liberation to offer the highest devotion to the Guru as one would to God (Vac. Gaḍh. 3.26, Vac. Var.5; also SU 6.23). This paramount devotion would be expressed by such acts of reverence and adoration as bowing before the Guru, anointing him with sandalwood paste, offering him garlands and other auspicious paraphernalia and, more generally, acting in ways that would please him, including being honest, humble and charitable to others. All such actions form a part of devoutly associating with the Guru through one's deeds.

To serve or associate with the Guru verbally – 'by word' – is to praise his divine nature, redemptive virtues and liberative role. Swaminarayan explains in other sermons that this can take the form of singing devotional songs in praise of his glory or discoursing upon śāstric statements revealing the nature of the Guru, especially as eternally transcending māyā and serving as the medium through whom Parabrahman can be reached and through whom Parabrahman lives, loves and liberates. For example, after making the important revelation in Vac. Gaḍh. 1.71 that when God manifests for the purpose of granting liberation to the jīvas, he is always accompanied by his Akṣaradhāma, he goes on to instruct:

> Therefore, a devotee of God should realise that the form of God along with his Akṣaradhāma is present on this earth, and he should also explain this fact to others.

In sharing the revelation that God continues to be accessible on earth – here and now – and that the way to liberation remains open to all through the human-abode of God, i.e. the Akṣarabrahman Guru, the seeker's own conviction of the Guru's divinity and liberative potency is fortified, and with it his/her own spiritual bond with the Guru.

To serve or associate with the Guru mentally – 'by thought' – can take many forms, and is perhaps the most profound of the three, as it naturally and inescapably feeds into each of the others.

Firstly, as Gunatitanand Swami mentions, associating with the Guru by thought is to 'not allow any disbelief towards him', that is, to fully accept his pure, divine, transcendental self. Swaminarayan relates this as a way to rising above one's own māyic tendencies. For example, in a remarkable statement in Vac. Gaḍh. 1.58, he corresponds the soul's purity and impurity with its understanding of the Guru's purity and impurity.

> If one realises the truly great Puruṣa to be absolutely lust-free, then, even if one is as lustful as a dog, one will also become lust-free. Conversely, if one perceives the fault of lust in the great Puruṣa, then no matter how lust-free one may be, one becomes full of intense lust. In the same manner, if one views the great Puruṣa to be full of anger or avarice, then one becomes full of anger and avarice. Therefore, if one understands the great Puruṣa to be absolutely free of lust, avarice, gluttony,[23] egotism and attachment, one will also become free of all of those impurities and become a staunch devotee.

Thus, an important way of mentally associating with the Guru is to meditate upon his pure, redemptive qualities, especially the attributes of his being as Akṣarabrahman.

Swaminarayan also describes the powerful tool of reminiscing times of personal interaction with the Guru. It will not always be possible to be with him or near him, yet vividly recalling past encounters can be just as fulfilling and liberative, Swaminarayan explains (Vac. Gaḍh. 1.3, Gaḍh. 1.38, Gaḍh. 2.35, Jet.3).

Expanding this further, Swaminarayan instructs offering 'mānsī pūjā' to the Guru (Vac. Var.5). This is a form of mental worship which mirrors all the outer actions of devotional worship mentioned above, but performed within, as a form of visualisation. Swaminarayan assures this can be just as efficacious as physically performing pūjā, *if* it is accompanied with deep adoration and reverence (Vac. Sār.3). He elaborates upon this form of worship in great detail in Vac. Gaḍh. 3.23, explaining that it is a potent method by which a devotee can 'increase his love' for the manifest form of God and 'gain tremendous spiritual fulfilment'.

This all-important mental relationship with the Guru is expanded further still when Swaminarayan instructs developing a spiritual 'oneness' with the Guru by constant contemplation and profound love. This demands further elucidation, and so forms the subject below of the concluding section of this chapter on liberation.

'Oneness' with the Brahmasvarūpa Guru Earlier in this chapter, we understood that liberation is a state of perfect spiritual purity and maturity, in which the soul becomes brahmarūpa – literally, 'like Brahman'. This not only entails eradicating māyic impurities born of a material self-misunderstanding but, more positively, acquiring the qualities of

[23] Gluttony in this context refers to not just overeating but includes an excessive liking for tasty food.

Akṣarabrahman. Swaminarayan explains in Vac. Gaḍh. 2.31 how both are made possible.

> The jīva, however, has associated with the body, the senses and the sense-objects. As a result of this improper association, the jīva has become one with the body, senses, etc. After forsaking their association, the jīva realises, 'My self is Brahman, which transcends and is free from māyā.' If one associates with Brahman through continuous contemplation in this manner, the jīva acquires the virtues of Brahman. . . .
>
> The jīva remains continuously attached to māyā . . . Only when one continuously associates with Brahman, one's inspirer, through contemplation – as previously described – is that attachment broken.

This constant contemplation on the Brahmasvarūpa Guru as one's true self is the antidote, Swaminarayan explains, to the improper association the soul has forged from time immemorial with its māyic bodies and surroundings across countless life-experiences through transmigration.

As we saw earlier, Swaminarayan also instructs in Vac. Gaḍh. 2.3:

> One should develop a oneness between one's jivātman and that Brahman.

In Vac. Gaḍh. 3.38, Swaminarayan calls for a spiritual connection with the Guru by similarly instructing:

> One should also attach one's jīva to the Bhakta of God, the great Sādhu.

Gunatitanand Swami expounds in SV 2.41 on why this association leads to receiving Akṣarabrahman's qualities, i.e. becoming brahmarūpa:

> First, one should attach one's jīva to the Ekāntika [Sādhu]. That Sādhu is absorbed in God, so he has the qualities of God, and so the Sādhu's qualities are imbibed by whoever associates with [the Ekāntika Sādhu].

Then stressing the absolute essentiality of this form of association with the Guru, he ends the sermon with the following pronouncement:

> Whether one observes this method today or after a thousand lives, ultimately, there is no alternative but to observe it.

We find similar instructions or statements in the Upaniṣads for identifying the finite soul with Akṣarabrahman. For example, the famous proclamation in BU 1.4.10 is 'Aham brahmā'smi {I am Brahman}'. Bhadreshdas explains this as a meditation of the form 'My self is Akṣara; the Brahmasvarūpa Guru is my self',[24] in line with the contemplation offered

[24] BU-SB 1.4.10, p. 49.

by Swaminarayan above in Vac. Gaḍh. 2.31. Hereby the aspirer of liberation becomes wholly absorbed in the divine Guru and rises above his/her current māyic awareness and self-understanding to the pure, transcendental brahmic state of liberation. Here and in other similar Upaniṣadic statements (CU 6.8.7,[25] MāU 1.2,[26] BU 4.4.5,[27] IU 16[28] and BU 5.15.1[29]), Bhadreshdas is keen to clarify that any predicated identity of the individual soul with Brahman is indicative of the brahmarūpa state, when the soul shares many of Akṣarabrahman's qualities and becomes worthy of the highest devotion to Parabrahman. The ontological distinction between jīvas/īśvaras and Brahman nevertheless remains securely intact.[30]

Elsewhere in the Upaniṣads, we find actual instructions to know or meditate on that Brahman as one's own self (e.g. TU 2.5.1,[31] MuU 2.2.5[32] and MuU 2.2.6[33]). One such series of instructions can be found allegorically in MuU 2.2.4, where one is called upon to 'target' Akṣarabrahman with one's soul, the arrow, and 'strike it unflinchingly'. Like an arrow lodged in its target that becomes one with it, so, too, the aspirer of liberation makes the Guru his/her focus and becomes one with him {śaravat tanmayo bhavet}. The imagery continues from the earlier verse in MuU 2.2.3, where the oneness is explained as taking on aspects of the Guru's nature {tadbhāva}.[34] Bhadreshdas describes this as a form of awareness {anusandhāna}, contemplation {anucintana} and engrossment {sanlagnatā}.[35]

A term that Swaminarayan often uses to establish this sense of oneness with and constant awareness of the Guru is 'ātmabuddhi', literally 'self-perception' or perception of selfhood. When directed to developing it 'with' or 'in' the Guru, it comes to mean 'perceiving the Guru as one's self' as part of an assimilative relationship. Swaminarayan instructs in Vac. Jet.1:

> One should develop a conviction of one's ātman as follows: One should develop ātmabuddhi with the Sant who has attained the manifest form of God, and one should believe only that Sant to be one's self.

[25] CU-SB 6.8.7, pp. 278–9. [26] MāU-SB 1.2, p. 313. [27] BU-SB 4.4.5, pp. 269–70.
[28] IU-SB 16, p. 24. [29] BU-SB 5.15.1, p. 327. [30] See also BS-SB 1.3.5, p. 90.
[31] TU-SB 2.5.1, pp. 373–4. [32] MuU-SB 2.2.5, pp. 273–4.
[33] MuU-SB 2.2.6, pp. 275–6. For the meaning of 'Aum' as Akṣarabrahman, see, for example, KaU 2.15–16, PU 5.2, MāU 1.1–2, TU 1.8.1, CU 1.1.1, CU 1.4.1 and BG 8.13.
[34] For a discussion in the Brahmasūtras about realising the Akṣarabrahman Guru as oneself in order to receive his qualities, see the Akṣaradhyadhikaraṇa in BS-SB 3.3.32–3, pp. 335–6.
[35] MuU-SB 2.2.3–4, pp. 271–3. For a similar emphasis on constant and engrossing awareness of Brahman, see Bhadreshdas's definition of 'brahmacarya' in KaU-SB 2.15, p. 102; PU-SB 1.2, p. 175; MuU-SB 3.1.5, p. 286; CU-SB 8.4.3, pp. 358–9 and BG-SB 8.12, p. 184, and also of 'brahma vyāvaharan' in BG-SB 8.13, pp. 185–6.

'The purpose of being profoundly attached to the Sant' in this way, Swaminarayan explains, 'is that he [the Brahmasvarūpa Guru] has the ability of penetrating the barriers' of māyā. As we learned earlier from this same sermon, māyā is otherwise impregnable. Swaminarayan thus concludes:

> All should imbibe this principle, as it is the very life of everyone.

In various other sermons, Swaminarayan explains more about what he means by such 'ātmabuddhi', or what such 'ātmabuddhi' translates to in practical ways as part of a spiritual aspirant's endeavours towards liberation from māyā or ajñāna.

In the state of ignorance, the soul falsely identifies with the material body with a sense of I-ness ('I am male/female'; 'I am white/black/brown'; 'I am fat/thin/tall/short'; 'I am attractive/ugly'; 'I am clever/dumb'; etc.) and regards all that is associated with it as 'mine' ('My house, my car, my money, my assets, my belongings, my power, my fame, my talents, my relatives, etc.'). According to Swaminarayan, this is the very definition of māyā (Vac. Gaḍh. 3.39). To rise above such a māyic understanding, one must identify with something which is eternally beyond māyā and has the ability to lift one from it, i.e. Akṣarabrahman. Swaminarayan thus instructs that it is not the body with which one should have ātmabuddhi (a perception of selfhood) but the māyā-transcending Guru. All notions of 'I' and 'my' should now be directed to the Guru, i.e. 'I am Akṣara. I am Brahman. The Guru is my self.'

Seen another way, just as the soul enlivens, inspires, activates the body and senses – without which a person can do or be nothing at all – now, the Guru becomes, as if, the aspirant's very soul, enlivening, inspiring, activating it in every aspect of life.

One important way in which this should manifest is as a life of perfect devotion to God, for the Guru is first, foremost and always the perfect devotee himself. He provides a model of the redeemed life for all others to emulate. Thus, if 'oneness' with Brahman is an acquisition of the Guru's virtues, in becoming more like him (Brahman-like, or brahmarūpa), it follows that these brahmic qualities promote and enhance the highest devotional relationship of the aspirant with God, itself a mark of liberation. While this is not a simple exercise in the external imitation of the Guru, the aspirer of liberation nevertheless has an example on which to model his/her sustained efforts and intentions, and craft a spiritually pure life immersed in God, like the Guru's.

This should not, however, be reduced to a purely exemplarist understanding of the Guru's role. He actively makes possible and available liberation by way of his unique ontological position as Akṣarabrahman. This is most evident in two important ways: firstly, the aspirers of liberation assimilate from him their brahmic qualities, to become brahmarūpa; and secondly, he serves as the medium through whom they can most fruitfully offer devotion to Parabrahman and, in return, receive Parabrahman's loving grace. This dual role of the Brahmasvarūpa Guru helps explain his central position in Swaminarayan Hindu theology.

Swaminarayan also explains that such ātmabuddhi with the Guru most readily manifests itself as concentrated spiritual love,[36] what Bhadreshdas calls 'prakṛṣṭānurāgodbhava',[37] because the aspirer of liberation is now attached to the Guru, not the body or its affiliates. The Guru becomes the priority, the ultimate focus of all attention and efforts, not worldly matters or māyic pleasures. Even while diligently fulfilling every personal and social responsibility, all actions, thoughts and intentions of the aspirant are now imbued with a spiritual awareness of the Guru and thus take on a wholly devotional character and spirit. This frees the aspirant of his/her karmic bondage. Swaminarayan therefore instructs:

> For a person who desires his own liberation, nothing in this world is more blissful than God and his Sant. Therefore, just as a person has ātmabuddhi towards his own body, he should similarly have ātmabuddhi with God and his Sant. (Vac. Gaḍh. 3.7)

Extending this to include relatives of the body, and specifying the relationship as one of profound love, Swaminarayan states elsewhere:

> One should develop affection for God's Sant just as one has affection for one's wife, son, parents or brother. Due to this affection, then, the jīva becomes absolutely fulfilled. (Vac. Gaḍh. 2.59)

> If a person maintains profound love towards the Ekāntika Sādhu of God just as resolutely as he maintains profound love towards his own relatives, then the gateway to liberation opens for him.[38] (Vac. Gaḍh. 1.54)

[36] It is useful to note that a further connotation of the term 'sevā' is derived from its usage in defining the Sanskrit verb-root 'bhaj', meaning worship or devotion. This also helps explain how service of or association with the Guru is a form of loving devotion.

[37] This is found in the Ātmagṛhītyadhikaraṇa (BS 3.3.15–18), where Bhadreshdas equates 'gṛhīti' {literally, 'acceptance'} to 'buddhi' {perception}, thus centring the discussion on ātmabuddhi. He extols such Guru-centred self-perception as the best and most important means to serving Parabrahman. BS-SB 3.3.15–18, pp. 323–6.

[38] This is an expanded translation by Swaminarayan of BP 3.25.20:

'The wise sages know: affection [for others] firmly binds the soul. However, if that same affection is directed towards the Sādhu, the gateway to liberation is opened.'

Swaminarayan's tenor is that the Guru is the gateway to liberation. A profound and loving association with him opens that gateway.

In another important statement, Swaminarayan emphasises:

> Intense love for the Satpuruṣa is itself the means to realising one's ātman, is itself also the means to realising the greatness of the Satpuruṣa, and is itself also the means to having the direct realisation of God. (Vac. Var.11)

Swaminarayan's striking insight here is that love for the Guru not only leads to a realisation of the Guru and the self, with whom the individual develops a spiritual connection, but also of God. It again points to the substantive presence of Parabrahman within the Brahmasvarūpa Guru, and explains the Śvetāśvatara Upaniṣad's call to offer the highest devotion to the Guru on par with that offered to God (SU 6.23).

All of these aspects are recapitulated in the Vedaras, where Swaminarayan repeatedly calls upon such ātmabuddhi with Akṣarabrahman. For example, in one segment of the letter, after narrating the cosmic powers of Akṣarabrahman, he adds that that Akṣarabrahman 'is among us', referring to the Brahmasvarūpa Guru in human form. Swaminarayan then instructs:

> O Paramahansas! One should develop ātmabuddhi with him [Akṣarabrahman], and with that thought, become a jīvan-mukta [i.e. a living liberated soul]. (VR 166)

Elsewhere in the letter he writes:

> He who offers upāsanā to Puruṣottama Paramātman while realising one's self to be one with Akṣara is worthy of great honour.

However, Swaminarayan clarifies in the same passage that there should be no perception of selfhood with Parabrahman.

> He who does not have a servant-master relationship with Puruṣottama, but behaves as if one with him, is worthy of scorn. (VR 214)

In yet another part of the letter, Swaminarayan makes reference to himself as 'Parabrahman Puruṣottama' before explicitly instructing:

> O Paramahansas! Offer upāsanā to me while having ātmabuddhi with that [Brahman]. (VR 158)

In many ways, this is the essence and foundation of Swaminarayan Hindu theology, by which all of its doctrines are illumined and consummated, including the end and means to liberation: upāsanā – loving worship

Figure 7 An image of Gunatitanand Swami (right) alongside Swaminarayan, representing the core Akṣara-Puruṣottama or Akṣarabrahma-Parabrahman doctrine of Swaminarayan Hindu theology. It follows Swaminarayan's teachings, for example in Vac. Gaḍh. 2.3, and Vedāntic instructions, such as in MuU 1.2.13, to know both Akṣara/Akṣarabrahman and Puruṣottama/Parabrahman. (1996. Oil on canvas, 38 × 51 in (96 × 130 cm). Image courtesy of Swaminarayan Aksharpith)

informed by correct theological knowledge – is to be offered to Swaminarayan as Parabrahman/Puruṣottama (albeit through his most accessible form, the current Brahmasvarūpa Guru), after realising oneself as brahmarūpa/akṣararūpa by spiritually and lovingly associating with that same Akṣarabrahman Guru. This is why this theological system of Swaminarayan Hinduism is traditionally referred to as Akṣara-Puruṣottama upāsanā,[39] and the classical appellation for the Swaminarayan school of Vedānta is **Akṣarabrahma-Parabrahma-Darśana** (Figure 7).

This fittingly concludes this introductory exposition of Swaminarayan Hindu theology.

[39] For a more extensive discussion of the meaning of 'Akṣara-Puruṣottama Upāsanā', see Brahmadarshandas, *Vacanāmrut Rahasya*, vol. III, pp. 195–214.

CHAPTER 12

Afterword
The Way Forward

Even after such an extensive exposition, our work in theology is not complete, because our understanding of God can never be complete. Indeed, to know God at all is to understand his infinite, unfathomable greatness, and so, so too must our trek along the path of theological learning be unending. If we are to pause at all, it must be to reflect upon not how far we have reached, but to where we can still go forth. What new avenues of theological reflection, analysis and description can this study now open up? Into which directions can we expect – *need* – to see this learning being taken? It is to these opportunities for new scholarship that I now dedicate the epilogue of this book.

The Swaminarayan Tradition

From the beginning, I have been at pains to stress that this book attempts, by all measures, a brief introduction to Swaminarayan Hindu theology. It is the necessary first step in presenting a doctrinal account of a living Hindu tradition *qua* theology.

Precisely because this book is an introduction, it has needed to be sufficiently broad, providing an overview of all the major themes of Swaminarayan Hindu theology and how they function together. The mass of content, including the copious source material from foundational texts upon which the exposition is necessarily grounded, has sometimes precluded a certain depth of analysis, but, to be fair, the expectation of this primary task could only have been to provide an overview and thereby lay the groundwork for subsequent theological reflection and analysis. This necessarily and largely descriptive enterprise thus serves as the first of many rounds of more critical theological work to follow.

Moreover, now that this basic account is in place, we are in a position to explore not only deeper but also wider and farther into this vast theological landscape. The exposition will hopefully function as an entrée, opening up the Swaminarayan tradition to new voices and alternative discussions, perhaps paralleling its Abrahamic counterparts. For example, could there now be scope for subsidiary disciplines within Swaminarayan Hindu theology – philosophical, philological, exegetical, practical? Subjects and themes such as Vacanāmrut Studies, Vacanāmrut Hermeneutics, Sampradāyic History, Pastoral Theology, Moral Theology, 'Sampradāyology' (as in Ecclesiology), rituals, liturgy, devotional piety and many others require attention. Even within Systematic Theology, there are new and different ways in which to think and to configure that thinking, to plumb and push the depths of our theological understanding.

As we venture further out, the hope is that Swaminarayan Hindu theologians of all denominations, as well as other theologians interested in Swaminarayan Hinduism, will also be able and willing to address secular concerns and concerns of modernity (as we shall shortly consider below), where theology meets, intersects, collides and coalesces with other fields of study and interest. Similarly, with the help of this introductory theological account, scholars of other disciplines – religion, South Asian studies, history, anthropology, political science, etc. – will have access to more nuanced understandings of Swaminarayan Hinduism to enrich their own scholarship.

In many ways, then, this is an enthusing time for scholarship on the Swaminarayan Hindu tradition. Being over two hundred years old, it can neither be considered all that young, nor very old. Yet it continues to be invigorated with fresh insights and new theological work from within the tradition, as noted in detail in the Prolegomenon (see Section 'Theological Scholarship in Swaminarayan Hinduism' in Chapter 1). Generally, though, much more work is needed in English to properly articulate the complex, sophisticated and exigent theological ideas of Swaminarayan Hinduism. When more experts develop, they will surely lead each other into finer debate and harder discussion, from which will gradually emerge more theological literature. As a corollary, they may also help develop the current vocabulary and conceptual apparatus of Hindu theology and even theology, so that in turn these disciplines, too, can be broadened and enriched.

Challenges to Swaminarayan Hindu Theology

A useful and important stimulant for the advancement of Swaminarayan Hindu theology is acknowledging the challenges that it currently faces or might soon face. As scholars accept these challenges, they will have to continue asking difficult questions of themselves and the tradition, questions that bear upon the life of the faithful community and its place in an increasingly interconnected, interdependent world. With humility and courage, and through prayer and grace, as they think and work hard to articulate meaningful responses, the result will surely be even more fine scholarship being produced.

Looking forward, I foresee these challenges coming from three main corners.

Other Swaminarayan denominations: As I declared at the outset, while I attempt to articulate Swaminarayan Hindu theology in this book, I write from within one of the many denominations of this rapidly expanding Hindu tradition, specifically from within the BAPS Swaminarayan tradition. It espouses, to use the classical appellation, Akṣarabrahma-Parabrahma-Darśana as the conclusive truth revealed by Swaminarayan. Scholars of other denominations within Swaminarayan Hinduism, located within their own schools of thought, may beg to differ on this interpretation, on my systemisation and exegesis of Swaminarayan's teachings from the Vacanāmrut (based on my own study and understanding of mainly BAPS Swaminarayan texts), or even on Bhadreshdas's rendering of the Vedānta canon. Such diverse voices are to be expected in such a religious tradition, especially where multivalent texts and authorities, both theological and historical, can be open to nuanced readings.

This provides us with an opportune juncture to delineate very briefly some of the key doctrinal differences of other Swaminarayan groups. These denominations are often identified according to the names of the places in Gujarat, India, where they were founded. While it is not possible here to cover the full gamut of denominations within Swaminarayan Hinduism, I should be clear about the criteria for the ones I have chosen: they are four of the oldest and largest denominations, those with the most striking variations in doctrine and/or those whose doctrines can be properly traced to available textual sources. Many other denominations, while still independent of these four, may or may not differ on actual doctrine, but, importantly, lack technical source material from which any clear summary can be gleaned. Notwithstanding the inevitable generalising that this entails, even within each denomination,[1] the following should still provide a useful, albeit cursory, overview of some of the fundamental and most common points of divergence, as I have understood them, from the system exposited in this book. My effort has been to source each point to the

[1] The task is made all the more intractable because of internal inconsistences between certain texts of a denomination, sometimes even within a single text. As is mentioned below, these texts need to be studied much more thoroughly than is possible here.

respective denomination's key texts, i.e. those which have been authored, edited, published or commissioned by key figures within that denomination.

Vartal and Ahmedabad denominations

- There are three eternal metaphysical entities {tattva}: jīva, māyā and Parabrahman.[2] The five metaphysical distinctions {bheda} of jīva, īśvara, māyā, Akṣarabrahman and Parabrahman are subsumed within these three entities.[3]
- Swaminarayan and liberation are accessible through the mūrtis {sacred images} of Swaminarayan that are ritually installed in mandirs by the 'ācārya', who must be a collateral descendant of Swaminarayan.[4]
- These ācāryas are another form of Swaminarayan, but not to be worshipped.[5]
- Swaminarayan himself is identical to all other avatāras, but not ontologically distinct from them.[6]
- Akṣaradhāma, the abode of God, is non-different to Goloka, Vaikuṇṭha and all other abodes of God.[7]
- Nitya-vibhūti, 'the eternal realm', is a distinct metaphysical substance, of which the abode of God is composed.[8]
- The abode of God also hosts divya-mahiṣīs, i.e. 'queens' of God, thus accepting a gender distinction among liberated souls.[9]

[2] Sadguru Ghanshyamcharandas, *Ādhyātmika Tattvākhyāna*, Harijivandas Shastri (ed.) (Vadtal: Harijivandas Shastri, Vadtal Swaminarayan Temple, 1973), p. 257; Nandkishordas Purani, *Ajñānadhvāntabhāskara* (Muli: Soni Maganlal Kalidas, Swaminarayan Temple, 1924), pp. 3–42; Sadguru Swamishri Swayamprakashdasji, *Uddhav Sampradāynī Mārgdarśikā* (Ahmedabad: Shri Swaminarayan Mandir Kalupur, 1998), p. 12; Harjivandas Shastri, *Vacanāmrut-Bhūmikā* (Vadtal: Shastri Harjivandasji, Swaminarayan Temple, 1972), p. 252.

[3] Harijivandas Shastri, *Mānameya-Prakāśikā* (Vadtal: Vadtal Swaminarayan Temple, 1949), pp. 114–15; Swayamprakashdasji, *Uddhav Sampradāynī Mārgdarśikā*, p. 17; Satyaprasaddasji Swami, *Vaidik Sampradāy ane Guru Parampāra* (Gandhidham: Shri Swaminarayan Gurukul, 2005), pp. 33–5.

[4] Hitendrabhai Naranbhai Patel, *Dharmavaṁśī Ācārya Pad* (Ahmedabad: Mahant Swamishri, Swaminarayan Mandir Kalupur, 1995), pp. 50, 52; Chotalal Maganlal Patel, *Upāsanā Darpaṇ*, 2nd edn (Charadva: Sadguru Shastri Swami Gopalcharandasji, Swaminarayan Mandir, 1976), pp. 52–3.

[5] Patel, *Dharmavaṁśī Ācārya Pad*, pp. 53–4.

[6] Harjivandas, *Mānameya-Prakāśikā*, pp. 477–92; Gordhan M. Patel, *Sarvoparī Upāsanānu Rahasya* (Vadtal: Shri Swaminarayan Mandir, 2009), pp. 1–170, esp. 1, 12, 22, 73; Ramdasji Swami, *Śhudhdh Sarvoparī Upāsanā* (Vadtal: Shri Swaminarayan Mandir, 2009), pp. 1–114, esp. e.g. pp. 34–40; Harijivandas, *Vacanāmrut-Bhūmikā*, pp. 203–29.

[7] Harijivandas, *Mānameya-Prakāśikā*, pp. 509–10, 511–13; Patel, *Sarvoparī Upāsanānu Rahasya*, pp. 85, 150; Ramdasji, *Śhudhdh Sarvoparī Upāsanā*, pp. 50–69; Harijivandas, *Vacanāmrut-Bhūmikā*, pp. 238–39, 242–51.

[8] Harijivandas, *Mānameya-Prakāśikā*, pp. 500–13; Harijivandas, *Vacanāmrut-Bhūmikā*, pp. 118, 238–42.

[9] Harijivandas, *Mānameya-Prakāśikā*, pp. 454–9; Ramdasji, *Śhudhdh Sarvoparī Upāsanā*, pp. 52–3; Harijivandas, *Vacanāmrut-Bhūmikā*, pp. 164–81, 344–7.

- Some souls, called nitya-muktas, are eternally liberated, i.e. have never entered into māyic bondage and transmigration.[10]
- Overall, the doctrines align closely with the Viśiṣṭādvaita school of Vedānta.[11] (See further below for how this specifically differs from the Akṣarabrahma-Parabrahman school.)

Maninagar denomination[12]

- Five realities transcend māyā. These are, in ascending order, mūla puruṣa (i.e. īśvara), vāsudeva brahman (i.e. Brahman), mūla akṣara, the divine light of Parabrahman (called Akṣaradhāma) and Parabrahman himself.[13]
- There are two Akṣaradhāmas. The higher Akṣaradhāma is the formless, divine light of Parabrahman's form,[14] within which the liberated souls (anādi muktas and parama ekāntika muktas) reside. Mūla akṣara (the lower Akṣaradhāma) hosts the mūla akṣara muktas, who are inferior to and distinct from the other liberated souls.[15]
- There are three types of liberated souls: ekāntika mukta, parama ekāntika mukta and anādi mukta.[16]

10 Harijivandas, *Mānameya-Prakāśikā*, pp. 253, 465–70, 504; Harijivandas, *Vacanāmrut-Bhūmikā*, pp. 184, 311–13; Satyaprasaddasji, *Vaidik Sampradāy ane Guru Paramparā*, pp. 31, 35.

11 Ghanshyamcharandas, *Ādhyātmika Tattvākhyāna*, p. 269; Nandkishordas, *Ajñānadhvāntabhāskara*, pp. 1–42; Muktanand Swami, *Brahmamīmāṃsā* with *Pradīpa* by Gopalanand Swami, P. B. Aṇṇaṅgarācārya (ed.) (Vadtal: Anand Prasad Maharaj, Swami Narayan Temple, 1952), pp. xxiii–xlviii, esp. pp. xlviii, 2; Harijivandas, *Mānameya-Prakāśikā*, pp. xxxiv, 1, 523; Harijivandas, *Vacanāmrut-Bhūmikā*, esp. pp. 12–13; Satyaprasaddasji, *Vaidik Sampradāy ane Guru Paramparā*, pp. 33–44; Balramdas Muni, *Viśiṣṭādvaita-Bhāskara* (Vadtal: Harjivan Shastri, Swaminarayan Mandir, 1986), pp. 1–29.

12 This is the largest of a number of independent groups who all trace their lineage to Abji Bapa.

13 E.g. Vacanāmrut with *Rahasyārtha Pradīpikā Ṭīkā* of Śrī Abjī Bāpāśrī, Ishwarcharandasji Swami (ed.) (Maninagar: Shri Anandimukta Sadguru Shri Muktajivandasji Swami Suvarna Jayanti Mahotsav Smarak Trust, 1959), Gaḍhaḍā 1.1, p. 29; Ibid. Gaḍhaḍā 1.7, pp. 42–7; Ibid. Gaḍhaḍā 1.33, pp. 113–14; Ibid. Gaḍhaḍā 1.45, pp. 140–7.*Rahasyārtha-Pradīpikā* is a commentary on the Vacanāmrut by Abjī Bāpāśrī, edited by Ishwarcharandasji Swami (not to be confused with the biographer of Yogiji Maharaj). However, it should be noted that the Vacanāmrut edition used by this denomination differs in key sermons from the edition used by the Vartal and Ahmedabad denominations, which is the same edition used by the BAPS denomination and many others.

14 E.g. Abjī Bāpāśrī, *Rahasyārtha Pradīpikā Ṭīkā* Loyā 13, p. 347.

15 *Śrī Abjī Bāpāśrīnī Vāto*, Ishwarcharandasji Swami (ed.) (Ahmedabad: A. M. Abjībāpāśrī Smārak Trust, 1975), I, p. 191; Abjī Bāpāśrī, *Rahasyārtha Pradīpikā Ṭīkā* Gaḍhaḍā 1.1, p. 29; Ibid. Gaḍhaḍā 1.7, p. 37; Ibid. Kāriyāṇī 7, p. 281; Ibid. Loyā 10, p. 338; Dharmaswarupdas Shastri, *Śrījī-Sammata-Viśiṣṭādvaita-Siddhānta-Sāgara* (Ahmedabad: Bahechardas Shankarbhai Mistry, 1936), pp. 190–5; *Śrījīvanprāṇ Svāmībāpānī Vāto* (Maninagar: Shri Swaminarayan Gadi Sansthan Shriji Sankalpmurti Adya Acharya Pravar Dharmadhurandhar 1008 Shri Muktajivan Swamibapa Suvarna Jayanti Mahotsav Smarak Trust, 1981), I, p. 93.

16 Abjī Bāpāśrī, *Rahasyārtha Pradīpikā Ṭīkā* Gaḍhaḍā 1.12 p. 54; Muni Swami Keshavpriyadasji Purani, *Śrī Abjībāpāśrīnu Jīvan-Vruttānt* (Vrushpur: Gopalji Kanji Patel, 1957), pp. iv–vii; *Śrījīvanprāṇ Svāmībāpānī Vāto*, I, p. 141.

- Anādi muktas reside engrossed in the divine form of Swaminarayan, one with him yet distinct, as sweetness is in honey or sugar dissolved in milk.[17]
- These anādi muktas are also forms of Swaminarayan, called svarūpāvatāras, who manifest on earth from him and thereafter return into him.[18]
- Swaminarayan remains manifest only through his pratimā {sacred images}, and so only they should be the focus of devotion.[19]

Junagadh denomination[20]

- Jīvas are considered to be 'fluid' in nature. By association with Parabrahman, who has a form, the souls, too, take on a form in their state of liberation, just as water turns into ice when placed in a freezing cold environment.[21]
- The liberated souls in Brahmadhāma have bodies composed of their own sentiency, not nitya-vibhūti.[22]
- Akṣarabrahman has only two forms: one which is the divine light of Parabrahman, wherein liberated souls reside; the other has a distinct form and is in the service of Parabrahman in Brahmadhāma.[23]
- Liberated souls serve Parabrahman in Brahmadhāma in various ways, such as by becoming his ornaments.[24]
- Some souls, called nitya-muktas, are eternally liberated and have always served Parabrahman in Brahmadhāma.[25]

[17] Ishwarcharandasji, *Śrī Abjībāpāśrīnu Jīvan-Vruttānt*, pp. 11–14; Abjī Bāpāśrī, *Rahasyārtha Pradīpikā Ṭīkā* Gaḍhaḍā 1.51, p. 141; Ibid. Loyā 13, p. 347; Ibid. Gaḍhaḍā 3.33, pp. 686–7; Muni Swami Keshavpriyadasji Purani, *Śikṣāpatrī-Rahasyārtha* (Ahmedabad: Hirjibhai Bhimjibhai Chavda & Vitthaljibhai Keshavjibhai Dave, 1966), pp. 14–17; Dharmaswarupdas, *Śrījī-Sammata-Viśiṣṭādvaita-Siddhānta-Sāgara*, pp. 57–69.

[18] Dharmaswarupdas, *Śrījī-Sammata-Viśiṣṭādvaita-Siddhānta-Sāgara*, pp.153–5.

[19] E.g. Abjī Bāpāśrī, *Rahasyārtha Pradīpikā Ṭīkā* Vartāl 10, p. 551; Ibid. Gaḍhaḍā 3.2, p. 619.

[20] This refers to the teachings of Krishnavallabhacharya, the founder of a denomination based at Junagadh.

[21] Krishnavallabhacharya, *Śrī-Svāminārāyaṇa-Darśana* (Junagadh, India: Shri Harisharanagati Mandal, 1983), Śrauta 5, p. 4.

[22] Krishnavallabhacharya, *Śrīharivākyasudhāsindhoḥ Brahmarasāyaṇa-Bhāṣyam* (Varanasi and Delhi: Chaukhambha Orientalia, 1980), I, Gaḍhaḍā 1.1, p. 31; Krishnavallabhacharya, *Śrī-Svāminārāyaṇa-Darśana*, Śrauta 12–13, pp. 10–12.

[23] Krishnavallabhacharya, *Brahmarasāyaṇa-Bhāṣya* Gaḍhaḍā 1.1, p. 30; Ibid. Gaḍhaḍā 1.12, p. 156; Ibid. Gaḍhaḍā 1.21, p. 268; Krishnavallabhacharya, 'Śrīguṇātītabrahmopaniṣat' in *Akhila-Bhūmaṇḍalīya-Sāmpradāyika-Mukti-Vyavasthā tathā Tattvaprabhāvalī* (Junagadh: Author, 1970), 3.5, p. 150.

[24] Krishnavallabhacharya, *Brahmarasāyaṇa-Bhāṣya* Gaḍhaḍā 1. I, p. 31; Krishnavallabhacharya, *Śrī-Svāminārāyaṇa-Darśana*, Śrauta 6–7, pp. 5–7.

[25] Krishnavallabhacharya, *Śrī-Svāminārāyaṇa-Darśana*, Śrauta 3, pp. 2–3.

Understanding the finer intricacies, proper bases and historical development of these differences would need to be the subject of a much more detailed piece of work. Still, as each denomination defends its system, arguing theologically and respectfully using valid theological texts and accepted professional methods, they will continue to contribute to the wider corpus on Swaminarayan Hindu theology, thereby advancing the field as a whole.

Other schools of Vedānta and Hindu traditions: Questions to Swaminarayan Hindu theology will also be posed from other Hindu traditions, many of which will already have established commentaries on the same Vedāntic texts, while others will draw from a completely different canon. Again, with key interpretative differences that bear significantly upon a school's theology, respectful discussions on topics such as the nature of God, the soul, the world and liberation, and on the way to liberation, the role of religious authority, the sources of valid theological knowledge, etc. will hopefully bear mutually fruitful results in refining ideas, arguments and methodology, even if without producing conclusive answers. After all, we need not have to agree to be able to learn from one another. Knowing where, why and how we disagree can be just as productive.

The wider community of theologians and other scholars: In time, like Christian theology and other traditions before it, Swaminarayan Hindu theology will also be placed under examination from modern, post-Enlightenment scholarship. How, for example, will it hold up when seen through the lens of postmodernism? If, or when, the likes of George Lindbeck, Hans Wilhelm Frei, Stanley Hauerwas or other proponents of post-liberal theology scrutinise its doctrines, premises, truth-claims, how will Swaminarayan Hindu theologians respond? What may have seemed axiomatic to them will suddenly be viewed with suspicion and ambiguity. How will the foundational revelatory texts of the tradition, considered sacred and infallible to the community of faithful, fare when subjected to the 'hermeneutics of suspicion' and other forms of literary criticism?

Embarking even further outside the crucible of religion, the Swaminarayan tradition, like other faiths, will also face questions from (atheistic) social and political scientists about the role and value of its religious position in postmodern society, including on important issues of public value and interest, such as social equality and justice, abortion, euthanasia, capital punishment, bio-ethics and many others. How and on what doctrines and texts will theologians draw upon to argue one way or the other? These are all interesting prospects and, as of yet, largely part of

He is always infinitely more powerful than jīvas, īśvaras, māyā, akṣara-muktas and Akṣarabrahman and is their independent controller, inspirer and śarīrin {presiding soul}. By his wish, he grants the fruits of all the jīvas' and īśvaras' actions. He is the inspirer of their ability to will, know and do.

This Parabrahman Puruṣottama Nārāyaṇa is imperceptible by māyic senses and inner faculties. While still remaining in Akṣaradhāma, by his own divine resolve and out of compassion, for the ultimate liberation of infinite jīvas and īśvaras and to fulfil the wishes of his devotees, he manifests with all his divine virtues, powers, etc. in human form in each brahmāṇḍa and becomes visible to all.

That manifest form of Parabrahman Paramātman is Sahajanand Swami Maharaj, Shri Swaminarayan Bhagwan. He is the absolute focus of worship for us all. To forever continue his worship in a manifest form even after he retracts his earthly manifestation, he forever remains fully manifest in his immanent form through the Akṣarabrahman Guru.

He [Parabrahman] is the cause of all avatāras; he is the master of them all, the avatārin. When, by his special wish, he pervades a jīva or an īśvara for a particular task, an avatāra manifests. The sentient beings of each of these avatāras are ontologically different from each other. Like these avatāras, the sentient beings of Vāsudeva and the Caturvyūha, and the twenty-four mūrtis, i.e. Keśava, etc., are ontologically different from one another.

Akṣarabrahman

Akṣarabrahman is distinct from Parabrahman. Like Parabrahman, it is one, eternal and a sentient entity and it transcends the three guṇas. It is forever divine, replete with infinite redemptive virtues, devoid of all māyic qualities and forever faultless. The form, qualities, powers, etc. of this Akṣarabrahman are dependent only on Parabrahman. And by the eternal will of Parabrahman, it is the cause, support, controller and śarīrin of the entire insentient and sentient creation and pervades it.

Although Akṣarabrahman is ontologically one entity, it serves in four different ways.

In its Cidākaśa form, Akṣarabrahman pervades within and outside of the infinite brahmāṇḍas and upholds them.

In the form of [Akṣara]dhāma, Akṣarabrahman is the divine abode of Parabrahman, the personal form of Akṣarabrahman and the infinite akṣaramuktas. There is only one such Akṣaradhāma; it is eternal and forever transcends the three [māyic] guṇas. Only liberated souls who have attained similarity[3] to Akṣarabrahman are able to enter it.

In the personal attendant form in that Akṣaradhāma, Akṣarabrahman has, like Parabrahman, a divine human-shaped form complete with two arms and all other features. He remains forever engrossed in the service of Parabrahman and is the ideal for the akṣara-muktas.

And in the form of the Guru as the eternal and complete vessel of Parabrahman, that Akṣara manifests in a human form with Paramātman in each brahmāṇḍa so that through his [Akṣara's] divine association he can make the jīvas and īśvaras who are bound [in the cycle of births and deaths] brahmarūpa, establish in them the highest level of unflinching faith, grant them ultimate liberation and forever let them experience the manifest presence of Paramātman through himself. He [the Akṣarabrahman Guru] protects the traditions of the Sampradāya and graces all with the experience of the highest bliss. Gunatitanand Swami, Bhagatji Maharaj, Shastriji Maharaj and Yogiji Maharaj have manifested in this succession of Akṣarabrahman Gurus. And this succession continues forever. At any one time, the path of ultimate liberation remains open through only one such Guru.

Māyā

Māyā is composed of the three guṇas; it is eternal while continually mutating, insentient, a material cause of creation, i.e. infinite brahmāṇḍas, and the diverse mysterious power[4] of Paramātman. As the cause of ego and attachment for jīvas and īśvaras, māyā has been the cause of their transmigration since eternity. Akṣarabrahman and Parabrahman are forever totally aloof from and beyond māyā and are its śarīrin.

Īśvara

Īśvara is an eternal sentient entity distinct from Parabrahman, Akṣarabrahman and jīva. In comparison to Akṣarabrahman and Parabrahman, īśvaras are extremely powerless; but compared to jīvas, they possess more power and knowledge. Paramātman, by his will, assigns them to the tasks of creation, etc. of the brahmāṇḍas. Like the jīvas, these īśvaras are countless in number, subtle

[3] See footnote 2.

[4] This is in the sense of a device or instrument wielded by and distinct from Paramātman, as a sword is the 'power' of a soldier.

in form like an atom, possess the qualities of indivisibility, etc., have consciousness as their form, are knowers, doers of good and bad karmas, and experiencers of the fruits of those karmas. They have been bound by māyā since eternity.

Pradhāna Puruṣa, Virāṭa Puruṣa, the devas presiding over their senses and inner faculties, Brahmā, Viṣṇu, Maheśa, etc. are all sentient beings of the īśvara category, and these beings are ontologically separate from each other.

Jīva

Jīva is an eternal sentient entity distinct from Parabrahman, Akṣarabrahman and īśvara. These jīvas are countless, subtle in form like an atom, possess the qualities of indivisibility, etc., have consciousness as their form, are knowers, doers of good and bad karmas, and experiencers of the fruits of those karmas. They have been bound by māyā since eternity.

Sādhanā and Benefits

To attain ultimate liberation, mumukṣus {aspirers of spiritual liberation} should profoundly love Parabrahman Puruṣottama Bhagwan Swaminarayan and the manifest Akṣarabrahman Guru, through whom Parabrahman manifests fully and continuously, with a sense that they are faultless and supremely divine and [when meeting either of them] that he is the manifest form of Parabrahman before their eyes. By firmly associating with him [i.e. that manifest form] through thought, word and deed they should please him immensely.

Jīvas and īśvaras seeking liberation who endeavour in this way, through the grace of Parabrahman, having achieved ekāntika dharma, become brahmarūpa, that is, attain similarity[5] to Akṣarabrahman, and attain the highest devotion to Parabrahman. All their miseries and faults are destroyed forever, and while alive, they experience the highest bliss of Paramātman.

By the wish of Paramātman, such a brahmarūpa devotee, on leaving the [physical] body, attains the Akṣaradhāma of Paramātman via arcimārga {a divine path}. There, with a brahmic body, while subserviently[6] serving the Lord of Akṣaradhāma, Parabrahman, by doing his darshan, he forever enjoys divine bliss.

[5] See footnote 2. [6] See footnote 1.

The Meaning of Akṣara-Purushottam Upāsanā

Akṣara-Purushottam upāsanā is not the worship of two entities – Akṣara and Puruṣottama. Rather, it means to become akṣararūpa [like Akṣara] and worship Puruṣottama, i.e. to become brahmarūpa [like Brahman] and worship Parabrahman. Therefore, when Parabrahman in human form returns to his abode, he suppresses the presence of the Brahmasvarūpa Guru and himself remains manifest on earth through him. Therefore, an aspirer of liberation who profoundly associates with the manifest Guru is, in fact, worshipping Paramātman himself.

The meaning of the 'Swaminarayan' mahāmantra is incorporated into this very meaning of Akṣara-Puruṣottama upāsanā. That is, to become like 'Swami', i.e. akṣararūpa, and subserviently offer devotion and upāsanā to 'Narayan', i.e. Parabrahman Puruṣottama Nārāyaṇa.

Conclusion

Thus, these theological principles are Vedic, eternal, revealed by Shriji Maharaj [Bhagwan Swaminarayan] and propagated by the Guṇatīta Guru Paramparā. Therefore all devotees of the Bochasanwasi Shri Akshar Purushottam Swaminarayan Sanstha should consolidate their understanding in this way and explain it to other aspirers of liberation.

Jai Swaminarayan from Shastri Narayanswarupdas
[Pramukh Swami Maharaj]
Guru Purnima, Samvat 2064 [18 July 2008], Bochasan

Glossary

Presented here are very brief explanations of certain Sanskrit, Gujarati and English terms commonly encountered in Swaminarayan Hindu theology. This will help the non-specialist reader better understand the system presented in this book. For further explanations or explanations of terms not included here, readers should refer to the index and the respective discussions within the exposition itself. The Appendix also provides useful summaries of certain key terms and concepts.

adhikaraṇa – This refers to a single or, more typically, group of sūtras within the Brahmasūtras forming a point of inquiry and debate, usually with a prima facie opposing view, leading to a concluding statement with supportive arguments.

Akṣara/Akṣarabrahman – This is one of the five eternal metaphysical realities, second only in transcendence to Parabrahman and forever untouched by māyā. Though ontologically one entity, Akṣarabrahman serves in four different forms: as the abode of Parabrahman, known as Akṣaradhāma; within Akṣaradhāma as the exemplary devotee of Parabrahman; in human form on earth, as the Brahmasvarūpa Guru; and as Cidākāśa, the all-pervading, conscious space that supports everything (except Parabrahman). *See also* Akṣaradhāma, Brahmasvarūpa Guru, Cidākāśa.

Akṣaradhāma – This is the name of the divine, transcendental abode of Parabrahman Puruṣottama, where he is forever seated before countless liberated souls who have attained qualities similar to those of Akṣarabrahman. It is a form of Akṣarabrahman.

akṣararūpa – 'like Akṣara'. This refers to the highest spiritual state, of liberated souls, wherein a jīva or īśvara attains certain qualities of Akṣarabrahman so that it is free of all māyic influences and can offer the highest devotion to Parabrahman, forever enjoying his supreme bliss.

akṣara-mukta – A jīva or īśvara that has attained ultimate liberation and who resides in Akṣaradhāma with a brahmic body.

antaḥkaraṇa – 'inner faculty'. This refers to the complete mind, which comprises four aspects, each characterised by its individual functions and named accordingly. It is called the 'manas' when generating thoughts and desires; the 'buddhi' when consolidating thoughts, making decisions and resolutions, forming convictions, or discriminating; the 'citta' when repeatedly contemplating or focussing; and the 'ahaṃkāra' when forming a sense of being or self. Each of the four functionalities is also referred to as an antaḥkaraṇa, and so antaḥkaraṇa is often used in the plural.

antaryāmin – 'indwelling controller'. This refers to God as the indweller and to his power to reside within all beings and things, by which he governs all of their actions and knows all of their thoughts and feelings.

aṇu – This refers to the fundamental, smallest building block of creation. When translated as 'atom', for convenience, it is used in its pre-modern or philosophical sense, meaning an infinitesimally minute particle.

anu-praveśa – 're-entering'. A term referring to the special empowering presence of Parabrahman, beyond his inherent pervading of all beings and things, by which they can fulfil certain tasks. For example, he specially enters within a selected īśvara for its manifestation as an avatāra, or within māyā (Mūla-Prakṛti), an akṣara-mukta (Mūla-Puruṣa), Pradhāna-Puruṣa, etc. as they successively engage in the creative process.

anvaya – 'not separate'. When used for Parabrahman, this term implies his immanent form, which inherently exists within all sentient beings and insentient matter. This is opposed to his vyatireka (or distinct) form residing in Akṣaradhāma.

ātman – 'soul' or 'self'. This refers primarily to the pure jīva, distinct from the physical, subtle and causal bodies, i.e. the spiritual self beyond its material body, senses, mind and worldly desires. More generally, it can mean that which pervades, inspires and governs. Thus, it can also refer to Parabrahman and Akṣarabrahman as the pervader, inspirer and governor of the physical and non-physical world, the śarīrin.

avatāra – A divine being that manifests on earth to fulfil various tasks at the behest of Parabrahman. It is metaphysically an īśvara, but is empowered and divinised by the special presence of Parabrahman, its lord.

avatārin – This refers to Parabrahman, as the cause and lord of the avatāras. He is distinct from and superior to them ontologically, because the avatāras are all īśvara in being.

avidyā – 'ignorance' or 'anti-knowledge'. Antithetical to true knowledge, this refers to a false understanding of reality. It is the root cause of pain and suffering, from which spiritual aspirants seek liberation. It is synonymous with māyā as ignorance.

axiom – This term refers to a proposition that is not susceptible to proof or disproof. Its truth is assumed to be self-evident, i.e. it is accepted as being true without the need for proof or argument.

Bhagavad-Gītā – This is one of the most popular texts of Hinduism. It comprises a dialogue between Arjuna, the warrior, and Kṛṣṇa, his charioteer and īṣṭadeva, at the outset of the battle between the feuding cousins, the Pāndavas and the Kauravas. It forms a portion of the epic Mahābhārata (Bhīṣma Parva, chapters 25–42) in which Kṛṣṇa enlightens Arjuna on dharma, karma, bhakti, jñāna, yoga, Brahman and Parabrahman, among other themes. It forms a part of the Prasthānatrayī, or triadic Vedānta canon.

Brahmā – This refers to an īśvara being who is assigned to be the creator of various life-forms within each brahmāṇḍa. He forms one part of the trinity of īśvaras, along with Viṣṇu (the sustainer) and Śiva (the destroyer), who are deputed by Parabrahman to oversee a brahmāṇḍa. This should not to be confused with Brahman, i.e. Akṣarabrahman, who is the second-highest of the five eternal entities.

Brahman – *See* Akṣara/Akṣarabrahman.

brahmāṇḍa – This refers to a system of fourteen realms {lokas}, including Mṛtyuloka (or earth), of which there are countless during any one time. It loosely refers to 'world'.

brahmarūpa – 'like Brahman'. A term referring to the enlightened state of being when one has qualities similar to those of Brahman, i.e. Akṣarabrahman. It is synonymous with akṣararūpa. *See* akṣararūpa.

Brahmasūtras – This is a highly technical Sanskrit treatise composed of extremely succinct, esoteric aphorisms, called sūtras. It attempts to systematise and harmonise the teachings of the Upaniṣads. It is also known as the Vedānta-Sūtras, Uttara-Mīmāṃsā-Sūtras and Vyāsa-Sūtras, and forms one part of the Prasthānatrayī, or triadic Vedānta canon.

Brahmasvarūpa Guru – This refers to the human embodiment of Akṣarabrahman, who manifests on earth along with Parabrahman. Parabrahman lives on and works through the Guru thus making himself accessible to humans so that they may worship him, experience him and strive towards ultimate liberation. The Brahmasvarūpa Guru is also referred to by such names as the Satpuruṣ, Uttam Bhakta, Ekāntik Bhakta, Ekāntik Sant, Param Ekāntik Sant and Param Bhāgvat Sant.

brahmatanu – A divine body, composed of brahmic consciousness, received by all liberated souls residing in Akṣaradhāma.

brahmavidyā – 'knowledge of Brahman'. This refers to the highest spiritual knowledge, conceived in Swaminarayan Hindu theology as the knowledge of Parabrahman and Akṣarabrahman, which leads to the realisation of the ultimate reality and to the ultimate liberation for the soul.

caitanya – 'sentience'; consciousness. This is the fundamental quality of all living things that distinguishes them from material objects.

Cidākāśa – This is the impersonal, shapeless form of Akṣarabrahman; the eternal, conscious space that pervades and supports all of creation.

darshan – 'seeing'. This refers to the seeing of, in particular, sacred images and holy persons. It is an act of religious worship, performed with deep reverence, adoration and meditative awareness.

Darśana – A term that refers to a classical system or school of Hindu thought that expounds the nature of reality and way to realising it.

devatā – 'deity'; god.

efficient cause – This refers to the maker of an object who transforms the raw material into the object itself. For example, the potter is the efficient cause of an earthen pot. *See also* material cause.

Ekāntika Dharma – This is a fourfold system of theological praxis comprising dharma – righteous living by observing the moral codes of scripture; jñāna – realisation of oneself as the ātman, distinct from the body; vairāgya – dispassion towards worldly pleasures; and bhakti – selfless devotion to God while realising his greatness. It is also known as Bhāgavata Dharma.

epistemology – This refers to the study of knowledge, specifically its nature, limits and sources, i.e. what we know and how we know it.

exegesis – A term that refers to the elaboration or critical interpretation of a (usually sacred) textual source.

hermeneutics – This is the branch of theology and philosophy that deals with exegesis, specifically the principles, techniques and tools of interpretation.

guṇa – This refers to a basic characteristic of māyā, of which there are three in total: sattvaguṇa ('goodness'), leading to calmness, awareness, compassion, etc.; rajoguṇa ('passion'), leading to desire, self-interest, bravado, etc.; and tamoguṇa ('darkness'), leading to anger, fear, dejection, etc. All beings are influenced by a combination of these three qualities until they are liberated from māyā.

guṇātīta – 'transcending the guṇas'. This adjective qualifies something that is beyond the influence of all māyic qualities, i.e. that which is divine. It especially describes Parabrahman and Akṣarabrahman. *See also* guṇa.

Guru Paramparā – This refers to the unbroken succession of Brahmasvarūpa Gurus who serve as the medium of Parabrahman on earth through whom he is accessible and ultimate liberation is possible.

iṣṭadeva – 'preferred deity'. A term that refers to the beloved God chosen as the focus of one's worship.

īśvara – This is one of the five eternal metaphysical realities. It is a finite sentient entity, much like a jīva in that it is still shrouded by māyā, but a higher being endowed with special powers and knowledge for fulfilling various functions within a particular brahmāṇḍa. Examples include Virāṭa Puruṣa, Brahmā, Viṣṇu and Śiva, and those divinities who enliven the various forces of nature, such as Sūrya, Candra, Varuṇa, etc.

jada – 'insentient'. This refers to the non-living, i.e. those things that are material, or without consciousness.

jīva – This is one of the five eternal metaphysical realities. It refers to a distinct, individual soul, i.e. a finite sentient being. All jīvas are bound by māyā, which shrouds their inherently radiant self characterised by existence, consciousness and bliss.

jñāna – 'theological knowledge'. Within the matrix of Ekāntik Dharma, this also refers to a realisation of the self as ātman.

kūṭastha – Literally meaning immovable, as if braced on or like an anvil, this adjective qualifies that which is stable and unchanging, i.e. immutable.

līlā – This refers to the activities of God, including creation, characterised as divine play, i.e. gracious, selfless, joyful and liberative. This is in contrast to human activities, which are born of desire and subject to karma.

material cause – This relates to the raw material out of which something is made. For example, clay is the material cause of an earthen pot. *See also* efficient cause.

māyā – This is one of the five eternal entities, the only one which is insentient. It is an instrument of Parabrahman that constitutes the base substance from which the material world is formed. By nature, it is characterised by the three guṇas. In its dormant state, before the time of creation, it houses all jīvas, īśvaras and elements. It is inspired by, controlled by and dependent upon Parabrahman and Akṣarabrahman. It also forms the ignorance that shrouds jīvas and īśvaras from which spiritual aspirants seek liberation. *See also* guṇa, Prakṛti.

metaphysics – This is a branch of philosophy that deals with reality and the investigation into its nature, i.e. what is real and how it is so.

Mṛtyuloka – 'realm of death'. A name that refers to earth, where everyone is subject to death. It is also the only one of the realms in a brahmāṇḍa where human birth and ultimate liberation are possible.

Mūla-Prakṛti – This is the name used for the primordial form of māyā when it is engaged in the creative process. *See* Prakṛti.

Mūla-Puruṣa – This is the designation given to an akṣara-mukta inspired by Akṣarabrahman to engage with māyā, or Mūla-Prakṛti, to initiate the creative process. It is also called Mahā-Puruṣa or Aksara-Puruṣa.

mukta – 'liberated'. This refers to a liberated soul, free from the bondage of māyā.

mukti – 'liberation'. This refers to the elevated spiritual state of the soul where it is free of all the binding and defiling forces of māyā and is able to offer unhindered devotion to Parabrahman, enjoying his undisturbed supreme bliss.

mumukṣu – 'aspirer of liberation'. This refers to an individual seeking liberation from the cycle of births and deaths.

mūrti – A sacred image infused with the presence of God, Gurus or other deities used in religious services to offer worship.

nirākara – 'without form'.

nirguṇa – 'without guṇas'. A term that qualifies something that does not have any of the three māyic qualities of sattvaguṇa, rajoguṇa and tamoguṇa, i.e. that which is divine. It also refers to the quality of being extremely subtle or minute.

niścaya/niṣṭhā – 'steadfastness'. This refers to religious conviction or resolute faith.

nitya – 'eternal'. A term that describes that which exists forever, without beginning or end.

ontology – This is the branch of metaphysics within philosophy concerning the study of existence and the nature of being. 'Ontological' therefore relates to the very nature of something, in its most fundamental sense of being.

pañcaviṣaya – This is a collective term referring to the five types of experiences, or pleasures, enjoyed by the soul through its five cognitive senses, i.e. the multitude of sights, sounds, smells, tastes and touches.

Parabrahman – God, the supreme existential reality. Also known as Puruṣottama and Paramātman, he is the highest of the five eternal entities.

Paramātman – 'supreme self' or 'super-soul'. This refers to God, especially as he who indwells, inspires and governs all beings and things. *See also* Parabrahman.

paramhansa – This refers to one of the 500 monks of the highest order ordained by Swaminarayan during his ministry. Swaminarayan held them to lofty standards of worldly renunciation and spiritual understanding.

Pradhāna-Prakṛti – A term that refers to the countless parts of Prakṛti created from itself when it is stirred from its dormant state by Mūla-Puruṣa. Each Pradhāna-Prakṛti goes on to join with an īśvara, which was previously dormant within māyā, to form a Pradhāna-Puruṣa pair. *See* Pradhāna-Puruṣa.

Pradhāna-Puruṣa – This refers to one of the countless pairs of Pradhāna-Prakṛti and an īśvara, from which, subsequently, a brahmāṇḍa is created along with the twenty-four elements, from which, in turn, the jīvas and īśvaras receive their respective bodies and the whole of creation is formed.

Prakṛti – A term that refers to the primordial form of māyā that engages with Mūla-Puruṣa (an akṣara-mukta) to form Prakṛti-Puraṣa, from which countless pairs of Pradhāna-Puruṣas are formed, each of which in turn go on to create a brahmāṇḍa. Because of its primal role, it is also referred to as Mūla-Prakṛti, Mahā-Prakṛti, mahā-māyā or mūla-māyā.

Prakṛti-Puruṣa – A configuration of māyā instrumental in the protological process. It refers to the pairing of Mūla-Prakṛti and Mūla-Puruṣa, from which countless pairs of Pradhāna-Puruṣas are formed for the creation and sustenance of each brahmāṇḍa.

Prasthānatrayī – This is the collective term for the triadic Vedānta canon, namely, the Brahmasūtras, Upaniṣads and Bhagavad-Gītā. It is considered essential for exponents of Vedānta schools to demonstrate that their system of doctrines is grounded in the Prasthānatrayī by providing supportive interpretations of these revelatory texts in commentaries.

Puruṣottama – 'supreme being'. God. *See* Parabrahman.

revelation – This refers to the communication of divine truth by God to humans by which they can come to know him. This can take many forms, including, though not limited to, such knowledge being committed to writing, i.e. scripture.

sākāra – 'with form'.

saguṇa – 'with guṇas'. A term that can be used to qualify something that possesses the three māyic qualities or, when referring to Parabrahman and Akṣarabrahman, to indicate that they possess divine qualities and liberative virtues but are not totally attributeless or impersonal. In another sense, it also refers to the quality of being extremely vast.

sampradāya – A religious tradition, usually marked by a succession of gurus leading a community of worshippers.

śarīra – 'body'. A technical term that refers generally to that which is pervaded, inspired and governed by the soul. In particular, it refers to the physical and non-physical world, which is pervaded, inspired and governed by Parabrahman, its śarīrin.

śarīrin – 'soul'. This technical term refers generally to that which pervades, inspires and governs the body. In particular, it refers to Parabrahman as the pervader, inspirer and governor of the physical and non-physical world, his śarīra.

satkāryavāda – The doctrine of causality that accepts an effect is pre-existent in its cause as a different state. In other words, new substances are not created, since they always exist; they only change state. Thus, what one sees as 'new' is not a new or different substance, but merely the same substance in a different state. For example, a gold necklace is nothing but the gold it is made of in a different form; it is not a new substance apart from the gold itself.

Satsaṅga – This refers to the fellowship of practitioners within the Swaminarayan Hindu tradition. When used in the lowercase, it invokes the full gamut of theological belief and praxis practised within the religious community of devotees, most essentially under the guidance of the Brahmasvarūpa Guru.

satsaṅgī – A member of the Satsaṅga fellowship, referring specifically to the community of Swaminarayan Hindu practitioners.

satya – 'true'. This is a technical term referring to that which is real, in existence.

siddhānta – A conclusive principle or doctrine.

soteriology – The area of theology concerning salvation. In this book, it pertains to mukti, i.e. the liberation of the soul.

sūtra – An aphorism or short phrase comprising the basic unit of the Brahmasūtras.

Sūtrakāra – A designation that refers to the author of the Brahmasūtras, known as Bādarāyaṇa Vyāsa.

svāmi-sevaka-bhāva – This refers to the master–servant relationship between God and individual souls. The devotee subserviently serves God out of deep adoration, reverence and gratitude and a profound realisation of one's inferiority before and utter dependence upon the almighty supreme reality. The relationship is therefore not one of subjugation enforced by an oppressive overlord, but of loving reverence and willing obedience to God.

theology – The study of religious beliefs where the focus of inquiry is God, marked traditionally by attention to and interpretation of scriptural authority. It is therefore described, most simply, as 'God-talk'.

Upaniṣads – This is a collection of canonical sacred texts forming the fourth portion of the Vedas, after the Saṃhitā (hymns), Brāhmaṇa (manual of rites and rituals) and Āraṇyaka (forest treatises). They contain profound discussions about the nature of ultimate reality, traditionally believed to have been revealed to enlightened seers thousands of years ago. These revelations were transmitted orally for generations before being committed to script. The Upaniṣads are also commonly referred to as Vedānta, and form one part of the Prasthānatrayī.

upāsanā – 'sitting near'. A term that refers to the loving worship of God informed by correct theological knowledge, allowing a personal relationship with him. More generally, it can refer to a tradition's framework of fundamental principles regarding the nature of God and the mode of worshipping him.

utpatti sarga – The protological process or order of creation marking the origins of the universe. It begins with the will of Parabrahman, which is received by Akṣarabrahman, who then inspires a liberated soul in Akṣaradhāma, who in turn engages with Prakṛti to initiate a sequence of creative activity until all life-forms are composed.

Vacanāmrut – 'immortalising ambrosia in the form of words'. This is a compilation of 273 spiritual discourses delivered by Swaminarayan between 1819 and 1829, meticulously noted and compiled by his senior disciples in his presence and verified by Swaminarayan himself. This text is regarded by the faithful of the Swaminarayan tradition as the primary revelatory scripture by which its doctrines are established and articulated, based on the distinctive belief that Swaminarayan, as the self-manifestation of Parabrahman, is both the source and subject of revelatory knowledge comprised within it.

Vedānta – 'conclusion of the Vedas'. A system of thought embodied in the Upaniṣads revealing the conclusive teachings of the Vedas, centring primarily on the nature of God, the self, the world, reality and personal experience. Also called Uttara Mīmāṃsā, 'the latter inquiry', it constitutes one of the six systems of inquiry known as the Darśanas.

Vedāntin – An adherent or proponent of a particular school of Vedānta, though sometimes referred exclusively to Advaita Vedānta.

Virāṭa Puruṣa – This is a sentient being of the īśvara category who is the inner soul of each brahmāṇḍa and therefore has the physical brahmāṇḍa as its gross body. He is formed as part of the protological process by one of the countless pairs of Pradhāna- Puruṣas. The creation, sustenance and dissolution of the brahmāṇḍa are his three states of being. He is also known as Vairāja Puruṣa or Virāṭa Brahmā.

vyatireka – 'distinct'; separate. When used for God, this term refers to his transcendental self, residing in Akṣaradhāma, as opposed to his anvaya (or immanent) form, by which he is inherent throughout creation and present through the Brahmasvarūpa Guru.

Bibliography

Primary Texts

Sanskrit and Translations from Sanskrit

Balramdas, Muni, *Viśiṣṭādvaita-Bhāskara* (Vadtal: Harjivan Shastri, Swaminarayan Mandir, 1986).

Bhadreshdas, Sadhu, *Brahmasūtra-Svāminārāyaṇa-Bhāṣyam* (Ahmedabad: Swaminarayan Aksharpith, May 2009).

Bṛhadāraṇyakopaniṣat-Svāminārāyaṇa-Bhāṣyam (Ahmedabad: Swaminarayan Aksharpith, April 2012).

Chāndogyopaniṣat-Svāminārāyaṇa-Bhāṣyam (Ahmedabad: Swaminarayan Aksharpith, April 2012).

Īśādyaṣṭopaniṣat-Svāminārāyaṇa-Bhāṣyam (Ahmedabad: Swaminarayan Aksharpith, December 2009).

Śrīmad-Bhagavad-Gītā-Svāminārāyaṇa-Bhāṣyam (Ahmedabad: Swaminarayan Aksharpith, January 2012).

Svāminārāyaṇa-Siddhānta-Sudhā (Ahmedabad: Swaminarayan Aksharpith, 2016).

Bhagwatpriyadas, Sadhu, 'Śrīsvāminārāyaṇa-Bhakti-Vicāra', unpublished PhD thesis, Bharatiya Vidya Bhavan, Mumbai (1972).

Bhaktipriyadas, Sadhu, 'Bhagavat-Svāminārāyaṇīya-Dharma-Darśanam', unpublished PhD thesis, Bharatiya Vidya Bhavan, Mumbai (1972).

Chaitanyanand, Muni, *Śrī Jñānavilāsa*, with Hindi translation by Swami Narayanprasaddas (Varanasi: Hariprakashdas Shastri, Swaminarayan Temple, n.d.) – no.14 in C023–092.

Dharmaswarupdas Shastri, *Śrījī-Sammata-Viśiṣṭādvaita-Siddhānta-Sāgara* (Ahmedabad: Bahechardas Shankarbhai Mistry, 1936).

Ghanshyamcharandas, Sadguru, *Ādhyātmika Tattvākhyāna*, Harijivandas Shastri (ed.), (Vadtal: Harijivandas Shastri, Vadtal Swaminarayan Temple, 1973).

Gopalanand, Swami, *Bhagavadgītā Saṭīka*, translation by Sadhu Madhavdas (Vadtal: Kothari Gordhanbhai on behalf of Viharilalji Maharaj, 1889).

Īśādidaśopaniṣad Bhāṣya, translation by Shastri Shvetvaikunthdas (Varanasi: Shri Hariprakash Shastri, 1970).

Brahmadarshandas, Sadhu, *Bhāratīya Darśannī Rūprekhā*, 2 vols. (Ahmedabad: Swaminarayan Aksharpith, 2007).

Brahmavidyānā Amūlya Grantho: Vacanāmrut ane Svāmīnī Vāto (Ahmedabad: Swaminarayan Aksharpith, 2008).

Brahmavidyāno Rājmārg: Svāminārāyaṇīya Sādhanā (Ahmedabad: Swaminarayan Aksharpith, 2008).

Brahmavidyānu Darśan: Svāminārāyaṇīya Tattvajñān (Ahmedabad: Swaminarayan Aksharpith, 2008).

Karmasiddhānt ane Punarjanma, 2 vols. (Ahmedabad: Swaminarayan Aksharpith, 2002).

Vacanāmrut Rahasya 1: Advitīya Ādhyātmik Granth, Vacanāmrut (Ahmedabad: Swaminarayan Aksharpith, 1999).

Vacanāmrut Rahasya 2: Svāminārāyaṇīya Tattvajñān (Pūrvārdh), 2nd edn (Ahmedabad: Swaminarayan Aksharpith, 2001).

Vacanāmrut Rahasya 3: Svāminārāyaṇīya Tattvajñān (Uttarārdh) (Ahmedabad: Swaminarayan Aksharpith, 2001).

Vacanāmrut Rahasya 4: Svāminārāyaṇīya Sādhanā (Pūrvārdh) (Ahmedabad: Swaminarayan Aksharpith, 2005).

Vacanāmrut Rahasya 5: Svāminārāyaṇīya Sādhanā (Uttarārdh) (Ahmedabad: Swaminarayan Aksharpith, 2005).

Dave, Harindra, *Akṣarnā Yātrī: A Biography of Harshad T. Dave*, 2nd edn (Mumbai: Arvind H. Dave, 2013).

Dave, Harshad T., *Akṣarbrahma Guṇātītānand Svāmī*, 7th edn, 2 vols. (Ahmedabad: Swaminarayan Aksharpith, 2000).

Bhagvān Śrī Svāminārāyaṇ, 6th edn, 5 vols. (Ahmedabad: Swaminarayan Aksharpith, 2013).

Brahmasvarūp Śāstrījī Mahārāj, 5th edn, 2 vols. (Ahmedabad: Swaminarayan Aksharpith, 2007).

Brahmasvarūp Śrī Prāgjī Bhakta, 9th edn (Ahmedabad: Swaminarayan Aksharpith, 2008).

Dave, Ramesh, *Ekāntik Dharmanā Dhārak Satpuruṣ* (Ahmedabad: Swaminarayan Aksharpith, 1980).

Svāminārāyaṇ Dharma ane Viśvanā Dharmo, 2nd edn (Ahmedabad: Swaminarayan Aksharpith, 1986).

Svāminārāyaṇ Sampräday ane Bhāratīya Sampradāyo (Ahmedabad: Swaminarayan Aksharpith, 1980).

Harjivandas, Shastri, *Vacanāmrut-Bhūmikā* (Vadtal: Shastri Harjivandasji, Swaminarayan Temple, 1972).

Ishwarcharandas, Sadhu, *Brahmasvarūp Yogījī Mahārāj*, 3rd edn, 6 vols. (Ahmedabad: Swaminarayan Aksharpith, 2010).

(ed.), *Yogī Gītā*, 18th edn (Ahmedabad: Swaminarayan Aksharpith, 2006).

(ed.), *Yogī Vāṇī*, 2nd edn (Ahmedabad: Swaminarayan Aksharpith, 2010).

Ishwarcharandasji Swami, Sadguru Shri (ed.), *Śrī Abjī Bāpāśrīnī Vāto*, 2 vols. (Ahmedabad: A. M. Abjibapashri Smarak Trust, 1975).

Keshavpriyadasji, Purani Muni Swami, *Śīkṣāpatrī-Rahasyārtha* (Ahmedabad: Hirjibhai Bhimjibhai Chavda & Vitthaljibhai Keshavjibhai Dave, 1966).
Śrī Abjībāpāśrīnu Jīvan-Vruttānt (Vrushpur: Gopalji Kanji Patel, 1957).
Kothari, Madhavlal Dalsukhram (ed.), *Śrījīnī Prasādīnā Patro* (Ahmedabad: The editor, 1978).
Krishnavallabhacharya, *Akhila-Bhūmaṇḍalīya-Sāmpradāyika-Mukti-Vyvasthā*, 4th edn (Jamvanthali: Shri Harisharanagati Mandal, 2005).
Nandkishor, Swami, *Ātyantik Kalyāṇ* (Bhuj: The author, 1958).
Narayanmunidas, Sadhu et al., *Vhālu Lāge Svāminārāyaṇ Nām* (Ahmedabad: Swaminarayan Aksharpith, 2002).
Nishkulanand, Swami, *Bhaktacintāmaṇī* (Ahmedabad: Swaminarayan Aksharpith, 2010).
Nityanand, Swami, *Śrī Bhagavadgītā Satīk* (Ahmedabad: Patel Narandas Vastaji, Swaminarayan Temple Kalupur, 1895).
'Parthāro' in *Vacanāmrut* (Ahmedabad: Shri Dharmada Pustak Prasidhi Fund Samiti, Swaminarayan Mandir Kalupur, 1899).
Patel, Chotalal Maganlal, *Upāsanā Darpaṇ*, 2nd edn (Charadva: Sadguru Shastri Swami Gopalcharandasji, Swaminarayan Mandir, 1976).
Patel, Gordhan M., *Sarvoparī Upāsanānu Rahasya* (Vadtal: Shri Swaminarayan Mandir, 2009).
Patel, Hitendrabhai Naranbhai, *Dharmavaṁśī Ācārya Pad* (Ahmedabad: Mahant Swamishri, Swaminarayan Mandir Kalupur, 1995).
Pramukh, Swami Maharaj, *Svāminārāyaṇ Darśannā Siddhāntono Ālekh* in Vacanāmrut, 30th edn (Ahmedabad: Swaminarayan Aksharpith, 2015), pp. vii–xviii.
Prasadanand, Swami, *Sadguru Prasādānand Svāmīnī Vāto* (Ahmedabad: Shri Swaminarayan Mandir Kalupur, 1995).
Ramdasji, Swami, *Śhudhdh Sarvoparī Upāsanā* (Vadtal: Shri Swaminarayan Mandir, 2009).
Satyaprasaddasji, Swami, *Vaidik Sampradāy ane Guru Parampāra* (Gandhidham: Shri Swaminarayan Gurukul, 2005).
Shastriji, Maharaj, 'Brahmasvarūp Svāmīśrī Śāstrījī Mahārājnī Divyavāṇī', transcript of audio recording, published in *Svāminārāyaṇa Prakāś*, 469–70 (November–December 1977), 462–9.
Shriharidas, Sadhu, *Sanātan Dharma Abhigam*, 4th edn (Ahmedabad: Swaminarayan Aksharpith, 2006).
Shrutiprakashdas, Sadhu, *Akṣarbrahma Nirupaṇ: Vaidik tathā Sāmpradāyik Śāstronā Ādhāre* (Ahmedabad: Swaminarayan Aksharpith, 2009).
Dhārmik Stotram: Cintan ane Darśan (Ahmedabad: Swaminarayan Aksharpith, 2001).
Śrī Svāminārāyaṇ Sampradāymā Avatār-Avatārī Nirupaṇ, 2nd edn (Ahmedabad: Swaminarayan Aksharpith, 2010).
Svāminārāyaṇ Mahāmantra: Arth ane Mahimā (Ahmedabad: Swaminarayan Aksharpith, 2002).

Svāminārāyaṇ Vedānt Darśan: Ek Rūprekhā (Ahmedabad: Swaminarayan Aksharpith, 1985).
'Upāsanā', *Samāmnāya: Journal of the Maharshi Veda-Vijñāna Academy*, 5–6 (1996–1997), 136–47.
Śrījīvanprāṇ Svāmībāpānī Vāto, 2 vols. (Maninagar: Shri Swaminarayan Gadi Sansthan Shriji Sankalpmurti Adya Acharya Pravar Dharmadhurandhar 1008 Shri Muktajivan Swamibapa Suvarna Jayanti Mahotsav Smarak Trust, 1981).
Svāmīnī Vāto, 21st edn with added footnotes and appendices (Ahmedabad: Swaminarayan Aksharpith, 2015).
Swayamprakashdasji, Sadguru Swamishri, *Uddhav Sampradāynī Mārgdarśikā* (Ahmedabad: Shri Swaminarayan Mandir Kalupur, 1998).
Vacanāmrut, 30th edn with added footnotes and appendices (Ahmedabad: Swaminarayan Aksharpith, 2015).
Vacanāmrut with *Rahasyārtha Pradīpikā Ṭīkā* of Shri Abji Bapashri, Swami Ishwarcharandasji (ed.), (Maninagar: Shri Anandimukta Sadguru Shri Muktajivandasji Swami Suvarna Jayanti Mahotsav Smarak Trust, 1959).
The Vachanāmrut: Spiritual Discourses of Bhagwān Swāminārāyan, translation by Sadhus of BAPS Swaminarayan Sanstha (Ahmedabad: Swaminarayan Aksharpith, 2014).
Vaghela, B.G., *Bhagvān Svāminārāyaṇnu Samkālīn Lokjīvan*, 3rd edn (Ahmedabad: Swaminarayan Aksharpith, 1988).
Vedaras, 3rd edn (Ahmedabad: Swaminarayan Aksharpith, 1978).
Viharilalji Maharaj, *Harilīlāmrut*, 4 vols. (Ahmedabad: Swaminarayan Aksharpith, 1997).
Vivekpriyadas, Sadhu (ed.), *Lī. Śāstrī Yajñapuruṣdāsjī*, 3rd edn, 2 vols. (Ahmedabad: Swaminarayan Aksharpith, 2007).
Viveksagardas, Sadhu, *Kariṣye Vacanam Tava* (Ahmedabad: Swaminarayan Aksharpith, 2010).
Yogī Gītā Marma (Ahmedabad: Swaminarayan Aksharpith, 2009).

English, Hindi and Braj Bhasha

Amrutvijaydas, Sadhu, *100 Years of BAPS: Foundation, Formation, Fruition* (Ahmedabad: Swaminarayan Aksharpith, 2007).
Anandswarupdas, Sadhu (ed.), *Śrī Svāminārāyaṇ Darśan: Ek Cintan* (Ahmedabad: Swaminarayan Aksharpith, 2004).
Brahmbhatt, Arun, 'The BAPS Swaminarayan Community' in Helen R. Ebaugh and Stephen Cherry (eds.), *Global Religious Movements Across Borders: Sacred Service* (Farhnam, UK and Burlington, VT: Ashgate, 2014), pp. 99–122.
'The Swaminarayan Commentarial Tradition' in Raymond Brady Williams and Yogi Trivedi (eds.), *Swaminarayan Hinduism: Tradition, Adaptation, and Identity* (New Delhi: Oxford University Press, 2016), pp. 138–55.
Kim, Hanna, 'The BAPS Swaminarayan Temple Organisation and its Publics' in John Zavos, Pralay Kanungo, Deepa S. Reddy, Maya Warrier and Raymond Brady Williams (eds.), *Public Hinduisms* (New Delhi: Sage, 2012), pp. 417–39.

'Svāminārāyaṇa: Bhaktiyoga and the Akṣarabrahman Guru' in Mark Singleton and Ellen Goldberg (eds.), *Gurus of Modern Yoga* (New York: Oxford University Press, 2014), pp. 237–60.

'Transnational Movements: Portable Religion and the Case Study of the BAPS Swaminarayan Sanstha' in Brian A. Hatcher (ed.), *Hinduism in the Modern World* (New York: Taylor & Francis/Routledge, 2015), pp. 48–64.

Muktanand, Swami, 'Śṛī Bhagavad Gītā Bhāṣya', unpublished handwritten manuscript, Akshardham centre for Applied Research in Social Harmony, Access No. 221B (1882).

Mukundcharandas, Sadhu, *Bhagwan Swaminarayan: An Introduction* (Ahmedabad: Swaminarayan Aksharpith, 2007).

Paramtattvadas, Sadhu, 'The Ontological Distinction between Brahman and Parabrahman in the Swaminarayan Vedanta Tradition', unpublished M.St. dissertation, University of Oxford (2007).

and Raymond Brady Williams, 'Swaminarayan and British Contacts in Gujarat in the 1820s' in Raymond Brady Williams and Yogi Trivedi (eds.), *Swaminarayan Hinduism: Tradition, Adaptation, and Identity* (New Delhi: Oxford University Press, 2016), pp. 58–93.

Shrutiprakashdas, Sadhu, 'Bhāratīya Dharmadarśana meiṅ Avatāravāda' in R.C. Sinha, Jata Shankar and A.D. Sharma (eds.), *Dimensions of Philosophy: Dr S. P. Dubey Felicitation Volume* (Delhi: New Bharatiya Book Corporation, 2012), pp. 42–9.

'Dārśanik Sāhitya aur Sanskṛtabhāṣā', *Dārśanika Traimāsika: Journal of Akhila Bhāratīya Darśana Pariṣad*, 58.1 (2012), 11–18.

'Ekāntika Dharma: Bhāratīya Dharmadarśana ke Itihāsa meiṅ Vismṛt Sādhanā' in R.N. Mehta (ed.), *New Dimensions of Indology: Dr Praveen Chandra Parikh Felicitation Volume* (Delhi: Bharatiya Vidya Prakashan, 1997), pp. 33–42.

'Sāṅkhyadarśanāntargata Prakṛtipuruṣa Śrī Svāminārāyaṇa Darśana ke Sandarbha meiṅ', *Dārśanika Traimāsika: Journal of Akhila Bhāratīya Darśana Pariṣad*, 36.1 (1990), 60–71.

'Śrī Rāmānujīya Viśiṣṭādvaita meiṅ Jīvanmukti' in Nitish Dubey (ed.), *Seśvara Vedānta* (Delhi: New Bharatiya Book Corporation, 2006), pp. 167–75.

Śrī Svāminārāyaṇ Darśan: Sanātan Dharmagranthoṅ ke Paripreksya meiṅ (Ahmedabad: Swaminarayan Aksharpith, 2005).

'The Theory of Caturvyūha in Pañcarātra', *Journal of the Ananthacharya Indological Research Institute*, 10 (2011–2012), 92–6.

Srivastava, R.S., Sadhu Ishwarcharandas, Sadhu Atmaswarupdas and Sadhu Anandswarupdas (eds.), *New Dimensions in Vedanta Philosophy*, 2 vols. (Ahmedabad: Bochasanwasi Shri Aksharpurushottam Sanstha, 1981).

Trivedi, Yogi, *Bhagwan Swaminarayan: The Story of His Life* (Ahmedabad: Swaminarayan Aksharpith, 2014).

Vakil, Suresh, *The Concept of Aksharabrahman in the Philosophy of Shri Swaminarayan* (Ahmedabad: Swaminarayan Aksharpith, 1985).

Williams, Raymond Brady, *Swaminarayan Hinduism: An Introduction* (Cambridge University Press, 2001).

Williams, Raymond Brady and Yogi Trivedi (eds.), *Swaminarayan Hinduism: Tradition, Adaptation and Identity* (New Delhi: Oxford University Press, 2016).

Secondary Sources

Abraham, William J., 'The Offense of Divine Revelation', *Harvard Theological Review*, 95 (2002), 251–64.

Athansius, *The Incarnation of the Word of God*, newly translated by a religious of C.S.M.V. School of Theology (London: Bles, 1944).

Barth, Karl, *Evangelical Theology*, translation by Grover Foley (New York: Holt, Rinehart and Winston, 1963).

Bhagvatsinhji Maharaja (ed.), *Bhagavadgomandal* (Rajkot: Pravin Prakashan, 1986).

Bhattacharya, Taranath (ed.), *Vācaspatyam*, 7 vols. (Varanasi: Chaukhamba, 1962).

Bhattoji, Dikshit, *Vaiyākaraṇasiddhāntakaumudī*, Gopal Datt Pande (ed.), (Varanasi: Chaukhamba Surbharati Prakashan, 1987).

Bhimacharya, *Nyāyakośa*, 4th edn (Pune: Bhandarkar Oriental Research Institute, 1973).

Bonhoeffer, Dietrich, *The Cost of Discipleship*, 6th edn, translation by Reginald H. Fuller, revised by Irmgard Booth (London: SCM Press, 1962).

Brunner, Emil, *Revelation and Reason*, translation by Olive Wyon (London: SCM Press, 1947).

Carman, John Braisted, *The Theology of Rāmānuja: An Essay in Interreligious Understanding* (New Haven, CT and London: Yale University Press, 1974).

Clooney, S.J., Francis X., *Comparative Theology: Deep Learning Across Religious Borders* (Oxford and Malden, MA: Wiley-Blackwell, 2010).

Hindu God, Christian God: How Reason Helps Break Down the Boundaries between Religions (Oxford: Oxford University Press, 2001).

'Restoring "Hindu Theology" as a Category in Indian Intellectual Discourse' in Gavin Flood (ed.), *The Blackwell Companion to Hinduism* (Oxford: Blackwell, 2003), pp. 447–77.

Theology After Vedanta: An Experiment in Comparative Theology (Albany: State University of New York, 1993).

Coburn, Thomas B., '"Scripture" in India: Towards a Typology of the Word in Hindu Life', *Journal of the American Academy of Religion*, 42.3 (1984), 435–59.

Deussen, Paul, *The Philosophy of the Upanishads*, 2nd edn, translation by Rev. A.S. Geden (New Delhi: Oriental Books Reprint Corporation, 1979).

Sixty Upaniṣads of the Veda, translation by V.M. Bedekar and G.B. Palsule, 2 vols. (Delhi: Motilal Banarsidass, 1980).

The System of the Vedanta, translation by Charles Johnston (Delhi: Low Price Publications, 1990).

Dikshitar, P. Venkateswar (ed.), *Pārāśarya Saṃhitā* (Mannargudi: Sri Venugopalaswami Temple and Sri Annaswami Iyengar Vidwat Sabha, 2005).

Edelmann, Jonathan, *Hindu Theology and Biology: The Bhāgavata Purāṇa and Contemporary Theory* (New York: Oxford University Press, 2012).

Flood, Gavin (ed.), *The Blackwell Companion to Hinduism* (Oxford: Blackwell, 2005).

Goswami, Tamal Krishna, *A Living Theology of Krishna Bhakti: Essential Teachings of A. C. Bhaktivedanta Swami Prabhupada*, edited with Introduction and Conclusion by Graham M. Schweig (New York: Oxford University Press, 2012).

Guinness World Records 2009 (London: Guinness World Records, 2008).

Gupta, Ravi M., *The Caitanya Vaiṣṇava Vedānta of Jīva Gosvāmī: When Knowledge Meets Devotion* (Oxford and New York: Routledge, 2007).

Halbfass, Wilhelm, *India and Europe: An Essay in Understanding* (Albany: State University of New York, 1988).

Healy, Nicholas M., 'What is Systematic Theology?', *International Journal of Systematic Theology*, 11 (2009), 24–39.

Hendry, George, *Theology of Nature* (Philadelphia: Westminster, 1980).

Hodge, Charles, *Systematic Theology*, 3 vols. (Grand Rapids, MI: William B. Eerdmans, 1940).

Jackson, Roger and John Makransky (eds.), *Buddhist Theology: Critical Reflections by Contemporary Buddhist Scholars* (Richmond, UK: Curzon, 2000).

Jhabwala, S.H., *Gita and its Commentators* (Bombay: Popular Prakashan, 1960).

Jones, Gareth (ed.), *The Blackwell Companion to Modern Theology* (Oxford: Blackwell, 2004).

Joshi, Jayshankar (ed.), *Halāyudhakośa* (Lucknow: Hindi Samiti, 1967).

Kaufman, Gordon D., *An Essay on Theological Method*, 3rd edn (n.p: American Academy of Religion, 1995).

Kelsey, David H., *Eccentric Existence: A Theological Anthropology*, 2 vols. (Louisville, KY: Westminster John Knox Press, 2009).

Lakshmitatacharya, M. E. (ed.), *Viśiṣṭādvaitakośa*, 6 vols. (Melukoṭe: Sanskrit Sanshodhan Sansat, 1983).

Lallurama, Jeevarama (ed.), *Shrimad-Bhagvad-Geeta Containing Eight Commentaries* (Mumbai: Gujarat Printing Press, 1912).

Lipner, Julius, *The Face of Truth: A Study of Meaning and Metaphysics in the Vedāntic Theology of Rāmānuja* (Albany: State University of New York Press, 1986).

Madhavacharya, Sayana, *Sarvadarśansaṅgraha* (Pune: Bhandarkar Oriental Research Institute, 1924).

Madhva, *Aṇubhāṣya with the Commentary Tattvaprakāśikā of Śrī Chalāri Śeṣācārya*, R.G. Malagi (ed.), H.P. Malledevaru (general ed.), (Mysore: Oriental Research Institute, 1985).

Shatprasna-Atharvana-Mandukya Upanishads with English Translation and Notes According to Sri Madhvacharya's Bhashya, translation by K.T. Pandurangi (Chirtanur: Sriman Madhva Siddhantonnahini Sabha, 1986).

Srī Madhvācārya Brahmasūtrabhāsya with Three Glosses, R. Raghavendra Acharya (ed.), 2nd edn, 3 vols. (Mysore: Oriental Research Institute, 1992).

Sūtra-Prasthānam and Upaniśat-Prasthānam in Sarva-Mūla-Granthāḥ (Bangalore: Akhila Bharata Madhwa Maha Mandala Publications, 1969).

Mani, Vettam, *Purāṇic Encyclopaedia* (Delhi: Motilal Banarsidass, 1975; reprinted 1989).

McGrath, Alister E. *Christian Theology: An Introduction*, 4th edn (Oxford: Blackwell, 2007).
Melton, J. Gordon and Constance A. Jones, 'Reflections on Hindu Demographics in America: An Initial Report on the First American Hindu Census', a paper presented at the Association for the Study of Religion, Economics & Culture meeting in Washington, D.C., 7-10 April 2011; accessible at http://www.thearda.com/asrec/archive/papers/Melton_Hindu_Demographics.pdf.
Migliore, Daniel L., *Faith Seeking Understanding: An Introduction to Christian Theology*, 2nd edn (Grand Rapids, MI & Cambridge, UK: William B. Eerdmans, 2004).
Mukundadeva, Madhava, *Adhyāsa-(Parapakṣa)-Girivajrākhyo Grantha* (Vrundavan: Shri 108 Nimbark Mahasabha, 1936).
Muraleemadhavan, P.C. (ed.), *Indian Theories of Hermeneutics* (New Chandrawal Delhi: New Bharatiya Book Corporation, 2002).
Nimbārka, *Vedānta-pārijāta-saurabha of Nimbārka and Vedānta-kaustubha of Śrīnivāsa: Commentaries on the Brahma-sūtras*, translation and annotations by Roma Bose, 3 vols. (Calcutta: Royal Asiatic Society of Bengal, 1940–1943).
Okita, Kiyokazu, *Hindu Theology in Early Modern South Asia: The Rise of Devotionalism and the Politics of Genealogy* (Oxford: Oxford University Press, 2014).
Otto, Rudolf, *India's Religion of Grace and Christianity Compared and Contrasted*, translation by Frank Hugh Foster (London: Student Christian Movement Press, 1930).
Owen, Huw Parri, *Christian Theism: A Study in Its Basic Principles* (Edinburgh: T. & T. Clark, 1984).
Padmapadacharya and Subrahmaṇya Śāstrī (eds.), *Pañcapādikā with Commentaries by Prakāśātman, Akhaṇḍānanda and Viṣṇubhaṭṭopādhyaya* (Varanasi: Mahesh Anusandhan Sansthan, 1992).
Paramtattvadas, Sadhu, 'Renunciation in Dietrich Bonhoeffer's The Cost of Discipleship', unpublished M.St. essay, University of Oxford (2007).
'The Role of Imagery in St Athanasius's The Incarnation of the Word of God', unpublished M.St. essay, University of Oxford (2007).
Patil, Parimal G., 'A Hindu Theologian's Response: A Prolegomenon to "Christian God, Hindu God"' in Francis X. Clooney, S.J. (ed.), *Hindu God, Christian God: How Reason helps Break Down the Boundaries between Religions* (Oxford: Oxford University Press, 2001), pp. 185–95.
Pereira, José (ed.), *Hindu Theology: Themes, Texts & Structures*, 1st Indian edn (Delhi: Motilal Banarsidass, 1991); originally published as *Hindu Theology: A Reader* (New York: Doubleday, 1976).
Ramanuja, *The Gadyatraya of Rāmānuja*, translation by M.R. Rajagopala Ayyangar (Madras: M.R. Rajagopala Ayyangar, n.d.).
Śārīrakamīmāmsā Śrībhāṣya (Brindaban: Mohalla Gyan Gudarhi, 1937).
Śrī Rāmānuja Gītā Bhāṣya with Text and English Translation, translation by Swami Adidevananda (Madras: Sri Ramakrishna Math, 2001).

Vedārthasaṅgraha (Melukote: Sanskritsanshodhan Sansat, 1991).
The Vedāntasūtras with the Commentary by Rāmānuja, part 3, translation by George Thibaut, *The Sacred Books of the East*, translation by various oriental scholars, Max Müller (ed.), vol. xlviii (Oxford: Clarendon Press, 1904).
The Vedāntasūtras with the Śrībhāṣya of Rāmānujācārya, translation by M. Rangacharya and M.B. Vardaraja Aiyangar, 2nd edn, 3 vols. (New Delhi: Munshiram Manoharlal, 1988–1991).
Rambachan, Anantanand, *A Hindu Theology of Liberation: Not-Two Is Not One* (Albany: State University of New York, 2015).
Ram-Prasad, Chakravarthi, *Divine Self, Human Self: A Comparative Theology from Two Gita Commentaries* (London and New York: Continuum, 2013).
Rangachar, M.E., *The Philosophy of Viśiṣṭādvaita* as *Expounded by Śrī Vedānta Deśika in the Nyāya-siddhāñjana* (Bangalore: Sri Nityananda, 2000).
Rangaramanuja, *Prakāśikā on Īśa-Kena-Kaṭha-Praśna-Muṇḍaka-Māṇḍukyānandavalli-Bhṛgūpaniṣadaḥ* (Pune: Anandashram Mudranalaya, 1947).
Sadhale, Gajanana Shambhu (ed.), *The Bhagavad-Gītā with Eleven Commentaries*, 3 vols. (Delhi: Parimal, 1992).
Sarasvati, Madhusudana, *Bhagavad-Gita with the Annotation Gūḍhārtha Dīpikā*, translation by Swami Gambhirananda (Delhi: Advaita Ashrama, 1998).
Shankara, *The Bhagavad Gita with the Commentary of Adi Sankaracharya*, translation by Alladi Mahadeva Sastry (Madras: Samata, 1998).
Brahmasūtra with Śaṅkarabhāṣya (New Delhi: Motilal Banarsidass, n.d.).
The Brahmasūtra Śāṅkara Bhāṣya with the Commentaries: Bhāmatī, Kalpataru and Parimala, K.L. Joshi (ed.), 2 vols. (Delhi: Parimal, 1987).
Brahmasūtraśāṅkarabhāṣyam with Commentaries Ratnaprabhā by Govindānanda, Bhāmtī by Vācaspati, Ānandagirīya by Ānandagiri, and also Nyāyanirṇaya, 2nd edn (Mumbai: Nirnayasagar Press, 1909).
Eight Upaniṣads with the Commentary of Śaṅkarācārya, translation by Swami Gambhiranand, 2 vols. xxxiv & xxxviii (Oxford: Clarendon Press, 1890–1896).
Sharma, Arvind, *The Hindu Gītā: Ancient and Classical Interpretations of the Bhagavadgītā* (La Salle, IL: Open Court, 1986).
Sharma, B.N.K., *The Brahmasūtras and their Principal Commentaries: A Critical Exposition*, 2nd edn, 3 vols. (New Delhi: Munshiram Manoharlal, 1986).
Shrinivasacharya, *Vedāntakaustubha in Brahmasūtranimbārkabhāṣyam*, 4 vols. (Delhi: Chaukhmba Sanskrit Pratishthan, 2000).
Shukla, Dinanath, *Bhāratīya Darśana Paribhāṣā Kośa* (Delhi: Pratibha Prakashan, 1993).
Srinivasa Chari, S.M., *Fundamentals of Viśiṣṭādvaita Vedānta: A Study Based on Vedānta Deśika's Tattvamuktākalāpa* (Delhi: Motilal Banarsidass, 1988).
The Philosophy of the Vedāntasūtra (New Delhi: Munshiram Manoharlal, 1998).
Sudarshana, Suri, *Śrutaprakāśikā on Rāmānuja's Śrībhāṣya*, 2 vols. (Mysore: Shri Vedanta Deshika Vihara Sabha, 1959).

Taylor, Mark, *Erring: A Postmodern A/theology* (Chicago: Chicago University Press, 1984).

Timm, Jeffrey R. (ed.), *Texts in Context: Traditional Hermeneutics in South Asia* (Albany: State University of New York, 1992).

Vallabha, *Aṇubhāṣya on the Brahmasūtra with the Commentary Bhāṣyaprakāśa and Super-commentary Raśmi on the Bhāṣyaprakāśa*, Mulchandra Tulsidas Teliwala (ed.), 4 vols. (Delhi: Akshaya, 2005).

Valpey, Kenneth, *Attending Kṛṣṇa's Image: Caitanya Vaiṣṇava Mūrti-Sevā as Devotional Truth* (Oxford & New York: Routledge, 2006).

Van Buitenen, J.A.B., 'Akṣara', *Journal of the American Oriental Society*, 79.3 (1959), 176–87.

Rāmānuja's Vedārthasamgraḥ, annotated translation and critical edn (Poona: Deccan College Postgraduate and Research Institute, 1956).

Vanhoozer, Kevin J. (ed.), *The Cambridge Companion to Postmodern Theology* (Cambridge: Cambridge University Press, 2003).

Vedanta, Deshika, *Adhikaraṇa-sārāvali with Two Commentaries: Adhikaraṇa-cintāmaṇi and Sārārtha-ratna-prabhā* (Madras: Sri Nilayam, 1974).

Vidyaranyamuni, *Vivaraṇa-prameya-saṅgraha* (Kashi: Achyutgranthamala Karyalaya, 1940).

Ward, Keith, *Concepts of God: Images of the Divine in Five Religious Traditions* (Oxford: Oneworld, 1993).

Religion and Community (Oxford: Clarendon Press, 2000).

Religion and Creation (Oxford: Clarendon Press, 1996).

Religion and Human Nature (Oxford: Clarendon Press, 1998).

Religion and Revelation (Oxford: Clarendon Press, 1994).

Index